THE CLEAR SPIRIT

Twenty Canadian Women
and their Times

Published on the occasion of
the Centennial of Canadian Confederation and
subsidized by the Centennial Commission

THE
CLEAR
SPIRIT

Twenty Canadian Women

and their Times

Edited by MARY QUAYLE INNIS

PUBLISHED FOR THE
CANADIAN FEDERATION OF UNIVERSITY WOMEN BY
UNIVERSITY OF TORONTO PRESS

Foreword

As ITS NATIONAL centennial project, the Canadian Federation of University Women decided to publish a book of biographies of Canadian women. Many University Women's Clubs and Alumnae Associations, the Canadian Federation of University Women itself, and some individual members have all contributed money and suggestions to make this book possible. It has been in the full sense a co-operative effort. We are especially grateful to Mrs. M. J. Sabia, President of the C.F.U.W., for advice and generous interest.

To young women of the future who regard university training as a matter of course and are free of all levels of all professions, this book may show what women could do before academic doors opened to them and also how their own freedom was gradually won.

We wish to thank the Centennial Commission most heartily for encouragement and for indispensable financial assistance.

The Editorial Committee appointed by the C.F.U.W. owes a particular debt of gratitude to Mary Quayle Innis, the editor of the volume, who undertook her task with enthusiasm and skill and brought it to completion at a propitious time. We thank also the authors, who responded cheerfully to the invitation to contribute and put vitality of their own into their accounts of a group of vital people.

VIDA PEENE
Chairman, Editorial Committee, C.F.U.W.

Contents

Introduction

MARY QUAYLE INNIS

A PROJECT FOR a book of biographies of Canadian women faces an editorial committee immediately with great numbers of vigorous and accomplished individuals among whom a choice must be made. The committee charged with preparing such a book for the Canadian Federation of University Women decided first of all to include only those who were no longer living and then to attempt to choose representatives of the various regions of Canada, of women's still more various activities and women whose work had been of national significance. The book would be a celebration, as well, of the women writers who would be asked to prepare the biographies.

The length of such a book as this is quite arbitrary, limited by finances and considerations of sensible space. It could be much longer for there is no lack of outstanding Canadian women. Several more books could be produced containing the stories of different women as distinguished and gifted as these; a choice had to be made, a line drawn somewhere.

The women included in such a book were to have spent a significant part of their lives in Canada, a decision which ruled out Mrs. Simcoe, for instance, and Mrs. Jameson and which barred also the musicians and actresses who for economic reasons had until recently to make their careers outside Canada. Their achievements, alas, have become part of the artistic story of Britain and the United States.

It could be asked, also, where are the members of women's traditional professions—the teachers, nurses, librarians? The multitude of candidates proved defeating and most of them were outstanding on the local rather than the national level. And for those finally included, there are other companions—the workers for women's rights and for temperance, the women historical writers like Kathleen Lizars and Agnes Laut, the women rather bleakly referred to in reference books as "versifiers," and the ringing classification "heroine," with Laura Secord, Madeleine de Verchères and Abigail Becker, and Mrs. Portlock, a "Bible woman." The firsts represented here have companions too—the first woman doctor, the first woman school inspector, the first woman lawyer. It is too early to find an Eskimo woman for inclusion but outstanding Eskimo women will soon appear. If this book provokes readers to go on searching for and informing themselves about the achievements of Canadian women—if it is followed by other such books—our earnest wish will be fulfilled.

As the biographies assembled, we began to see a theme, a unity. Far-spaced as they were in time and distance, there are striking similarities between the women in this book. Nearly all of them were born and grew up on farms, as of course most Canadians did well into the twentieth century. The earlier ones had a short formal education—high school and normal school marked a top achievement. A surprising number lost their mothers or both parents in early childhood and were brought up by aunts or grandmothers. Most had hard and strenuous early lives. And all had within them a powerful driving force—a long-held and steadily-held-to ambition which nothing could shake or defeat. Such desires had to be strong to push through the barriers set up by tradition, by disapproval, and even active opposition. And in spite of very real struggles—or because of them—most of these women lived long, full, vigorous lives. In view of the current controversy over marriage versus career, it should be noticed that several of them carried on their careers while bringing up their children and running their homes and apparently saw—and created—no conflict at all. They were criticized but so were the unmarried career women.

Pioneers must, since this is Canada, begin the story and we have four of them. They were all fighters as pioneers must be if they are to survive. Madame de La Tour fought English and French rival claimants and she and Mère Marie de l'Incarnation, along with Susanna Moodie and Catharine Traill, fought the deep forest, loneliness, homesickness and privation. Women, however strong, take the shape of their period and Mère Marie brought her great executive ability to the service of her church and her order. But her work helped to build also the new colony of Quebec. The literary Strickland sisters, pressed by poverty and sharp new experience, wrote their invaluable records of the beginnings of Upper Canada.

Writing was an acceptable activity for a woman and Laure Conan and Pauline Johnson emerge as early dedicated writers. Laure Conan sheltered behind her pen name but Pauline Johnson ventured onto the public platform, divided and driven by the pressures of her Indian and white inheritance.

Adelaide Hoodless was one of the first of an honourable line—the woman with a cause. Seeing a need, she advanced on it with all her eloquent force and by so doing pushed forward women's organized activities. She was a homemaker and kept, in spite of criticism, to the feminine domain though she made that include the speaker's rostrum.

The next step was into men's own world. Cora Hind, the crop analyst and agricultural expert, Maude Abbott, the doctor, Emily Murphy, the magistrate, in their several spheres moved into what had been solely masculine professions and began the long campaign for tolerance and acceptance which has by no means ended yet. Spearheaded by Magistrate Murphy, the five indomitable "Persons" forced their way into government and opened a path for their inheritor, another undefeatable woman, Agnes Macphail, who in turn blazed a trail which too few follow.

Artists could be professional by this time and we have Emily Carr, world-praised at last after her long neglect, L. M. Montgomery and Mazo de la Roche, world-known also in their separate fields; in the studies printed here we gain fresh insight into their creative lives.

Another trail-blazer, Alice Wilson, was one of the first women to make a place for herself in science—in her case, the formidable science of geology. The illustration of Dr. Wilson with her hammer explaining rocks to a group of men in itself documents a revolution.

And then that very modern and yet traditional figure—the volunteer—in this case Margaret McWilliams. Like Mrs. Hoodless, she took up causes in which she deeply believed and with her university training and her relentless energy made a career of them. With Maude Abbott and Alice Wilson she represents women as university graduates, achieving at last full educational experience. The continuous thread of women's advance and development gleams through the stories of these twenty Canadian women.

These biographies display the very real struggle of able and forceful women against very real obstacles. It is easy and partly right to blame men and their vested interests for making women's path difficult. But only partly right—many barriers are built and kept in repair by women themselves, tradition-bound, envious or timid. Advance sometimes seems slow but, as this book shows, for an able and determined woman obstacles make the road intriguing.

The writers of these biographies are as interesting as the women about whom they write and nearly as various. They are young and elderly and in between, university teachers and journalists, professional women and housewives. They were commissioned to write not panegyrics or "inspirational" accounts but documented, serious biographies based on the social history of the subject's time and place. As a result of their efforts we hope that the dust and stir of early Winnipeg, for example, or the dreamy charm of "The Island," or the forest loneliness of Upper Canada are palpable to the reader.

Twenty women stand forth, vividly alive. Holding hands, they would draw together not just the century of Canada's political existence but the whole span of her history.

ACKNOWLEDGMENTS

Aside from my happy association with the authors of the book I should like to pay tribute to the Editorial Committee of the Canadian Federation of University Women. Vida H. Peene was named chairman of this Committee, which included Dr. Bertha Bassam, recently retired Director of the School of Library Science of the University of Toronto and Mrs. A. S. Morton, a former president of the Canadian Federation of University Women. Three other C.F.U.W. members served as advisors: Mrs. Henry F. Angus of Vancouver, Miss Constance Hayward of Wolfville, Nova Scotia, and Mme. Victor Trepanier of Quebec. Miss Francess Halpenny, Managing Editor of the University of Toronto Press, gave generous and invaluable help at every stage of the work. To all these the editor is deeply indebted and profoundly grateful.

The Contributors

ETHEL GRANGER BENNETT (Mrs. H. A. Bennett) was born in England, educated at the University of Toronto and the University of Wisconsin, and is the wife of the retired president of Victoria College, University of Toronto. She has been a professor of French and is the author of historical novels, *Land for their Inheritance* (Toronto: Ryerson Press, 1955), *A Straw in the Wind* (Toronto: Ryerson, 1958), and *Short of the Glory* (Toronto: Ryerson, 1960), and a contributor to the *Dictionary of Canadian Biography*, vol. I.

FLORA HAMILTON BURNS was secretary to managers of the Bank of Montreal in Victoria and later private secretary to Col. N. L. D. Maclean, M.P. She has contributed to various publications as a free lance journalist and wrote and broadcast for the CBC a series of scripts on West Coast history. A close friend of Emily Carr, she has prepared broadcasts on the painter and directed the Hudson's Bay Company exhibition "The World of Emily Carr" in Vancouver and Victoria in 1962.

MICHELINE DUMONT-JOHNSON (Mme Rodrigue Johnson), is a licentiate of the Université de Montréal and has taught history and literature at the Ecole Normale Cardinal-Léger, in Montreal. She has published a selection of the writings of Laure Conan in the collection "Les Classiques Canadiens" and a portrait of Laure Conan in *Les Cahiers de l'Académie canadienne-française*, vol. 7, *Profils littéraires*. Her home is in Montreal, she is married to a sociologist and she has a daughter.

DORIS FRENCH was born in Saskatchewan, is a writer and broadcaster and the mother of two children. She was co-author with Margaret Stewart of *Ask No Quarter,* the life of Agnes Macphail (Toronto: Longmans, 1959), and author of *Faith, Sweat and Politics* (Toronto: McClelland and Stewart, 1962), the story of Canadian labour pioneers. She has published many stories and articles and is now CBC commentator at CBO, Ottawa.

KENNETHE M. HAIG was born on a farm at Alexander, Manitoba, and graduated from the University of Manitoba. She was a reporter and editorial writer on the *Winnipeg Free Press* and has published several books, *Precedent to Precedent,* an account of Canada's rise to responsible government, *What Mean These Stones,* a history of Kildonan church, and *Brave Harvest,* a biography of E. Cora Hind.

ELEANOR T. HARMAN was born at North Battleford, Saskatchewan, and attended the University of Saskatchewan and the University of Toronto. She worked in several publishing firms and is now Assistant Director of the University of Toronto Press. She is co-author of four books on Canadian history (*A Student's Workbook in Canadian History,* 1946; *The Story of Canada,* 1940; *Canada in North America, to 1800,* 1960; *Canada in North America, 1800–1901,* 1961), author of articles on Canadian history and scholarly publishing, and editor of *The University as Publisher,* 1961.

RUTH HOWES (Mrs. F. H. Howes) was born and educated in the United States. She lived on a farm near Millet, Alberta, and has been untiringly active in the Women's Institute, becoming Alberta president, national vice-president and holding many other offices. She attended as a delegate the conferences of the Associated Country Women of the World in Toronto, Ceylon and Edinburgh, and is assistant editor of the *Federated News,* the A.C.W.W. publication. She and her husband have now retired to Millet; they have three daughters and fourteen grandchildren.

DOROTHY LIVESAY MACNAIR was born in Winnipeg and educated at the University of Toronto. Her home was in Clarkson next to Mazo de la Roche's "Trail Cottage." Two of her volumes of poems, *Poems for People* and *Day and Night,* have received the Governor-General's Award for Poetry and she has frequently written for Canadian journals and CBC documentary programmes. Her most recent volume of poetry, *The Colour of God's Face,* results from her experience in teaching English at an African training college in what is now Zambia. She has been teaching creative writing at the University of

British Columbia and lives in Vancouver. She is a widow with a grown son and daughter.

ELIZABETH LOOSLEY is a graduate of the University of Toronto in modern languages and of the University of Toronto Library School. She worked in the Reference Division of the Toronto Public Library, at the Leaside Public Library and at the Adult Education Service at Macdonald College, Ste. Anne de Bellevue. She was editor of *Food for Thought* and assistant to the general editor of the *Dictionary of Canadian Biography*. She has published many scholarly articles in professional journals and was joint author, with John R. Seeley and R. Alex Sim, of *Crestwood Heights: A North American Suburb* (Toronto 1960), and author of *Residential Adult Education: A Canadian View* (Toronto, 1960).

MÈRE MARIE EMMANUEL, o.s.u., was Daisy Chabot, a graduate of the University of Western Ontario, docteur ès lettres of the University of Ottawa and docteur en philosophie of Université Laval. She is a professor at the Collège des Ursulines at Quebec and head of the department of French of the Collège feminin de Québec. She is the author of *Marie de l'Incarnation d'après ses lettres* (Ottawa 1946); *Marie de l'Incarnation* in the collection "Les Classiques Canadiens" (Fides, 1963); *Tant femme que rien plus* (Québec 1964), and contributor to the *Dictionnaire biographique du Canada*, vol. I.

ANNE MONTAGNES (Mrs. Ian Montagnes) has an M.A. in English from the University of Toronto. She is a free lance writer, a reviewer for the *Globe and Mail*, and is the mother of two children.

JESSIE BOYD SCRIVER, M.D., C.M., F.R.C.P. (C), F.A.A.P., graduated in Medicine from McGill University in 1922 in the first class to graduate women in that faculty. She taught Paediatrics in the University and practises her specialty in Montreal. Her husband, now retired, and her son are both doctors and professors of medicine at McGill.

CLARA THOMAS (Mrs. Morley Thomas) was born in Strathroy, Ontario, graduated from the University of Western Ontario and received her Ph.D. from the University of Toronto. Her thesis subject, the life and writings of Anna Jameson, has led to a biography to be published by the University of Toronto Press. She is assistant professor of English at York University and has two sons.

ELIZABETH WATERSTON (Mrs. Douglas Waterston) was born in Montreal, attended McGill University and has a Ph.D. in English

from the University of Toronto. She has taught English at Sir George
Williams University in Montreal, at the University of Western
Ontario, and has recently been appointed associate professor of
English at the University of Guelph. She has written a number of
scholarly articles, *Pioneers in Agriculture* (Toronto: Clarke, Irwin,
1957), a book for children, *Composition for Canadian Universities*
(Toronto: Macmillan, 1964), a text-book, and contributed two chapters to *Literary History of Canada* (University of Toronto Press,
1965). She is the mother of five children.

BETTY JANE WYLIE (Mrs. W. T. Wylie) has an M.A. in English
from the University of Manitoba. She has published articles in the
Winnipeg Free Press and various magazines, and done radio and
television work. She has produced several plays, written three puppet
plays presented in Winnipeg schools, and is now working on a special
centennial puppet play. She has four children.

THE ILLUSTRATIONS

It is not easy to find portraits of women who lived in Canada's early days
before the advent of photography. No authentic personal portrait of
Madame de La Tour exists. Mère Marie de l'Incarnation appears in a
photograph of the beautiful sculpture by Bourgault "qui s'est inspiré du
monument d'Emile Brunet." The Strickland sisters had their pictures taken
only when they were very old and drawings of them as young women
have been made by John Elphick from early sketches.

Pauline Johnson is shown wearing the beautiful white gown she wore
in 1894 in her first London season: "my first English dinner dress." Cora
Hind, on the other hand, appears in the fringed and beaded coat in which
she liked to astonish her friends. The portrait of Mrs. Hoodless is reproduced from the one which hangs at Macdonald Institute at Guelph and
in the Dominion Archives. Alice Wilson is shown at Billings Bridge creek
on a 1951 field trip. Margaret McWilliams is examining a volume presented to her at the time she gave up her Current Events classes.

We are grateful to the authors who provided portraits and wish to make
the following acknowledgments. The picture of Laure Conan was kindly
made available by Fides, Boulevard Dorchester, Montreal, and that of
Agnes Macphail was taken for the *Globe and Mail*. The portrait of Mazo
de la Roche is by Charles Aylett. Emily Murphy's picture was provided
by her daughter Miss Evelyn G. Murphy and McDermid Studios Ltd.,
Edmonton, and Mrs. McClung's by her daughter Mrs. H. M. Atkinson.
For the picture of Emily Carr we thank the Provincial Archives, Victoria,
D.C.; for that of Dr. Alice Wilson, the Geological Survey of Canada. Mrs.
McWilliams' comes from Jack Ablett, *Winnipeg Free Press* and Mazo de
la Roche's from Miss Caroline Clement.

THE CLEAR SPIRIT

Twenty Canadian Women
and their Times

Fame is the spur that the clear spirit doth raise . . .
To scorn delights, and live laborious days. . . .

MILTON, *Lycidas*

Madame de La Tour

1602-1645

ETHEL M. G. BENNETT

ACADIA HAS FURNISHED many a theme for poets and dramatists from the fierce conflicts which characterize its early history. English and French, Catholics and Huguenots fought and quarrelled on its shores. Charles de Saint-Etienne de La Tour during his life-span saw it pass to the English three times. Its importance as a coastal region guarding the gulf and "great river of Canada" was not always recognized by France; consequently its early colonization was haphazard and lack of understanding and wise direction from the home land led to many quarrels among rivals. The story of Madame de La Tour, who is often called the heroine of Acadia, is the story of one of these conflicts.

About her early life various assertions have been made but few facts definitely established. Françoise-Marie Jacquelin, to give her her maiden name, was born in France, probably about the year 1602. Her father was a barber of Le Mans, says one historian, but this is an example of the many statements about her which can be neither verified nor refuted. One version of her story is that at an early age she ran away from her barber father to join a band of strolling players and later, under the name of Mlle Desnoyers, became a famous

Parisian actress, attracting a succession of titled admirers; then, when her popularity was declining and her lovers deserting her, she listened to a proposal from Desjardins, an agent from La Rochelle, who had been commissioned by his employer Charles de La Tour, lieutenant-governor of Acadia, to find a woman of good physique with a tidy sum of money and send her across the sea to marry him.

A twentieth-century descendant of La Tour, however, claims for her a more conventional past: she was the daughter of a family which belonged to the *haute noblesse* of France, and Charles de La Tour had met her on one of his brief visits to the old land.

Whatever the truth about her origins and her life in France, of one thing we can be sure: when she had once decided to join La Tour in the new world, she became completely devoted to him and his cause. Active and courageous, she proved a daring and resourceful ally in the quarrel in which she found him involved—a quarrel which filled all her married life and which was, in the end, to be the cause of her death.

Unfortunately, the truth about that quarrel is difficult to establish, for it has been obscured by the intense partisanship of those who have recorded it. The bitterness and animosity of the seventeenth century have been perpetuated even into the twentieth. As recently as the 1930s accounts have appeared maintaining that La Tour's rival was an unprincipled grasper after power and La Tour a patriotic hero cheated of his rights, or that La Tour was a traitor and a libertine and Charles de Menou d'Aulnay his victim and a saint.

No one has ever suggested that Charles de La Tour was a saint. He had some very evident human weaknesses. But, to judge by the variety of people who were friendly to him in different crises of his chequered career, he also had personal charm. Amiable and obliging yet capable of sudden outbursts of temper when his honour was touched, indolent yet on occasion recklessly ready to seize an opportunity for action, he seems to have combined the pride and courtliness of a seventeenth-century French gentleman of birth and breeding with the easy-going, laughter-loving ways of the tribe of savages among whom he had spent his youth. His new wife no doubt found it easy to fall in love with him and she never swerved in her loyalty.

To understand the quarrel in which Mme de La Tour took such an active part, it is necessary to familiarize oneself (as she no doubt did) with the events of her husband's life in Acadia before their marriage.

He had been on these coasts for thirty years. In 1610, he and his father, Claude de Saint-Etienne de La Tour, had left France with Jean de Biencourt de Poutrincourt et de Saint-Just, whose intention was to make a permanent settlement on lands granted to him around Port-Royal (Annapolis Royal today). Here, as a member of De Monts' colony (still famous today because of the celebrated *Ordre de Bon Temps*), Poutrincourt had spent the merry winter of 1606. De Monts' colony had been withdrawn the following year, however, and now, under new arrangements, Poutrincourt was returning with fresh hope. But that hope, too, was destined to be short-lived. In 1613 the English under Samuel Argall came up the coast from Virginia and destroyed the French settlement. Poutrincourt was once more forced to return to France.

His nineteen-year-old son, Charles de Biencourt de Saint-Just, unwilling to abandon Acadia to the English, decided to remain in the neighbourhood, and Charles de La Tour, now aged seventeen, decided to stay with him. A few other Frenchmen joined them and with these and some friendly Micmacs, the two youths roamed about in the forests and along the coasts, maintaining themselves as best they could while waiting for the French to return. That their homeland would send out a force sufficient to protect her rights to that region must have seemed to them a reasonable hope—indeed a certainty. In France land was the basis of wealth. Here were vast riches which the king would surely consider worth the effort of holding.

They waited in vain. In the tenth year of this roaming life, Biencourt died. His father had, meanwhile, met his death in military service in Europe, and such rights as the son had inherited passed to his young friend and companion Charles de La Tour. The latter, still expecting the French to return eventually, built himself a fort at Cape Sable (Fort Lomeron) on the southwest end of the peninsula (Nova Scotia). He could hardly hope to establish a settlement of any importance until he obtained support from France, but he did build up a fur trade. The fishing vessels which came yearly to the Acadian coast enabled him to maintain communications of a sort with the old land; there is evidence that he had more or less regular commercial relations with Macquin and Georges, a firm of ship-chandlers in La

Rochelle. His mode of life, however, seems to have been that of the Micmacs rather than that of a civilized French gentleman. He had children by a woman of the tribe, a union blessed by a missionary priest when the occasion offered; and to his credit be it said that he had his three daughters legitimized. One of them, Jeanne, seems to have been with him fairly constantly and later married a French gentleman who had received land grants in Acadia.

The French court, meanwhile, was still showing no interest in this coast. Such colonizing efforts as were made were centred on the new colony which Champlain had established far up the river St. Lawrence; but even it was left to the mercy of trading companies, who failed to promote settlement. In 1627, however, Cardinal Richelieu, newly risen to power, began to concern himself with the possessions of France in the New World. He organized the Compagnie des Cent-Associés to supersede former trading companies and be responsible for settling the country. Charles de La Tour now sought to have his position recognized by this powerful minister and the new trading company. Since France and England were at war, Richelieu would surely appreciate the advantage of a French stronghold on the Acadian coast. From his fort on Cape Sable, La Tour wrote letters to both king and cardinal. In one, dated at Fort Lomeron July 25, 1627, he "humbly requests His Majesty not to allow such a beautiful and excellent country, so rich in resources, to be lost to France." He declares his intention of continuing to maintain himself there if his strength is equal to his courage and enterprise; if it is not, he will "die with glory in the service of Your Majesty." For all his wild living, it is evident that he could command the language of a courtier and, to him as to most French gentlemen of his age, his *gloire* was something for which he would fight to the death.

The letter had some effect. In 1628, among the ships of Richelieu's new company bringing supplies to the New World, was one destined for Fort Lomeron, and on it was the elder La Tour coming to join his son. But English vessels under command of the Kirkes captured Roquement's little fleet, remained in the Gulf of St. Lawrence to blockade the river, succeeded in starving out Quebec, and finally, after Champlain had been forced to surrender that fortress, took both Champlain and Claude de La Tour to England as prisoners. The country passed to the English. Of all the vast region known as New

France, only Charles de La Tour's fort on Cape Sable remained in French hands.

The story of Charles's father, interesting though it is, has no place here except as it concerns the career of his son. In England, Claude de La Tour became interested in Sir William Alexander's plan for establishing a New Scotland in the very region where he himself had once hoped to settle with Poutrincourt. He joined Alexander's company and accepted a baronetcy of Nova Scotia. Indeed, his enthusiasm carried him further; he accepted a baronetcy for his son. No doubt he thought Charles would be glad of such support after his long years alone. And the Scots, to be sure, were not, like the English, the traditional foes of France but had often been her allies.

Charles, meanwhile, knowing nothing of his father's action, was maintaining his position on Cape Sable (he had now changed its name to Fort St. Louis) and hoping for aid from France. Instead of French ships, however, it was British vessels which, on a day in 1630, appeared in front of his fort. On board were the elder La Tour and his new allies, sailing in with complete confidence, sure that they would be welcome. But Claude had misjudged his son. Instead of receiving the British with joy and agreeing to join them at once, as his father had promised he would, Charles declared that he "would rather die than be so base as to betray his King" (Champlain's account). According to Nicolas Denys, a contemporary though not an eye-witness, the British attacked Fort St. Louis, but Charles drove them off. The Scots, none too pleased with La Tour senior, sailed away to their destination at Port-Royal. Later, records Champlain, Charles succeeded in "bringing his father back to the path of duty."

In July, 1631, while negotiations were still going on between France and England for the restoration of Canada to France, Charles de La Tour received a document which justified his boast to the British that he had "a master able to appreciate his loyalty." Richelieu had nominated him to the king as lieutenant-governor in the land of Acadia and His Majesty had ratified the nomination. With this commission La Tour must have felt that his future as a French gentleman of importance in the New World was assured, especially as, in the following year, the treaty of Saint-Germain-en-Laye restored to France all her possessions in North America. When Louis XIII sent out a French officer named Isaac de Razilly to receive the surrender of Port-Royal from the Scots and be governor, Razilly recognized La Tour's commission and made no attempt to interfere with him. There was plenty of room for both of them.

Razilly had landed at La Hève, on the seaward coast across the peninsula from Port-Royal, and he made this the site of his main settlement. La Tour had by this time been granted permission to build a fort at the mouth of the St. John River and, about 1635, he moved there from Fort St. Louis, although the latter remained in his control. But in that same year Razilly died. A gentleman named Charles de Menou d'Aulnay, who had been a lieutenant under him, now succeeded him and began at once to claim authority over all Acadia, including the lands granted to La Tour. He moved the settlement to Port-Royal, which the Scots had had to vacate. Now two hostile Frenchmen faced each other across the forty-five mile stretch of the Baie Française (Bay of Fundy). Each sent appeals to the king asking for confirmation of his rights. The royal answer, dated February, 1638, hardly improved the situation. It purported to define the limits where each was to command "in order that the boundaries should not be a subject of controversy"; but by it His Majesty gave to d'Aulnay the mainland from the Bay of Fundy down the coast (the coast on which Fort La Tour at the mouth of the St. John was situated), and to La Tour the peninsula where Port-Royal was. Each was designated by the title of lieutenant-governor, and they were expected to share the fur trade between them. Having thus set down conditions which made conflict inevitable, the letter ended by enjoining upon each not to interfere in the affairs of the other.

This was the situation when Françoise-Marie Jacquelin arrived in Acadia. There had probably been no actual violence as yet, but jealousy and resentment were at a pitch which might precipitate an outburst at any moment. The circumstances of Marie's arrival and marriage are far from clear. According to one story, it was in connection with them that the first blow was struck. In the summer of 1640 (this account says), La Tour brought her across the Bay of Fundy in order to have the marriage solemnized by the Capuchins in d'Aulnay's fort. But La Tour had ecclesiastics in his own fort, who belonged to the Récollets, a rival Franciscan order. It seems hardly likely that he would so acknowledge the superior authority of d'Aulnay's priests. The story goes on to state that, when La Tour sailed in with his bride-to-be, d'Aulnay was absent from Port-Royal and the couple were refused admission; and that, on the way home, La Tour met d'Aulnay's vessel and attacked.

Whether or not Marie's married life had so violent a beginning, it is certain that there were, about this time, encounters between the two rivals which resulted in bloodshed. Any other woman than Françoise-Marie might well have been dismayed by the prospect before her. Her position as wife of one of His Majesty's lieutenant-governors promised to be very different from anything she could have pictured. The fort, with its cluster of rough wooden buildings inside a palisade of upright logs, looked more like part of the surrounding forest than like the residence of a royal official. And there was no sign of any other human habitation as far as the eye could see.

Fort La Tour was situated, as excavations begun in 1955 have proved, on Portland Point at the edge of the present city of Saint John, New Brunswick. Built on the shore near the mouth of the St. John River, it had hills rising behind it and in front a harbour opening into the Bay of Fundy. Though man had as yet left scarcely a mark of his presence, the strong forces of nature were manifest everywhere: the might of the rising tide, which Marie would see daily submerging islands in the bay and which, building up to tremendous heights, surged around the very knoll on which the fort stood, making it an island; clouds of birds, often so thick that the sun could not pierce through them; dark forests of tall fir and pine from which came a pungent, exhilarating tang, but from which, also, there might issue at any moment silent-footed savages or strange wild animals. Unfamiliar noises would assail her ears night and day. Nicolas Denys, one of her contemporaries in Acadia, records among those that disturbed him the honking of wild geese at night; the thud of salmon leaping upstream and falling back with a whack and a splash into shallow water; the hammering sound of beavers beating with their tails to pound mud into the walls of their dams. And every day, in regular recurrence, Marie would hear the roar of the distant falls rising in a crescendo that filled the air like thunder, then gradually sinking into silence.

To explore her new environment, she had the choice of footpath or rowboat. It was on foot that she would first approach the falls. Climbing up a densely wooded slope and proceeding through the

forest on top, she would suddenly find herself on the brink of a
precipice; for here the St. John River had cut itself a channel through
the white limestone of the hill. When the tide was ebbing, the waters
of sea and river, all rushing at once to crowd through the narrow
chasm and impeded by rocky ridges and islands, sent foam and spray
leaping high in the air; then, having hurled themselves over the last
obstacle, they plunged on in swirls and eddies to sweep around the
end of the promontory. Soon, however, the violence of sound and
motion began to diminish, until, after a few hours, the waters had
entirely lost their frantic haste and subsided into slack and silence.
Then, gradually, began a movement inland, mounting in force until
the rising tide overpowered the current of the river and sent a flood
of water pitching backwards, to tumble on the reverse side of the
rocks and go surging up the gorge.

It was a violent and amazing spectacle. Even today, though both
the volume of the river and the height of the Fundy tides have
dwindled, though railway and road bridges cut the view and the
white limestone cliffs have been blackened by city air, tourists still
stand for hours to watch it.

To Mme de La Tour, however, her surroundings were not just
scenery. A determined woman intent on establishing a home here,
she was concerned with their practical aspect. The reversing falls
served as a barrier to protect the river. Hostile ships, whether they
came from d'Aulnay or from the English, could not steal up that
waterway to attack Fort La Tour from the landward side, for it was
only at brief intervals, a few minutes just after half-tide, that it was
possible for any boat to pass. Wild life might disturb her slumbers,
but it provided furs and food. Besides the leaping salmon, there were
gaspereaux, a less agile fish easily caught in the weir which Charles
had set up, across on the marshy side of the channel. There were
also lobsters. Denys mentions some with front claws that would hold
a pint! And there was, of course, a variety of game. But fish and game
had each their seasons. What the fort lacked was staples. Charles
had to import his grain from France. That could be remedied if land
were cleared so that his men could grow their own. He had advertised
for settlers in a gazette in France some years ago, but so far the men
whom he had succeeded in attracting showed no desire to clear and
till land; they preferred hunting, fishing, and trading. Trade was of

course important, and, fortunately, the St. John bore many fur-laden canoes on its current. But there were over a hundred men in her husband's service and they all had to be fed, as well as paid. Some of them had been Charles's followers all through his days and years of hardship and poverty. Marie would no doubt have liked to see them comfortably established now, and girls brought out from France to marry them and help them settle on land. There was excellent land available: above the falls, the river ran through a pleasant valley with gentle slopes and grassy meadows, where agriculture might be very successful.

The home which Françoise-Marie Jacquelin had envisaged for herself and her husband in the New World was not a primitive dwelling with the bare essentials of survival, but one which should have some degree of comfort, even of elegance. This is indicated by fragments of attractive pottery and fine glass found in the excavations at Saint John and probably brought out by her from France. In fact, the value of the jewelry, furnishings, and other household effects in the fort was later estimated at ten thousand pounds. Marie no doubt felt that the residence of Charles de Saint-Etienne de La Tour, lieu-tenant-governor of Acadia, should have the amenities proper for a French gentleman, so that he might live with dignity in this land where for so many years he had wandered like a homeless savage. She might well have pictured a future in which he would be a feudal lord with tenants and tilled lands to provide him a comfortable living. Yet how could he spare funds and men for the clearing and tilling of land, when he needed all the strength he could muster to protect himself from his enemy across the Bay?

D'Aulnay, so Nicolas Denys maintained, was a man who could brook no rival. He would not rest until he had driven Charles out. Denys spoke from bitter experience for he himself had already been driven out. An enterprising man full of zeal for developing the country's resources, he had, in Razilly's time, not only established the first sedentary fisheries, but also started a lumber industry at La Hève. The planking and beams which his carpenters prepared were carried back to France by the ships which brought Razilly's provisions. But after Razilly's death, d'Aulnay refused to allow him any space on the ships and even forbade him to use the harbour. He had to abandon the whole site, timber and all. Now he had established himself up on the island of Miscou, far enough away from d'Aulnay to be safe.

Charles de La Tour, his new wife surely resolved, would not be driven out so easily. The thought of anyone trying to dispossess him would fill her with wrath and indignation. Charles had been on this coast for thirty years, had spent his whole life maintaining French rights here. Alone, he had kept a foothold for France and had bravely withstood attempts to seduce him from his loyalty, not hesitating to defy the English and the Scots and even his own father. D'Aulnay had arrived in time of peace and done nothing but step into another man's shoes. Why should *he* have authority to deprive Charles of his rightful place? Was Charles's commission as lieutenant-governor to be null and void?

D'Aulnay soon showed that he considered it so. After the encounters of 1640, he had sent letters to France laying complaints against La Tour, charging that he was abusing his authority and living a disorderly life in his fort. (One of the disorders mentioned was that he allowed psalm-singing, a Huguenot practice.) Since d'Aulnay's father in Paris had influence with Richelieu, the complaints received attention. The result was that His Majesty issued an order for La Tour to come to France to answer the charges, and left it to d'Aulnay to see that he obeyed. Considering, no doubt, that this summons justified him in taking action, d'Aulnay now seized La Tour's fort on Cape Sable and, though he had been expected to preserve it for coastal defence, burned it to the ground, together with the Récollet residence and chapel connected with it. La Tour, meanwhile, had received a letter from his agent in France, advising him to look to himself and guard against d'Aulnay's designs. Marie and her husband, convinced now that their enemy would stop at nothing, were constantly on the alert.

On August 17, 1642, a sail appeared in the Bay and entered the channel which led to their harbour. Charles at once sent one of his lieutenants to set up a swivel gun on the opposite shore, ready to fire on the vessel at any sign of hostility. It anchored at some distance and from it was launched a small boat which set out rapidly toward the fort. As it drew nearer, the La Tours saw that it was rowed by four sailors and had three gentlemen passengers seated in it. One of the latter raised a trumpet to his mouth and proclaimed their mission. They were the bearers of a decree recently issued in France and entrusted to the Sieur d'Aulnay. "The Sieur d'Aulnay de Charnisay" they designated him, "Governor and Lieutenant-General of His Majesty throughout all the coasts of Acadia." La Tour could hardly refuse to listen to a royal decree, whatever hopeful suspicions he may have entertained about its authenticity. He allowed the boat to land, and listened with due courtesy while d'Aulnay's envoy began to read. "Given at Paris, this 23rd day of February in the year of Our Lord sixteen hundred and forty-two," he began. Then, after a lengthy preamble, came the words of the decree itself. It ordered La Tour to yield himself and his fort at once to d'Aulnay, who would take him prisoner to France.

La Tour's temper flared. No gentleman who prized his honour could brook such a summons. He seized the document in his strong hands and crumpled it into a ball. Using violent language to the envoys, he ordered them thrown into his dungeon; then he had a shot fired from his fort's cannon and immediately the swivel gun on the other shore roared out at d'Aulnay's vessel, which hastily set sail back across the Bay while the La Tours stood triumphantly on their ramparts hurling insults after the departing foe.

That Marie was wholeheartedly with her husband in this defiance there is little doubt. Indeed, according to charges which d'Aulnay made later, she was the main cause of his "contempt and rebellion." Women of dauntless fighting spirit were not unknown in the France of her day. "Musketeers in petticoats" one writer has called them. The most celebrated is no doubt La Grande Mademoiselle, who took an active part in the wars of La Fronde and fought on the walls of her city of Orléans. Mme La Tour, fighting in the New World for her home and her husband, could compare favourably with her in enterprise and physical courage. Perhaps she had qualms at times at the thought that the paper which Charles had treated so contemptuously might really have been a genuine summons from His Majesty and that d'Aulnay, in that case, could now produce witnesses to swear at the French court that Charles was a rebel. In any case, the prisoners down in the dungeon would certainly be his enemies henceforth and, once released (as they would have to be; it would cost too much to feed them), their stories could do incalculable damage.

Summer ended without further sign of the enemy. Winter came and things were still peaceful. But the lull, the La Tours surmised, was only because d'Aulnay had gone to France to press his charges. They had little hope that he had decided to leave them in peace. Indeed, before the month of March, 1643, was out, they saw his ship once more at the entrance to their channel. Then arrived a second vessel. Each, according to the report of La Tour's scouts, was of three hundred tons and had thirty guns. A small pinnace soon joined them. The La Tours, having no vessel of any size to send against them, had to endure the sight of them day after day, swinging idly at anchor just out of reach of gunfire from the shore. Their fort was being blockaded, and they were infuriatingly helpless.

Early on the morning of May 21, in the dim pre-dawn light, a sentry on the ramparts espied a small boat creeping around the shore toward the fort. He ran hastily to report to his master, who at once came out and hailed it. It proved to be the longboat from a new arrival, the *Saint-Clément*, an armed vessel sent out from La Rochelle by La Tour's agent, loaded with supplies for the fort. She had safely completed her ocean voyage and rounded Cape Sable the previous day, but had then found herself prevented from reaching her goal; for, sailing up the Bay of Fundy, she had seen three vessels coming to meet her. Recognizing one of them as d'Aulnay's, and realizing that their object was to capture the *Saint-Clément* and her cargo, Captain Mourron had turned and fled down the Bay. He dared not risk an encounter, for his ship was of only 140 tons. By gaining the open sea, he had escaped them for that day. When darkness had fallen, he sailed cautiously up the Bay again and, from a safe distance, launched the longboat to take a letter to the fort announcing his plight. In it he asked for instructions, for unless La Tour could aid him in some way, he saw no possibility of delivering his cargo.

That Captain Mourron had been allowed to equip an armed vessel and sail from a French harbour with supplies for Fort La Tour seemed evidence to Charles and Marie that the French court was not so unfavourably disposed to them as they had been led to believe. This was an encouragement, but it did not solve the present dilemma. How could they get the much-needed food for guns and men? On board the *Saint-Clément* were also two passengers whom Marie was expecting to add to her household staff as "waiting women." (She was, it seems probable, by this time the mother of a son.) The *Saint-Clément* must be brought safely into harbour. But how? Only by help from outside, that was plain. The one possible source of such help was Boston, eighty leagues down the coast. La Tour had already established trade relations there, and had acquaintance with some of the town's merchants. Charles and Marie devised a plan.

"Accompanied by his intrepid wife," says Parkman, La Tour slipped out of the fort in the night, rowed stealthily past d'Aulnay's blockading vessels, and by dawn was on board the *Saint-Clément*. He gave orders to the captain to sail down to Massachusetts Bay. In France later, Captain Mourron filed a report of the voyage (as all ships' captains were required to do on their return home), in which he says that La Tour took upon himself the responsibility for any risk this might involve. It was quite possible, of course, that the English of the Bay, alarmed by the unexpected appearance of a French vessel, might offer some resistance to the *Saint-Clément*'s approach. There had been plenty of violent incidents between French and English on this coast to justify suspicion. The "three-hilled city of the Puritans," however, not anticipating any attack, had become careless about defence, and the *Saint-Clément*, sailing in past Castle Island, was inside the harbour before the Boston citizens had any warning of it. Governor John Winthrop in his journal tells how startled they were, and remarks on the impression made by La Tour's courtesy and forbearance. "If he had been ill-minded toward us, he had such opportunity as we hope neither he nor any other shall ever have the like again," for Castle Island was deserted and La Tour could have landed on it and turned its cannon upon the town. Winthrop goes on to describe the colourful incidents of this visit. He makes no mention of Marie de La Tour, but if she was not present, she would certainly hear all about it on her husband's return. La Tour went to religious services, listened to Puritan preachers, and was generally courteous and friendly. On training day in Boston, he watched with generously expressed admiration the 150 Boston soldiers exercising on the common; then put on an expert performance of his own with forty men from the *Saint-Clément*. He had soon succeeded in hiring ships and men, for Governor Winthrop allowed him "a free mercate" (market), and drums beat in the streets of Boston for volunteers. Afterwards, however, there was a great deal of argument, sustained by many biblical quotations, criticizing the governor for allowing men to go. Was it lawful, questioned the Puritan elders, to aid an idolater? This seems sufficient proof that, whatever respect La Tour had shown for the religion of his hosts, he had not denied his own.

The criticism of the governor's decision came too late to interfere with La Tour's success. He had already secured, at a price (£520 a month sterling), three English ships and a frigate. With this reinforcement he and Captain Mourron sailed back up the coast. While d'Aulnay with his ships watched the fort on the St. John, thinking he had his rival blockaded there, the *Saint-Clément* and the English ships suddenly appeared in his rear. Recognizing defeat, d'Aulnay fled across the Bay to Port-Royal, pursued by La Tour and the English. Now, instead of being blockaded, La Tour was the blockader. He sent some of the English in with a letter to d'Aulnay, asking him for an explanation of his action in destroying Fort St. Louis and demanding damages. But d'Aulnay refused to open the letter, so the English reported, because La Tour in addressing it had not styled him Lieutenant-Governor of all Acadia. La Tour, in anger, sailed in for an assault. With his own men and a few of the Englishmen who volunteered, he attacked a mill, which was defended by d'Aulnay's men. Three of the latter were killed and the mill burned. Then La Tour, considering that he had done enough damage to make d'Aulnay stay in his own territory for a time, sailed back across the Bay and with his English escort entered his own fort.

Whatever Marie may have thought of the fighting and the destruction which her husband had wrought at Port-Royal, of one thing she could be sure—d'Aulnay would hasten to report it to France. Somehow the justification of Charles's conduct must be laid before the French court. D'Aulnay had had no right whatever to interfere with the *Saint-Clément*, which had left France with full permission to deliver the necessary cargo. But who was there to plead Charles's case at court? He had no influential father in Paris. And if he himself left Fort La Tour, d'Aulnay would no doubt seize and destroy that fort as he had Fort St. Louis. Marie made up her mind. *She* would go to France. The *Saint-Clément*, lying in the shelter of Partridge Island, was being loaded with furs for the return voyage. Fortunately they had had a fairly successful trade. With peltry she could negotiate in France for the following year's supplies and then proceed to Paris to present her husband's case. The English vessels, whose term of hire was not yet up, waited to escort the *Saint-Clément* out of the harbour.

She arrived at La Rochelle on October 9, 1643. It was a time of confusion and disorder in France, for the great cardinal and his royal master had both died and the country was under the new minister Mazarin and the Queen Regent, mother of the five-year-old king. Perhaps that is why Marie was able to unload her cargo unmolested, in spite of the charges of d'Aulnay, who had also reached France. She succeeded in negotiating for a ship to take provisions to Fort La Tour.

But her pleading of her husband's case at court that winter proved vain. D'Aulnay's "charge" was that La Tour had allied himself with the English to attack him, with the aim of driving the French out of Acadia. A decree of March 6, 1644, condemned La Tour for contumacy because he had not appeared in France when summoned. It also forbade Mme de La Tour to send any aid to him, or to return to Acadia herself, on pain of death. Marie did not for a minute consider obeying such a prohibition. Learning of the preparations which d'Aulnay was making to strengthen himself against Charles, she succeeded in getting a message off warning her husband that his rival had prevailed against him at court and was now collecting soldiers, ammunition, and ships with which "to subdue him." Then the courageous lady, eluding the French authorities, made her escape to England. Here she hired an English ship to carry her back to her husband and his imperilled fort.

She had lost no time. Before the end of March she set sail from Southampton. The ship under Captain Bailey had, as cargo, goods which Marie was taking for her husband's Indian trade, but also merchandise for New England. Marie's anxiety, increased by the slowness of the crossing, rose to heights of angry impatience after the ship had actually reached the coast of America; for the captain, instead of hastening as directly as possible to enter the Bay of Fundy as he had contracted to do, kept going out of his way to trade at different points on the coast, even up the St. Lawrence itself. Then, when at last they approached Cape Sable and were about to round it, another vessel accosted them. It was d'Aulnay's newly acquired ship, *Le Grand Cardinal*; and it was on the lookout for Mme de La Tour. But that resourceful woman was not to be taken by surprise. She had already disappeared below the hatches, after instructing the captain to say that this was a London vessel bound for Massachusetts Bay. D'Aulnay could hardly insist on boarding and searching an English ship, but

his appearance had accomplished part of his purpose—it had turned
Captain Bailey aside from the goal his passenger was so impatient
to reach. He now continued his way down the coast to Boston.

Roger Williams may well have been on this ship, for he arrived
in Boston at the same time as Mme de La Tour, bringing with him
the charter for his colony of Rhode Island, dated London, March 14,
1644. (One writer suggests that the six months on the ocean with
this strong-minded Puritan turned the lady into a fanatical Protestant,
and that this accounts for a violent scene she is said to have had later
with the Récollets in her fort.)

It was September 17 when Captain Bailey entered the harbour of
Boston. We can imagine Marie's wrath and frustration at finding
herself, after a six months' voyage, still eighty leagues from her home.
Her anger against Captain Bailey would be heightened, if possible,
when she discovered that Charles had been in Boston and had left
just the week before. He had received her letter of warning and had
once more come to the English to seek help. It was more than a year
since she had seen him or had any news of him or her family. Besides
the infuriating disappointment of having missed him, she must have
felt concern for his safety. The *Mountjoy*, the English ship which
had accompanied him, was only a small pinnace, and d'Aulnay's *Grand
Cardinal* was no doubt still on the prowl.

The long delay in reaching Fort La Tour had other serious aspects.
Mme de La Tour's merchandise in the hold of Captain Bailey's vessel
would now be too late for trade on the St. John. In addition to the
loss of that revenue, she herself would now be put to the expense of
hiring ships to take her home. Captain Gibbons, a Boston friend of
the Sieur de La Tour, and other merchants to whom the Frenchman
owed money, agreed with Mme de La Tour that she had grounds for
a lawsuit against Captain Bailey. She took action at once. For four
full days, Governor Winthrop tells us, the hearing lasted, and then
judgment was given. Mme de La Tour was awarded £ 2,000 damages.

Captain Bailey protested the judgment and refused to pay. Marie
had him arrested. He obtained the freedom of his person by delivering
on shore cargo to the value of £ 1,100. But this was merchandise
destined for the merchants of Charleston, just across the Charles River
from Boston, and they objected. In the disputes which followed,
Marie, anxious to get home and despairing of collecting her £ 2,000,

offered to sign a promissory note as payment to anyone who would furnish her with ships to escort her to her fort. A certain Captain Paris declared himself willing to accept such terms and secured three vessels for her. She finally wrested from Captain Bailey a money payment of £100—a sum sufficient to discharge her debts for food and lodging in Boston—and accepted such security as he offered for the balance of the sum awarded her. It took a few days to get the arms and provisions for the escort of ships which Captain Paris was to command, and she signed a note in his favour for £700, to be paid in peltry when the ships reached Fort La Tour. Then at last, on board his ketch of forty-three tons and six guns, she sailed out of Boston harbour and was on her way up the coast. But even the weather seemed conspiring to keep her from Charles. Contrary winds beat the ships back, fog and sleet enshrouded them. It was the end of December, 1644, before they at last entered the mouth of the St. John River.

She must have felt a great joy in the reunion with her husband and son—the baby who had had to be left in the care of waiting women. But the fort was in even a worse state than she had feared. Lack of merchandise and d'Aulnay's blockade had ruined trade. The few furs which Charles had been able to collect by roaming the region himself amounted, according to Captain Paris's reckoning, to only £172 of the £700 promised in the lady's note. Charles was constrained to add a gold chain of the value of thirty or forty pounds which he was very reluctant to part with (perhaps it was a wedding gift brought from France by Marie), and which he stipulated should be redeemable "in case it possibly may."

Because of the fort's scarcities, Marie felt that Charles should go to Boston again. She herself had found the people there well disposed toward her; though d'Aulnay, as she had discovered during her stay, was sending envoys to the Massachusetts Bay authorities in an effort to discredit Charles. He would not succeed, she felt sure. Captain Gibbons, at least, would remain friendly, and other New England merchants to whom Charles was in debt would surely be anxious to help him; they would not want him to lose his fort. There might also be a possibility of extracting more money from Captain Bailey. In the end, Charles agreed. D'Aulnay's ships, it was thought, had been badly damaged in the winter's storms; he would not venture forth again until the weather was better, and he would never suspect that anyone else would be foolhardy enough to do so. If Charles left now, he could be back before the enemy knew that he had gone. So he set out on the strongest pinnace they had, taking with him an escort from the fort's soldiers.

After he had left, his wife made a discovery which must have added greatly to her anxiety. Charles had told her that, while he had been out hunting moose and beaver skins to pay his debts, d'Aulnay had sent one of his lieutenants into the fort to try to seduce the men from their allegiance, but that all the lieutenant had got for his pains was jeers and curses. Now she began to perceive that d'Aulnay's enticements of fine food and good wages were having more weight with some of the men than Charles had realized. Moreover, the Récollet priest, Fr. André, apparently having forgotten d'Aulnay's destruction of the Récollet chapel on Cape Sable three years ago (though he had been one of those who had claimed damages at the time) was now wavering in his loyalty. Perhaps the documents which d'Aulnay's emissary had displayed had convinced him that Charles was a rebel; perhaps he was reluctant to remain in a fort which was under the command of a Huguenot mistress, and one, moreover, who had sent her husband to seek aid from the "foes of God." He had an exchange of harsh words with Mme de La Tour, after which he and his fellow-priest announced their intention to leave. This was a deciding factor for some of the hesitating men. In addition to the risk of remaining with scanty food in the fort of a man who had been declared a traitor, they now had to face the possibility of fighting and perhaps dying with no one there to grant them absolution. Eight of them decided to go with the priests. In a leaky boat and with a small supply of Indian corn, they started on their voyage across the Bay. If storms came up, they might never reach their goal.

Winter dragged to its end. Marie had no means of knowing whether Charles's pinnace had reached Boston harbour, or whether the deserters had arrived safely at Port-Royal and reported his going. If d'Aulnay knew of the commandant's absence from the fort, he would no doubt seize the opportunity to attack.

In the middle of March, 1645, sails were sighted far down the channel and she sent a small boat to reconnoitre. It returned in haste. Hovering around Partridge Island were two ships of d'Aulnay's, the

Grand Cardinal and a smaller vessel. Day after day, week after week, Mme de La Tour and her men watched. The sails remained in sight but did not advance up the Bay. Then, on the 12th of April, they came swiftly in on the mounting tide. D'Aulnay had decided to attack.

Marie had only forty-five soldiers left in the fort, and no one to whom she was willing to entrust its defence. She took command herself. Her men were too few, her ammunition too scant, for her to consider mounting cannon in a strategic position along the shore, as Charles had done on d'Aulnay's appearance three years ago. D'Aulnay, who lacked neither men nor guns, seized the opportunity to do so. Marie soon realized that she was about to be bombarded from both land and sea.

Meanwhile, however, a small boat was being lowered from the *Cardinal*. As it rowed toward the fort, her sentries recognized the men in it—Fr. André and six of the men who had left with him. Mme de La Tour's first thought was that they were returning to aid her, and she allowed them to enter her fort. But when they began to mingle with her men, she quickly discovered her mistake. They were urging her soldiers to desert her, enticing the ill-fed men with tales of the good food with which d'Aulnay would reward them. But in her fort were men who were passionately loyal to her. They took quick action against the intruders, driving them out at gunpoint and restraining any who would have followed them; she herself, according to one of the men who later turned traitor, hurled insults at them and in her fury seemed ready to tear their eyes out. Shortly afterward, d'Aulnay began his bombardment.

Meanwhile, Charles, having found the Boston merchants less quick than he had hoped to respond to his appeal, had despatched a small boat back to his fort with such food and ammunition as he had been able to procure. In it he had sent also one of his own personal servants with a letter for his wife to tell her he would be with her in a month. (He no doubt hoped by that time to be accompanied by English ships.) One of d'Aulnay's vessels intercepted the little boat, and neither her husband's letter nor the supplies he had sent ever reached Mme de La Tour.

D'Aulnay now hastened to press his attack before La Tour should rejoin his wife with reinforcements. For three days and three nights Mme de La Tour and her men withstood it. They inflicted such damage on the besiegers that the *Grand Cardinal* was forced to withdraw with a hole in her keel, listing and seemingly ready to sink. But she finally came to rest on a sand-bar out in the channel below the gaspereaux weir. The report was that twenty of d'Aulnay's men were killed and thirteen wounded.

The next day was Easter Sunday. Confident that d'Aulnay, a devout Catholic, would not attack on that day, Mme de La Tour ordered her men to take a well-earned rest. Once again her enemy sent some of his men to try to seduce the weary soldiers from their allegiance; once again the fort's defenders drove them out with threats and curses. The invaders had, however, before being forced out, succeeded in making secret arrangements with a hired Swiss soldier named Hans Vannes. During his watch the next morning, d'Aulnay's men made a swift onslaught upon the palisade. He failed to give any alarm. Mme de La Tour suddenly saw the assailants within her outer walls. She summoned all her little garrison and rushed to the ramparts.

D'Aulnay now called upon her to surrender. Neither she nor her men were in any mood to listen. She answered by running up La Tour's standard on the bastions and firing a volley from the fort's cannon. Then d'Aulnay's trumpeters shouted a message offering parley. The lady commandant's first impulse was to hurl back more defiance; but when he offered to spare the lives of all within the fort if she would surrender, she yielded. There was now no hope for the fort. If d'Aulnay would give quarter to all her men, she must surrender and save their lives. After he got possession, however, d'Aulnay changed his mind. He decided that the men should all be hanged "pour servir de mémoire et d'exemple à la posterité" of the consequences of such obstinate rebellion. Two were spared: the Swiss who had betrayed the fort and another man who saved his own life by acting as executioner. Mme de La Tour, according to Nicolas Denys' account, was forced to be present at the executions, wearing a rope around her neck as if she were a criminal. (Denys was not an eyewitness; he is reporting what he heard.)

A heart-broken and desperate prisoner, Marie tried to communicate with her husband. He might even now be on his way with help for the defence of the fort. He must be warned that it was in the hands of the enemy; otherwise he might fall into a trap. She wrote a letter which she planned to entrust to the friendly Micmacs. But she was caught in the act and thereafter kept under strict surveillance. Frustrated, she "fell ill of spite and rage" according to the statement of André Certain, one of d'Aulnay's officials entrusted with the task of drawing up a report on the capture of the fort.

The Capuchin missionary Pascal de Troyes says that he visited her several times and exhorted her to abjure the heresy she had professed at Boston, and that she did so before she died. For various reasons, however, his report, as well as that of André Certain, is suspect.

After three weeks of imprisonment, Mme de La Tour died.

In Boston there was a rumour that d'Aulnay had poisoned her. André Certain asserts that neither she nor her waiting women nor her little son suffered any harm. (This is the only mention of the son, and since nothing further is known of him, it is assumed that he died in early childhood.)

Having lost his fort and being still in debt to the Boston merchants, La Tour took refuge in Quebec for several years. When, in 1650, d'Aulnay met his death by drowning, La Tour went to France to present his case. The French court exonerated him completely of all charges of treachery and rebellion, and appointed him Lieutenant-Governor of Acadia, with all his former possessions restored.

Three years after d'Aulnay's death, Charles de La Tour married the widow, his declared purpose being "to establish peace and tranquillity in Acadia and harmony and concord between the two families who have governed it."

"Peace and tranquillity in Acadia" was a dream not to be realized in La Tour's lifetime. But he, yielding to circumstances, managed by negotiation and adjustment to maintain himself and his family at Fort La Tour until his death in 1666.

It is through the children of his third marriage that Charles de La Tour's posterity in Canada claim their descent. But it is Françoise-Marie Jacquelin who is remembered as "the most remarkable woman in Acadia's early history" and the first European woman to have made a home in what is now the Province of New Brunswick.

BIBLIOGRAPHY

Dictionary of Canadian Biography.
NICOLAS DENYS, *The Description and Natural History of the Coasts of*

North America, ed. W. F. Ganong, Champlain Society Publications, II. Toronto, 1908.

Winthrop's Journal "History of New England," ed. J. K. Hosmer. *Original Narratives of Early American History,* ed. J. F. Jameson. New York, 1908.

A. Couillard Després, *Charles de Saint-Etienne de la Tour.* Arthabaska, 1930.

Emile Lauvrière, *Deux traîtres d'Acadie et leur victime: les Latour père et fils et Charles d'Aulnay.* Paris et Montréal, 1932.

2

Marie Guyart de l'Incarnation

1599-1672

MARIE-EMMANUEL CHABOT

A LA FIN du XVIe siècle, la France plonge encore dans l'atmosphère chevaleresque de la Renaissance. Il y a du panache dans l'air et sur les chapeaux, on rêve de se signaler au service du roi, d'entreprendre des voyages au long cours. En Touraine, le roi et les seigneurs habitent les plus magnifiques jardins du royaume.

C'est dans cette contrée d'équilibre et de beauté que Marie Guyart naît le 28 octobre 1599, au foyer de Florent Guyart, maître boulanger, et de Jeanne Michelet alliée aux fameux Babou de la Bourdaisière. Chez les Guyart, on conserve le souvenir d'un aïeul illustre, membre de l'escorte qui, envoyée par Louis XI en Calabre, amena au château du Plessis le thaumaturge François de Paule.

Dans ses *Relations*, Marie raconte quelques traits de son enfance écoulée dans la paroisse Saint-Saturnin. Elle parle de la charité envers les pauvres qu'elle soulageait parfois avec excès : « Je ne saurais dire comme je les aimais. » De bonne heure, elle manifeste un attrait sensible pour la piété : « J'allais souvent à l'église et me tenais là une bonne partie du jour. Mon cœur souhaitait avec ardeur cette communication, et j'étais si enfant que je ne savais pas que c'était là faire oraison. »

La nuit, Marie prolonge sa prière et voit passer le Seigneur en songe. Il lui sourit, lui demande : « Voulez-vous être à moi ? » Et la petite s'élance, répond un « oui » qui caractérise sa nature ardente et généreuse. Elle est bien celle acquiescera toujours aux volontés de Dieu.

Cependant, elle grandit dans la joie, dans une harmonie qui semble la destiner aux félicités du monde. Un jour, l'adolescente déclare son désir d'entrer au couvent. La voyant agréable et accorte, sa mère fait la sourde oreille et lui offre plutôt un époux. Loin de se révolter, Marie accepte volontiers le bon vouloir de Dieu, exprimé pour elle par la décision de ses parents. C'est ainsi qu'elle devient, à dix-sept ans, l'épouse de Claude Martin, négociant en soie. A cette heure décisive, Marie semble percer l'avenir et confie à sa mère : « Puisque c'est une résolution prise et que mon père le veut absolument, je me crois obligée d'obéir à sa volonté et à la vôtre ; mais si Dieu me fait la grâce de me donner un fils, je lui promets dès à présent de le consacrer à son service ; et si ensuite, il me rend la liberté que je vais perdre, je lui promets encore de m'y consacrer moi-même. »

Le 1er avril 1619, Marie Martin se rend en pèlerinage à l'Abbaye de Marmoutier pour demander la bénédiction de l'apôtre des Gaules sur l'enfent qu'elle va mettre au monde. Et le fils tant désiré naît le lendemain, en la fête de saint François de Paule, ami et protecteur de la famille Guyart. Au registre de la paroisse Saint-Pierre des Corps, se lit encore l'acte de baptême de Claude Martin junior.

En ménage, Marie ne connaît pas le bonheur. Quoiqu'elle aime beaucoup son époux, elle traverse des épreuves qu'elle refusera d'expliciter. Six mois plus tard, Claude Martin meurt prématurément. Marie reste veuve à vingt ans. La voilà ruinée, plongée dans une foule d'embarras. « Diverses affaires, écrit-elle, m'apportèrent de nouvelles croix beaucoup plus grandes qu'une personne de mon sexe, de mon âge, de ma capacité les eût pu porter. » On pourrait la croire à la merci du découragement et des exploiteurs, mais elle se tourne vers le ciel : « L'esprit de Dieu qui m'occupait intérieurement me remplissait de foi, d'espérance et de confiance, me faisait venir à bout de tout ce que j'entreprenais. »

En quelques semaines, Madame Martin liquide le commerce de son mari et retourne habiter chez son père. Bien sûr, le désir de se consacrer à Dieu lui revient impérieux, mais l'heure n'est pas propice : son fils au berceau la réclame tout entière. Toutefois, Marie résiste aux instances de ses proches qui veulent la remarier. Au fait, de nombreux partis se présentent.

Mais elle a déjà fait son choix définitif : désormais, elle appartiendra à Dieu qui lui donne des marques de dilection extraordinaire. Cet Amant dévoile ses exigences absolues. Le récit qu'elle a laissé de la vision de 1620 marque son entrée officielle dans la voie mystique, son baptême de sang :

> Un matin que j'allais vaquer à *mes* affaires que je recommandais instamment à Dieu avec mon inspiration ordinaire : *In te Domine speravi ; non confundar in aeternum...* je fus subitement arrêtée, intérieurement et extérieurement, et par cet arrêt subit, le pensée de mes occupations me fut ôtée de la mémoire. Lors, en ce moment, les yeux de mon esprit me furent ouverts et toutes les fautes, péchés, et imperfections que j'avais commis depuis que j'étais au monde, me furent représentées avec une distinction et clarté plus certaine qu'aucune certitude humaine. Au même instant, je me vis toute plongée dans des flots de sang et mon esprit fut convaincu que ce sang était celui du Fils de Dieu, de l'effusion duquel j'étais coupable par tous les péchés qui m'étaient représentés et que ce Sang précieux avait été répandu pour mon salut...

En se resaisissant, Marie se trouve en face de l'église des Feuillants. C'est à cet ordre qu'appartient Dom Raymond de St-Bernard qui deviendra son premier directeur spirituel.

Loin de se diriger vers le couvent, ou de mener une vie retirée dans le monde, Marie, pourtant avide de solitude et de silence, accepte, en 1621, d'aller vivre chez sa sœur Claude, épouse de Paul Buisson fort engagé dans « le tracas des affaires temporelles ». Chargés, pour tout le royaume, des transports commerciaux sur eau et sur terre, les Buisson possèdent une troupe de serviteurs, des entrepôts, des écuries, des quais le long de la Loire.

Tout d'abord, Marie Martin assume les travaux du ménage, le soin des domestiques malades, les tâches les plus viles de la maison. Délicate, elle s'acquitte même en cachette de toutes les besognes humiliantes, pour les épargner à ses compagnes.

Mais en 1625, les Buisson ouvrent les yeux : dans leur sœur, ils découvrent soudain une femme de tête, un chef capable de gérer toute l'entreprise. Voilà Marie contre-maîtresse, comptable, cheville ouvrière d'une des plus grandes firmes de transports du royaume de France. Eclate alors le génie pratique de Mme Martin, son parfait équilibre, son aisance à se « sanctifier dans le tracas » . Elle passe des jours entiers dans une écurie servant de magasin. A minuit, elle s'attarde sur le port à faire charger ou décharger des marchandises. Pour compagnie ordinaire, des crocheteurs, des charretiers, une soixantaine de chevaux. Une autre crierait au surmenage ; Mme Martin trouve tout facile et rien dans ce brouhaha ne la détourne de sa grande « application » à Dieu. Attentive à la prospérité d'une maison de commerce, au bien-être de « la plus grande famille de toute la province » , elle fait chez les Buisson son premier « noviciat » , s'apprête à « porter les tracas et les travaux de la Nouvelle-France » .

En 1535, Angèle Mérici avait fondé, à Brescia, un Institut très souple qui rassemblait des femmes résolues de travailler à l'éducation des filles. Cinq ans plus tard, le 27 janvier 1540, Mère Angèle mourut après avoir dicté sa Règle. La Compagnie de Sainte-Ursule comptait alors 150 membres agréés par le Saint-Siège. Toutefois, l'époque n'était pas prête à comprendre cette forme de vie religieuse séculière, sans clôture et sans habit distinctif.

Vers 1568, saint Charles Borromée appella les filles d'Angèle dans son diocèse de Milan et leur proposa la vie commune. Bientôt, la Compagnie de Sainte-Ursule passa en France et connut une ère de prospérité en Provence.

Dès 1608, les Ursulines gagnèrent Paris. C'est là que la Compagnie devint l'Ordre de Sainte-Ursule en acceptant la clôture et les vœux solennels. Dans ces cadres plus rigides, les moniales se trouvaient en harmonie avec l'esprit contemporain et avec les instructions du Concile de Trente qui n'avait pas prévu la formule futuriste d'Angèle Mérici. Du monastère de la rue Saint-Jacques à Paris, sortirent une quinzaine de maisons qui, à leur tour, en fondèrent trente d'autres. Simultanément, six Congrégations surgirent en terre française. A celle de Bordeaux se rattachait le monastère des Ursulines de Tours qui nous a donné Marie de l'Incarnation.

Depuis 1625, les Ursulines sont installées dans la petite Bourdaisière, logis du XVIe siècle, en bordure de la rue du Petit-Pré. Chaque fois que Marie passe en face du monastère, elle se sent comme emportée vers les moniales qui mènent une vie à la fois active et contemplative, pleinement conforme à son attrait mystique et apostolique.

Le 25 janvier 1631, Mme Martin quitte son vieux père et son fils Claude sur lequel les Buisson promettent de veiller. Heure d'agonie où elle se sent comme écorchée vive, « séparée en deux ». Pour se rassurer, elle a besoin de penser que l'Eglise a béni sa décision, que Dieu lui demande ce sacrifice héroïque.

Une fois en clôture, elle connaît quelques jours d'apaisement, mais les épreuves l'assaillent bientôt : tentations de dégoût, critiques des gens du monde et des religieuses, ruses de son fils Claude pour apitoyer sa mère et la forcer à retourner à la maison. Profitant des travaux de construction, il s'introduit au réfectoire, passe la tête dans la grille de la chapelle, dirige même l'attaque du monastère avec des gamins armés de pierres et de bâtons. « Rendez-moi ma mère ! Je veux ma mère ! » clame-t-il. Marie distingue la voix de son enfant et les plaies du 25 janvier 1631 recommencent à saigner. Seul le Seigneur réussit à la consoler en lui promettant « avec un grand amour » qu'il prendra soin du jeune Claude Martin.

Après un noviciat avec des compagnes à peine sorties de l'adolescence, Mme Martin prononce ses vœux de religion, le 25 janvier 1633, en la chapelle Saint-Michel.

Mère Marie s'adonne aux œuvres de l'Institut, est nommée sous-maîtresse des novices. Il lui arrive de donner des conférences où percent son originalité et ses charismes particuliers. Une secrète intuition lui laisse entendre que le monastère de Tours n'est pour elle qu'un lieu de passage, que Dieu lui prépare une mission unique dans l'Eglise.

En 1634 le secret se dissipe. En songe, Marie de l'Incarnation se promène avec une dame séculière dans un grand pays « plein de montagnes, de vallées et de brouillards épais ». Un homme « vêtu de blanc » les accueille et les conduit jusqu'à une petite église où se tient la Vierge Marie. Ce pays, c'est le Canada. Marie y voyage en esprit et « dans toute la terre habitable » où se trouvent des âmes raisonnables appartenant à Jésus-Christ. Au début, elle pense que sa profession de religieuse cloîtrée lui interdit de s'embarquer pour le Nouveau Monde. Pourtant, l'appel devient plus pressant, et peu à peu les obstacles apparemment insurmontables se lèvent un à un.

Sans se mettre à la recherche de la dame du songe, Marie de l'Incarnation la trouvera en Mme de la Peltrie, jeune veuve conquise aux missions de la Nouvelle France par la lecture des *Relations* des Jésuites.

Un jour le Père Le Jeune lance un appel pressant : « Si les excès, si les superfluités de quelques dames de France s'employaient à cet œuvre si saint [celui de la fondation d'un couvent de religieuses enseignantes au Canada], quelles grandes bénédictions elles feraient fondre sur leur famille ! » Mme de la Peltrie exulte ; elle prend l'invitation au sérieux, se détermine à consacrer non seulement sa fortune, mais sa personne aux missions de la Nouvelle-France.

Là encore, que de combats : un père qui s'obstine à vouloir remarier sa fille, une famille qui s'indigne de voir la jeune veuve dilapider ses biens. Pour calmer ses proches, Mme de la Peltrie simule un mariage avec M. de Bernières-Louvigny, trésorier du roi en la ville de Caen. A Paris, elle consulte M. Vincent, le Père Condren de l'Oratoire et les Pères Jésuites qui lui révèlent les projets de Marie de l'Incarnation.

A ce moment, il faut lire les lettres de Mère Marie pour comprendre sa prudence et son audace. D'une part, elle s'en remet au conseil des personnes sages et ne veut nullement se précipiter dans une aventure « en apparence contre toute raison humaine » ; d'autre part, son désir missionnaire la dévore, un instinct intérieur lui dit qu'avec le Seigneur elle viendra à bout de ses desseins. Que son confesseur et sa supérieure la rabrouent, l'accusent de présomption, elle garde la paix, voire une pointe d'humour. Certes, elle n'est qu'une pauvre sœur à mettre derrière la porte, mais que sont les obstacles dans la main du Tout-Puissant ? « Des pailles et des toiles d'araignées qu'il peut détruire en un moment. »

En novembre 1638, les événements se bousculent. Mme de la Peltrie entre en relation avec Mère Marie et les préparatifs du départ s'organisent. Peu importe que les Messieurs de la Compagnie des Cent-Associés refusent d'embarquer Mme de la Peltrie et ses religieuses ! Elle frétera un navire à ses frais. Le 13 février 1639, Mme de la Peltrie arrive chez les Ursulines de Tours. On se reconnaît, on se détermine à partir pour le Canada. Reste cependant à solliciter l'autorisation de Mgr Bertrand d'Eschaux, archevêque de Tours, réputé très sévère. On appréhende un refus. Tout au contraire, Son Excellence se trouve très honoré de donner des filles pour un si pieux dessein.

Sœur Marie de Saint-Bernard, jeune ursuline de 22 ans, s'offre pour la mission du Canada. On l'accepte, et par reconnaissance envers saint Joseph qui a patronné sa vocation, elle change son nom en celui de Marie de Saint-Joseph.

Jusqu'à présent, les Buisson ont pris soin de l'éducation de Claude Martin. Ç'a été leur manière de payer leur dette de gratitude envers Marie qui les a obligés pendant dix ans. Mais voici qu'ils inventent un odieux moyen pour entraver le départ de Marie de l'Incarnation : ils menacent de révoquer la pension qu'ils versent au jeune homme. Encore une fois, Marie triomphe en répondant qu'elle ne mise plus sur le secours des hommes.

Le 22 février, Mgr d'Eschaux reçoit en son palais les deux ursulines missionnaires, Mme de la Peltrie et Charlotte Barré, sa fille de compagnie. Il leur commande de partir au nom de l'obéissance et elles entonnent l'*In exitu Israel* et le *Magnificat*. Le cortège roule vers Paris en passant par Amboise et Orléans. Ici, Claude, maintenant agé de 20 ans, rencontre sa mère et fait volontairement le sacrifice de ne plus jamais la revoir en ce monde.

A la dernière minute, à Paris, l'archevêque refuse de laisser partir une ursuline du Faubourg St-Jacques, ne voulant pas l'exposer « au péril de la mer et des barbares ». Nos voyageuses trouvent une troisième compagne à Dieppe et s'embarquent le 4 mai, à bord du *Saint-Joseph*, pour le Nouveau Monde.

Trois *Hospitalières* fraternisent avec les Ursulines. Imaginons une traversée de trois mois sur une mer grosse de banquises et de pirates. Un immense iceberg frôle le navire et menace de le fendre en deux. A Tadoussac, les passagers se jettent si fièvreusement dans la chaloupe qu'ils tremblent de couler à fond sous le navire.

Dans la soirée du 31 juillet 1639, on campe à l'Ile d'Orleans. Le lendemain, une chaloupe envoyée par M. de Montmagny les conduit à Québec.

C'est fête chômée le premier jour du mois d'août. Dans son agenda de réception, M. le Gouverneur a inscrit un *Te Deum* à l'église de Notre-Dame de Recouvrance, un vin d'honneur au fort Saint-Louis, un feu d'artifice pour célébrer la naissance du dauphin et l'arrivée des religieuses missionnaires.

Le lendemain, randonnée à Sillery, réserve des sauvages. Madame de la Peltrie et les Ursulines ouvrent larges leurs bras aux petites filles des bois, les caressent et tentent de les apprivoiser. Noël Négabamat, chef chrétien de la bourgade, confie sa fille aux Ursulines.

A la Basse-Ville, la vie religieuse s'organise dans une petite maison prêtée par le sieur Juchereau des Châtelets. Cette espèce de taudis aux murailles et à la toiture ajourés, Marie de l'Incarnation l'appelle finement son « Louvre ». Pour se garantir du froid, on couche dans des coffres tapissés de serge.

Soudain se déclare une épidémie de petite vérole. Le « Louvre » sert d'hôpital. On range les malades sur le plancher ; la réserve de toile, les draps, les guimpes, les serviettes et les bandeaux passent en bandages. Toutes les séminaristes sont atteintes et quatre succombent. Comble de malheur, on craint que les sauvages n'attribuent cette calamité au baptême, à la présence des religieuses, et ne reprennent leurs enfants.

Au contraire, les petites séminaristes continuent d'affluer en si grand nombre qu'il faut songer à bâtir. A l'automne de 1642, les Ursulines entrent dans leur nouveau monastère de la Haute-Ville. Rien de terminé : les plafonds ne sont que des madriers rangés à la hâte sur des poutres. Même en brûlant 175 cordes de gros bois dans les quatre cheminées, on souffre du froid. Doublement, parce que Mme de la Peltrie est partie pour Montréal avec M. de Maisonneuve et Mlle Mance, et, dans l'espoir d'établir un second monastère d'Ursulines à Ville-Marie, Mme la Fondatrice a retiré tous ses meubles. Mère Marie s'est laissé tout enlever sans aucune répugnance. Maintenant, les séminaristes couchent sur des peaux de castor prêtées par les Messieurs de la Compagnie. Loin de blâmer Mme de la Peltrie, Mère Marie s'inquiète de son amie et ne peut douter « que ses intentions ne soient bonnes et saintes ».

Au fait, en voulant participer à toutes les fondations, Mme la Fondatrice compromet l'œuvre précaire des Ursulines de Québec. La situation est si grave que le retour en France semble imminent. Toutefois, Mère Marie garde son courage et son invincible confiance en Dieu.

Après avoir songé de se rendre en canot jusqu'aux missions du lac Huron, Mme de la Peltrie rentre à Quebec dans l'automne de 1643. Ces dix-huit mois d'absence ont paru un siècle.

Dès 1641, Marie de l'Incarnation avait opéré la fusion de ses Ursulines appartenant à deux congrégations différentes (Paris et Bordeaux). Cet arrangement établi dans la plus grande paix avait assuré l'unité et la stabilité du groupe. Restaient la rédaction des Constitutions adaptées au pays et aux obligations des religieuses européennes qui venaient tour à tour grossir le nombre des missionnaires. Ces Constitutions sont rédigées en 1647 par le Père Jérôme Lalemant, supérieur des missions de la Nouvelle-France. Inspiré et soigneusement revu par Marie de l'Incarnation, ce manuscrit reste un monument d'équilibre, d'adaptation, un traité de vie spirituelle plutôt persuasif que normatif. L'idéal d'une ursuline s'y dessine avec un heureux mélange de contemplation et d'action. Telle que décrite, la religieuse n'apparaît pas écartelée entre la prière et l'œuvre d'éducation. C'est la moniale unifiée qui continue d'aimer Dieu en instruisant les petites filles. Tout le secret de Marie de l'Incarnation éducatrice se trouve là.

Pour mieux évangéliser les sauvages, elle se met à l'étude des langues indiennes, compose des grammaires et des dictionnaires. Rien ne la rebute. Elle commence par débarbouiller ses séminaristes toutes enduites de graisse. Entre deux prières, il faut leur apprendre à vivre, leur montrer qu'on ne jette pas de savates dans le potage. Au début, les séminaristes manifestent beaucoup de docilité, mais bientôt l'ennui les travaille. Hop ! elles sautent par-dessus la palissade et regagnent la forêt de leur enfance. Marie sait bien qu'il ne sert de rien de vouloir franciser les sauvages; mais le roi l'ordonne. Seuls quelques sujets d'élite arrivent à prendre les habitudes et la culture européenne. Les autres, quoique très intelligentes, tiennent à garder leur langue et leurs coutumes.

Sur le point de la foi, c'est autre chose : Marie de l'Incarnation connaît d'immenses succès apostoliques. Ses séminaristes servent Dieu comme des anges et les adultes que l'on catéchise à la grille, ou dans le monastère, se comportent comme des convertis exemplaires, des chrétiens des premiers âges de l'Eglise. Dans sa correspondance, Mère Marie rapporte plusieurs traits édifiants de ses néophytes. Elle les aime tant, les trouve parfois si éloquents qu'elle ne quitterait pas la place pour aller entendre le plus grand prédicateur de l'Europe.

Tout compte fait, certaines filles françaises lui paraissent beaucoup plus difficiles, « plus savantes en matières dangereuses » que les enfants des bois. Chez les Ursulines, on leur apprend l'écriture, l'arithmétique, la piété et les bonnes mœurs. Il se trouve de gentilles demoiselles parmi les pensionnaires et les externes. Les premiers registres ont conservé les noms de familles marquantes : tels de Repentigny, Bourdon, de Chavigny, Couillard, Marsolet, de la Poterie. Comme ces familles vivent pour la plupart dans une extrême gêne causée par la rareté de l'argent, elles paient la pension des élèves en nature, c'est-à-dire en cordes de bois, en cochons gras et en barils d'anguille salée. Quelques-unes se préparent à prendre la relève, à devenir de ferventes novices. Elles font la consolation de Mère Marie qui les considère à bon droit comme des sujets très qualifiés. L'ère des tâtonnements semble close. Mais dans la nuit du 30 décembre 1650, le feu anéantit le monastère jusque dans ses fondements. Pieds nus dans la neige, **Marie de l'Incarnation** et ses compagnes chantent le *Te Deum*. Témoin de ce spectacle insolite, un honnête homme s'écrie : « Il faut que ces filles-là soient folles, ou qu'elles aient un grand amour de Dieu ».

Après l'incendie, plusieurs se demandent si la Providence prépare par là le retour des Ursulines en France. Mais Marie de l'Incarnation, âme de toute l'entreprise, tient ferme. Elle attend dans la paix l'heure et les moyens de rétablir son œuvre. Encore une fois ses talents de femme d'affaires vont opérer des prodiges.

J'avais, écrit-elle, un instinct intérieur que toute cette charge me tomberait sur le dos, qu'il me faudrait recommencer tout de nouveau, et j'en avais une appréhension naturelle, que je n'osais déclarer de crainte de m'opposer à la volonté de Dieu. Tous nos amis, surtout le R. P. Ragueneau, les Pères de sa maison et M. D'Ailleboust, notre Gouverneur, crurent qu'il ne fallait pas demeurer plus longtemps sans prendre une résolution. L'affaire ayant été mûrement consulté, tous furent d'avis qu'il nous fallait rebâtir, et qu'à moins de cela, il n'y avait nulle apparence de pouvoir subsister en ce pays.

Alors, Mère Marie fait abattre les masures jusqu'aux rez-de-chaussées, et se met à l'œuvre avec un courage surhumain. Elle sait bien que le départ des Ursulines découragerait une grande partie des colons et compromettrait l'éducation des petites Françaises qui, en un sens, sont plus en péril que les sauvages. Pendant les travaux, Mère Marie installe la communauté dans la maison de Mme de la Peltrie, et les classes se font tout simplement sous des toits d'écorce et de verdure.

Et le nouveau bâtiment sort de terre; le voici au carré de la muraille, on monte les cheminées, on lève la charpente. Mais les artisans et les manœuvres coûtent les yeux de la tête. Mère Marie doit les payer jusqu'à cinquante-cinq sols par jour. Livre de comptes en main, elle précise qu'il faut débourser plus de trente livres par jour. Quatre bœufs de labour traînent le bois et le sable, et la pierre se tire sur place. Les Pères Jésuites ont prêté huit mille livres, mais Mère Marie en doit bien vingt mille. A certains jours, elle crie famine :

Croiriez-vous que pour quarante à cinquante personnes que nous sommes, y compris nos ouvriers, nous n'avons plus que pour trois fournées de pain, et nous n'avons nulles nouvelles des vaisseaux qui apportent le rafraîchissement à ce pays ? Je ne puis faire autrement que de me réjouir dans tout ce qu'il plaira à cette bonté paternelle de faire. Quelle en soit bénie éternellement !

Le 4 avril 1652, la Mère Marie de Saint-Joseph meurt à l'âge de trente-six ans. Marie de l'Incarnation nous a laissé une notice nécrologique de sa jeune compagne. Cette fille de grande famille apparaît gaie, musicienne, catéchiste populaire auprès des sauvages, ursuline exemplaire. Ses derniers mois s'écoulent dans un logis ouvert au froid, à la fumée, aux clameurs des enfants, à l'odeur de l'anguille. Marie de l'Incarnation devient volontiers son infirmière, la veille, la console, la traite comme son enfant selon la nature.

« Nous sommes dans notre nouveau bâtiment depuis la veille de la Pentecôte » (29 mai 1652), s'empresse d'écrire Mère Marie à ses amis de France. Décidément, il y a eu du miracle. Les Ursulines avaient tout perdu et voilà le monastère rebâti et remeublé. En tout, trente mille livres de dépenses. Sur cela, huit mille livres de prêts, très peu d'aumônes. Pourtant, il ne reste que quatre mille livres à payer à une personne qui en donne le fonds après sa mort, et ne s'en réserve que l'usufruit pendant sa vie. « Enfin, conclut Mère Marie, il y a vingt-quatre mille livres de pure Providence ».

Cependant, la colonie prospère et l'Eglise canadienne se trouve assez mûre pour recevoir un évêque. Mgr de Laval descend à Québec en 1659. Comme aucun logis convenable ne se trouve prêt à le recevoir, les Ursulines lui offrent l'hospitalité dans la maison de Mme de la Peltrie. Au cours de sa correspondance, Marie de l'Incarnation brosse le portrait de « Mgr notre Prélat ». Elle le trouve charitable, humble, extrêmement pauvre : « ce ne sera pas lui qui se fera des amis pour s'avancer et pour accroître son revenu, il est mort à tout cela. Peut-être, (sans faire tort à sa conduite), que s'il ne l'était pas tant, tout en irait mieux ; car on ne peut rien faire ici sans le secours du temporel ; mais je me puis tromper, chacun a sa voie pour aller à Dieu ».

Certes, « c'est un Saint », mais tout autre que Mère Marie. Vingt ans plus âgée que lui, elle pourrait être sa mère et sa conseillère. Toujours respectueuse envers l'autorité, elle garde toutefois son franc-parler. Quand Mgr de Laval menace de changer les Constitutions de 1647, elle s'alarme, « car, quand on est bien il faut s'y tenir, parce qu'on est assuré qu'on est bien, mais en changeant, on ne sait si on sera bien ou mal ». Sa Grandeur a laissé huit mois ou un an pour réfléchir, « mais, s'empresse d'écrire Marie, l'affaire est déjà toute pensée et la résolution toute prise : nous ne l'accepterons pas, si ce n'est à l'extrémité de l'obéissance ». Néanmoins, elle se tait pour ne pas aigrir la situation, car étant d'une haute piété, Monseigneur n'en reviendra jamais, s'il se persuade qu'il y va de la gloire de Dieu. Marie de l'Incarnation attribue tout cela au zèle du prélat, mais en matière de règlement, elle sait que « l'expérience doit l'emporter par-dessus toutes les spéculations ». Les Constitutions de 1647 sont enfin maintenues, moyennant quelques modifications qui annoncent des changements notables pour les années à venir.

Jusqu'à présent, Mère Marie a partagé toutes les vicissitudes de la colonie. Par sa prière et son amitié, elle a soutenu les missionnaires jésuites. Elle exalte leur courage et leur martyre, envie vraiment leur sort. Auprès d'elle, gouverneurs, officiers, concitoyens et Français de toutes classes viennent chercher lumière et réconfort. Avec les uns, elle cause d'oraison ; avec les autres, elle s'entretient des intérêts temporels de la Nouvelle-France. Elle a ses idées sur le commerce, la guerre, l'industrie, l'immigration. Quoi qu'on pense, l'extermination des Iroquois lui paraît urgente, et le tri des colons salutaire.

Justement, ces barbares multiplient leurs raids, terrifient la population et manquent effrontément à toutes leurs promesses. En 1660, Marie de l'Incarnation raconte que son monastère a été mis en état de siège. La place est convertie en fort gardé par vingt-quatre hommes et une douzaine de grands chiens. Enfermée dans le dortoir, Mère Marie fait le guet toute la nuit, de crainte d'alarme. En 1665, le roi envoie M. de Tracy et son régiment pour mettre les barbares à la raison. Mère Marie s'intéresse de près aux expéditions du Vice-Roi, bienfaiteur et ami des Ursulines.

Confidente des hommes importants de la colonie — MM. d'Ailleboust, de Repentigny et du Vicomte d'Argenson — Mère Marie devient aussi l'admiratrice de l'Intendant Talon, « sous qui, dit-elle, le pays s'est plus fait et les affaires ont fait plus de progrès que depuis que les Français y habitent ».

Sur les dernières années de sa vie, Marie de l'Incarnation note l'évolution de son monastère et celle de la colonie. Que de changements depuis 1639 ! Il y a quelque trente ans, le centre de la Nouvelle-France comptait cinq ou six petites maisons bordées de forêts et de halliers.

Maintenant Québec est une ville, au delà et aux environs de laquelle se trouvent quantité de bourgs et villages, dans une étendue de plus de cent lieues... Nous avons pour l'ordinaire vingt à trente pensionnaires françaises qui nous donnent cent et vingt livres de pension. Nous prenons les filles sauvages gratuitement : encore leurs parents qui sont passionnés pour leurs enfants, croient nous obliger beaucoup... Pour les externes, nous avons toutes celles de la haute et basse-ville ; les Français nous amènent leurs filles de plus de soixante lieues d'ici, quoique Mgr notre Prélat ait établi des maîtresses d'école à Montréal.

En plus de ses nombreuses occupations, Mère Marie entretient une correspondance volumineuse. Tout compte fait, le nombre approximatif de ses lettres atteindrait le chiffre énorme de 12 à 13,000. Ecrites, la plupart, la bride sur le cou, dans les quelques semaines de la navigation, ces missives s'adressent à ses bienfaiteurs. La liste conservée dans les archives énumère des noms de tout rang, des clercs, des laïcs, des moniales de différents ordres, même les religieuses de Port-Royal. Marie prend tous les tons. D'abord, celui du récit qui fait de ses lettres des sources précieuses d'histoire coloniale, un document irremplaçable pour les années allant de 1639 à 1672.

Variée, Marie brosse des fresques immenses, des fonds de scène, des gros plans, des détails pittoresques. Les personnages gesticulent, parlent, selon leur tempérament. Il y a des plumes, des tambours, des processions, des canons, des flèches et des cris de guerre dans ces pages. Pour s'amuser, Marie s'arrête même à décrire son compatriote des Groseilliers, décoré de l'Ordre de la Jarretière. Elle enregistre aussi quelques harangues des sauvages, orateurs nés, comédiens passés maîtres dans l'art du mime. A preuve, ce discours de l'Indien Kiatsoton :

Il en tire un autre qu'il attache au bras du sieur Couture en disant tout haut : « C'est ce collier qui vous amène ce prisonnier. Je ne lui ai pas voulu dire lorsque nous étions encore en notre pays : Va-t'en, mon neveu, prends un canot et t'en retourne à Québec. Mon esprit n'aurait pas été en repos, j'aurais toujours pensé et repensé à part moi : Ne s'est-il point perdu ? En vérité, je n'aurais point eu d'esprit si j'eusse procédé de cette sorte. Celui que vous nous avez renvoyé a eu toutes les peines du monde en son voyage ». Alors il commença à exprimer ses peines, mais d'une manière si naturelle, qu'il n'y a point de comédien en France qui exprime si naïvement les choses, que ce Sauvage faisait celles qu'il voulait dire. Il avait un bâton à la main qu'il mettait sur sa tête pour représenter comme ce prisonnier portait son paquet. Il le portait ensuite d'un bout de la place à l'autre, pour exprimer ce qu'il avait fait dans les sauts et dans les courants d'eaux, où étant arrivé, il lui avait fallu transporter son bagage pièce à pièce. Il allait et venait, représentant les tours et retours de cet homme. Il feignait heurter contre une pierre, puis il chancelait comme dans un chemin boueux et glissant. Comme s'il eût été seul dans un canot, il ramait d'un côté, et comme si son petit bateau eût voulu tourner, il ramait de l'autre pour le redresser. Prenant un peu de repos, il reculait autant qu'il avait avancé ; il perdait courage, puis il reprenait ses forces. En un mot, il ne se peut rien voir de mieux exprimé que cette action, dont les mouvements étaient accompagnés de paroles qui disaient ce qu'il représentait. « Encore, disait-il, si vous l'eussiez aidé à passer les sauts et les mauvais chemins, le reste aurait été supportable. Si au moins, en vous arrêtant et pétunant, vous l'eussiez regardé de loin et conduit de la vue, cela nous aurait consolé : mais je ne sais où étaient vos pensées de renvoyer ainsi un homme seul parmi tant de dangers. Je n'en ai pas fait de même au regard de Couture, je lui ai dit : Allons, mon neveu, suis-moi, je te veux rendre en ton pays au péril de ma vie ». Voilà ce que signifiait le second collier.

Puis, la plume s'attendrit, aborde les problèmes spirituels, ne se refuse pas aux confidences. Entre toutes, les lettres destinées à Dom Claude Martin sont les plus riches de tendresse de nouvelles, de conseils et d'encouragements. Après le départ de sa mère pour la Nouvelle-France, Claude est devenu moine bénédictin de la Congrégation de Saint-Maur. A partir de 1652, il est élu tour à tour prieur, assistant, définiteur et président des chapitres généraux de son ordre. C'est pour lui que Marie rédige la *Relation* de 1654, sorte de traité mystique sur ses grâces d'oraison. Pour obtenir cette faveur, le fils avait longtemps insisté : « Puisque vous m'avez abandonné dans ma jeunesse, il est juste que vous me dédommagiez en me racontant toute votre vie d'intimité avec le Seigneur. »

Et le fils, émerveillé, se trouve en possession d'un grand roman d'amour. Etape par étape, il suit l'itinéraire mystique de sa mère. Il apprend qu'elle a été d'abord une petite fille privilégiée, assez pure pour voir passer le Seigneur dans ses rêves. Puis, il la voit grandir. Belle, harmonieuse, sans aucun complexe, elle a des velléités de vocation monastique, et se marie quand même, puisque ses parents le désirent. Maintenant, Claude entre dans la chair et dans l'esprit de sa mère. Comme elle l'a aimé ! Comme les Tourangeaux l'admiraient ! Au point de se retourner pour la mieux regarder.

Si le Seigneur l'a comblée, il a, d'autre part, beaucoup exigé d'elle : le sacrifice de son enfant, de sa liberté, de sa patrie, voire des consolations sensibles dont il l'avait d'abord comblée. A travers les lignes, Claude entend les soupirs de sa mère, ses déchirements. Ses joies aussi, ses extases de plus en plus simples. Tout d'abord exultante, elle va s'unifiant de plus en plus, au point d'entrer dans un état de quiétude voisin de la vision béatifique. Au fait, elle en arrive à « respirer » le nom de Dieu, sans figure, sans parole, comme abîmée dans la Trinité dont elle a reçu d'ineffables communications.

Et comme tout cela est bien dit : d'un trait, avec le charme et la fraîcheur de la sensation première, dans un français de grande classe. C'est que Marie possède des dons d'écrivain, un dynamisme à l'abri de tout vieillissement.

La dernière fois que Dom Claude a vu sa mère, il a trouvé « son abord doux, sa taille belle et son visage un peu riant » . Cette physionomie faite de gravité, de vigueur et d'amabilité possédait toute l'harmonie des contrastes. Dans sa jeunesse, elle a eu des excès de complaisance et de vivacité naturelle, mais avec la grâce de Dieu, elle a conquis une parfaite maîtrise de sa personnalité.

D'une santé robuste, Marie de l'Incarnation affronte les rigueurs du climat, de la pauvreté, du surmenage. A la fin de sa vie elle souffre d'un flux épatique qui lui enlève l'appétit et l'empêche de se tenir à genoux. Elle s'appuie sur une canne et poursuit jusqu'aux limites sa carrière d'héroïsme. Epuisée par trente-trois ans de corvées apostoliques, Marie de l'Incarnation meurt le 30 avril 1672, vers six heures du soir. Ses dernières paroles avaient été pour les petites sauvagesses et pour son fils : « Dites-lui que je l'emporte avec moi en paradis. »

Le peintre de M. de Courcelles s'empresse de fixer les traits de l'illustre visage, mais son pinceau malhabile ne réussit pas à reproduire la gloire de la Mère spirituelle de la Nouvelle-France.

Héritier des papiers de sa mère, Dom Claude Martin publie une biographie de Marie de l'Incarnation en 1677. A cette occasion, Mgr de Laval lui expédie un panégyrique résumant toute la carrière et toutes les vertus de la première supérieure des Ursulines de Québec :

Dieu l'ayant choisie pour donner commencement à l'établissement des Ursulines en Canada, lui avait donné la plénitude de l'esprit de son Institut. C'était une parfaite supérieure, une excellente maîtresse des novices ; elle était capable de tous les emplois de la religion. Sa vie, commune à l'extérieur, mais très régulière et animée d'un intérieur tout divin, était une règle à toute sa communauté. Son zèle pour le salut des âmes et surtout pour la conversion des Sauvages était si grand et si étendu qu'il semblait qu'elle les portait tous dans son cœur, et nous ne doutons point qu'elle n'ait beaucoup contribué par ses prières à obtenir de Dieu les bénédictions qu'il a répandues sur cette Eglise naissante.

Rome reconnaît l'héroïcité des vertus de la Vénérable Mère Marie de l'Incarnation, en juillet 1911. Pour la proclamer bienheureuse, nous attendons deux miracles approuvés par les autorités pontificales.

Au mois de mai 1964, les restes de Mère Marie ont été déposés dans un oratoire attenant à la chapelle, décorée par Noël Levasseur, en 1724. Sur une plaque de granit canadien, on a gravé un nom, deux villes, deux dates extrêmes :

MARIE GUYART DE L'INCARNATION

NEE A TOURS LE 28 OCTOBRE 1599

DECEDEE A QUEBEC LE 30 AVRIL 1672

Au-dessus, se trouve le tableau exécuté par Botoni en 1878. Mère Marie donne audience aux pèlerins, et son œuvre continue au Canada français. En 1966, l'Union Canadienne des Moniales de Sainte-Ursule compte trois provinces : Québec, Trois-Rivières, Rimouski. En tout, un millier de religieuses qui ont essaimé au Japon et en Amérique du sud.

Pour répondre aux désirs de Vatican II, les filles de Marie de l'Incarnation ont rajeuni leurs méthodes et leur habit religieux ; simplement, comme Mère Marie elle-même l'a fait pour mieux servir en terre canadienne.

En avril 1964, un grand événement a resserré les liens entre la France et le Québec : la bénédiction de la chapelle St-Michel, restaurée par l'association Touraine-Canada. C'est dans ce sanctuaire que Marie de l'Incarnation fit profession, le 25 janvier 1633. Du monastère des Ursulines de Tours, établi en 1625, subsiste encore un long bâtiment rectangulaire flanqué de deux pavillons. Maintenant, ses toits abritent l'internat du Lycée Choiseul. La petite Bourdaisière, premier logis des Ursulines, construit au XVe siècle, demeure presque intact avec son revêtement de brique et de pierre, sa tourelle d'escalier polygonale.

En ces lieux de pèlerinage tourangeau et québecois se trouvent le souvenir et la présence de Marie Guyart de l'Incarnation. Mais pour la rencontrer, et dialoguer avec elle, il faut surtout lire et méditer ses écrits. C'est là que sa grâce de chef continue d'opérer des conquêtes, sans doute moins spectaculaires que celles de 1666, mais toujours profondes et toutes à la gloire de son « Grand Dieu » .

BIBLIOGRAPHIE

La Vie de la Vénérable Mère Marie de l'Incarnation, première Supérieure des Ursulines de la Nouvelle-France, tirée de ses lettres et de ses écrits, éditée par Dom CLAUDE MARTIN. Paris, 1677.

Lettres de la Vénérable Mère Marie de l'Incarnation, première supérieure des Ursulines de la Nouvelle-France, éditées par Dom CLAUDE MARTIN. Paris, 1681.

Ecrits spirituels et historiques, publiés par Dom CLAUDE MARTIN, ... réédités par Dom ALBERT JAMET, avec des annotations critiques, des pièces documentaires et une biographie nouvelle. Paris et Québec, 1929–1939, 4 vols.

Le Témoignage de Marie de l'Incarnation, Ursuline de Tours et de Quebec. Texte préparé et publié avec une introduction par Dom ALBERT JAMET. Paris, 1932.

HENRI BREMOND, *Histoire littéraire du sentiment religieux en France*, tome VI. Paris, 1926.

Marie de l'Incarnation, fondatrice du monastère des Ursulines de Québec, par une religieuse ursuline de Québec. Québec, 1935.

PAUL RENAUDIN. *Une grande mystique française au XVIIe siècle, Marie de l'Incarnation, Ursuline de Tours et de Québec: essai de psychologie religieuse*. Paris, 1935.

J. L. BEAUMIER. *Marie Guyart de l'Incarnation, fondatrice des Ursulines au Canada, 1599–1672*. Trois-Rivières (Canada), 1959.

ANDRÉ RETIF. *Marie de l'Incarnation et la mission*. Tours, 1964.

EDITOR'S NOTE

Readers are referred to Mère Marie-Emmanuel's full account of Marie de l'Incarnation in English in the *Dictionary of Canadian Biography* and in French in the *Dictionnaire biographique du Canada*.

3

The Strickland Sisters

SUSANNA MOODIE 1803–1885

CATHARINE PARR TRAILL 1802–1899

CLARA THOMAS

ONLY A FEW CANADIANS now living can personally recall either of the two Strickland sisters whose lives and achievements form so important a part of the story of Upper Canada's settlement. Dr. Lily Mathieson of Belleville, whose long medical career was itself notable among the achievements of Canadian women and who died as recently as 1966, remembered being introduced to Mrs. Moodie, a venerable old lady who greeted her kindly, but whose age and dignity filled her with tongue-tied awe. Recollections of Mrs. Traill, whose long and active life extended well into the nineties, are more commonly available and are always tributes to a gentle, joyful, and strong personality. Distanced by time as we are, we can perhaps appreciate more fully than could those who knew the two ladies personally both the great adventures and the marked successes that form the story of their lives.

Catharine Parr Traill and Susanna Moodie were the youngest daughters of Thomas Strickland of Reydon Hall in Suffolk. Of his family of nine children, six were ultimately famous in varying degrees for their writings; Catharine and Susanna claim double recognition and remembrance, as settlers in Upper Canada and as recorders of its life.

The Stricklands were proud of a distinguished lineage. Thomas, born in 1758, was descended from wealthy and influential Stuart supporters and more remotely, as he and all his family believed, from Catharine Parr, the sixth wife of Henry VIII. His daughters, Agnes and Elizabeth, whose *Lives of the Queens of England* commanded both public acclaim and scholarly respect, were impelled to their subject by family pride as much as by their bent toward historical research. "I derive my descent from John, Duke of Lancaster, fourth son of Edward III, and eight of the early queens of whom I have written," wrote Agnes.

Thomas Strickland spent his working life as master and manager of the Greenland docks, in London. He retired in his late forties, partly because of ill health—he was, his daughters say, a "martyr to the gout" —and partly because he could now afford to live at ease as a country gentleman and to devote himself to his absorbing interest, the education of his family. First he rented Stowe House, a pleasant rural property near the town of Bungay in Norfolk, the home of Catharine's and Susanna's early years. Then in 1808 he bought Reydon Hall, near Southwold, in Suffolk, henceforth considered the Strickland family seat, remembered with pride and nostalgia by his emigrant children and maintained, until the 1850s, by their mother and sisters.

Mr. Strickland had married twice: his first wife, a grand-niece of Sir Isaac Newton, died with the birth of their first child, a little girl who died in infancy. In 1793 he married Elizabeth Homer, the mother of six daughters, two sons, and a ninth child who died very young. Catharine, born in 1802, and Susanna, in 1803, were the youngest of the daughters. Mrs. Strickland was a willing and an able partner in her husband's educational system, undertaking the instruction of the younger children as her husband supervised the lessons of the older ones. The scope and the rigour of the undertaking are impressive to contemplate, but it was by no means an unusual phenomenon among cultivated English families. As the childhood of the Mills, Burneys, Austens, Martineaus and scores of others less notable indicates, many parents considered the education of their children their personal task as well as their parental responsibility.

Mr. Strickland had a fine library, some of it a legacy from his first wife, and at least one book, Pope's *Iliad*, Sir Isaac Newton's own copy. Catharine recalled how she and her sisters "ransacked the library for books":

We dipped into magazines of the last century. . . . We tried history, the drama, voyages and travels, of which latter there was a huge folio. We even tried 'Locke on the Human Understanding.' We wanted to be very learned just then, but as you may imagine, we made small progress in that direction, and less in the wonderfully embellished old tome, *Descartes' Philosophy.* . . . We turned to the *Astrologer's Magazine* and so frightened the cook and housemaid by reading aloud its horrible tales of witchcraft and apparitions that they were afraid to go about after dark (Traill, *Pearls and Pebbles,* p. viii)

The Strickland educational régime was practical as well as literary. No money was spent on toys, for the children were encouraged to make their own. Often Mr. Strickland would suggest a project and would give them materials and tools to work with; "There are two ways to make this thing," he would say, "a right way and a wrong way, now try and find out the right way." His influence on the children was strong and the success of his methods great—had he known that Catharine, Susanna, and Samuel were to spend their maturity as pioneers in Upper Canada, he could not have done more to equip them for their future rôles.

Periods of freedom balanced the rigour of the working hours. Mr. and Mrs. Strickland and all their children delighted in a country life. They celebrated May Day according to the old customs, crowning Catharine, "Katie," with garlands and paying her homage as she sat on a grassy bank. The sisters rambled daily in the woods and by the river. Their special delight was a "secret garden" carefully laid out, planted and tended, the site of play-actings, readings, and recitations devised and directed by Agnes and Elizabeth. Katie often accompanied her father while he fished. She was the one of them all who went beyond healthy enjoyment of the out-of-doors to an inquiring interest in everything she beheld: the configuration of a cloud, the stamen of a flower, the precise markings on a butterfly. To her these were matters both to see and to record, and by her interest, which matched his, she gave her father great pleasure.

Reydon Hall was near the town of Norwich and it may well be that Mr. Strickland had chosen to settle close to that community, which, at this time, was particularly notable for the liveliness of its intellectual life and the presence of an active circle of intelligentsia. The Taylor and the Martineau families were centres of a group whose interests went far beyond the provincial into every branch of European learning. Mr. Strickland joined this milieu and made it available to his daughters when he bought a house in the town. He began to spend his winters there, sending the boys to Dr. Valpy's school, which the sons of John Galt later attended, and giving the various daughters who accompanied him access to the city library as they became old enough to range further abroad in their reading.

As was to be expected among such a group of literary-minded and imaginative children, writing stories for fun had begun very early. Part of the pleasure of the enterprise was in its necessarily surreptitious nature; in a day when Jane Austen's family insisted that she keep handy a piece of muslin to throw over her writing at the approach of visitors, when Harriet Martineau wrote her prize-winning essays on the world's religions in a cold bedroom between five and seven o'clock in the morning, the similarly well-brought-up young Stricklands were certainly not encouraged to "scribble such trash." Even the finding of writing materials for this frivolity was a serious problem. Catharine recounts her joy and Susanna's as they came upon a large store of paper, blotting paper, and pens at the bottom of an old chest, the property of an uncle who had died. The girls began a tale for children, each day reading an episode to their sister Sara, who was a sympathetic listener and a kind critic. They were concerned to keep their project from their mother and their eldest sister Eliza, fearing equally the parental authority of the one and the sarcastic tongue of the other. When they were, inevitably, found out, they retrieved their manuscript only under promise to use it for curl-papers!

In the spring of 1818, Mr. Strickland was suddenly informed of the failure of a firm in which he had heavily invested. The shock of the loss of much of his private income was aggravated by an acute attack of the arthritis which periodically crippled him. He died at Norwich, attended by Eliza, Agnes, and Catharine who had spent the winter with him there. During the next year, while their father's affairs were being settled and the town house disposed of, Eliza and Catharine remained at Norwich. Eliza was much involved in business matters, since she had been trained as her father's secretary and confidante. As a result, Catharine was left free to wander in the town, to read and to return to the writing which continued to charm her. She was the first of the sisters to achieve publication, thanks to the kindness of a family friend who found a manuscript on her writing-table and, instead of lecturing her on wasting time in telling stories, sent it to Harris's Publishing House in London. A month later, to the astonishment of the whole family, he brought her news of the acceptance of her story and a fee of five golden guineas.

Catharine's success, *The Blind Highland Piper and Other Tales*, was the first trickle in what became a Niagara of words from the pens of the Strickland sisters. In straitened circumstances, literate and highly articulate, enchanted by the process of writing as well as by its products, Eliza, Agnes, Jane, Catharine and Susanna busily scribbled. Among them all, only Sara refrained; she had already been the willing listener for the younger girls, and no doubt her opportunities for continuing the rôle were endless.

The Stricklands' success was in large part determined by the growing demand for light and polite reading material, suitable for ladies of all ages, much of it published in the many "Annuals" which flourished in the 1820s. "Christopher North" of *Blackwood's* condescended to women writers of the day as "the swarm that came out with the Annuals," and characterized their works as elegant, highly moral trifles, designed for the "elderly young lady" who could not be expected to tire eyes or brain with *The Faerie Queene* or *Paradise Lost*. In the early days of their writings the Strickland sisters' works fitted into either this category or that of the highly moral and cautionary children's tale. As they gained a reading public and some confidence in success, however, their works diverged radically according to their predominant talents and interests: Agnes and Eliza toward English and Scottish historical research, Jane to Roman history, Susanna to fiction and poetry, and Catharine to works in which fact was always uppermost.

The years of the 20s passed pleasantly enough for the sisters. They lived for the most part at Reydon Hall, going to London from time to time to visit cousins and to enjoy a wider society and city contacts. At home they were busy housekeeping, sewing and writing, their way of life considerably curtailed since their father's death, but still secure enough for the present, though lacking in the "expectations" of legacies or marriage settlements that formed a background to the attractions of many young women of marriageable age. Catharine was of enviable and equable temperament; from earliest childhood she had been happy and adaptable, the favourite of her father and yet unenvied by her sisters whose reminiscences of her converge in agreement—"Katie never saw a sorrowful day." Susanna was far less even in her disposition, given to great enthusiasms and sudden depressions. "A curly-headed emotional creature," the elder sisters found her, "rather Keatsian in appearance." For a time she departed radically from genteel orthodoxy and was converted to Methodism, perhaps influenced by sister Sara's first husband who was, to the family's consternation, a Dissenter. She was often caught up in humanitarian causes, and it was on one of her visits to London, at the home of Thomas Pringle, Secretary of the Anti-Slavery Society, that she met Mr. Moodie, her future husband.

John Moodie, born in 1797, was the fourth son of Major James Moodie of Melsetter in the Orkneys. He had joined the Royal Fusiliers in 1813 and after seeing service and suffering a severe arm wound in 1814, was released on half-pay in 1819. He joined his brother Benjamin in South Africa, their father's property in Orkney having been lost to the family. Another brother, Donald, joined them, married and settled in South Africa, but after ten years of adventurous but rather rootless life, John returned to England. His *Ten Years in South Africa*, published by Bentley in 1835, shows him to be a keen observer, a vivid writer, and a brave man, though certainly a traveller rather than a settler.

Like the Stricklands, Mr. Moodie rejoiced in a romantic ancestry, tracing descent from the Norwegian Earls of Orkney and from William Moodie, Bishop of Caithness, 1455–60. Less remotely, in 1746, his grandfather had led a force against the Jacobite rebels in Orkney and had brought to justice Sir James Stewart, adherent of the Pretender and murderer of an earlier, loyal Moodie. In background and in experience, John Moodie was a glamorous figure and in 1831 he and Susanna "married for inclination," as she says, taking no thought then of their financial future. They moved to Southwold, near Reydon Hall, and here before long Captain Thomas Traill, a fellow officer and brother Orkney-man, came to visit. Mr. Traill had been at Balliol College before joining the army. Sir Walter Scott's son-in-law and biographer, John Lockhart, had been a close friend and he was on easy terms with Edinburgh's literary men. His anecdotes of Scott, Jeffreys, and "Christopher North" charmed Susanna, and his combination of well-read, entertaining companion and practical man of affairs completely won Catharine. Mr. Traill was a widower; his wife had been dead for some years, and two sons were living with his relatives in the Orkneys. When he came to Southwold, he was already considering emigrating to Canada where, as a half-pay officer, he would qualify for one of the land grants being offered as inducements to gentlemen-emigrants.

Romantic attraction aside, it speaks well for Thomas Traill's good sense that he recognized in Catharine Strickland the attributes of a pioneer-wife. For her part, Catharine was predisposed to an interest in Canada because her younger brother, Samuel, had emigrated in 1825. By 1831, Samuel's Canadian experiences were an adventure saga in themselves: he had married, had a son, bought and partially cleared two hundred acres in Otonabee township near the town of Peterborough, lost his first wife, married again, spent three years in the service of the Canada Company, had two more children and was now on the point of selling his property near Peterborough and buying new land ten miles back in the bush, a holding which he called Reydon, after the family home. Samuel's reports to his family were full of optimism and enthusiasm and were, no doubt, a large factor in influencing Thomas Traill's decision to settle in the Peterborough district.

In May, 1832, Catharine and Thomas Traill were married. After a trip to Edinburgh and Kirkwall, in Orkney, to introduce the bride to the Traill relatives, they planned to seek their family fortunes in Canada. Catharine speedily found favour with her husband's family, so much so that they demurred at the plan of emigration: "Truly, she was a lovely bright thing to take out to the untracked wilds of a colony." However, with good wishes and the keenings of the Traills' old Orkney nurse mingling in their ears, and a promise of hospitality in the Canadian Highland settlement of Glengarry, from the chieftain of the Macdonalds himself, they set off on their Atlantic voyage. Their ship, the last of the season, sailed from Greenock on July 7; they reached Quebec on August 15.

Meanwhile, Mr. Moodie too had decided to emigrate, though Susanna dreaded the prospect and opposed it with all her influence.

In retrospect, her husband's decision seemed shockingly sudden: in reality, he and Thomas Traill had probably explored the possibilities for some time before their departure. Certainly one of Susanna's sisters warned her of Mr. Moodie's "mania" to emigrate before she would allow her mind to consider a possibility so obnoxious to her.

The Traills' marriage and their Canadian plans were bound together; to both, Catharine brought all the capabilities, the calm optimism, and the common sense of her nature. She accepted their economic need and believed in the opportunity for founding and preserving their family fortunes in Canada. Susanna had married with no such plan in mind. She was dismayed and rebellious at the economic situation that made emigration the seemingly prudent course, and with all allowance made for her considerable propensity toward self-dramatization, the record of her feelings at this time rings true and is painful to read: "I seldom awoke without finding my pillow wet with tears." She had consented, finally, "for my husband's sake, for the sake of the infant," and "it seemed both useless and sinful to draw back." It was not physical privations which she dreaded, but "the loss of the society in which I had moved, the want of congenial minds, of persons engaged in congenial pursuits, that made me so reluctant to respond to my husband's call." John Moodie was, like his wife, strongly disposed toward the literary and intellectual life—that had been one of the bases of the attraction between them. Susanna describes him as "a lover of ease," as "the poet, the author, the musician, the man of books, of refined taste and gentlemanly habits." Yet "the half-pay of a subaltern officer, managed with the most rigid economy, is too small to supply the wants of a family; and if of good family, not enough to maintain his original standing in society." (*Roughing it*, ch. xi.) Though, years later, Susanna was to blame herself that she had resisted the plan, that "like Lot's wife, I still turned and looked back, and clung with all my strength to the land I was leaving," her forebodings about the wisdom of their venture proved all too true. Neither partner was equipped, mentally or physically, for a life in the bush.

The Traills reached Quebec on August 10, 1832, and the Moodies, with their baby daughter Katie, some three weeks later. Each of the sisters recorded her early Canadian experiences, Catharine in letters to her mother which, edited of intimate personal comment, were published in 1836 in Charles Knight's "Library of Entertaining Knowledge" as *The Backwoods of Canada*. The series of sketches which Susanna wrote and which we know as *Roughing it in the Bush*, was not collected and published until 1852, though five of them appeared in John Lovell's Montreal periodical, the *Literary Garland*, in 1847, and the entire work gives the impression that its major portion was written while Mrs. Moodie was still a settler in the backwoods. These two books are notable, both as first-hand accounts of the exigencies of pioneer life and as revelations of the impact made by frontier conditions upon two talented women of identical backgrounds but very different personalities. Catharine Traill's work was written to "give information regarding the domestic economy of a settler's life" and "to afford every possible information to the wives and daughters of emigrants of the higher class who contemplate seeking a home among our Canadian wilds" (*Backwoods*, p. 1). Susanna's work was written, she says, for quite the opposite purpose: "If these sketches should prove the means of deterring one family from sinking their property, and shipwrecking all their hopes, by going to reside in the backwoods of Canada, I shall consider myself amply repaid for revealing the secrets of the prison-house, and feel that I have not toiled and suffered in the wilderness in vain" (*Roughing it*, ch. xix). Their opposition in purpose and viewpoint detracts nothing from the unique quality of each work and adds an important dimension of interest to the two considered as complementary documents of pioneer experience.

The cholera epidemic, which doubled the hazards of emigrating in the 1830s, was in one of its peak periods when the Traills reached Canada. Because of the delay in getting their goods through customs, they had to stay in Montreal during a hot, sultry spell of August weather, and, on the day when they were, thankfully, to leave, Catharine became ill with the cholera. Its onset was sudden and its pain intense, but its duration was, mercifully, brief. She survived, largely owing, by her account, to the care she received from two Irish serving girls and a conscientious doctor, whose remedies "were bleeding, a portion of opium, blue pill, and some sort of salts—not the common Epsom." After a confinement of several days, she was able to begin the journey, "though still so weak that I was scarcely able to support myself."

The trip by stage to Lachine did nothing to hasten her convalescence —she was sometimes "literally bruised black and blue." From Lachine to Prescott by steamer and stage was pleasant, however, particularly as the neat and attractive farms which she glimpsed along the way gave her encouragement for the future. "We also are going to purchase wild land, and why may not we see our farm, in process of time, thought I, equal these fertile spots."

From Prescott to Cobourg they travelled on the *Great Britain*, "the finest steamer we had yet seen," and on September 1 they left Cobourg in a light wagon for the twelve-mile trip to Rice Lake. It took only a superficial observation of the wild country through which they were now passing, coupled with remarks made to them by an experienced settler who was a fellow-traveller, for the Traills to begin to modify their expectations of achievement, and to adapt to the realities of life in the woods with the rational common sense that was their hallmark: "I began to apprehend that we also had taken too flattering a view of a settler's life as it must be in the backwoods. Time and our own personal knowledge will be the surest test, and to that we must bow. We are ever prone to believe that which we wish." (*Backwoods*, Letter v.)

The "apology for a steamboat" that was to take them up the Otonabee ran aground some four miles before the scow that finished the journey to Peterborough was to meet them. The Irish oarsmen were disgruntled and drunk when they finally arrived on the scow, and, after an angry scene, they stranded their passengers about three miles from Peterborough, leaving them no choice but to walk. Catharine's initiation to the forest was this forced march, an exhausting and frightening climax to her journey. The path was impeded by fallen trees, they could scarcely keep their guide in sight, she fell into a stream and "thus I was wet as well as weary." It was nearly midnight when they reached Peterborough, and found a place to rest for the night. But, in recounting this sorry introduction to the district which was to be her home, Catharine adds a postscript which is typical of quick ability to gain equilibrium: "I can now smile at the disasters of *that* day, but at the time they appeared no trifles, as you may well suppose."

Samuel Strickland, who was clearing his land in Douro township, ten miles from Peterborough, started for town immediately the word of his sister's arrival reached him. With his help and advice, Thomas Traill was able to draw his 400-acre government grant on land adjoining Strickland's in Douro and Verulam townships. Samuel had achieved the second stage of successful settling—he had moved from a shanty into a comparatively roomy log house on his own land; he insisted on sparing his sister and her husband the discomforts of a shanty experience by having them stay with him, his wife, and their three children, until the Traills' own log house should be finished.

The journey from Peterborough through the bush, on a road "that hardly deserved the name," was a trial of endurance:

If you could bear these knocks, and pitiless thumpings and bumpings, without wry faces, your patience and philosophy would far exceed mine;— sometimes I laughed because I would not cry. . . . Imagine you see me perched upon a seat composed of carpet-bags, trunks, and sundry packages, in a vehicle little better than a rough deal box set on wheels, the sides being merely pegged in so that more than once I found myself in rather an awkward predicament, owing to the said sides jumping out. In the very midst of a deep mud-hole out went the front board . . . as I could do no good, I kept my seat and patiently awaited the restoration to order. (*Backwoods*, Letter VII.)

The Traills were fortunate in having available to them the seven years' Canadian experience of Samuel Strickland; they were wise, both in availing themselves of it and in settling in the Peterborough area, one of the most thriving of Upper Canadian settlements. The Stewarts and the Reids, the founding families of the area, were successful and experienced in all the aspects of pioneer economy; further, the group was knit together by family relationships and friendships as well as by common experience: Samuel Strickland's second wife was the daughter of Mr. Reid, and Catharine and Mrs. Stewart became close friends.

The Backwoods of Canada records only the first three years of the Traills' Canadian experience, though for later editions Catharine added a supplement describing their reaction to the Rebellion of 1837. The 1836 edition, however, is exactly what it announces itself to be: a compendium of commentary on conditions and useful advice, given form by its narrative of personal experience. More than a third of the text deals with the experiences of their long journey to their land; the rest is weighted toward description of the flora and fauna, of the Indians, and of general customs and conditions that all settlers must meet. Success, given good sense and hard work, is taken for granted. Had Elizabeth Bennet and Mr. Darcy, well refined of their "Pride" and their "Prejudice," decided to emigrate for the future of their family, we would expect to find in them a capability, an adaptability, and a cheerful common sense similar to Catharine and Thomas Traill's.

Catharine was frankly delighted to be rid of the social pretentiousness that she deplored in England and as a ridiculous import to Canadian towns and villages: "we are totally without the fear of any Mr. or Mrs. Grundy; and having shaken off the trammels of Grundyism, we laugh at the absurdity of those who voluntarily forge afresh and hug their chains." Her mind was scientific, rational, and inquiring in its bent, accumulating and assimilating the facts and conditions of her new existence and organizing these to be passed on usefully to others. She saw their situation as a "Robinson Crusoe sort of life" and her naturally empiric mind accepted and welcomed the challenge.

Her love of nature, which went far beyond emotional enthusiasm to a scientist's patience and particularity, was, from the first, an absorbing hobby and must have been a major sustaining factor in the years of pioneer hardships. In an early letter she promises to collect a *hortus siccus* for her sister Eliza—"I now deeply regret I did not benefit by the frequent offers Eliza made me of prosecuting a study which I once thought dry, but now regard as highly interesting." She commenced a programme of self-tuition which led her beyond the status of amateur and which made her, finally, an international authority on Canada's plants and flowers. The beginnings of this future reputation are strongly marked in *The Backwoods*: she devotes two paragraphs only to her attack of cholera, but requires more than forty pages of her text to describe the birds, small animals, and particularly the flowers that she has observed around her home.

She is concerned that a truthful picture be given of the problems of emigration and is particularly anxious to instruct prospective emigrant women, both on the attitudes they should wisely develop and the skills they must anticipate acquiring. On the first she says, "we bush-ladies have a wholesome disregard of what Mr. or Mrs. So-and-so thinks or says. We pride ourselves on conforming to circumstances." Toward the latter purpose she reports at length on all the facets of housekeeping in the bush, and finally appends thirty-five pages of useful information of all kinds, including a collection of recipes for making maple-sugar, soft soap, candles, vinegar—processes which might well be unfamiliar to an Englishwoman but which were a necessary part of the knowledge of a Canadian housewife.

Catharine found Canadian society no rude shock to her understanding of class distinctions: "As a British officer must needs be a gentleman and his wife a lady, perhaps we repose quietly on that incontestable proof of our gentility, and can afford to be useful without injuring it." She considers that it is the quality of the Peterborough settlement that the "lower or working classes are well-disposed," perhaps underestimating her own and her husband's abilities to command both affection and respect. In any case, the Traills have no personnel problems:

Our servants are as respectful, or nearly so, as those at home; nor are they admitted to our tables, or placed on an equality with us except at "bees," and such kind of public meetings; when they usually conduct themselves with a propriety that would afford an example to some that call themselves gentlemen, viz., young men who voluntarily throw aside those restraints that society expects from persons filling a respectable situation. (Backwoods, Letter xv)

The final letter in the Backwoods of Canada carries a dominant note of satisfaction and optimism: "On the whole we have been fortunate, especially in the situation of our land, which has increased in value very considerably; our chief difficulties are now over, at least we hope so, and we trust soon to enjoy the comforts of a cleared farm" (Backwoods, Letter xviii). The book ends with no peroration, no recapitulating, but simply as a letter ends, and particularly a letter from Catharine Traill. She has been describing a strange light she observed in the winter sky which seemed like and yet strangely different from the aurora borealis. And then, suddenly, "I must now close this epistle; I have many letters to prepare for friends, to whom I can only write when I have the opportunity of free conveyance, the inland postage being very high. . . . Adieu, my kindest and best of friends."

Its several editions attest the book's success, both in terms of its declared purpose, as a manual for emigrants, and as "entertaining knowledge" for a wider reading public who were attracted by its low-keyed charm and air of authenticity. Some sixty pages of its text were used by N. P. Willis in his *Canadian Scenery* (1842), the work which was illustrated by the Bartlett prints so much in demand today.

The Moodies were not spared the first or shanty stage of settlers' life, as the Traills had been. They reached Cobourg on September 9, 1832, and decided to buy a partially cleared farm about eleven miles to the northwest, instead of going into the backwoods. They could not move into the house on their property, however, until its occupant "Old Joe R——" could be persuaded to leave. This he had promised to do "at the commencement of sleighing"; meanwhile, the Moodies rented a small log shack on an adjoining farm. On a rainy fall day, they, their infant daughter Katie, a guest, Tom Wilson, who had been a neighbour in England and whom they had encountered and befriended in Cobourg, and two servants, Hannah and James, were confronted with a building which Susanna thought "not a house, but a cattle-shed, or pig-sty":

I was perfectly bewildered—I could only stare at the place, with my eyes swimming in tears . . . a room with but one window, and that containing only one whole pane of glass; not an article of furniture to be seen, save an old painted pine-wood cradle, which had been left there by some freak of fortune. The rain poured in at the open door, beat in at the shattered window, and dropped upon our heads from the holes in the roof. The wind blew keenly through a thousand apertures in the log walls; and nothing could exceed the uncomfortableness of our situation. (*Roughing it*, ch. v)

By a combination of industry and ingenuity they managed to make the shack a tolerable temporary dwelling-place, only to move within a week because of the sale of the farm on which it stood. An old woman, Betty Fye, rented them her cabin for the exorbitant price of $20 and in it, only slightly better than "Old Satan's," their first dwelling, they spent their first Canadian winter.

In the spring, Old Joe finally vacated their own house, leaving it overrun with mice and garnished by a hidden dead skunk, less a matter of malice than the frontiersman's crude idea of a good joke on the "gentry." They were on their own land, however, and in their own home:

It looked beautifully clean and neat. Bell had whitewashed all the black, smoky walls and boarded ceilings, and scrubbed the dirty window-frames, and polished the fly-spotted panes of glass until they actually admitted a glimpse of the clear air and blue sky. Snow-white fringed curtains, and

a bed, with furniture to correspond, a carpeted floor, and a large pot of
green boughs on the hearth stone, gave an air of comfort and cleanliness to
a room which, only a few hours before, had been a loathsome den of filth
and impurity. (*Roughing it*, ch. IX)

For the first time, it was possible for Susanna to look on her surroundings with appreciation:

The banks of the little streams abounded with wild strawberries, which,
though small, were of a delicious flavour. . . . Every patch of cleared land
presented a vivid green to the eye; the brook brawled in the gay sunshine,
and the warm air was filled with soft murmurs. . . . Every object that met
my eyes was new to me, and produced that peculiar excitement which has
its origin in a thirst for knowledge and a love of variety. We had commenced gardening, too, and my vegetables did great credit to my skill and
care. (*Roughing it*, ch. IX)

In June, 1833, a second daughter, Agnes, was born, just as the
Moodies were beginning an unfortunate and misguided venture into
farming on shares. It is evident from the record that John Moodie was
hopeful of living in Canada as an English country gentleman, though
in retrospect Susanna reiterates, by precept and example, the folly of
such expectation. They engaged a man and his wife to live in the
shanty they had just left and to work the farm: "Moodie was to find
them the land, the use of his implements and cattle, and all the seed
for the crops; and to share with them the returns." The agreement
was a disaster; the couple took advantage of the Moodies' inexperience
and the wife boasted that they could cheat as they wished, and defied
the Moodies to stop them.

One season with unscrupulous share-croppers was enough for the
Moodies and more than enough for their resources. They began to
think of moving to the Peterborough district, where the proximity
of the Traills and the Stricklands would be reassuring and where the
experience of Samuel would help them to avoid such disastrous
arrangements as had already undermined their funds. Furthermore,
the infrequent news they got from Catharine was unfailingly encouraging—the Traills' experience, though hard, seemed pleasant in
comparison to their own. Early in 1834 Mr. Moodie completed
arrangements for the purchase of 66 acres on Upper Katchawanook
Lake, in Douro township. He also took up 200 acres of clergy reserves
adjoining it, and later bought another 100 acres nearby, for £150.

On a February morning they set off on the forty-five mile journey to their new home. Mrs. Moodie, the two children, a maid-servant, a hamper of poultry, and a dog and cat, were in one sleigh, driven by their guide, and another sleigh, driven by his brother, carried Mr. Moodie, their furniture, and such farm equipment as they had assembled.

It is at this point in *Roughing it in the Bush*, when her experience joins that of her sister, that the particular quality of the book as a whole manifests itself, as Susanna's talents and temperament, so different from Catharine's, are highlighted. From 1834 on, until both the Moodies and the Traills left the backwoods, their experiences ran parallel. Neither experienced a hardship that the other must not have undergone; yet how different are the tones of the two sisters in their records. Catharine can say "My dear sister and her husband are comfortably settled in their new abode, and have a fine spot cleared and cropped. We often see them, and enjoy a sweet chat of home." Susanna gives small space to such pleasant generalities; her record of bush life is dramatic, immediate, and specific:

In my sister's and brother's families, scarcely a healthy person remained to attend upon the sick [with ague and lake fever]. . . . After much difficulty, and only by offering enormous wages, I succeeded in procuring a nurse to attend upon me during my confinement. The woman had not been a day in the house before she was attacked by the same fever. In the midst of this confusion and with my precious little Addie lying insensible on a pillow at the foot of the bed—expected every minute to breathe her last—on the night of the 26th of August the boy I had so ardently coveted was born. The next day old Pine carried his wife (my nurse) away upon his back, and I was left to struggle through, in the best manner I could, with a sick husband, a sick child, and a new-born babe. (*Roughing it*, ch. XIII)

Catharine describes the logging-bee which raised their first home with gratitude and good nature:

The work went merrily on with the help of plenty of Canadian nectar (whiskey), the honey that our bees are solaced with. Some huge joints of salt pork, a peck of potatoes, with a rice-pudding and a loaf as big as a Cheshire cheese, formed the feast that was to regale them at the raising . . . we laughed and called it a *pic-nic in the backwoods*; and rude as was the fare, I can assure you, great was the satisfaction expressed by all the guests of every degree, our "bee" being considered so very well conducted. In spite of the difference of rank among those that assisted at the bee, the greatest possible harmony prevailed. . . . (*Backwoods*, Letter IX)

Susanna makes the logging-bee that raised their cabin the theme of an entire sketch. She begins with a flat statement of her opinion of bees in general: "They are noisy, riotous, drunken meetings, often terminating in violent quarrels, sometimes even in bloodshed." She continues with a vivid recreation of their bee, always disapproving in its undertones, but persuasively realistic and, above all, humorous, in its effect.

Susanna found the experience "odious"; she hated "these tumultuous disorderly meetings," and she was forced to officiate at three of them before sixteen acres were cleared for the Moodies' fall wheat. But her distaste did not close her eyes to their details, and in retrospect she was able to give to its record a dramatic colouring and an aura of slightly ribald celebration that rise above her disapproving admonitions. Malachi Chroak, pretending to play the bag-pipes on a set of bellows, pretending to see the ghost of his "owld grandmother" who taught him to sing, is drawn well and truly from life. In his vigour he somehow cancels out the disapproving figure of his hostess who at last retired to bed, worn out from the exertions of "that hateful feast" but still forced to endure the noise of the drunken revelry: "It would have been no hard task to have imagined these miserable beings fiends instead of men."

Susanna was, in fact, not a diarist, not a writer of calm expository prose, certainly not an instructress of prospective emigrants, but a gifted recorder of character, dialogue and incident, especially of a humorous nature. Her early life in Canada made a great impact on her creative powers, extending talents that she had exercised before—character drawing and the record of incident—and releasing another that she had scarcely practised—the ability to see with a humorist's slant and to communicate her amusement to others. She never lived comfortably with her comic vision, however, or rightly estimated its potential in her writing. In *Life in the Clearings* (1853), she confesses embarrassment at her life-long tendency to laughter:"I wish nature had not given me such a quick perception of the ridiculous—such a perverse inclination to laugh in the wrong place; for though one cannot help deriving from it a wicked enjoyment, it is a very troublesome gift, and very difficult to conceal. (ch. XVII)"

Susanna had written much fiction before coming to Canada. It had always been conventional, moral, sentimental, having to do with heroes, heroines, and villains of her own or higher social rank. In Canada she was thrust into the company of all sorts of people, few of whom were of her own social class and all of whom seemed different, often totally reprehensible, but almost always amusing. These people she could write of without inhibition and she captured a whole gallery of them, in the very accents in which she heard them speak. From the ship's captain to "the little stumpy Man," *Roughing it* is made memorable by these people and by their reported talk. Old Satan, Tom Wilson, Betty Fye, John Monaghan, Jacob and Malcolm come alive and occupy centre stage for a time; many others are recorded, as are the workers at the logging-bee, in vignettes only. In total, the book is alive with their many presences. There are a few persons she meets whose stories seem to demand her well-practised sentimental vein: the dying girl, Phoebe, is one of these, as is the strange, melancholy hunter, Brian. Even in these tales, however, she transcends her own sentimental convention as she sketches from the life.

In the service of her sketches, Susanna is recklessly self-revealing. It was natural for her to be the centre of her narrative, as Catharine is the narrator and centre of hers. But unlike her sister, Susanna, centre stage, becomes one of her own "characters": a prejudiced, class-conscious, ill-equipped pioneer, sometimes the butt of her own stories, sometimes the heroine, passionately revolting against her circumstances while slowly and uncomfortably adapting to them. Catharine quietly states the achievement, whether it be confidence in an assured social position or satisfactory relations with servants; Susanna dramatizes the struggle, with herself a storm centre.

In fact, she was no less gallant than Catharine: she endured the same hardships, bore two children while living in the most primitive conditions and won a succession of battles over fear and pride:

My husband and I had worked hard in the field; it was the first time I had ever tried my hand at field labour, but our ready money was exhausted . . . . we could not hire and there was no help for it. I had a hard struggle with my pride before I would consent to render the least assistance on the farm. . . . If we occasionally suffered severe pain, we as often experienced great pleasure, and I have contemplated a well-hoed ridge of potatoes on that bush farm as in years long past I had experienced in examining a fine painting in some well-appointed drawingroom. (*Roughing it*, ch. xiv)

Again and again, Susanna warns the "gentleman" against settling in the backwoods. He "can neither work so hard, live so coarsely, nor endure so many privations as his poorer but more fortunate neighbor," the industrious working man. John Moodie was unfitted, in more than his gentleman's status, for the life of a pioneer farmer. Both Samuel Strickland and Thomas Traill avoided the mistakes in judgment to which Mr. Moodie was prone and which he recites himself in the introduction to his *Scenes and Adventures as a Soldier and Settler* (1866). Besides the selling of his commission and the investing of his capital in steam-boat stock which paid him no return, he could not quickly come to grips with the necessities of a Canadian settler's life. For the preservation of her family, Susanna had to learn to be an efficient pioneer: the English lady who was a joke among her Yankee neighbours because she could not bake bread, learned to feed her family on whatever she could use—eel pie, dandelion coffee and, when poverty and hunger clamoured together, on their pet pig.

News of the Rebellion of 1837 was a great surprise to the Douro settlers, who had no thought of disloyalty to the Queen's government or representatives in Canada and who had been too isolated to be aware of the momentum of discontent. What they did hear was distorted by rumour: "that there was a war between Canada and the States; that Toronto had been burnt and the governor killed." Even the most conservative report had Toronto "besieged by the rebel force."

Thomas Traill and Samuel Strickland had already gone to join the loyal forces of the Crown before the Moodies heard of the outbreak. John Moodie, though partially disabled by an injured leg, hurried off the next day. The Queen's proclamation summoning all loyal gentlemen was an "imperative call of duty"; further, as Susanna reports their assessment of their situation, "our affairs were in such a desperate condition that Moodie anticipated that any change must be for the better." Mr. Traill left home on December 8 and was back again on the 12th, the party of about 200 volunteers which he had joined having been ordered to disperse at Port Hope. Mr. Moodie returned, temporarily, in a week, but he left for Toronto on January 8 to join, as captain, one of the new militia regiments which had been quickly formed for possible future defence against the rebels. Susanna was left with old Jenny and the children to look after the farm but her husband's pay enabled them to pay some of their pressing debts.

Meanwhile, the Traills had begun to consider moving from the backwoods; in 1838, after six years of rugged pioneering, they left the bush for the village of Ashburnham, now a part of Peterborough. Ever since coming to Canada they had worked at clearing and farming their original holding. Their success was not spectacular, though their industry and good sense were unremitting. Neither of them had been youthful when they married; by 1837 Thomas Traill was middle-aged. A few additional cleared acres every year did not balance the increasing difficulty of continuing back-breaking work in the forest. In contrast, Samuel Strickland, who had come to Canada as a young man of nineteen, had been able to devote all the years of his greatest energy to settling and he had succeeded accordingly.

Susanna endured the bush for about a year longer than her sister. In the spring of 1838, John Moodie came home for a brief leave and then returned to his regiment which he knew was to be reduced before long. Susanna was faced with loneliness, hard work, and a knowledge that the future, even with her husband at home, held no bright prospects. They were still several hundred pounds in debt, the steamboat stock was obviously worthless, "the returns from the farm scarcely fed us, and but for the clothing sent by our friends at home, who were not aware of our real difficulties, we should have been badly off indeed." In desperation, she finally wrote a statement of their situation to Sir George Arthur, the Lieutenant Governor, and asked him to continue Mr. Moodie in the militia. This letter she posted, with the encouragement of her brother-in-law, shortly before John Moodie was relieved of his duties and returned home in August, 1838.

The birth of their third son, in October, coincided closely with Sir George Arthur's response: Mr. Moodie was appointed pay-master to the militia in the Victoria district and though they knew that this was a temporary position it was another period of relief for them. Once again, Susanna was left with the children, and this time with an added deprivation, the removal of the Traills to Ashburnham. This time, too, she had several dangerous illnesses to contend with: the children caught scarlet fever, then Susanna herself was ill for ten weeks, and next the baby became so sick that, for several terrifying days, there seemed no hope for his survival.

Fortunately, there was one grand amelioration for Susanna during this dreary period. Mr. James Lovell of Montreal, who was beginning the periodical *The Literary Garland,* wrote to ask her to contribute to it, offering to pay her at any rate she set. She had made tentative efforts to write for publication since she came to Canada; she had been invited, for instance, to write for the *North American Review*, published in Philadelphia, and she had managed to send off several articles, "though the expense even of the stationery and the postage of the manuscripts was severely felt." But she had never been paid anything for her work and indeed had probably not even had the satisfaction of seeing it in print. Later offers from American editors she had refused because she could not afford to pay the postage of manuscripts to the States. Mr. Lovell's offer was welcome enough in monetary terms alone; as a lift to her morale, it was priceless—somewhere out of the wilderness readers still cared about literature, and Susanna Moodie was being sought after as an authoress. She set her price at $5 a page, probably a quarto page of eight sheets, since she says: "It required a great deal of writing to fill a sheet."

The gains to her family at first were small, but to Susanna there were now more possibilities in the future than she had dared hope for:

This opened up a new era in my existence. . . . I actually shed tears of joy over the first twenty dollar bill I received from Montreal. It was my own; I had earned it with my own hand; and it seemed to my delighted fancy to form the nucleus out of which a future independence for my family might arise. (*Roughing it*, ch. xvii)

The *Literary Garland* was published from 1838 to 1851 with Susanna Moodie a steady contributor of fiction and poetry, earning from twenty to forty pounds a year, "as time or inclination tempted me." She was by far its most prolific contributor; through her, Catharine Traill and the Strickland sisters who were still in England also found opportunities for publication. Although several of the *Roughing it in the Bush* sketches appeared in it in 1847 and much of her poetry is topically and patriotically "Canadian," most of Susanna's work for the *Garland* reverted to the conventionally moralistic, sentimental, and highly didactic fiction of the days before her marriage and emigration. As she began this enterprise, fictional ladies and gentlemen, gallant officers and politely reared young girls were a soothing escape from the log house where she "sat up and wrote by the light of a strange sort of candle that Jenny called 'sluts.' " Whenever she did write of her bush experiences, she detached herself from their reality by two points of view, the humorous and the admonishing; they did not blend smoothly in the finished work, but the voicing of each one of them sustained her, as the study and the record of nature fortified and satisfied her sister Catharine.

The militia regiments were disbanded in the summer of 1839 and once again John Moodie came home for a very scanty harvest, but this time uncertainty about their future was speedily relieved. Very shortly, he was offered the post of sheriff in the Victoria district, his centre to be the town of Belleville, from which he had already worked as paymaster. He hurried off to find a house and Susanna was left to dispose of their farm goods, crops, stock, and to prepare to join him when the first fall of snow should make moving by sleigh practicable: "Heartily did I return thanks to God that night for all his mercies to us; and Sir George Arthur was not forgotten in those prayers."

The sleigh-trip out of the wilderness was as cold and hazardous as their trip in had been seven years before. On that first trip, Samuel Strickland's home had been their goal and shelter; on this trip, he was organizer and guide. It took two days to travel the forty-odd miles between their farm and Belleville, but this time not a log cabin, but a "neat pretty cottage" awaited them.

The passage of time could not, however, be cancelled; Susanna's personal hesitancies and misgivings about her new life ring true and sad: "For seven years I had lived out of the world entirely; my person had been rendered coarse by hard work and exposure to the weather, I looked double the age I really was, and my hair was already thickly sprinkled with grey. I clung to my solitude." (*Roughing it*, ch. xviii)

When they moved from the bush, Catharine Traill and Susanna Moodie were in their late thirties; their early years in Canada were only introductory, considered in the perspective of their long lives. To mistake, or to present, the part for the whole because its compelling interest is, in each case, personally documented, is to distort and falsify the lives and achievements of the sisters.

The Traills lived in the village of Ashburnham until 1846 when they moved again to the country, this time to a partially cleared farm on the south shore of Rice Lake, near the village of Harwood. They named their home "Oaklands" and the rise on which it stood, Mount Ararat. For ten years they lived here with their family, which finally numbered nine, four sons and five daughters. Catharine, like Susanna, implemented their always meagre income by writing sketches and short tales, but unlike Susanna, she wrote fiction largely as a means of earning and not in any similar degree as an end in itself, a pleasure and a necessity of her personality. She was glad to move to "Oaklands" from Ashburnham, partly because of the increased scope the country gave to her botanical investigations. Here she wrote *The Canadian Crusoes* and *Lady Mary and her Nurse*, the children's books for which she is best remembered, and *The Female Emigrant's Guide*, a dictionary of useful knowledge for the pioneer woman and a useful companion-piece to *The Backwoods of Canada*.

Lady Mary and her Nurse, also published as *Afar in the Forest* and *Stories of the Canadian Forest*, is a collection of animal stories, sentimentally told, but with evident keen observation of the kinds and habits of Canadian animals. *Canadian Crusoes* is a minor classic among Canadian children's books. It is the story of two Scottish Canadians, Hector Maxwell and his sister Catharine, and their French-Canadian friend, Louis Perron. The three young people are lost on the Rice Lake plains, and in the course of their wanderings they learn the arts and crafts of survival in the wilderness. They are joined by a young Mohawk girl, Indiana, whom they have rescued from exposure and death at the hands of her tribe's enemies, the Ojibways. The story ends on a high note of romance: the French, Scottish, and Indian strains are united in the marriages of Louis and Catharine and Hector and Indiana.

Such a plot no more strains the bounds of credulity than does, for instance, *The Last of the Mohicans*. In fact, Catharine Traill was probably influenced by Cooper and almost certainly by Scott, in her own impulse toward the making of romantic Canadian legend. She was entirely herself, however, in the weight she gave to practical nature lore—the plot does not obscure the book's assembling of instructions for survival in the wilderness. It is in this aspect that *Canadian Crusoes* attracts curiosity and then admiration today; it was reprinted in 1923. The book carries heavy strains of sentimental melodrama and evangelical moralizing which are now outdated, but its voice of an expert telling plainly and clearly how to make, how to find, how to live in the Canadian woods is still clear and compelling. The title, *Canadian Crusoes*, is of course, a particularly happy choice, true to Catharine Traill's outstanding rational and empiric nature and to her own experience. Like the events of her own life, her characters' adventures are informed and directed by intelligence, common sense, and adaptability; a potentially hostile environment is dominated and put in its proper perspective, to be respected for its strengths and enjoyed for its beauties. In 1852, the book was published in London, given the prestige of her sister's name by the addition of "edited by Agnes Strickland," and in 1853 an American edition was published in New York. There were several later editions of both *Canadian Crusoes* and *Lady Mary and her Nurse*, but Catharine Traill received for them nothing more than the $50 that Thomas Nelson & Sons paid when they bought the copyright.

The Backwoods of Canada had been designed and had been successful as a basic text for emigrating gentlewomen. In 1854 Catharine Traill published *A Female Emigrant's Guide*, a more specific instruction manual, combining all sorts of useful information, and particularly stressing the food and medicinal possibilities of native Canadian plants and the various ways of preparing and cooking both plants and animals. From the lore of Indians, from observation of the habits of birds and animals, and from her own keen and constant observations and experiments, she had, after twenty years in Canada, assembled a complete dictionary of pioneer economy. The usefulness of the book in her own day is obvious—she even includes a calendar summary, instructing her readers on what they may expect of the weather and of plant and animal life, month by month, through the Canadian year. Its charm today, when we do not need its instruction, is in its harking back to things past, with all the simplicity, clarity, and expert knowledge that Catharine Traill commanded when she reported what she found and what she saw, what she knew and what she used.

In 1857 the Traills' home, "Oaklands," burned down. The disaster of fire, which had also afflicted the Moodies and which haunted Susanna's dreams, was a shock from which Thomas Traill did not recover. Their oldest son was married, but their youngest was only ten; they lost all their possessions, and after staying with Samuel Strickland for a time, they moved to a house of the Stewarts, friends and neighbours of the Otonabee days. There Mr. Traill died.

Catharine settled in the village of Lakefield where one of the daughters, Mary, began to teach school, and where the family could be under the benevolent eye of Samuel Strickland. She bought a home, "Westover," largely from a £100 windfall granted her by Lord

Palmerston in recognition of her literary and botanical work. He had been interested in Mrs. Traill by an English patroness, Lady Charlotte Greville, who had bought one of the collections of ferns and grasses that Catharine pressed and mounted, and who had subsequently provided her with other aristocratic patrons and, even more practically, with a screw-press for her botanical specimens.

In the major works of her later years, *Canadian Wild Flowers* (1868) and *Studies of Plant Life in Canada* (1884), she collaborated with her niece, the "little Addie" of *Roughing it in the Bush.* Agnes married Charles FitzGibbon, the son of Captain James FitzGibbon, a colourful figure in Upper Canada's early days, and commander of the troops sent to disperse the rebels at Montgomery's Tavern. Mrs. FitzGibbon, who, after the death of her husband, was married again to Colonel Browne Chamberlin, painted a distinguished series of Canadian wild flowers. Her aunt contributed the text for her work and, fair exchange, Agnes contributed the illustrations for her aunt's later work, *Studies of Plant Life in Canada.*

In the introduction to *Studies of Plant Life,* Catharine Traill described the progress of her self-education in botany during her years in Canada, and her ambition that her work might become a "household book, as Gilbert White's Natural History of Selborne is to this day among English readers." The text reflects Catharine herself; it has a candid, diary quality, an expectation that the reader's pleasure will match the writer's, and a literary flavour from the many poetic epigraphs chosen to complement her descriptions. She ranges from Chaucer to Longfellow, from Milton to William Cullen Bryant to find fitting tibutes to her flowers, and on one occasion she composes her own verses to the violet, "after the manner of Herrick."

Her work, though not scientifically botanical by the standards of the twentieth century, is remarkably precise and encyclopaedic to the lay reader. Usually, her method is to name a plant, by popular and latin names, to categorize it, and then to go into its special properties. For example, we find that the Marsh marigold, vividly recalled by its description, has leaves which are edible as "pot-herbs," while the May-apple, which she links to the Mandrake of age-old notoriety, has leaves of deadly poison. The fruit, however, is pleasant to eat, "sub-acid," and "is a fine preserve with white sugar and when flavoured with lemon peel and ginger." Goldenrod makes yellow or green dye, the milkweed fibre would give a long strong thread, a possible valuable addition to the manufacture of Canadian fabrics, mullein leaves have great healing properties and are also supposed to drive away rats and mice; "but this virtue may be only a fond illusion. Commend me rather to Miss Pussy." The combination of meticulously observed detail, of practical suggestion, and of affectionate familiarity with all the range of plant life gives a timeless attraction to her work.

She was eighty-two when her *Studies of Plant Life in Canada* was published; ten years later, she gathered together her final work, *Pearls and Pebbles*, a compendium of her personal recollections and her naturalist's observations. Meanwhile, she had received various tokens of the recognition she had earned, both as a Canadian pioneer and as a devoted naturalist. In 1883 she had been officially fêted in Ottawa; a fern which she had found growing near Lakefield had been named for her, "A. marginale (Swz.) var: Traillae"; finally, the government had granted her an island in Stoney Lake, a grant which Mr. Sandford Fleming described to her as "the smallest acknowledgment which is due to you for your life-long devotion to Canada."

She took possession of her new summer home in 1893, and enjoyed her summers in it until her death, in her 98th year, in 1899. She retained her enthusiasms and the faculties for enjoying them, living graciously with age as she had adapted gracefully to life. Her faith had always been sustaining to her, but in the works of her old age she voices more than orthodoxy, a conviction of the spirituality of all matter. The essay on her island closes with these lines:

> Nor think though men were none
> That heaven would want spectators, God want praise:
> Millions of spiritual creatures walk the earth
> Unseen, both when we wake and when we sleep.

The final essay in *Pearls and Pebbles* is at once a statement of her belief in the unity of all matter and the final affirmation of a benign life—"Something gathers up the fragments, and nothing is lost."

For forty-five years, until her death in 1885, Susanna Moodie considered Belleville her home. She did not have the trouble that she anticipated in adapting to a more complex and a more socially active environment, though when it became known that she was an "authoress" she or her children were sometimes embarrassed: "One of my boys was tauntingly told by another lad at school 'that his ma said that Mrs. M—— invented lies, and got money for them.' . . . The sin of authorship meets with little toleration in a new country."

Of a total family of seven children, two daughters and five sons, one daughter, Katie, was born in England; another daughter, Addie, and three sons, John A. D., Donald, and John S. who was drowned in the River Moira when he was eleven, were born in the bush; and two sons, George Arthur and Robert Baldwin, were born in Belleville. With her circumstances more settled and her family complete, Susanna's writing became more and more a career and a vocation, its income always a needed addition to the family funds. Between her and her husband there was total loyalty, affection, and respect, but her position, financial and social, was never quite as sure as she would have wished; it is impossible for an onlooker across the years to find John Moodie any more adaptable in his later career than he had been in the bush. His tenure as sheriff was an uneasy one, partly because he tried to deputize his duties to others and so incurred both public censure and court action, and partly because he was dissatisfied with his position and sporadically sought preferment from Sir George Arthur or from Robert Baldwin, the leader of the Reform party. The introduction to his *Scenes and Adventures as a Soldier and Settler* (1866) gives Mr. Moodie's version of his situation, but reveals through his words a man whose primary error was to hold fast to the fallacy of the emigrant "gentleman"—that as such and for that alone, Canada owed him a competence.

Their years in the bush had not stifled either the Moodies' spirit of adventure or their devotion to literature; indeed, experience had confirmed in both of them a certain conviction that their natural and most useful rôle was that of mentor to their fellow Canadians in matters both practical and cultural. In 1847 Mr. Joseph Wilson of Belleville was persuaded to finance and publish a periodical, the *Victoria Magazine*, with John and Susanna Moodie the editors and major contributors. They were, no doubt, encouraged in this enterprise by the success of the *Literary Garland*, but they hoped to attract a different clientele from its polite and relatively well-read subscribers. The *Victoria Magazine*'s title-page announces it as "a cheap periodical for the Canadian people" with its motto "The surest way to *obtain* is to *desire* success."

Anna Jameson, travelling in Canada in 1837, had been astonished at the numbers and the popularity of newspapers, both published locally and imported from America. In Susanna Moodie's opinion "the Canadian cannot get on without his newspaper any more than an American could without his tobacco," and she evidently hoped to extend this interest: "The Farmer, of all others, should be a reading man. . . . He has always plenty of time, during his daily labours, to arrange and digest in his mind the knowledge he has previously acquired." John Moodie's adventures in South Africa are serialized through several numbers; his reflections on "Religion and Loyalty," fulsomely rhetorical, counsel moderation and charity. Occasionally, as in his verse "Dan Simpson's song," Mr. Moodie shows an appreciation of the ridiculous as lively as his wife's. Susanna, for her part, contributed poems and sketches, notably a series of "Trials of a Travelling Musician," which she said that she set down just as they were told to her. These again display her ear for dialogue and dialect and her considerable success in reporting them, together with her keen sense of the comic, in both character and situation:

I now proceeded with the concert. The song of the drowning child saved by the Newfoundland dog drew thunders of applause. When the clamour had a little subsided, a tall man rose from his seat at the upper end of the room, and, after clearing his throat with several loud hems, he thus addressed me—"How do you do, Mr. H—— ? I am glad, sir, to make your acquaintance. This is my friend, Mr. Duby," drawing another tall man conspicuously forward before all the spectators. "He, too, is very happy to make your acquaintance. We both want to know if the dog you have been singing about belongs to you. If so, we should be glad to buy a pup." (*Victoria Magazine*)

The *Victoria Magazine* continued for twelve issues, ending in August, 1848. The Moodies seem to have been paid nothing for their industry, but the very existence of the twelve numbers is, today, a monument to their enterprise: "It was an earnest desire to encourage as much as possible native-born authors, and to make our magazine a medium through which they might gain the attention of the public; and we were not a little disappointed that the few articles we received from Canadian writers were not of a character to interest our readers. The Canadian people are more practical than imaginative." (*Mark Hurdlestone*, Intr.)

In 1851, the *Literary Garland* discontinued publication; it is likely that the loss of this outlet for her writing and the source of part of the family income prompted the publication of *Roughing it in the Bush*, in 1852. Many of the sketches of the Moodies' early experiences in Canada had already been printed. Now Susanna arranged them in chronological order, superimposed on them certain passages of comparison between living conditions in Canada "then" and "now," always favourable to the 50s and anticipating further progress, and gave them an introduction whose strong warning to gentleman-emigrants was carried in its overtones throughout the book.

Roughing it in the Bush, as we know it, is an uneasy amalgam of Susanna's fictional talent, her keenly felt and humorously observed experiences, and her cautionary admonitions. On publication it was deservedly enjoyed; it was also resented by those who felt that the conditions which Mrs. Moodie described had passed away, and that, therefore, her representations were misleading, or, at the least, snobbish. It must certainly be admitted that Susanna had not been careful enough in editing her earlier work before its collected publication. She made amends, however, by the speedy preparation and publication of *Life in the Clearings* (1853), with an introduction which is both an apology for offence given and an explanation of the position taken. She reiterates her warning to the gentleman-emigrant: "let him leave to the hardy labourer the place assigned to him by Providence, now undertaken, upon limited means, the task of pioneer in the great wilderness." But she balances this with an admission of the great gaps in her experience at the time of writing the sketches for *Roughing it in the Bush*, and with a statement of gratitude to Canada, the "country of my adoption—the great foster-mother of that portion of the human family whose fatherland, however dear to them, is unable to supply them with bread." Her earlier portraits of the rascally Yankee settlers who were at once the bane of her pioneer days and the source for some of her best sketches are now balanced by a tribute to "our enterprising, intelligent American neighbours." Their influence, she admits, has helped to produce a successful amalgamation of classes in Canada which she now finds desirable.

She based her sketches in *Life in the Clearings* on the framework of a travel narrative, a trip from Belleville to Niagara Falls. This structural device is not strong enough to support and dominate the sketches, and the book is memorable for the assembling of its parts rather than for the totality of its whole. Catharine Traill's powers of observing and reporting were predominantly exercised on her natural environment: Susanna's eye was always on individuals, and from them to their, and to her, social environment. Her descriptions of the trip itself read like romantic and sentimental "set pieces": the blue water glides by, the wooded hills recede in the distance, at the Falls "the wide world of tumbling waters are flashing and foaming in the sunlight." But the people she meets, the conversations she reports, the humorous anecdotes she tells, with herself as the central figure, are as vivid and persuasively "real" as the best of the Bush sketches, though marked by a more tolerant and less satiric tone.

Much of *Life in the Clearings* is, from our standpoint, social history, enlivened and authenticated by the presence of Susanna Moodie as its narrator. The chapters on "Camp Meetings," "Education," the "Lunatic Asylum" and the "Provincial Agricultural Show," the fore-runner of the Toronto Exhibition, are documentary accounts of aspects of Ontario life in the mid-nineteenth century and as such alone are to be valued. That they were recorded by a contemporary, a practised observer, and a writer with twenty years' experience of Canada is a large bonus of good fortune. Furthermore, in this work Susanna is determinedly positive and factual in her approach, at the same time offering us the interest and vigour of her opinions. She now speaks, not from a position of passionate reaction to a new and shocking environment, but confidently, secure in her status as a Canadian, the wife of an official of the courts, and a professional woman of letters; in none of these rôles does she wish to be misunderstood.

She believed that all writing, and particularly fiction, the work of "the despised and reprobated novelist," must and will subserve a moral purpose. "I look upon these authors as heaven-inspired teachers," she proclaims, thereby establishing a didactic purpose for her own work and explaining to us the inhibiting of certain of her own talents. She deprecates her own tendency to laughter, and takes care to announce in this book that certain anecdotes she reports, in a tone of humorous satire against the pretensions of the ignorant, were "told her by another." On the other hand, her admiration for the work of nine-teenth-century novelists, particularly Dickens and Thomas Hood, the "humane men" who command the reader to "step with them into these dirty abodes of guilt and wretchedness, and see what crime really is" encouraged the development of her own talent toward realistic writing. The chapters on the prison and its inmates, the lunatic asylum and its patients, and particularly her story of Grace Marks the murderess, are blood-chilling in their effect. Her talent toward the realistic-naturalistic portrayal of the suffering and degradation she deplored was a formidable one; its lack of development in her later writing is, like the lack of development of her comic and anecdotal veins, regrettable to us. To Susanna Moodie, however, both what she wrote and the way she wrote were dictated by her time and place in society, her reading public, and her own conception of her function as an authoress.

After *Life in the Clearings*, she wrote many novels, but in them she reverted to the romantic and sentimental vein that she had practised even before coming to Canada, and that had been the style of much of her *Literary Garland* work. *Flora Lyndsay, Mark Hurdlestone, The World Before Them, Matrimonial Speculations,* and *Dorothy Chance* are among her later works; most of them were first published in England by Bentley; some were reprinted in the United States, one as late as 1885, the year of her death. All were directed toward an English reader—the polite young lady and her eminently Victorian mother. There was in Canada, as Susanna Moodie well knew, little or no possibility of publication and an extremely small reading public. She was never without the necessity of writing to augment a small family income and in general her readers concurred in the admonition she reports from one English lady: "Don't fill your letters home with descriptions of Canada. Who, in *England*, thinks anything of *Canada?*" Prudently, she complied.

The lives of Catharine Traill and Susanna Moodie, considered solely in their physical aspects, are records of endurance, adaptation, and achievement, both impressive in themselves and as they typify the experience of thousands of pioneer women whose histories go unrecorded. Beyond that, Mrs. Traill and Mrs. Moodie are uniquely interesting among Canadian women—sisters of identical background, shared talents, but very different temperaments, whose lives and writings have left us a diverse panorama of the land, the people, and the institutions of nineteenth-century Ontario.

BIBLIOGRAPHY

SUSANNA MOODIE. *Roughing It in the Bush* was first published in London in 1852; selections may be read in the New Canadian Library series, Toronto, 1962, edited by CARL F. KLINCK.

—— *Life in the Clearings* was first published in London in 1853; a Canadian edition may be found in the Pioneer Books series, Toronto, 1959, edited by R. L. McDOUGALL.

TRAILL, C. P. *The Backwoods of Canada* was first published in London in 1836; selections are found in the New Canadian Library series, Toronto, 1966, edited by CLARA THOMAS.

—— *Studies of Plant Life in Canada*. Toronto, 1885.

—— *Pearls and Pebbles*. Toronto, 1894.

4

Pauline Johnson

1861-1913

ELIZABETH LOOSLEY

Pauline Johnson, the legend, is alive for every Canadian school child in her "Song my Paddle Sings." As for Pauline Johnson, the woman, it is highly unlikely that existing material will ever fully reveal her. Idolized by her friends, lionized by her concert audiences, almost a sacred tradition to the Canadian Indians, her *persona* is all that remains.

Emily Pauline Johnson was born March 10, 1861, on the reservation of the Six Nations near Brantford, Ontario, a Mohawk of the tribe that had come to take up lands on the Grand River in the exodus after the American Revolution. She was the youngest child of an English mother, Emily Susanna Howells (a relative of the American author, William Dean Howells) and a Mohawk father, George Henry Martin Johnson, who had met his wife, the sister-in-law of the Reverend Adam Elliot, the Anglican missionary on the reservation, while living as an assistant and interpreter in the Elliot household. Much has been made of Pauline Johnson's "royal" Indian descent from the mythical founders of the League of the Iroquois, an aura which greatly enhances the legend. But F. D. Reville, a former editor of the *Brantford Exposi-*

tor and husband of Jean Morton, a close girlhood friend of Pauline's, gives a different view of her ancestry in a letter dated November 19, 1929, and written to Frank Yeigh, who was gathering information for an article which later appeared in the *Canadian Bookman*:

I deleted the reference to Pauline having Indian "royal blood" descent, a statement so frequently made and just as inaccurate as the other allegation that her father was head chief of the Mohawks. As a matter of fact— and I knew the family very intimately—he was not a hereditary chief at all, and had that title conferred upon him quite late in life. Pauline's undoubted genius manifestly caused someone in the first place to initiate fairy stories regarding her descent. My own opinion is that she owed more to the Howells strain in her mother than anything else. (Public Archives of Canada, Manuscript Group 30, D 48.)

Wherever the truth may lie, it cannot be denied that Pauline's Indian forebears were eminent, both among their own people and the white men. Her great-grandfather, Jacob Johnson (Tekahionwake) was the godson of Sir William Johnson. Her grandfather, John Smoke Johnson, served with Sir Isaac Brock during the War of 1812. Here again the white strain appears, through Smoke Johnson's wife, Helen Martin, who was the daughter of a Mohawk chief, George Martin, and Catherine Rolleston, adopted into the tribe after her capture during a raid on the Pennsylvania settlements. This blending of Indian and white, this pull between two cultures, one closely dependent on nature and in decline and the other technological and dominant, is the real key to the personality of Pauline Johnson.

George Henry Martin Johnson, as befitted his distinguished Indian background, received an English education at school in Brantford and life at "Chiefswood," built for his white wife, reflected the cultured taste and extensive learning which made him fully the equal of Mrs. Johnson, herself a woman of high intelligence.

Little Pauline's education was wide, if informal. From her earliest childhood she was exposed to a library of the classics and the best contemporary writings, in which she was allowed to read as she pleased, developing a strong liking for poetry. Her eldest brother, Beverly, and her sister, Evelyn, were sent away to school but Pauline and Allen were educated for two years at home by a governess. Later Pauline spent three years at an Indian day school on the reservation and a further two years at the Central School in Brantford, finishing her studies in 1879. During these free childhood years she drew deeply from her environment: from the natural beauty of "Chiefswood" under its great trees, close to the river where her canoe always waited; from the Indian tales of her old grandfather, John Smoke Johnson; from the famous guests, eager to visit the idyllic estate on the Grand River—titled Englishmen, outstanding scholars, artists, and writers, men and women who made Pauline familiar with a great world beyond the reservation long before she herself became a part of it.

Her time was spent in the fashion of any well-to-do young woman of the period: in social activities; canoeing on the river; summer expeditions to Muskoka (which intensified her strong feeling for nature); parties; amateur dramatics; and visits to the homes of friends, young people from nearby Brantford, with whom she mingled freely, evidently experiencing no discrimination because of her Indian birth. Her own description of her home and family is given in "My Mother," the first episode in *The Moccasin Maker*, published in 1913, the year of her death in distant Vancouver. In this charming, nostalgic account, her early years are bathed in a golden light. But tragedy, even then, shadowed an otherwise carefree existence and it came, significantly, through white men. In January, 1865, when Pauline was not quite four years old, her father was severely beaten for his opposition to the illicit liquor traffic on the reservation. Again, in October, 1873, he was attacked by white enemies who resented his refusal to condone the theft of Indian timber. After years of impaired health, George Henry Martin Johnson died, February 19, 1884.

The sheltered, gracious pattern of life at "Chiefswood" was shattered, as there were no longer the financial resources to maintain it. Beverly, in Hamilton, and Allen, in Toronto, were already independent and it was only too evident that Pauline and Evelyn must support themselves. The dignified, spacious house on the Grand River was abandoned for rented quarters in Brantford, where Mrs. Johnson established a home for her two daughters. Evelyn went to work in the Indian office but Pauline found no such practical solution. She turned more seriously to poetry, which she had written, chiefly for her own enjoyment, from her childhood, and in which she was now encouraged by her friends, the Revilles. Her first published poems appeared in the short-lived New York magazine, *Gems of Poetry*, in 1884 and 1885. Although the monetary return was minimal, Pauline was beginning to build a literary reputation which brought her into contact with other Canadian writers. "A Cry from an Indian Wife" was accepted for publication in the Toronto periodical, *The Week*, II (1885), 457. Its editor was a young Canadian, Charles G. D. Roberts, who became a loyal and lifelong friend, sharing generously with her his friends, relatives, and influence. Her talent was beginning to be recognized in other quarters also. At two public events of some importance she was asked to read her own poems, composed for these occasions: at the re-interment of the famous Seneca orator, Red Jacket, and eight other Seneca chiefs, arranged by the Buffalo Historical Society at Forest Lawn Cemetery in Buffalo, October 9, 1884; and at the dedication of a statue to Joseph Brant, in Brantford, October 13, 1886.

The year 1889 marks the first international recognition of Pauline Johnson's poetry. She was twenty-eight. Her work had been appearing regularly in *The Week* and occasionally in other periodicals, which led naturally to the inclusion of two poems "In the Shadows" and "At the Forge" in *Songs of the Great Dominion*, a poetry anthology compiled by William Douw Lighthall of Montreal. The eminent English critic, Theodore Watts-Dunton, selected these poems for particular attention in the London *Athenæum*, hailing Pauline Johnson as a North American Wordsworth, sounding a new note—"the note of the Red Man's Canada." The yearning of a country, centuries old, for a renewal of primitive vitality was satisfied by even the slightest treatment of nature, pure and undefiled, foreshadowing the tremendous success Pauline was later to enjoy in London society, the London revealed in all its decadent splendour by Henry James, also a North American. But the half-white Indian woman of cultured upbringing could not become the pre-European "savage," nor could her poetry deny its British and Victorian inspiration, derived as it was from the library at "Chiefswood." The Pauline Johnson legend, however, was evolving and the Watts-Dunton critique established her as a literary personage in Great Britain as well as Canada. Nevertheless, a letter from the aged John Greenleaf Whittier, dated March 4, 1891, and evidently written in response to a gift of Pauline's poems, does not reflect the enthusiasm of Watts-Dunton. "They have strength as well as beauty, and study and patient brooding on thy work will enable thee to write still better," was his sober, Quaker dictum.

Pauline's developing literary reputation, while personally gratifying, had by no means solved her precarious financial future. On Saturday, January 16, 1892, when Pauline was thirty-one, fate took a hand in her affairs, reshaping the course of her life. She had been invited by Frank Yeigh, president of the Young Liberal Society of Toronto, to take part in a concert on this date at the Art Gallery rooms of the Ontario Society of Authors, together with such outstanding figures as Wilfred Campbell, Duncan Campbell Scott, and W. D. Lighthall. More than any others of this distinguished group, Pauline made an immediate impact on the audience (one which was to be repeated again and again throughout the years), when she recited her two dramatic poems, "A Cry from an Indian Wife" and "As Red Men Die." So vivid was her presentation that Mr. Yeigh lost no time in capitalizing on his discovery. A second appearance, this time alone, was arranged for February 19, 1892, in Association Hall, Toronto ("The Song my Paddle Sings" was composed for the occasion). Pauline had at last found a way to use her literary talent for her own support. But it was a long and frequently rough road which led her over the vast distances of her own country, to Great Britain and the United States. For the following twenty years she was to be a nomad.

During 1893 and 1894 Pauline toured the Atlantic provinces intensively. In this period she continued to write—"Indian Medicine Men and their Magic," appeared in the *Dominion Illustrated Monthly* I (1892), 140–143, and "Iroquois of the Grand River" in *Harper's Weekly*, XXXVIII (1894), 587–89—but her ambition centred around the publication of her poetry. The money earned through her recitals and her now established literary reputation made it possible for her to leave for London in the summer of 1894 with letters of introduction from His Excellency the Earl of Aberdeen, Governor-General of Canada; from Lieutenant-Colonel the Hon. G. A. Kirkpatrick, Lieutenant-Governor of Ontario; and from the Reverend William Clark, Trinity College, Toronto. Thus she was assured an entrée into the highest literary, political, and social circles of Victorian London: the London of Ruskin, Swinburne, and Shaw; of Millais, Burne-Jones, and Alma-Tadema; of Maude Adams, Julia Arthur, Mrs. Patrick Campbell, Ellen Terry, Sir Henry Irving, and Sarah Bernhardt. Pauline's contact with this glittering world came largely through the great London hostesses, who vied with one another to secure her as an attraction at evening parties, where she appeared in Indian dress, a piquant combination of the noble savage and the gracious woman, who could be hired as an entertainer but who could also mingle, in her own right, with the august guests, some of whom had been received at "Chiefswood," her own home. The success she enjoyed did not deflect her from her objective in coming to London. Her first volume of poetry, *The White Wampum*, accepted by John Lane of the "Bodley Head," was received with enthusiasm on its publication in 1895, after Pauline's return to Canada. Included in it were poems which had already become popular: "As Red Men Die," "The Song my Paddle Sings," and "In the Shadows," one of the two poems which had first attracted Watts-Dunton.

The appearance of the volume, however, did nothing to alleviate her precarious financial situation. Her recitals, therefore, were more necessary than ever and she immediately started on her first tour of Canada, an exhausting succession of cities and towns, none too well linked by rail and flung across a continental wilderness. To each she gave her utmost and in the giving received warm response from her audiences and acquired a deep love for the country she felt to be uniquely hers through the Indian ancestors to whom it had once belonged. A now elderly woman, who, at the age of fifteen, heard her in St. Mary's, Ontario, commented that it was impossible to forget her. "I still shudder, it was so real when she recited 'When Red Men Die.' Of course there was no radio, no TV, and a concert like that was a great event and the whole town was there."

Certain cities Pauline made particularly her own. Winnipeg was one and Vancouver another. And it was in Winnipeg, in the winter of 1897, that the second decisive event in her life took place: her meeting with Walter McRaye, who was to be her manager and co-star for the remainder of her career. Lorne Pierce, in a postscript to McRaye's own book, *Pauline Johnson and her Friends* (Toronto, 1947), has given a brief outline of the life of this man, fifteen years younger than Pauline, who was as closely associated with her as any other human being, a friendship which, together with her concert career, alienated Pauline from her own family but which, on the other hand, made it possible for her to endure the rigorous schedule to which she was bound. McRaye, a pseudonym for McCrae, was also a Canadian and a professional entertainer, reciting the *habitant* poems of W. H. Drummond. It was natural that he and Pauline should be drawn together as transients in a strange city at Christmas time. They gave several joint recitals, then parted until they met again in Peterborough in the spring of 1899. In the autumn of 1900 they again joined forces. From that time, until Pauline's retirement in 1909, they travelled together, covering every part of Canada, visiting London in 1906, and many sections of the United States. McRaye, who knew Pauline so well, must assume much of the responsibility for the impenetrable legend surrounding her, for it was he, together with her sister Evelyn, who systematically and ruthlessly eliminated all personal references from her papers and correspondence after her death.

The year 1898 had been a crucial one for Pauline, the woman. Her mother, to whom she was deeply devoted, died on February 23, 1898, and Pauline finally cut all ties with Brantford and the "Chiefswood" of her happy childhood. Her engagement to Charles Drayton of Toronto, Assistant Inspector of the Western Loan & Savings Company of Winnipeg, announced in the *Brantford Expositor*, Wednesday, January 26, 1898, was broken later in the year for reasons that remain unknown but there can be no doubt that the blow was severe.

Pauline's second book of poetry, *Canadian Born*, was published in 1903, a much inferior collection in comparison with her earlier poems. In 1906, she made her second visit to London, accompanied by McRaye, but this venture, too, fell short of her first triumph. "'Drawing Rooms' were no longer popular; other forms of entertainment had taken their place. We made our first public appearance in London at Steinway Hall . . ." is McRaye's account of their reception. They performed, however, to a distinguished audience, which brought Pauline to the attention of Sir Gilbert Parker and Sir Arthur Pearson, owner of the *Daily Express*, to which she contributed a series of articles. Even more important was her meeting with Chief Joe Capilano, of the Squamish Mission of North Vancouver, who headed a delegation of British Columbia Indians, appealing to King Edward VII himself for protection against white violation of ancient tribal and fishing rights. This friendship was later to give Pauline the inspiration for *Legends of Vancouver*, her finest prose work.

Then came the return to Canada and yet another gruelling circuit. "In the summer of 1907," says McRaye, "we toured all over the middle western states for the Slayton Lyceum Bureau of Chicago—Chautauquas that took us as far west as Boulder, Colorado. . . ."

It was now seventeen years since Pauline Johnson had had her memorable first night in Toronto and the strain of time and travel had told on her health. She was thinking of retirement, McRaye tells us:

New York, Boston, Philadelphia, and many parts of the United States had paid her tribute as a brilliant artist and woman. Every village, town, and city in her native land knew and loved her. Vancouver was the city she liked best; it had always given us friendly audiences and I think we had appeared there over a dozen times. . . . I arranged to go across the Rockies and, after a good-bye performance in Kamloops [1909], she said farewell to public life and settled down in a cosy flat in the suburbs of Vancouver.

An unidentified and undated newspaper clipping among the Pauline Johnson material in the Mills Memorial Library, McMaster University, reports an appearance of Pauline Johnson and Walter McRaye in Winnipeg in these last years. "Though traces of her recent illness are noticeable she is fast regaining strength. Of course, her beautiful hair is gone, a severe attack of brain fever being the cause of this."

It was also in 1909 that McRaye married Lucy Betty Webling, a London actress, who toured with him in Pauline's place until 1914, when he enlisted in the Canadian Army Medical Corps. Lorne Pierce discreetly refrains from drawing any inference that his marriage in any way influenced Pauline's decision to retire (or vice versa)—and again the legend remains intact.

Pauline's intention was to earn her living as a free lance writer. Her renewed friendship with Chief Joe Capilano flowered into *Legends of Vancouver*, in which she lovingly shaped the ancient tales of his people into prose of surprising sensitivity and beauty. Before the series (first published as separate articles in the *Vancouver Province*) was completed, Pauline was stricken with cancer of the breast, discovered too late to be operable. The *Legends*, gathered into a book and published through the kindness of her friends, provided much of the desperately needed financial support during her two years of illness. On March 7, 1913, Pauline Johnson died at the age of fifty-two, in a Vancouver nursing home, heroic to the end in her devotion to her friends and to her writing. Her ashes were buried in her beloved Stanley Park. Tributes poured in from the whole of Canada and from Great Britain. The woman was dead, only the legend lived.

There are only two clues to the personality of Pauline Johnson: the accounts of her friends (fuel for the legend); and her own writings (not too revealing). The Brantford Historical Society owns many early photographs, which show her as a slender, short, dark, and exceedingly handsome girl, sometimes with a brooding expression, and always fashionably dressed. "Contrary to the usual with Indian women, she had outrun the fading time of beauty by ten years at least, an English heritage truly, and was at her best in charm and looks at thirty-five." That she was physically beautiful, with the magnetic attraction of an actress, is self-evident through the impact which she made on audiences and individuals alike. Her Canadian and English tours brought her hosts of "friends" among the famous as well as the simple people of the small towns, farms, and ranches. The devotion she aroused was strong enough to surround her to the end with genuine love and concern, after illness stripped the glamour from her. The Brantford Historical Society possesses a photograph of this period, taken with Betty McRaye, showing her as a gaunt, emaciated, middle-aged woman, her Indian features more pronounced than in her youth.

The tribute from Pauline's biographer, Mrs. William Garland Foster, wife of a British Columbia journalist, is typical of those written by her friends:

The keynote of Pauline Johnson's soul was loyalty. . . . She seemed to have epitomized in her being all the loyalty, all the fealty of the great aboriginal race from which she descended. Her ability to make friends was as remarkable as her genius and was in some way part of it. While her charming personality brought her many friends, it was the beauty of her character that kept them. . . . For the men who were responsible for discovering her genius she had the warmest gratitude. . . . Always Pauline Johnson's kindness was proverbial.

In any appraisal of her character, there is always the danger of categorizing certain qualities as "Indian" or "white." Yet loyalty, generosity, and gratitude *are* Indian characteristics to which she gave full and free expression. But in her closest relationships, these qualities were not enough to bring her happiness, either in marriage or within her own family, where her most intimate tie was with her white mother. She and her sister Evelyn were almost completely estranged for many years. When they were reunited in the last days of Pauline's life, the meeting was too painful for Pauline to endure, for it was only Evelyn's sense of family duty and her eagerness to settle details of the "Chiefswood" estate that brought her to Vancouver. Her favourite brother, Allen, did *not* visit her, although, according to Mrs. Foster, he sent his sister a newspaper clipping stating that she was "in actual want and had lost the use of her right arm," a gesture that hurt and angered Pauline to the point of fury. There were, however, flowers from Allen at her funeral! The legend had separated her from the more conventional lives of her sister and brothers, although each, in his or her own way, had come to terms with the white world, if not with one another.

But Pauline was the only member of her family to function in that white world largely on the strength of her Indian background, both in her literary productions and in her dramatic art. There is no doubt that Pauline was passionately proud to be an Indian but it is also true that she traded on that very pride to earn her living. How far she was conscious of this it is impossible to say. Norman Shrive, in his penetrating essay, states: "Pauline Johnson, the person, knew the Indian and could perceive the artificiality that had become associated with him. The irony is, however, that she in some respects became part of that artificiality, either deliberately or unknowingly. That it was the latter is perhaps indicated by the lapse in her powers of discrimination when she applied them to poetry." And once she had embarked on her recitals, she was no longer accepted as an individual in her own right but as the "Mohawk-princess" poetess, a role played at depth until the legend stood between her and reality.

"It was not with the individual that Pauline Johnson was in love. Like all poets she was in love with Love, just as she was in love with life itself. All artists, creators, poets, crave affection. It cannot be otherwise, for the great drain of vitality consequent upon the creation of a masterpiece demands a draught of the healing springs of life." Time has reversed this pronouncement of Isobel Ecclestone MacKay. It is precisely because Pauline Johnson drank so sparingly from the "healing springs of life" that her work is not truly great. Limited by her constant travels, increasingly trapped in the legend, Pauline's relationships were inevitably sporadic and, to some degree, superficial. It is not without significance that she and Walter McRaye invented a whole group of imaginary companions, in almost childlike fashion, to while away the tedious hours on the road. And could that passionate "love poetry," which so impressed her contemporaries, spring from the same need? Mrs. Foster primly answers "There were several engagements, but something always intervened, as if subconscious influence protected her from entering a domestic life, which would have been death to that art which was the well spring of her being." And in the end that art betrayed her.

"There came a time, after her last trip abroad [1907]," Mrs. Foster states, when "her friends in the east lost sight of her. She was losing much of her beauty with illness and the passing years, and perhaps had some natural hesitancy about making the necessary re-adjustments from youth to age. And, too, she was weary with the long round of effort in pleasing the public." Yet it was only when the legend disintegrated that a courageous, indomitable woman, capable of anger as well as love, independent and proud, yet generous and grateful, was finally revealed. It was what Walter McRaye calls "the stoicism of her race," shining through the white inheritance, that enabled her to counter death with the poem, "And He Said, Fight on," inspired by Tennyson's "The Revenge," read so many years before in the quiet library at "Chiefswood."

Pauline Johnson's own writings reveal the Indian-white dualism in many ways. Quite apart from the conscious, professional use of her Indian heritage, her early experiences did not predispose her to accept or to honour the white race. She did, after all, grow up on the Six Nations reservation, although admittedly in a favoured position, and thus could not avoid the contrast between her own treatment and that of her Indian neighbours. The brutal beatings which indirectly brought about her father's death affected her deeply. In her poetry the Indian invariably is the hero in any conflict with the white man, running the gamut from an idealized, romantic, prehistoric figure to the poor, victimized "Cattle thief" or "Corn husker." In her prose she is divided. "In the Beginning," a short story in *The Moccasin Maker*, deals with a favourite theme—marriage between an Indian or half-breed woman and an Englishman (usually endowed with fair, curly hair, blue eyes, and a handsome physique). Even with due allowance for Victorian melodrama, it is difficult to accept her depiction of the white missionary who intervenes to prevent his nephew from marrying his half-breed student.

". . . You can't trust her." His [the missionary's] eyes grew smaller, more glittering, more fascinating then, and leaning with an odd, secret sort of movement towards Lawrence, he almost whispered, "Think of her silent ways, her noiseless step; the girl glides about like an apparition; her quick fingers, her wild longings—I don't know, but with all my fondness for her, she reminds me sometimes of a strange snake. . . ."
They were the last words I [Esther, the half-breed] ever heard uttered by either that old arch-fiend or his weak, miserable kinsman. . . .

But before Esther takes her revenge, she contemplates her sleeping lover.

. . . As I bent over him the fulness of his perfect beauty impressed me for the first time; his slender form, his curving mouth that almost laughed even in sleep; his fair tossed hair, his smooth, strong-pulsing throat. God, how I loved him!

Then there is that odd mixture that gives its title to the collection of boys' stories, *The Shagganappi*. Fire-Flint Larocque, son of a French father and an Indian mother, product of an Indian school on a western reservation, protégé of the Governor-General, arrives, miraculously, at the "great Eastern college in Ontario," with an outfit that includes "silk socks, silk shirt, top-coat lined with mink, an otter collar. . . ." Shag mingles with the aristocracy of Montreal through Hal Bennington, son of Sir George Bennington, for whom Shag's father once acted as cook on a western tour. The astounding climax, in which Hal confesses that his own mother is a half-breed, a secret well-kept by the noble Shag, leaves the latter undisputed leader of the school and thus entitled to read the address on the occasion of the visit of his old friend, Lord Mortimer, Governor-General of Canada. Here Shag, the half-breed, wins by being more English than the English themselves!

Occasionally Pauline Johnson wrote only about white characters, usually sympathetically. "The King Georgeman," also included in *The Shagganappi*, is a highly melodramatic and sentimental account of a self-sacrificing Englishman, a visitor in the West and at first despised as a tenderfoot, who nurses a small-pox victim back to health at the risk of his own life, thus converting a hardened criminal into a useful citizen.

Yet neither story seems realistic in any human sense. Again Pauline may be catering, unconsciously, to the current public stereotype of the "superior" white race, a practice which she herself had condemned in reverse with perception, wit, and irony, in a newspaper article published in the *Toronto World*, May 22, 1892, entitled "A Strong Race Opinion on the Indian Girl in Modern Fiction."

But when Pauline was able to forget the white-Indian pull, she wrote with rare insight, pride, and even tenderness, about the ways of her people, in prose that perfectly conveyed her theme. "Hoolool of the Totem Pole" and "A Night with North Eagle," both of which appear in *The Shagganappi*, as well as her *Legends of Vancouver*, show her at her best as a writer. Tenas, little son of the west coast Indian woman, Hoolool, has a dream of "baby totems," which leads his mother, a widow, to make small totems for sale, similar to the large one she has refused to sell, even to buy food.

By nightfall, it [her work] was completed, and by the fitful fire-light Hoolool painted and stained its huddled figures in the black, orange, crimson and green that tribal custom made law. The warmth of the burning cedar knots dried the paints and pigments, until their acrid fragrance filled the little room, and the child's eyelids dropped sleepily, and in delighted happiness he once more snuggled into his blanket bed, the baby totem hugged to his little heart. . . .

Here the woman speaks and not the legend, completely at one with the Indian Hoolool, bent over her fire and her carving. And it is here, in such prose as this, that Pauline Johnson can make her claim to be a Canadian writer of note, fully justifying the identification which she invariably and consciously made with the Indian side of her heritage.

The pull of the two cultures is again evident in Pauline's attitude towards religion. George Henry Martin Johnson was an Anglican, who represented his church as well as his people on many important occasions. His father, John Smoke Johnson, regularly attended the Mohawk chapel on the reservation and he is buried in its churchyard, with his Bible and his tomahawk beside him. Pauline, in her youth, was a communicant of the Church of England and in the last days of her life it was an Anglican clergyman of Vancouver, the Reverend C. C. Owen, who visited her frequently to administer communion, who conducted her funeral service in Christ Church, and who later led the "brief and simple" rites when her ashes were buried in Stanley Park. A memorial service was also held in His Majesty's Chapel of the Mohawks, near Brantford, Ontario, where a large boulder marks the Johnson family plot.

What was Pauline Johnson's real religion? She has left such poems as "Brier," "Easter," "Christmas," "Penseroso," which are conventional in the extreme. "A Prodigal," which begins "My heart forgot its God for love of you," is a much more sincere confession of the inadequacy of human love, measured against the divine love of God. Mrs. Foster, Pauline's biographer, holds the view, as does Walter McRaye, her intimate friend, that she deeply believed in the "Great Tyee," who did not "so materially differ from the God of the Anglo-Saxons." In her prose, she wavers between an almost violent antipathy towards orthodox Christianity ("As It was in the Beginning"; "Her Majesty's Guest"; and "The Derelict," all included in *The Moccasin Maker*) and a more sympathetic attitude towards the Christian faith, but without any seemingly deep commitment to it. When she was dying, Mr. Owen asked her how she could face death with such courage and cheerfulness. She replied that her example was Robert Louis Stevenson (incidentally a devout Christian). Her faith, deeper than she herself probably knew, is beautifully revealed in the words of the little child to his mother, again in "Hoolool of the Totem Pole":

"You have two names—'Marna' [mother, in Chinook] and 'Hoolool'— yet you are the same. Maybe it's that way with the two Great Tyees, the white man's and ours. . . ."

Patriotism was always a strong facet of Pauline Johnson's character, yet as it is revealed in her work, it is frequently jingoistic and cheap. As one who knew Canada from coast to coast in a way that few of her contemporaries had known it, she had a deep and passionate love for and appreciation of its varied landscape, which shine through her nature poetry and some of her prose. Intensely British and Canadian in her loyalty, she could, nevertheless, achieve the ultimate in triteness, when she wrote with patriotism rather than nature or her own people as her theme. "Canadian Born" shows her at her worst:

We've yet to make our money, we've yet to make our fame,
But we have gold and glory in our clean colonial name,
And every man's a millionaire if only he can brag
That he was born in Canada beneath the British flag.

Her nonchalant, even whimsical attitude towards the Russo-Japanese War strikes a jarring note, after the world events of the past half-century:

> So take off your cap
> To the brave little Jap
> Who fights for Chrysanthemum land.

But though Pauline Johnson may have lacked political understanding, her boys' story, "Gun-shy Billy," in *The Shagganappi*, shows clearly that, underneath the flippancy, she hated the futility of war:

> He saw only a simple grave in the open veldt in far-away Africa—a grave that he, himself, had heaped with stones formed in the one word "Canada." At the recollection of it, poor Billy buried his aching head in his hands. The glory had paled and vanished. There was nothing left of the terrible war but the misery, the mourning, the heartbreak of it all!

From such scattered fragments it is difficult to construct any coherent or definitive portrait of Pauline Johnson but it does seem clear, as Norman Shrive believes, that "much of the popular interest in Miss Johnson today is still stimulated by the essential non-literary aspects of her career—her Indian heritage, her dress, her skill as a stage performer and her personality." Yet, as he points out, Pauline Johnson's literary reputation must not be underestimated. (Roy Daniells reminds *his* readers, "Her collected poems, *Flint and Feather* (1912), have been in demand for fifty years.") Popular demand to the contrary, Professor Shrive concludes that contemporary critics, notably A. J. M. Smith, do not concede that Pauline Johnson is either a lyric poet of note or an adequate interpreter of the Indian to the white man. "Her best work is not to be found in her Indian poetry at all but in one or two pretty and very artificial little lyrics." Professor Shrive's own verdict is not quite so drastic:

> Pauline Johnson actually was one of the few people who saw through the new popular image of the Indian and who said so in writing. Aside from certain prose pieces in *Legends of Vancouver* some of the most perceptive, the most unaffected writing she did was in private letters to friends and in some fugitive newspaper articles, writing that reflects an author of distinction more than the Pauline Johnson of the stage and of "The Song my Paddle Sings."

Today Pauline Johnson is not remembered for the full range of her literary output. A few of her poems, notably the incomplete selection included in *Flint and Feather*, appeal particularly to young Canadians exposed to them in school. Her prose is largely neglected. Nor is there any way of knowing what Pauline Johnson herself would have chosen to write if the circumstances of her life had allowed her leisure and financial independence. There are indications that her talent was greater than contemporary modes of expression or the state of Canadian literature could convey. But when one actually sees the white brocade dress, worn time and time again on concert platforms from Newfoundland to British Columbia or the Indian costume which doubled for it, critical pronouncements from a safe and comfortable distance do not seem entirely just. Only a gallant and indomitable woman with her back to an economic wall would have dared or have had the inner resources to create a legend which has stubbornly withstood the attacks of our super-sophisticated twentieth-century critics. Let him who can barn-storm a continent, writing prose as well as poetry (with no help from the Canada Council) cast the first stone!

BIBLIOGRAPHY

So much has been written about Pauline Johnson that a comprehensive bibliography would not add greatly to the little actually known of her personal life. The following selection gives the salient material without too much repetition and appraises her contribution to Canadian literature more soberly than her contemporary admirers.

Manuscripts

Unexamined manuscripts exist at "Chiefswood," near Brantford, Ontario, now a museum (Mrs. Joyce Smoke, Curator). There are also some papers in the possession of Mr. and Mrs. Andrew Jamieson, Ohsweken, Ontario. Unpublished reminiscences of Evelyn Johnson are in the hands of Dorothy Keen and Martha McKeon of Toronto. These form the basis for two recent articles by Mollie Gillen in *Chatelaine*, XXXIX (1966), No. 2, 25, 40–49; No. 3, 39, 96–102, which are highly romanticized and do not add to Mrs. Foster's well-documented biography.

The Brant Museum, Brantford, Ontario, has many photographs and other mementoes of Pauline Johnson and the Johnson family, including some letters. The Douglas Library, Queen's University, Kingston, Ontario, holds manuscript poems and letters sent to H. O'Brien, 1894–1903. The Mills Memorial Library, McMaster University, Hamilton, Ontario, has miscellaneous material: newspaper clippings, notes, accounts, programmes, a letter or two, etc. There are scattered references to Pauline Johnson in the Yeigh Papers, which are divided between the Public Archives of

Canada, Ottawa, and the Ontario Department of Public Records and Archives, Toronto.

Printed Sources

ROBERT AYRE, "Pauline Johnson" in "Canadian Writers of the Past," IX, *Canadian Forum*, XIV (1933), 17.

ANNIE H. FOSTER, *The Mohawk Princess: Being Some Account of the Life of Tekahion-wake (E. Pauline Johnson)* (Vancouver, 1931). This still remains the most comprehensive and useful biography of Pauline Johnson. While the author shares the contemporary enthusiasm, she provides a full account of Pauline's life, supporting her statements with sound documentation, not always complete.

E. PAULINE JOHNSON, *Flint and Feather: The Complete Poems of E. Pauline Johnson (Tekahionwake)*; with introduction by Theodore Watts-Dunton and a biographical sketch of the author; illustrated by J. R. Seavey (Toronto, 1926).

—— *Legends of Vancouver*: a new edition with an introduction by Marcus Van Steen and illustrated by Ben Lim (Toronto, 1961).

—— *The Moccasin Maker* (Toronto, 1913).

—— *The Shagganappi*; with introduction by Ernest Thompson Seton (Toronto, 1913).

—— *The White Wampum* (London, Toronto, Boston [1895]).

KLINCK, CARL F. *et al.* (eds.), *Literary History of Canada: Canadian Literature in English* (Toronto, 1965), 425–26; 752. Contains brief appraisals of Pauline Johnson as a writer in longer articles by Roy Daniells and Munro Beattie.

WALTER JACKSON McCREA [Walter McRaye, *pseud.*], *Pauline Johnson and Her Friends* (Toronto, 1947).

—— *Town Hall Tonight* (Toronto, 1929).

N. SHRIVE, "What Happened to Pauline?" *Canadian Literature*, XIII (1962), 25–38. Dispassionate and perceptive appraisal of Pauline Johnson as a writer, stressing her ability in prose and her witty, lucid comprehension of the Indian role in Canadian fiction.

MARCUS VAN STEEN, *Pauline Johnson: Her Life and Work* (Toronto, 1965). Consists of a long introduction and a casual sampling of poetry and prose. A much less substantial work than the title intimates.

[THEODORE WATTS-DUNTON], unsigned review of *Songs of the Great Dominion* . . . , ed. W. D. Lighthall (London, 1889), *Athenaeum; Journal of Literature, Science, and the Fine Arts, Music, and the Drama*, No. 3231 (Sept. 28, 1889), 411–13.

FRANK YEIGH, "Memories of Pauline Johnson," *Canadian Bookman*, XI (1929), 227–29.

5

Laure Conan

1845-1924

MICHELINE DUMONT

"Non, je ne laisserai pas parler de moi dans la préface de mon livre. Si j'avais pensé que cela vous viendrait jamais à l'esprit, je serais morte bien des fois avant de vous prier de présenter mon roman au public." Voilà ce qu'écrit Laure Conan, le 4 mars 1884, à l'abbé Casgrain, grand ami des lettres canadiennes. Cette déclaration est bien caractéristique de la première romancière du Canada français, car jamais un écrivain ne fut plus avare de confidences sur sa vie personnelle que Laure Conan.

Aussi est-il bien téméraire de tracer le portrait de cette femme énigmatique. A peine croit-on avoir saisi quelques traits, que l'image s'estompe dans un nouveau brouillard. Et l'on reste déçu devant tant de questions restées sans réponse. D'abord, d'où vient ce beau nom de Laure Conan ? Pourquoi Félicité Angers l'a-t-elle choisi pour signer ses romans et ses articles ? Où l'a-t-elle trouvé ? C'est peine perdue, personne ne le sait.

Femme mystérieuse, entrée par hasard et sans y participer vraiment dans un milieu à la fois littéraire et patriotique, écrivain estimable et estimé, Laure Conan est inséparable de sa seconde identité, celle de

Félicité Angers. Les deux physionomies s'expliquent, se complètent l'une l'autre. Personnalité double ? Non. On dirait plus justement qu'elle fut une personne divisée, tour à tour attirée par le silence et la parole. C'est le paradoxe étrange d'une vie marquée à la fois par l'anonymat et la célébrité. Célèbre, Laure Conan le fut durant sa vie ; elle l'est toujours depuis, par l'intérêt qu'elle provoque chez les critiques littéraires, les étudiants et les professeurs de lettres. Anonyme, Félicité Angers le fut de par sa volonté propre ; elle le reste aujourd'hui à plus d'un égard tant elle se livre peu dans les rares documents qu'elle nous a laissés.

On sait que Félicité Angers est née à La Malbaie en 1845. Elle est la fille d'Elie Angers, forgeron de son métier et de Marie Perron, commerçante. Les ancêtres de la famille Angers sont arrivés au pays en 1667.

Grâce au double labeur des parents, les six enfants Angers peuvent poursuivre des études supérieures à Québec. Félicité, pour sa part, est pensionnaire au couvent des Ursulines. Elle semble y prendre des goûts littéraires. Tout au moins, on sait qu'elle y mérite plusieurs fois le privilège de transcrire ses compositions françaises dans le cahier d'honneur de la maison : *Le Papillon littéraire*. Elle reçoit à la distribution des prix un ouvrage fort sérieux, typique des pensionnats d'alors : *Les Heures sérieuses d'une jeune personne*. Malgré la sévérité d'une telle lecture, à une époque où on était volontiers romantique, Félicité Angers en fait son livre de méditation quotidienne. Mieux, elle se prend d'admiration pour l'auteur, Charles de Sainte-Foye. De l'aveu même de Laure Conan, cet auteur spirituel représente Charles de Montbrun, le père d'Angéline de Montbrun (premier roman de Laure Conan, écrit en 1881), figure paternelle que l'on peut d'ailleurs retracer dans les autres ouvrages de la romancière. A vrai dire, il y a là une clef de l'énigme que pose Félicité Angers. En effet, Charles de Sainte-Foye semble marquer si profondément l'adolescente, puis l'adulte, que toute leur vie affective en sera marquée. C'est ce que l'on peut déduire, semble-t-il, de l'œuvre de l'écrivain, où transparaît toujours une sorte de refus, un angélisme, une impossibilité d'aimer, de pouvoir en tirer une quelconque satisfaction. En somme, Félicité Angers apparaît comme ayant été formée dans un climat spirituel aux accents jansénistes particulièrement vifs. Elle cherche d'ailleurs à s'y maintenir si l'on considère qu'elle ajoute à sa lecture spirituelle de base une lecture de chevet, *Mes Prisons*, de Sylvio Pellico, dont le contenu ne l'éloigne pas de préoccupations où le devoir se confond avec le pardon.

Cette ambiance spirituelle et intellectuelle s'accorde d'ailleurs fort bien avec le cadre de vie retirée que mène Félicité Angers. Elle ne quitte pas La Malbaie, sinon pour effectuer quelques excursions dans les environs, à l'Ile-aux-Coudres, à Tadoussac. La seule occupation qu'on lui connaisse, consiste à entretenir le jardin de la maison paternelle. Elle y cultive des roses qui font l'admiration de tout l'entourage. Il y a tout lieu de croire qu'elle rédige aussi un journal intime. Sans aucun doute, Félicité Angers n'est pas satisfaite de la vie qu'elle mène. Elle sent le besoin de s'exprimer davantage. Elle décide donc de devenir Laure Conan : elle sera écrivain.

Cette décision allait faire d'elle une pionnière sans le savoir. En effet, Laure Conan est la première femme à pénétrer dans le monde des lettres au Canada français. Pour son entrée, elle publie à 33 ans, soit en 1878, un premier roman dans *La Revue de Montréal*. C'est *Un Amour vrai*. Comme l'a écrit un critique, « cette histoire de conversion est bien ce qui peut s'écrire de plus affligeant dans ce genre de littérature dite d'édification ». L'héroïne de *Un Amour vrai* décide de renoncer à un amour légitime pour obtenir la conversion de celui qu'elle aime. Le ton un peu mièvre, la thèse si évidente font de ce premier roman une œuvre bien faible. Aussi cette publication ne fait-elle aucun bruit. Les lecteurs n'ont même pas la curiosité de connaître l'identité de cette Laure Conan. Sans doute pensent-ils que ce pseudonyme cache la personnalité de quelque prêtre amateur des belles-lettres.

Pourtant, lorsqu'en 1881–2 *La Revue canadienne* publia *Angéline de Montbrun*, l'étonnement et la curiosité firent bientôt place à l'admiration. Quelques indiscrétions révélèrent aux lecteurs que l'auteur était une canadienne authentique dont le talent se révélait soudainement au public. On salua l'événement de tous côtés. On parla d'Eugénie de Guérin. On expliqua qu'à l'instar du Cardinal Wiseman, auteur de *Fabiola*, elle avait élevé le roman à une dignité toute nouvelle de sorte que son ouvrage pouvait être mis entre toutes les mains.

Cependant, les lecteurs ne s'avisèrent pas de l'importance de cette publication. A une époque où de rares romanciers racontaient maladroitement des récits touffus où s'agitaient des personnages inconsistants, la première romancière de notre littérature se cantonnait au contraire dans une vision intérieure des événements et des êtres. Dans la première partie de son roman, pour raconter l'idylle de Maurice Darville et Angéline de Montbrun, elle choisit le procédé des lettres, si propre aux confidences, aux analyses. On peut lui chicaner le caractère un peu artificiel de cette technique, l'irréalité de cet amour qui ne semble pas se confronter à la réalité, et surtout ce personnage indécis de Maurice Darville, sorti tout armé de son cerveau. Il n'en reste pas moins que ces lettres préfabriquées rivalisent de délicatesse et de subtilités. De sensiblerie aussi, mais une sensiblerie toute disposée à se transformer en une sensibilité étonnante de profondeur. La seconde partie du roman s'en trouve toute transfigurée. On sait, en effet, que l'héroïne, Angéline de Montbrun, éprouvée par la mort de son père, se voit défigurée par un accident et rompt aussitôt après ses fiançailles. C'est ici qu'Angéline fait l'apprentissage de la tristesse et découvre péniblement le chemin de la résignation. Une fois admis un certain caractère malsain dans cette vocation à la souffrance, il faut avoir l'honnêteté d'en apercevoir la justesse de l'analyse. Chaque nuance intérieure y est mesurée avec adresse. On suit avec intérêt les méandres de cette évolution spirituelle qui avance à la recherche de l'équilibre et de la paix. On sent que Laure Conan connaissait à fond les ressources cachées de son univers intérieur. Et on devine que dans ces *Feuilles détachées* du journal intime d'Angéline de Montbrun, elle se raconte elle-même avec une sincérité et une complaisance mal déguisées. Masochiste, elle en devient savante, ou va jusqu'au lyrisme dans l'évocation de ses tourments.

Nous comprenons mieux maintenant pourquoi Laure Conan tenait tant à ce qu'on ne parle pas d'elle dans la préface de son roman. Dans cette lettre dont il était question au début de ce texte, Laure Conan disait également à l'abbé Casgrain : « Je suis bien trop peu de chose pour occuper ce redoutable public de ma personnalité. Et si la vie m'a été triste et amère, je ne veux ni m'en plaindre, ni qu'on m'en plaigne. Je ne tiens pas à faire pitié. Pas davantage je ne voudrais me faire une parure de ma pauvreté ni de mes tristesses. Vous me direz peut-être qu'il y a là une fierté sauvage, une sensibilité maladive. Peut-être. Mais enfin, je suis ce que je suis et je n'y puis rien. »

Qu'avions nous besoin, au demeurant, des confidences de l'abbé Casgrain ? Nous découvrons la vraie Laure Conan en filigrane, à travers tous ses romans. Au fond, les critiques de l'époque ne s'y trompaient pas de beaucoup quand ils parlaient prudemment d'autobiographie au sujet d'*Angéline de Montbrun*. En devenant Laure Conan celle-ci n'avait pas cessé d'être Félicité Angers, la solitaire demoiselle de La Malbaie. L'écrivain puisait dans l'expérience personnelle de sa vie privée la matière première de son œuvre. Félicité Angers, c'est un peu Cendrillon au foyer. Et la magie d'une marraine qui s'appelait l'invention romanesque lui a permis de mettre en valeur les réserves cachées d'une âme tout en nuances et de laisser apparaître Laure Conan, image vieillotte et naïve d'une femme très douce qui a su révéler au public les charmes certains de l'introspection subtile. Par cette transposition, Cendrillon va au bal. Faut-il lui en vouloir si elle n'obéit pas à la légende et redevient grillon au premier coup de minuit pour se consumer dans le devoir et y entraîner ses héroïnes ? D'ailleurs, on ne doute plus de la ressemblance entre Laure Conan et Angéline de Montbrun quand on lit cette lettre que la romancière écrivait à une admiratrice : « Merci de vos bonnes paroles pour Angéline. C'est mon enfant de prédilection. J'ajouterais qu'on m'a blessée en me disant du mal de Maurice, et on m'en a tant dit... Je le trouve malgré cela digne d'être aimé. »

On le voit, *Angéline de Montbrun* est à plus d'un égard, un roman capital. D'abord, il révèle les conflits profonds qui furent le lot de Félicité Angers, et les critiques n'ont pas fini d'épuiser les thèmes qu'il contient. D'un autre côté, il est le premier roman d'analyse de notre littérature, et à ce titre, il mérite une place d'honneur dans la production romanesque canadienne. Ce fait mérite qu'on s'y arrête. Car il ajoute un relief tout particulier à la vocation de Laure Conan. Et si l'apparition d'un écrivain est toujours intéressante à expliquer, elle le devient encore plus quand cet écrivain est une femme qui ouvre des chemins encore inexplorés.

On peut deviner que le destin de Félicité Angers fut tissé de chagrins, d'introversion, de frustrations, de fermeture sur soi. En s'affirmant dans la création romanesque, en devenant Laure Conan, elle se délivrait intérieurement. Plus tard, en s'engageant dans la littérature patriotique, comme on le verra, elle donnerait un sens positif à sa vie. Cette interprétation est certainement plausible. Si séduisante qu'elle soit, elle ne résout pourtant pas la difficulté d'expliquer dans son contexte social la vocation de Laure Conan.

Le monde littéraire de 1880 à Québec ou à Montréal est un univers clos où gravitent quelques poètes, journalistes, prêtres et critiques. Leur réputation ne s'étend pas au delà du cercle étroit de leurs intimes. Le public qui les lit est peu nombreux. La société québécoise, repliée sur elle-même, n'a pas connaissance, pour ainsi dire, des activités de ses écrivains. Le monde féminin, en particulier, est tenu presqu'à l'écart de ces activités. On saisit alors le caractère surprenant de l'apparition de Laure Conan : non seulement une femme est entrée dans le monde de la littérature, mais elle a inauguré chez nous la tradition du roman psychologique. Que la société canadienne-française de 1880 ait engendré une Laure Conan, c'est là une belle énigme, surtout quand on réalise que l'auteur n'est pas issu d'un de ces cercles privilégiés de la capitale ou de la métropole, mais d'un village aussi reculé que La Malbaie. Au bout du compte, on ne peut avancer que de timides hypothèses pour expliquer cette émergence. Chose certaine, Laure Conan est un être marginal.

La romancière apporte cependant une explication étrange à sa vocation. Elle écrit à son protecteur l'abbé Casgrain : « J'éprouve le besoin de me justifier d'avoir essayé d'écrire. Permettez-moi de vous dire que les circonstances ont tout fait ou à peu près. Ma volonté, je vous l'assure, y a été pour bien peu de choses. La nécessité seule m'a donné cet extrême courage de me faire imprimer. » Cette explication est plus surprenante encore que la vocation littéraire de Laure Conan. Félicité Angers serait donc devenue Laure Conan dans le désir de gagner sa vie. Dans un pays et à une époque où le métier d'écrivain était le plus sûr moyen de ne pas gagner d'argent, cette ambition a de quoi rendre sceptique. Or, fait plus invraisemblable encore, Laure Conan a réussi à vivre de sa plume. Cette femme n'a pas fini de nous étonner.

Après la publication d'*Angéline de Montbrun*, ce roman dont l'importance et l'intérêt pour la connaissance de l'auteur sont déjà apparus, Laure Conan s'est engagée dans la littérature patriotique mais sans cesser pour cela de traiter ses sujets sous l'angle de la psychologie des personnages. En 1886, elle manifeste cet intérêt patriotique par une brochure *Si les Canadiennes le voulaient*. Sous la forme d'un dialogue assez maladroit, elle concrétise ce qui lui semble l'essentiel du patriotisme en politique, insistant sur le rôle de la femme dans ce domaine. Le personnage principal, M. de Vagemmes, ressemble à s'y méprendre à Charles de Montbrun, le père d'Angéline. On devine ainsi Laure Conan influencée par son père spirituel même dans ses ouvrages impersonnels.

En 1889, elle découvre les *Relations des Jésuites*. Ses personnages seront désormais tirés de l'histoire canadienne. C'est alors qu'elle publie ses deux romans qui ont le plus grand succès auprès du public : *A l'œuvre et à l'épreuve* (1891), où elle évoque la vie de Charles Garnier, l'un des huit martyrs canadiens ; et *L'Oublié* (1900), dans lequel elle se plaît à retracer la carrière de Lambert Closse, l'un des défenseurs de Ville-Marie. Dans chacun de ces romans apparaissent des figures féminines dont la consistance psychologique ressort d'une manière remarquable. Dans *A l'œuvre et à l'épreuve*, Gisèle Méliand accepte de renoncer à son amour pour Charles Garnier quand elle apprend que celui-ci veut se dévouer auprès des indigènes du Canada. Dans *L'Oublié*, la figure d'Elisabeth Moyen est une des mieux réussies de Laure Conan. La jeune femme de Lambert Closse est d'ailleurs étudiée avec tant de complaisance que le personnage de Lambert Closse paraît lui-même secondaire à côté de cette héroïne.

A la même époque, Laure Conan s'est également tournée vers le journalisme. Retirée de 1893 à 1898 au monastère des religieuses du Précieux-Sang à Saint-Hyacinthe, elle dirige *La Voix du Précieux-Sang*, annales religieuses qu'elle rédige presqu'à elle seule. Son écriture perd alors en authenticité ce qu'elle gagne en abondance. Mais l'écrivain peut, grâce à ces travaux, gagner honorablement sa vie. Après ce premier contact avec le journalisme, Laure Conan publie ensuite dans un très grand nombre de revues. Elle collabore activement au premier journal féminin du Canada français, *Le Journal de Françoise*, et parfois, elle reprend de vieux articles, les rajeunit d'un titre nouveau et les publie dans une autre revue. Il lui arrive même de réclamer impérieusement ses honoraires auprès de ses nombreux éditeurs. Elle a vécu de sa plume certes ! Mais à quel prix ! Elle sacrifie aux goûts de l'époque et multiplie les articles où la religiosité dispute la place d'honneur au patriotisme ému. Elle s'intéresse à toutes les questions qui soulèvent l'opinion publique. Elle est de toutes les bonnes causes, religieuses et patriotiques de préférence. Elle ne refuse jamais sa collaboration, bien qu'elle entende agir à sa manière, dans le silence de son bureau de travail. Ainsi en 1910, elle collabore au Congrès Antialcoolique de Québec en publiant *Aux canadiennes*. Elle collabore au Congrès Eucharistique de Montréal, la même année, en publiant *Jeanne Le Ber, adoratrice de Jésus-Hostie*. Si on lui demande sa participation concrète, elle refuse avec fermeté et ce n'est que longuement suppliée qu'elle va déposer une gerbe de fleurs, lors de l'inauguration du monument de Jeanne Mance, dans la cour de l'Hôtel-Dieu de Montréal.

On retrouve ici le paradoxe de sa double physionomie. Effacée et timide dans une société qu'elle fuit comme la peste, Laure Conan a l'audace des faibles dès qu'elle écrit. Elle n'hésite pas à correspondre avec les écrivains les plus en vue des milieux littéraires du Canada français. Elle va chercher les correspondants jusqu'en Europe : Julie Lavergne, Carmen Sylva (la reine de Roumanie), voire même René Bazin. Elle signe Laure Conan, bien sûr, ces messages impersonnels et distingués. Car Félicité Angers reste étrangère à toute cette activité et ne sera jamais que la « Tante Fé » de ses nombreux neveux et nièces ; ou encore, la sœur du notaire de La Malbaie, un peu ridiculisée par les gamins qui montent en épingle des comportements qu'ils jugent excentriques. Elle a par exemple, cette habitude d'assister à une messe matinale le dimanche, et de revenir enchapeautée et enrubannée à la grand-messe, juste pour écouter le sermon. Le curé s'est d'ailleurs si bien conformé à ce rite qu'il attend qu'elle arrive pour commencer son prône !

Cet effacement rend sa carrière bien spéciale. D'une part, elle est privée de cet aspect mondain ou militant qui a si bien caractérisé plusieurs femmes de lettres à qui elle avait ouvert la voie. D'autre part, elle est tissée d'un labeur ininterrompu et se distingue par là de ce que l'on observe chez ces écrivains qui se contentent des lauriers que leur a mérité une publication qui a fait du bruit. Il reste que dans sa production copieuse et variée, la tradition a eu vite fait d'établir un choix sévère. Rien n'est demeuré ou presque, de tous ces articles qu'elle envoyait sans discrimination, aussi bien à une revue considérable, telle que *La Revue canadienne*, qu'à une obscure et éphémère feuille paroissiale. Devoirs d'écolière où elle résumait honnêtement ses lectures ; textes sans âme qui vont de l'hagiographie la plus traditionnelle aux biographies historiques d'une authenticité médiocre ; des réflexions les plus banales sur le patriotisme aux méditations religieuses les plus inattendues. Boileau des lettres à sa manière, Laure Conan collige ses articles en volumes et publie en 1913, *Physionomies de saints* et en 1917, *Silhouettes canadiennes*.

Il ne faut pas croire, cependant, que la romancière cède complètement le pas à la journaliste. Mais Laure Conan est devenue plus réticente avant de livrer une œuvre au public. Elle se laisse aller à reprendre un texte du début de sa carrière. En 1883, elle avait écrit *A travers les ronces*, qui avait paru dans *La Revue canadienne*. Cette nouvelle paraît en 1919 sous un nouveau titre, *L'Obscure Souffrance*. La romancière a pratiqué quelques coupures dans ce texte un peu mélodramatique et on sent un certain malaise dans l'évolution du récit. *L'Obscure Souffrance* reprend le thème de la piété filiale déjà abordé dans *Angéline de Montbrun*, mais cette fois dans une pénible histoire d'alcoolisme. La même année, Laure Conan publie *La Vaine Foi*, où l'on fait la rencontre d'une héroïne aux prises avec les problèmes de la foi vécue. Ces deux nouvelles sont écrites sous la forme d'un journal intime et on y retrouve le goût de Laure Conan pour les analyses psychologiques. L'inspiration en est cependant bien froide et la romancière, guindée dans son nouveau rôle de figure publique, ne retrouve plus les accents d'*Angéline de Montbrun*.

Enfin Laure Conan n'hésite pas à se tourner également vers le théâtre. Elle écrit *Aux jours de Maisonneuve*, adaptation dramatique de *L'Oublié*, le plus populaire de ses romans. Une troupe d'amateurs accepte de monter le spectacle en 1920, au Monument National de Montréal. Le succès, plus que médiocre, chagrine beaucoup l'auteur qui s'en plaint à plusieurs de ses amis. Elle cherche la cause de l'échec dans le jeu maladroit des comédiens ou même dans le mauvais goût des costumes. Il lui semble qu'avec de beaux costumes, bien authentiques, sa pièce pourrait avoir un éclatant succès. Cette vieille dame de 75 ans ne pouvait s'imaginer que la faute en était plus justement à sa propre inexpérience de l'écriture dramatique. La tentative vaut cependant d'être rappelée, car elle témoigne de la grande vitalité de Laure Conan.

Heureusement, il n'était pas écrit que sa carrière se terminerait sur un échec. L'opiniâtreté inlassable qui avait toujours caractérisé la romancière, allait lui permettre de donner à son public un véritable chant du cygne. En 1921, la maladie vient interrompre ses activités. Elle se retire à la villa Notre-Dame-des-Bois à Sillery, où les religieuses de Jésus-Marie ont une maison de repos. C'est là qu'elle commence l'œuvre à laquelle elle pense depuis si longtemps, l'œuvre qu'elle veut laisser à son public comme un testament spirituel. A l'âge de 79 ans, Laure Conan a la force de retrouver le ton enthousiaste de *L'Oublié* et de *A l'œuvre et à l'épreuve*. Elle trace d'une main ferme, le tableau de l'occupation de Québec en 1759. Elle raconte avec ferveur, l'amour naissant de Thérèse d'Autrée, la jeune Française, pour le beau lieutenant canadien, Jean de Tilly. Elle pose clairement les données du dilemme qui déchire le cœur de son héros : faut-il retourner en France et mériter ainsi l'amour de Thérèse d'Autrée ou rester au pays pour soutenir le peuple brisé par la tourmente de la défaite ? L'amour ou le devoir ? Voilà bien le problème qui a hanté toute la vie de Laure Conan. En le transposant ici dans un cadre patriotique, elle donnait par ailleurs à ce dilemme toute la dimension spirituelle dont elle était capable ; car la romancière avait finalement cédé le pas à la patriote. Du moins le croyait-elle. Rien de plus assuré que l'esprit de l'écrivain. Et cependant, rien de moins calme que le cœur de la femme. Ecoutons une dernière confidence. Au moment où Laure Conan écrivait ce dernier roman, elle dit à un de ses nombreux correspondants, l'abbé Lionel Groulx : « J'aime mon héros. N'allez pas le dire. » Un tel aveu a de quoi désarmer. Mais il n'était pas écrit que l'amour serait, même une seule fois, victorieux dans les œuvres de notre première romancière. Lorsque Jean de Tilly choisit courageusement son devoir envers la patrie, on devine la romancière, fidèle à son éthique personnelle. Mais on sent aussi que dans ce choix, elle voudrait entraîner avec elle toute la nation canadienne. Ce dernier roman s'intitule *La Sève immortelle* ; Laure Conan l'a terminé alors qu'elle était agonisante.

Le 6 juin 1924, Laure Conan mourait à l'Hôtel-Dieu de Québec. L'année suivante, *La Sève immortelle* était édité par les soins de son ami Sir Thomas Chapais. Laure Conan fut inhumée au cimetière de La Malbaie. Mais aujourd'hui, on connaît davantage le monument que quelques-uns de ses concitoyens ont érigé sur l'emplacement de la maison qu'elle avait habitée si longtemps et qui a malheureusement été détruite. Les admirateurs de Laure Conan peuvent également trouver à la Pointe-au-Pic un petit musée où ont été recueillis un très grand nombre des objets de la romancière. Partout d'ailleurs où elle est passée, à Saint-Hyacinthe, à Sillery, au couvent des Ursulines, on conserve les reliques de la première femme qui illustra les lettres canadiennes.

A parcourir les journaux de juin 1924 à Québec ou à Montréal, on a l'impression que la disparition de Laure Conan a provoqué une sorte de deuil national. Les journalistes lui consacrent des éditoriaux. Les pages féminines retracent la carrière de cette grande dame de notre littérature. On publie de nombreux textes de la romancière. En fait, si la mort de Laure Conan n'a pas été sentie par l'ensemble de la population, il n'en reste pas moins qu'avec elle disparaissait un témoin particulièrement saisissant de son époque et une pionnière dont on ne mesure pas assez la véritable audace. Elle a créé chez nous une tradition romanesque qui, avec Germaine Guèvremont, Gabrielle Roy, a fourni quelques-uns des plus grands romans de la littérature canadienne. De plus, elle a inauguré dans notre société, le journalisme féminin, lui donnant au départ un cadre de respect et de haute tenue. On peut même dire que sans y avoir participé activement, elle n'a pas été étrangère aux différentes victoires féminines du début du siècle, telles que le droit de vote et le droit pour les femmes d'accéder à des carrières dites masculines.

Quant à son œuvre, il est possible aujourd'hui d'en établir les véritables dimensions. Un de ses romans, *L'Oublié*, a reçu une récompense prestigieuse : il a été couronné par l'Académie française en 1903. Un autre roman, *A l'œuvre et à l'épreuve*, a été traduit en anglais dès 1909 sous le titre de *The Master Motive*. Cette consécration de popularité qu'est la traduction n'a pas été méritée par beaucoup de romanciers canadiens, surtout dans les premières années du XXe siècle. Ces deux témoignages attestent concrètement le succès populaire de ces deux ouvrages avant la seconde guerre mondiale.

La Sève immortelle a perdu son public avec la transformation de l'idéologie nationaliste dans la province de Québec. Mais *Angéline de Montbrun*, qui avait été éclipsée par la popularité des romans historiques, est de nouveau dans l'actualité littéraire. En 1950, la collection du « Nénuphar » (Fides) accueillait *Angéline de Montbrun* parmi les ouvrages fameux qui ont illustré la littérature canadienne. Dès lors, les critiques se penchaient de nouveau sur ce roman et y retrouvaient cette fois des thèmes inédits, freudiens ou sociologiques. Tout récemment on donnait un cours sur *Angéline Montbrun* à l'Université de Montréal. La réputation de Laure Conan a même franchi la frontière de la langue puisqu'une étudiante de l'Université de Toronto a écrit sa thèse de doctorat sur la première romancière canadienne.

Succès de critique, pourrait-on dire. Et pourtant, simultanément, on pouvait voir Laure Conan figurer dans la collection « Les Classiques canadiens » ainsi que dans le cahier de l'Académie canadienne-française intitulé *Profils littéraires*. C'est dire que les esprits les plus divers s'entendent pour accorder à Laure Conan une place de choix parmi les pionniers de la littérature canadienne-française.

BIBLIOGRAPHIE

MICHELINE DUMONT, *Laure Conan*, dans "Les Classiques canadiens." Montréal, 1961.
Les Cahiers de l'Académie canadienne-française, vol. 7.

Adelaide Hunter Hoodless

1857-1910

RUTH HOWES

In Macdonald Institute at the University of Guelph, Ontario, hangs a portrait of a beautiful, serene woman, Adelaide Hunter Hoodless, and in the Dominion Archives in Ottawa hangs a copy of this portrait. Across Canada from east to west you will find other copies of this portrait in the Tweedsmuir Histories which have been compiled by more than 1,200 branches of the Federated Women's Institutes of Canada. Across the seas in England, Asia, Australia, New Zealand and Africa, the name and memory of Adelaide Hoodless are revered by more than seven million women.

Adelaide Hoodless worked tirelessly to help homemakers. During her fifty-two years of life she founded or helped to found the Young Women's Christian Association, the National Council of Women, the Victorian Order of Nurses, Macdonald Institute at Guelph, the School of Household Science affiliated with McGill University and the Women's Institute organizations which have spread around the world. She could hardly have dreamed that from the first Women's Institute at Stoney Creek, Ontario, would grow an organization with 3,350 branches and 72,000 members in every province of Canada and the Territories. Women's Institutes in countries on five continents are affiliated with other rural organizations in many lands through the Associated Country Women of the World, the largest organization of country women in existence, linking together 159 women's societies in 108 countries, states and provinces, women of all races, colours and creeds.

Adelaide Hoodless was herself born in a country home. Her grandfather, Joseph Hunter, with his wife, Jane, and fourteen children came to Canada from Monaghan in Ireland and settled in the Derry West section of the Township of Toronto, Peel County, in 1836. David Hunter, the fifth child, was about twenty years old and John, the youngest son, was about eleven at the time. When David married, he and his wife Jane settled near St. George, about forty-five miles from his father's house. Here in 1851 David Hunter bought a simple clapboard house on the Blue Lake Road in the beautiful countryside of Brant County.

It was a house dating perhaps from the 1830s, heated by stoves as the many stovepipe holes still indicate today. At the left of the hall is a large room, evidently the parlour, judging by its ornate baseboard. The door of this room has a lock so that the sacred precincts could be barred from exploring children. Upstairs there are now four rooms with sloping ceilings but when Adelaide Hunter lived there there were only three. The little back room was referred to as "the boys' room" and the one in front of it was "the girls' room". The pantry was lined with shelves and there all the foodstuffs were stored except, of course, the fruits and vegetables, cream and milk which were kept in the big, cool cellar. For some time the house had an east wing which contained the summer kitchen and woodshed but this was taken down some years ago and sizable lilac bushes grow now where it once stood.

In this house, "The Willows," South Dumfries, Brant County, Adelaide Hunter was born on February 27, 1857. She was the youngest in a family of twelve children. Her father died several months before her birth and she grew up in a home where there were privations, where everyone must help in the work of the home and the farm. From her early childhood she gained a knowledge and understanding of the problems of farm women which in later years moved her to help homemakers whenever she could.

"The Willows" was bought by the Federated Women's Institutes of Canada in 1959 and is known as the Adelaide Hunter Hoodless Homestead. The Homestead, when its furnishing is completed, will be a replica of a modest rural home of the period, nearly a hundred years ago, when Mrs. Hoodless lived there as a child. Already several rooms have been completely furnished and the committee is confident that the restoration will be completed by 1967; this is one of the Federated Institutes' Centennial projects. All articles have been gifts of groups and interested individuals, some of the most prized donated by the Hunter and Hoodless families and now coming back to the old home. The grounds have been landscaped in keeping with the character of the house. Two acres of land adjoining the Homestead have been purchased by the South Dumfries Township Council and the FWIC given the privilege of using them as parkland, in addition to the three acres of the site already owned by the organization and used as a picnic area.

It is not hard to imagine the little girl moving through these rooms with her many brothers and sisters, going down to the spring under the willows, playing in the woods, and trudging a mile and a quarter to the German school house. She must have been a very pretty child for the later portrait shows a handsome woman with broad forehead, delicate features, thick wavy hair and beautiful poise.

We know very little about her early years. As the youngest of twelve children in a fatherless home she probably had a public school education. But one schoolmate remarked tartly, "Adelaide went to ladies' college, but I don't know just what it did for her." This may have been during the time, before her marriage, when she lived with her older sister Lizzie, Mrs. Seth Charlton, in Cainsville, Ontario.

Nor do we know much about her sisters and brothers. Alex was the oldest, then Lizzie, Dr. John, and Joseph. Some of the brothers went to university and Adelaide grew up in a home of culture and uncompromising Presbyterian ethics with all the social graces that come of natural charm and a gentle background. There is no doubt that her personal appeal helped her over many difficult places but she never depended on this characteristic. She was straightforward and fearless, stating her case clearly and making her cause plead for itself. Perhaps her experience as one of a large family gave her the emotional hardihood and the perseverance she needed to carry through some of her schemes in spite of criticism and opposition, just as her own youth on a farm no doubt gave her an understanding of the needs of farm women.

Her granddaughter, Miss Muriel Bostwick, of Hamilton tells this story. "When Mrs. Hoodless became engaged she said to her clergyman, 'Here I am, a strong Presbyterian and a Whig, planning to marry a man who is not only an Anglican but a Tory. What shall I do?' He replied, 'My dear, you can be a good Christian in any church, but stick to your politics.' Apparently she did, for the Hoodlesses attended the Anglican Church in Hamilton, but each stuck to his own politics."

The old family Bible records Adelaide's marriage which took place at Zion Church at Brantford, on September 15, 1881. The man she married, John Hoodless, born in Hamilton in 1854, was the son of a successful furniture manufacturer and dealer in that city. When he left school at twenty he had entered his father's business as a partner. The Bible also records the birth of four children: Edna Clarkson, born July 7, 1882; Joseph Bernard, born December 10, 1884; Muriel Adelaide, born July 27, 1886; John Harold, born January 23, 1888, and died at the age of 18 months.

We may imagine Mrs. Hoodless's active and happy domestic life with four small children and a busy and prosperous husband until the loss of her youngest child in 1889. It was the death of John Harold which stirred his mother to the work which she carried on for the rest of her life.

In those days one child in five died and every family had its small graves in the churchyard. But John Harold's mother refused to accept his death with resignation. She set to work to find out why her son had died, why so many other children died. When she learned that her baby's death had been caused by impure milk delivered to her home, she felt responsible for the tragedy and she decided that she must do everything in her power to bring within reach of all women the education necessary to prevent similar tragedies. Her purpose is shown in her own words, "Apart from my family duties the education of mothers has been my life work," and her convictions about the educational needs of women of her time centred around "a special attention to sanitation—a better understanding of the economic and hygienic value of foods and fuels and a more scientific care of children with a view to raising the general standard of the life of farm people."

In those days rooms were swathed in heavy curtains and laden with stuffed upholstery; windows were tightly shut for night air was known to have poisonous properties. Women wore long heavy skirts which gathered dust and hats to keep the sun from their faces. Flies swarmed in the kitchens and ice boxes were few and inefficient. Milk delivered through the streets in open cans was one of the principal causes of the "summer complaint" of which so many children died. Open wells led to epidemics and typhoid fever and few families had not lost at least one member from tuberculosis. From this background Mrs. Hoodless emerged to tackle the complacent ignorance of society.

In the autumn of 1889 a Young Women's Christian Association was organized in Hamilton and Mrs. Hoodless saw an opportunity to begin her work of informing women about nutrition and sanitation. One of the principal activities of the YWCA in its early years was its programme of classes in cooking. Mrs. Hoodless not only busied herself with these but persuaded the Hamilton School Board to send pupils to the YWCA cooking classes. Her work was facilitated by the fact that her husband was a member of the School Board and for ten years its chairman and in 1891 she herself was elected president of the Hamilton YWCA. The classes grew, soon more teachers were needed and the YWCA conducted teacher training classes. But about this time Mrs. Hoodless entered upon the wide sweep of her remarkable life work.

The Columbian Exposition at Chicago in 1893 was the rather dramatic starting point for a great many women's activities. The beautiful white Women's Building contained exhibits of women's work and a Women's Congress brought together representatives of women's groups from all over the world. Women had only recently been admitted to universities, they were restless and eager to launch into a new world of effort and responsibility.

Sixty Canadian women went to Chicago, Mrs. Hoodless heading the YWCA delegation. There the idea of a national organization was born; the women began to realize how much concerted national work would increase the effectiveness of their efforts to improve society. Mrs. Hoodless with characteristic vigour took the matter in hand. "Upon my return," she wrote later, "I wrote to every city and town in Canada. Where there were already established Associations I asked for their views etc.; where I did not know of any existing, I wrote the Mayor of the place, asking for information and if he would kindly place the letter in the hands of some responsible Christian woman who would assist me in my efforts to secure information. In all, I sent ninety letters; some were most courteously answered, others were ignored. The result was, on the 7th of December, 1893, we held our first conference in the YWCA Building, 18 Elm Street, Toronto."

At this first national conference twelve Associations were represented. Mrs. Hoodless was elected first vice-president. In 1895 she became the second president of the national YWCA. She was president for two years and for fourteen years president of the Hamilton YWCA.

The YWCA continued to be an important interest for Mrs. Hoodless but it was only one strand in the thick skein of her activities. Much more had happened as a result of the stimulating Chicago visit than the birth of the national YWCA of Canada, important as that was. It is intriguing to follow this development in the journal of Lady Aberdeen. The new Governor-General and his wife who had just arrived in Canada went at once to Chicago so that Lady Aberdeen could see the exhibits and talk to the other organization women assembled there. For Lady Aberdeen had been extremely active in initiating and encouraging women's movements in Great Britain, and Canada offered her a new field.

The United States National Council of Women, dating from 1888, and the British organization had formed an International Council of Women and at Chicago in 1893 Lady Aberdeen was elected its president. Lady Aberdeen and Mrs. Hoodless must have met at Chicago, and they must have talked about organizing a National Council of Women in Canada. On her way from Chicago to Ottawa, on October 26, Lady Aberdeen stopped in Hamilton "to talk to Mrs. Hoodless." On October 27 a great meeting was held in Toronto at the Horticultural Pavilion, later Allen Gardens. Ladies came—1,500 of them—and Lady Aberdeen spoke on the value of the recently organized Ladies' Union and similar groups in Britain. Then and there the National Council of Women was organized with Lady Aberdeen as president and Mrs. Hoodless as treasurer.

The next morning, October 28, Lady Aberdeen held the first committee meeting of the new Council with Mrs. Hoodless and four other ladies "to go over the constitution and rules." Afterward they had lunch at the YWCA on Elm Street. The National Council of Women was launched and in it Mrs. Hoodless was to find the platform for much of her domestic science work.

At the first annual meeting of the National Council in April 1894, Mrs. Hoodless presented a resolution that the National Council of Women do all in its power to further the introduction of domestic training for girls into the public school systems of Canada. When in 1901 the Standing Committee on Household Science was set up, Mrs. Hoodless became its convener so that she was connected with the development of household science in every Canadian province which took it up.

Mrs. Hoodless had led a delegation to interview the Hon. G. W. Ross, Minister of Education for Ontario, later premier of the province, and at his suggestion she began a series of addresses. Between the years 1894 and 1896 Mrs. Hoodless gave over sixty addresses to school boards and teachers' conventions, so that through her direct approach to the Department of Education in Ontario and New Brunswick, and through the efforts of the Local Councils in Nova Scotia, Manitoba, British Columbia, household science courses were established in each of these provinces.

As a result of her work the Ontario Legislature made domestic science and manual training permissive subjects in the public schools and gave grants to school boards which decided to introduce these subjects. Between 1893 and 1908 Mrs. Hoodless succeeded in having domestic science courses introduced in thirty-two centres, operating under school boards and other government organizations in addition to private schools.

As the new subjects attracted greater interest more teachers were needed and the National Council pressed for expanded teacher training facilities. In 1902 the Ontario School of Domestic Science was affiliated with the Ontario Normal College at Hamilton to train teachers for both public and high schools. Mrs. Hoodless enlisted the help of Lord Strathcona who was the largest contributor to this school. Similar schools were set up in Truro, N.S., Halifax, Montreal and Ottawa.

The demand for domestic science teachers increased rapidly and financing the school at Hamilton fell heavily on a few supporters. Fortunately Mrs. Hoodless was able to enlist the interest of the philanthropist, Sir William Macdonald, who donated funds to erect

a building for an Institute of Household Science at the Ontario College of Agriculture in Guelph. In 1903 the Normal School of Domestic Science was moved to Guelph. Influenced by Mrs. Hoodless, Sir
William Macdonald in 1905 announced his intention to found a
"magnificent college" at Ste. Anne de Bellevue near Montreal, in
affiliation with McGill University, for courses in agriculture and
domestic science. Similar centres were later established in all the
provinces. Fifteen years after the National Council of Women came
into being the public and the educational authorities had come to
accept household science as education rather than a "fool fad." Every
year Mrs. Hoodless gave a series of lectures to the students of
Macdonald Institute on "Ethical Training of the Homemaker" and
she gave addresses also at the Toronto Normal School.

Since Mrs. Hoodless was obviously the leader of the new movement,
she was asked by a publisher to write a textbook on domestic science,
which was published in 1898. At first each Local Council of Women
was asked to send in twenty-five "tried receipts" for the book. The
"little red book," as it was called, was ahead of its time in that it
contained calorie charts and chemical analyses and stressed the importance of meat, fruit, and fresh vegetables in the diet. Miss Muriel
Bostwick has one of these books. She writes, "I have in my possession
a book entitled 'Public School Domestic Science', authorized by the
Education Department of Ontario, published in 1898 by Copp Clark
Co. Ltd. of Toronto, written by Adelaide Hoodless, President of the
School of Domestic Science, Hamilton. This book covers chapters on
Relation of Food to the Body, Nutrition, Food and Economy, Cooking
of Food, etc., Recipes, Menus, Infants' Diets. It is interesting to read
now in view of the great advances in the knowledge of foods, housekeeping, etc."

All this was not accomplished without difficulties. There were the
natural obstacles of prejudice and conservatism when a new course
is suggested. And there were special obstacles inherent in the character of the period. Woman's place was in the home and she was
expected to stay there, venturing outside only to do church work or
perhaps attend the WCTU, the dominant women's organization at
that time. When the National Council of Women was started in
1893, a Toronto newspaper, *The Empire*, commented, "Hitherto it has
not been the correct thing, from a Canadian society standpoint, for

a woman to speak on a platform. But now for the first time a Governor General's wife has given a public address." The paper thought it possible that a change in public sentiment might follow.

But the National Council met with many problems from its own members as well as from critical outsiders. Lady Aberdeen wrote in her journal, "Of course women who have worked only on a church basis at first find it hard to grasp the broader national side; the idea of an organization simply designed to get all workers to know and appreciate one another, and to unite for common purposes, has been difficult to inoculate; however it has been done."

There was, for example, a veritable battle over the type of prayer to be used in opening National Council meetings and when silent prayer was decided upon, to avoid denominational differences, an Ottawa newspaper raised a new storm by the headline "N.C.W. against Lord's Prayer."

It was Mrs. Hoodless who had drawn together the local YWCA's into national unity and it was in her spirit of co-operation that the YWCA in 1914 entered into federation with the National Council of Women.

Mrs. Hoodless maintained that it was all wrong to educate, as was then done, both boys and girls along the same lines. Her lifelong advocacy of domestic science for girls and manual training for boys meant that girls should become homemakers and keep within the domestic framework. Of course Mrs. Hoodless herself was a contradiction of these demands for her life was spent in travelling and speaking, in meetings and committee work. Yet she was a woman of exceptional capacity and vigour and her family did not suffer because of her outside activities. Bernard, her son, paid this tribute to his mother:

Today one can hardly conceive that the attacks made upon her could have occurred. She was derided in the press and from the platform as one of those despised "new women." "Let her stay at home and take care of her family," was one of the pieces of advice most often handed out.

As to staying at home and taking care of her family, well! no mother was ever more devoted nor any home better managed. . . . She was a great mother, and her wonderfully developed mother instinct was large enough to include all classes and creeds. I think I could describe her no better than to say she was a woman with a great maternal instinct.

Her daughter declared:

As a homemaker she was an inspiration. Our old home, Eastcourt, was open house and she was the gracious centre around which everything revolved. Mother had travelled widely and there were always interesting people coming and going. . . . She had a stimulating and lovable personality that drew young and old alike. Yet she seemed to have time for everything. She used to say, "Women must learn not to waste valuable time on non-essentials" and I think much of her success was due to her wise choice of essentials and concentrating on same.

She was wise enough to enjoy some recreation for she played golf and was a member of the Hamilton Golf Club.

Mrs. Hoodless's ideas foreshadowed modern concepts of psychology in attributing to the home a crucial rôle in shaping the lives of children and through them the future of society. She wrote:

Domestic Science is the application of scientific principles to the management of the home. It teaches the value of pure air, proper food, systematic management, economy, care of children, domestic and civil sanitation and the prevention of disease. It calls for higher ideals of home life and more respect for domestic occupations. In short it is a direct education for women as homemakers.

The management of the home has more to do in the moulding of character than any other influence, owing to the large place it fills in the early life of the individual during the most plastic stage of development. We are, therefore, justified in an effort to secure a place for home economics, or domestic science, in the educational institutions of this country.

This conviction lay behind her often-used maxims: "You purify society when you purify the home"; and "A nation cannot rise above the level of its homes, therefore, women must work and study together to raise our homes to the highest possible level." She was fond of quoting Herbert Spencer's theory that "the welfare of the family underlies the welfare of society."

An appreciation published during Mrs. Hoodless's lifetime gives a picture of her and of her family life which helps to provide background for her many activities.

That she is a lady of strong mentality and liberal culture is shown forth between the lines of this review. She uses practical methods in working toward the ideal and has accomplished results the value of which is now widely acknowledged.

Mr. and Mrs. Hoodless have a son and two daughters; Joseph Bernard, B.S.A., Edna and Muriel. Their home is a magnificent, palatial residence, Eastcourt, standing in the midst of four acres and considered one of the handsomest in the city of Hamilton. Its architectural beauty is supplemented by many beautiful works of art and the adornments which wealth can secure and refined taste suggest.

Eastcourt provided comfort and security which must have had a contribution to make in themselves to her active life. It still stands but crowded now between newer houses, cut up into apartments, and made unrecognizable by an added front.

Lady Aberdeen in her tour of western Canada had seen many isolated frontier communities where women and their children had no nursing assistance and often no medical care. A district nursing scheme had been set up in England in 1887 and named in honour of Queen Victoria's jubilee. Thinking of this, she advocated a nursing scheme for Canada to be called, since it was 1897, the Victorian Order of Nurses. Mrs. Hoodless worked hard to promote this plan which, however, met with severe opposition. The Ontario Medical Association, which had not been consulted, passed a resolution of "most unqualified disapproval of the scheme on account of the dangers which must follow to the public." The plan was nevertheless pushed vigorously forward and several years later the doctors publicly admitted their conversion. Succeeding years have proved the worth of this organization. VON branches are found in larger cities and some of the smaller ones.

Mrs. Hoodless had been extremely active in several fields but in 1897 she entered a new one. She had attacked a professor of bacteriology who had given an address at an Experimental Union meeting at Guelph, asking him why nothing had been done for women and children while great efforts were being made to disseminate information about the care and breeding of livestock. She came closer to participation when she spoke at the Agricultural College at Guelph about the introduction of manual training and domestic science into the public schools, urging, "Girls should be educated to fit them for the sphere of life for which they were destined—that of homemaker— and this should be done by teaching Domestic Science in the Public schools." This statement attracted the attention of Mr. Erland Lee, a young farmer and secretary of the Farmers' Institute of Saltfleet township. He invited Mrs. Hoodless to speak at a Farmers' Institute meeting. The ladies invited to this meeting were greatly impressed with the idea she put forward that the women, like the men, should have an institute. Seeing their interest the chairman asked how many women would come to a special meeting the next Friday evening to form an institute, and thirty-five promised to come.

On that Friday, February 19, 1897 in Squire's Hall, Stoney Creek, Mrs. Hoodless found 101 women and 1 man, Mr. Lee, the chairman. She had brought with her Mrs. Rorer, an authority on domestic science. Bernard Hoodless wrote later, "It was my privilege as a boy to hitch up her favourite horse, Scotty, and drive her down to Stoney Creek on that stormy night of February 19, 1897. I can still remember that meeting in the old hall, up a rickety flight of outside stairs, and my sliding into a seat at the back and wondering what it was all about."

Mrs. Hoodless's speech that night was practical as well as inspirational. She pointed out that if men needed an organization which would enable them to grow better crops of hay, grain and fruit, and produce better livestock, then an Institute for the women would be equally helpful in their work. Indeed, she declared, it was much more necessary since women's work—homecraft and motherhood—was much more important than that of men, as it concerned the home and care of the loved ones who dwelt there.

The first regular meeting of the new Institute was held on February 25 when Mr. Lee presented the constitution he had drafted. It stated, "the object of this Institute shall be to promote that knowledge of household science which shall lead to the improvement in household architecture with special attention to home sanitation, to a better understanding of economics and hygienic value of foods and fuels, and to a more scientific care of children with a view to raising the general standard of health of our people."

At the next meeting two papers were read, entitled "Proper Food for Children" and "Art," and at the third meeting, "The Child in Health and Disease." At the end of its first year Stoney Creek Institute had 75 members.

The second Women's Institute was formed only four months after the first, at Whitby, and the third at Kemble in Gray County. Meetings opened with the Lord's Prayer and roll call and closed with the National Anthem, and each member paid twenty-five cents for expenses.

In December, 1902, twenty-four Institutes held a meeting at Guelph and the next year the first Women's Institute convention was held in the unfinished Macdonald College with Miss Martha Van Rensselaer from Cornell as the speaker. That year the Institutes had 4,500 members.

The interest of the Ontario Department of Agriculture was enlisted by Mrs. Hoodless to such effect that the Department gave the same money grants to Women's Institutes as to Farmers' Institutes and began in 1903 to send out lecturers, of whom Miss Laura Rose was the first. That summer 189 meetings were held in four weeks, each with a speaker sent by the government. In 1904 there were 149 Institutes with 5,433 members; in 1907 there were 500 Institutes. At Mrs. Hoodless's suggestion the motto "For Home and Country" was adopted in Ontario and is used today by thousands of Institutes in many countries.

One writer has described the special initiative and contribution of this movement: "It must have taken the courage of a pioneer to launch an educational movement for women who were right in the thick of their heaviest family responsibilities, most of them farm women with all that implies in the way of limited leisure time. And certainly it took a pioneer's vision to lay plans so sound that objectives are still adaptable to changing conditions, the program attracting women after more than half a century."

An institution which grows so phenomenally is obviously filling a need. The Women's Institutes with their purpose, "the broadening and enriching of rural life," have been called a rural university. They began with child care and home management. Government teachers gave condensed courses in cooking, dressmaking, and home nursing and government bulletins on such subjects were distributed. The work soon spread into many channels. Much energy was devoted to improving rural schools, providing playground equipment, introducing hot lunches, dental clinics, and medical inspection. Institutes helped to set up local libraries, cottage hospitals, rest rooms for country women in towns, to introduce music teaching, handicrafts such as rug and glove making, recreation facilities such as playgrounds and swimming pools. They encouraged amateur dramatics, choral singing, labour saving devices and improvements in homes, did war work, helped the Red Cross and the Navy League.

Meanwhile the Institutes had been spreading far beyond Canada's borders. A British Columbia Institute member, Mrs. Alfred Watt, had gone to live in England after the death of her husband. Efforts to form organizations for farmers' wives had been unsuccessful there until Mrs. Watt formed the first Institute in the Welsh village with the long name, called Llanfair for short, in 1915. The rapid spread which had occurred in Canada was now repeated. Two years later there were 40 Institutes in England and Wales. Miss Emily Guest from Ontario had at about the same time introduced Institutes to Scotland. In Belgium and France the Fédération des Cercles de Fermières served much the same purpose as the Institutes.

It was the Women's Institute of Canada which first thought of an international organization and approached the National Federation of Women's Institutes of England and Wales and the Women's Rural Institutes of Scotland. The idea was carried to the Scandinavian countries, Holland, France, Germany, New Zealand, Australia, India, Ceylon and other countries in Africa and Asia. In 1933 the international organization was formed in Stockholm—the Associated Country Women of the World. Now the ACWW comprises Institutes and similar organizations of country women in 108 countries.

Many have been the pilgrimages to Stoney Creek to honour the founder of the Institute movement. When the Associated Country Women of the World met in Triennial Conference in Canada in 1953, a thousand women went on such a pilgrimage to honour Mrs. Hoodless, and each one realized in a concrete way what this "Woman of Vision" had meant to all women, how great was the power of the idea of benefiting homemakers which had brought into being this world-wide organization of Country Women. At each Triennial Conference of the ACWW—whether it is held in Canada, Denmark, Ceylon, Melbourne or Dublin—this tribute is repeated. This educational movement for women was in reality the beginning of a great adult education movement and gave Canada a "blueprint for Extension Education."

It would be impossible to recount all the activities into which Mrs. Hoodless was drawn as her enthusiasm and responsibilities for domestic training increased. In her capacity as a lecturer she was one of the first women, if not the first, to be employed by the Ontario government. She was on an annual salary as a lecturer and instructor toward the end of her life. She represented technical education for Canada at the International Congress of Women held in London in 1899 where she was presented to Queen Victoria. And she was Canadian representative at the biennial meeting of the General Federation of Women's Clubs held in St. Louis, Missouri, delivering there an address on "Ethics in the Home."

In 1908 Mrs. Hoodless was commissioned by the Minister of Education of Ontario to visit and report on the trade schools recently established in the United States and the next year she was appointed to the Advisory Committee of the Carnegie Institute, Pittsburgh, on Technical Education, and at the time of her death was investigating the whole question of technical education and trade schools for girls. One of her last addresses, given at Milwaukee on this subject, caused widespread interest and comment in educational centres in the United States as well as Canada.

Influenced by Mrs. Hoodless, Mrs. Massey-Treble had in 1901 set up a School of Domestic Science at the Victoria Institute in Toronto. Mrs. Hoodless wished to establish a course in household science at some university to give teachers more advanced training. The government was not willing to commit itself to added expenditure, so Mrs. Hoodless set out on her own to secure the needed capital. She was scheduled to speak at a large meeting of club women in Massey Hall.

A friend wrote of that fateful evening: "On the eve of her 52nd birthday, she was scheduled to speak at a meeting of the Federation of Women's Clubs in Massey Hall, Toronto. 'My head is splitting,' she complained to her daughter, Muriel, at dinner, 'I can't drive the car tonight.' 'Bernard will take you,' her daughter reassured her. Despite her bad headache, she gave an inspired speech, which resulted in the subsequent founding of the Lillian Massey School of Household Science in Toronto. Half-way through her talk, while her audience was enthusiastically applauding, Adelaide Hoodless, smiling, sipped some water. Suddenly the crash of a glass was heard, and she fell to the floor, lifeless. She had given her life for her countrywomen."

Honours showered upon the memory of Mrs. Hoodless. A portrait was unveiled in Macdonald Institute the year after her death, a cairn set up in 1937 near her birthplace was unveiled by Lady Tweedsmuir and two years later members of the Scottish Rural Institutes dedicated a flagpole and flag in the park which surrounds the cairn. Bronze plaques were inscribed to her memory and in 1959 the Canadian Post Office issued a special stamp to honour the movement she had initiated, the Associated Country Women of the World.

Perhaps the memorial which would have pleased her most was the plaque placed at the Homestead on June 13, 1959, by the Ontario Archaeological and Historic Sites Board. The inscription reads:

ADELAIDE HUNTER HOODLESS 1857–1910

Adelaide Hoodless was born in this farm house and lived here until she married John Hoodless 1881. On February 19, 1897, she organized at Stoney Creek, the world's first Women's Institute. It was her belief that in this organization rural women could discuss their problems and work together to improve their standard of homemaking and citizenship. The movement spread rapidly throughout Ontario and later to other Provinces. Mrs. Hoodless, a natural leader and forceful speaker, introduced the teaching of domestic science into Ontario Schools and obtained funds for the building of Macdonald Institute at Guelph.

The National Historic Sites and Monuments Board erected a plaque June 2, 1962, proclaiming Adelaide Hunter Hoodless an eminent Canadian. This plaque is at the right of the front door of the Homestead and was unveiled by Mrs. Keith Rand, President of the Federated Women's Institutes of Canada.

1857–1910

Adelaide Hunter Hoodless

Founder of the Women's Institutes
Movement in Canada 1897, Pioneer
Advocate of the Teaching of
Domestic Science in Canadian Schools.

She was active in the Establishment of
the Macdonald Institute at Guelph,
Macdonald College at Ste. Anne de Bellevue,
and the National Council of Women.

To the Homestead will come women from Canada, the United States, and many parts of the world, from all walks and all races and creeds: the Young Women's Christian Association, the National Council of Women; the Home Economics Associations; the Victorian Order of Nurses; the Associated Country Women of the World: all interested in a Canadian woman of vision, Adelaide Hunter Hoodless.

BIBLIOGRAPHY

A variety of source material has been found useful by the author. Miss Muriel Bostock, the grand-daughter of Mrs. Hoodless, provided copies of letters and articles. Friends of the Hoodless family in Ontario have shared personal letters. There is material in the archives of Macdonald Institute at Guelph. References to Mrs. Hoodless occur in *Unfold the Years*, the history of the Young Women's Christian Association in Canada; *Proud Heritage*, the history of the National Council of Women in Canada; *Fifty Years of Achievements*, issued by the Federated Women's Institutes of Ontario; *Story of Women's Institutes*, by Robertson Scott, which records the W.I. movement in the British Isles. Newspaper clippings from the Brantford *Expositor*, the Paris *Star*, the Guelph *Mercury*, and the *Home and Country* (F.W.I.O.) have been useful. Stella Blair has made Mrs. Hoodless the subject of a play. Ethel Chapman has an article on Mrs. Hoodless in *Pioneers of Education* edited by Harriet Rouillard. Edith Rowles refers to her work in *Some Early Developments in Home Economics in the Colleges and Universities of Canada*. Marcus VanSteen contributed an article to the *Globe and Mail* (Feb. 27, 1960) entitled "A Voice That Cried in the Wilderness."

7

E. Cora Hind

1861-1942

KENNETHE HAIG

"Miss E. Cora Hind was rather terrifying. She was more positive about everything than most people are about anything." So wrote W. A. McLeod of the *Western Producer*. He records that he was astounded to learn that it took Miss Hind twenty years to get on the *Winnipeg Free Press* staff although she had made up her mind to do just that when she arrived in Winnipeg in 1882 fresh from the high school halls of Flesherton and Orillia, Ontario.

On a May morning of 1935 in the big City Room of that paper the staff had gathered. J. W. Dafoe, the Editor in Chief, speaking into the unaccustomed silence, for even the presses had stopped, asked Miss Hind's acceptance of the scarlet gown which after tomorrow's convocation she would be entitled to wear as a Doctor of Laws of the University of Manitoba.

The public service which you have rendered and which is thus recognized and rewarded, has been chiefly in connection with the development of Western Canada's great primary industry—agriculture. I shall not dwell on the extent, variety and value of these services but I shall venture to say that I do not think any other individual—and I am making no exception in the case of persons of high official position, has made a contribution comparable to yours.

Mr. Dafoe continued, remembering the years that only Miss Hind and he had experienced:

Apart from myself there is no one in the company gathered today who has been with the Free Press longer than you have been. When, after an absence of some years I came back to the Free Press in 1901 I found that, as part of your activities in a business which you were then conducting, you were supplying the Free Press regularly with reports dealing with agricultural and marketing matters. The wisdom of having you an all time member of the staff was so evident that an arrangement to this end was soon made. . . . As a specialist and authority in your particular field you have built a reputation which is world wide; and you could go nowhere where agricultural pursuits are intelligently followed, that you would not find yours a known and familiar name.

Miss Hind was speaking, her clear voice carrying her words easily:

I admit that I am among the most fortunate of women. I never had work which I did not like, and the years spent on the Free Press have been the happiest of my life. I am very much touched by knowing that the University Women's Club has put forward the suggestion that I should have this honour conferred upon me. . . . I treasure even more the fact that the Free Press has done me this great honour. You are my family, and I am very, very grateful.

A painting of her hangs among the agricultural great in the Royal Winter Fair Building in Toronto, her sapphire blue eyes still scanning the scene, her brown hair piled high, intelligence in every line of her face. It is by Kuch, the gift of the Canadian Women's Press Club, of which organization Miss Hind was a charter member.

It was more than fifty years before that 1935 day when two women had arrived in Winnipeg on the train from St. Paul, Cora and her aunt, Alice Hind. Ella Cora was born in Toronto in 1861, the only daughter and youngest child of Edwin and Jane Carrol Hind. When she was two years old her mother died and Aunt Alice Hind gathered up the three children and took them to their grandfather Hind's farm at Artimisia, Gray County, Ontario. Cora's father was a stone mason and some of his carving still adorns Osgoode Hall in Toronto and St. James Cathedral in Montreal. On a business trip to Chicago in 1866 he was stricken with cholera and died within a few hours. Grandfather's became the children's home and Aunt Alice, as Cora asserted,

"more than a mother to me." When the family moved to Flesherton
Cora continued at school there. Then came Uncle George Hind's
invitation to Orillia for the high school term. On her return to
Flesherton she found two cousins, the Jacques boys, visiting from
the fabulous west—at least the visitors would admit of no lesser
descriptive term. Presently Aunt Alice announced that she was going
west. "I'm going too," said Cora. So there they were on an August
day in 1882 all ready to disembark as the engine puffed importantly
into the station.

The train itself was not quite used to its exalted state and certainly
the inhabitants of Winnipeg were not. There were only 7,000 of
them and Winnipeg had not long been incorporated—long enough,
however, to have experienced a great boom when the song of the city
was the auctioneer early and late calling his building lot wares. Cora
used to observe that she had arrived the morning after. She was
sometimes a little plaintive about that for she had missed the beginning of the C.P.R. and she had missed the day when the boats steamed
down the Assiniboine and the Red. However, that first night the
travellers' rest was broken by the sound of a dynamite explosion. It
was the blowing up of Upper Fort Garry, only the gate left standing.
More room was already needed for the city to expand. Afterwards
Cora and Aunt Alice read Robert Hill's *History of Manitoba* and
knew afresh that the land to which they had come had a story, that,
not so long ago, it had been the centre of the great fur trade, and that
now, in the settlements stretching out from it, as the upright columns
of elevators began to rise, it was shaking its locks ready to become
the distributing centre of the whole northwest. Had Cora any pre-
monition that bright morning as she picked her first way along the
mud-encrusted plank sidewalk, and as her gaze swept away to the
horizon from which came a soft wind, that she was destined to become
a chronicler of this growth, to play an outstanding part in it, to carry
its name with hers to far countries, to become the most eminent
agricultural editor that this continent has produced?

She found the Free Press building that first morning and not long
after she set out to interview Editor Luxton. She explained to the
astonished gentleman that she would like a job on the paper. Perhaps
it was then as she watched his face and recognized prejudice that
her resolve stiffened; she said later, she had never started for any

place that she did not succeed in reaching. The detour at this date took the line of a visit to a lawyer's office and then to an establishment where typewriters were for sale, although in Winnipeg no one yet could use one. However she rented one for a month and started in with her two-finger practice. Aunt Alice helped, which was sporting of her, as she had wished Cora to be a teacher ("the profession had prestige"), which perhaps Aunt Alice thought her dress-making living-room-turned-work-room lacked. The thirty pecking days being accomplished back Cora went to the agent. Yes, the firm of Macdonald, Tupper, Tupper and Dexter had bought one "and had no one in the office who could operate it." Off she went slithering in the mud but determined. So E. Cora Hind became the first typist west of the Lakes.

At that office, which almost at once Cora made her own, there was plenty of business going forward in the settlement of deeds of halfbreed script sold by the owner during the big boom. Immigrants had begun their timid entry, the Railway was still building, now and again a farmer came in and as he waited talked to "the Lady" who seemed extraordinarily interested in his efforts to build up a farm in spite of the menace of the encroaching prairies. Now and then Cora would explain that she had been brought up on her grandfather's farm, and that she couldn't remember the time when he hadn't told her of his efforts. "She knew the points of a horse before she could read," Aunt Alice once explained. The two talked over things in the evenings in the rooms over the big store which Aunt Alice had metamorphosized into a home. Cora told all about the office, the partners, the students—whom Cora thought to herself might show more application—and the clients. Especially the clients and their agricultural problems. She knew the names of the twelve farmers who had furnished the grain in 1876 to the harassed runner of the Steele Briggs Company who had arrived by way of St. Paul and a lumber wagon with his story that Eastern Canadians had had a bad season and he must get good seed. He got it—857 bushels. It was seven years later, 1883, that she and Aunt Alice in their careful scanning of the newspaper read jubilantly that the C.P.R. had begun to build a terminal elevator at Fort William to hold more than one million bushels! They also found letters almost at once from *pro bono publico* asking what the C.P.R. meant! Where would they get the grain to fill it? Aunt Alice and Cora might well have had together a laugh of triumphant

prophecy although perhaps they did not, on these quiet evenings in a
frontier town, envision the ocean of grain moving out in season day
and and night carrying millions of bushels to the markets of the
world from Winnipeg, where more cars of grain were inspected than
in any other single point in North America. Cora's topic at supper at
another time would be the inspection system which had set up six
grades of wheat headed by Manitoba No. 1 Hard. Years later when
she travelled the wheat kingdoms she found that this inspection
system had become an international triumph, an inspiration for its
own development, and still Manitoba No. 1 Hard wore the crown.

Now and again she varied the agricultural topics by acquainting her
attentive aunt with bits of office drama. "Today I typed a brief which
was presented in court, the first of its kind used in Winnipeg." Long
after she told this incident to the Business and Professional Women's
Club of the City, of which she was an honorary member. Rows of
the members inspected their fingers which had tapped out a multitude
of such briefs.

Even in a pioneer town struggling with horse-drawn street cars and
ever-present mud, there were concerts and amateur plays in the old
theatre where the manager cautioned against too vociferous applause
lest the floor should give way. Of the usual life of young people Cora
seems to have seen little. Perhaps she was too weary after her strenuous
day in the office, and afterwards in her own public bureau; perhaps
it was the harassing anxiety never quite absent from her mind in
those days when she might hear the howl not of the coyote but of
the wolf at the door. "Sometimes we were down to bread and tea,"
she once related. Not for long though, this walking in the shadows;
for her the early days retained their excitement, their promise, their
never failing sunrises.

Sometimes to the flat came Dr. Amelia Yeomans, the first woman
doctor in town. She wished to talk over the desperate times she was
encountering with the miseries which intemperance brought with it.
Aunt Alice and Cora joined the W.C.T.U. The organization did not
sit about mourning the wide-open bars, or go by on the other side
when they heard of conditions in the local gaol. They brought these
conditions to the attention of Winnipeg's comfortable pew-fillers.
Cora wrote many of the speeches for the W.C.T.U. ladies as her
firm presently found out, although no criticism was made. Indeed the

gentleman who was to be Sir Hugh John Macdonald, beloved magistrate of Winnipeg, lent her what help he could. Cora also found time to assist the Margaret Scott Mission, aid which she continued through the years. And there were gayer moments. One of her friends, Mrs. R. J. Buchanan, went on a visit to Chicago and came back with a suit skirt fully eight inches from the floor! She walked down the street in it too and soon quite a crowd followed her. Mrs. Buchanan stuck to her guns and at last, despite expostulations as to what the world was coming to, other women followed her example, including Cora. Her heavy trailing skirts were things of the unwept past.

It was during these times that Red River fever (typhoid) stalked the streets. Small wonder since the water was hauled from the open river and delivered from door to door in a huge puncheon. Available hospital space was soon crowded to the doors. Many of the patients brought in from the prairies, carried in from the streets, had recently come to the West and were without friends. The town did what it could—everything but boil the water. One evening Cora, faltering, dropped into a chair at the flat, her eyes very bright, her cheeks scarlet, and Aunt Alice had to find the overworked doctor, Wilfred Good. Cora was babbling in delirium, back in her childhood in the east and Aunt Alice waited on her day and night. There was a long convalescence and for the next year or two, recounted Cora, "Aunt Alice met me on my return from the office with a glass of milk. Yes, we got our milk in those days by the frozen pound."

In 1893 Cora set up her own office and Winnipeg got its first public stenographer, indeed the first one west of the Great Lakes. "Miss E. Cora Hind" was sought after at her little office by all sorts and conditions of men, immensely relieved to be "shut" of the job of writing out their own reports by hand: wheat farmers and cattle men, prospectors, distinguished visitors paying a hazardous visit to the frontier, circus managers, missionaries. "From every one of them I learned something," reported Cora. That was only fair, for they were learning much more from her than was nominated in the bond. An elegantly turned out gentleman, a British diplomat, paused to inquire "what she thought of western Canadian prospects." He soon had his notebook out jotting down stories of new farms stretching out, of grain, livestock, of communities growing up. "There is Brandon not so far from here with its wheat fields golden around it; many communities along the railway which cannot get cars fast enough to take out the grain in the fall and there it waits piled in sacks by the right of way." The gentleman paid double Cora's fee.

Then came the day when a tall, athletic-looking gentleman with a clerical collar came to her office. Cora knew him: the Reverend James Robertson, D.D., home missions superintendent of the Presbyterian Church in Canada. Once Cora observed that there were three things the general public did not realize their indebtedness to: the daily newspaper and milk and bread. On reflection she could have added the nation's debt to the labours of the church. She was never to forget Dr. Robertson or the stories he told her of the building of the West, she following him every buckboard and lumber wagon mile. She kept in her memory stories of shacks made ready for "the Minister"; of small churches triumphantly building; of schools with classes on week days and services on Sunday. She herself had seen now and again a wagon packed high with provisions, with a man and woman and perhaps a child, driving "the team" out along Portage Avenue, out, out until they were lost in the distance.

It was in 1898 that Cora got her first chance at crop inspecting, a profession which was to make her name famous. Prospects were bright that spring, and summer softly wooed the fields. But autumn and the rains came. Day after day, night after night, rain, clouds and more rain. The crop could not ripen. Already Eastern Canada and the United States were asking, "What of the Western crop?" The clouds shifted into the lives of men. Wholesale firms in the East were becoming reluctant to ship any more goods. It was then that Colonel Maclean of the Maclean Publications in Toronto stepped into the picture. He had visited Winnipeg. He had been in Miss Hind's office. Cora's heart pounded when she read his telegram, "Would she make a survey?" She took the train west that night.

In those days before the Canadian Wheat Board took over marketing, wheat prices fluctuated widely according to the size and quality of the crop. Millers and financiers among others were intensely anxious to know whether the crop was of good quality and how large it would be, and therefore crop prediction was of vital concern not only to the West but to all Canada and the United States.

Aunt Alice, that high-couraged soul, had packed Cora's bag saying confidently that of course she would look after the office. She often assumed this role when in the years ahead Cora went off to conventions and other gatherings.

That first trip went as far west as Moose Jaw and then swung south back to Winnipeg. It set a pattern that Cora followed through the years, fanning out with the widening crop areas. It meant close scrutiny out the train windows and long chats with the trainmen, conductors, and brakeys, men knowledgeable about conditions. "Who is the best newspaper man?" a traveller once asked a brakey. Back shot the answer "Miss E. Cora Hind." The railroad men remained her friends and admirers through the years: east, west, north, and south. No doubt their good wishes added to the fragrance of the opulent bunch of roses which the vice-president of the C.P.R., Grant Hall, sent her each Christmas morning. There were also on this first trip stops at stations, with first a visit to the livery barn to secure a good team and driver. Cora in her heavy tweed suit and buttoned boots made careful surveys through the fields securing here and there a head of wheat and threshing it out in her small hands.

Her telegram finally reached Colonel Maclean: 35,000 acres frozen but she had seen much good grain and had noted good yields. Dr. Hind had made her first crop report. Gloom lightened somewhat along Winnipeg streets. The merchants took heart and goods shipments began once more to reach stores.

This was but one aspect of her public connection with the world of agriculture. Some years before, 1887 to be exact, Cora had heard some remarks in the office concerning the opening of the Winnipeg Grain Exchange. It had only a small room in the basement of the City Hall and only ten members. Ten forward-looking citizens but how they would have laughed in those early days if anyone had suggested that a young woman in an office not far away would in 1937 be welcomed and acclaimed by them, and hold from their unanimous hands a special membership to that institution. Through the years it would grow to twelve storeys and conduct on its busy floor—Cora darting hither and yon as the bidding went on—the biggest cash grain market in the world.

To her bureau in 1893 had come a committee of men asking, Would Miss Hind cover their convention for them? It was a dairy convention and Cora sat in, never for a moment bored, and wrote a report for the *Free Press*. Other agricultural conventions sought her aid and the report of their doings duly reached the *Free Press*. Never in her forty years did any agricultural meeting become humdrum to her. Dr. Hind had a genius, narrow if you will, but a genius nevertheless for agriculture; indeed a dedicatio᾿ that was akin to a spiritual force. For her, truly, agriculture was a partnership with God.

In the late nineties she became acquainted with Dr. J. W. Robertson, Dominion Dairy Commissioner. He found an intelligent listener for his recital of his efforts to encourage the dairy industry in Manitoba and the territories, soon to become Saskatchewan and Alberta. She heard his opinion that never could the West equal the standard of quality of butter set by the dairies of Quebec. When Manitoba began to gather in the blue ribbons in the international show at Toronto in 1918, she would have difficulty in suppressing her satisfaction, that is if she did suppress it, for she had made it a life work to attempt to get over to the benighted ranks east of the Great Lakes the worth and glory of the West. It often did not add to her popularity but Cora never paused to consider that. As the years wheeled, she noted the growth of dairy herds and the millions of pounds of butter exported. She sent out weekly market reports to creameries and cheese factories. Dr. J. A. Ruddick, now head of the Dairy Department of the Dominion Department of Agriculture, was often in her office telling her of the growth in the prairie provinces.

Sometimes she remembered back to that time in 1884 when the word had flashed through Winnipeg that Louis Riel was back among the lodges of the Métis, his kinsmen. Excitement burned down the streets and Winnipeg, at the centre of the long trails that radiated from it, was shaken when the word of Duck Lake and the ambush of Colonel Crozier and his police and volunteers reached it along the humming wire. Finally came the news that the rebellion was over and Cora, with the rest of the city and indeed the rest of Canada, breathed freely again. Still Aunt Alice and Cora were concerned. Beef for the troops had had to be imported! On their Sunday walks out beyond the planks they had become acquainted with the surging acres of grass and flowers. This was pasture—they knew good pasture—and importing beef! Cora asked her farmer friends who came to the office for an explanation. Livestock breeding had commenced; they could name four farmers in the business in quite a big way, but they were a little uneasy under Cora's scandalized eyes. Importing beef! Ten years later in 1895 Aunt Alice was cheered by the report brought by Cora that 22,000 head of beef cattle had been exported.

Brandon Experimental Farm had been opened in 1888, and its superintendent, Dr. S. A. Bedford, had got to know of this new help offered by Cora's bureau. He came in when he could to chat over prospects and found an eager listener ready to hear of his grain plots and his planting of small fruits. Here was a man after her own heart, a man who put his hand to the nail and his right hand to the workman's hammer—to the hoe anyway. Through the years Miss Hind got to know well the men at Ottawa and in the western capitals who were in charge of the agricultural experiments, knew them and held them in high esteem. Thus when she was in Brandon one day in 1892 it was not surprising that Dr. Bedford sent over a conveyance for her. He was almost shaking with excitement. Cora knew Red Fife as the favourite seed for wheat but also knew the anxious eyes which scanned the late August skies for signs of frost. She had heard of Dr. Saunders of Ottawa who with his sons, C. E. and A. P. Saunders, was engrossed in experiments to produce a wheat which would mature a few days earlier. In fact Cora had read every word she could about him. Dr. Saunders was in Brandon at this time with Dr. Bedford. He was trying experiments in the cross breeding of wheat. Miss Hind watched the careful work of the doctor's delicate fingers. It was a long, long task. In 1907 she got the word that the new wheat had arrived. It was seeded in careful plots. Marquis wheat had reached the prairies. Scientific agriculture now took its place in Miss Hind's table talk. She may have been somewhat overcome when she was made an honorary member of the Canadian Association of Technical Agriculturalists but her embarrassment was shared by none of her confrères. They had long regarded her as one of themselves.

For twenty years she had hoped for a place on the *Free Press* but she had not been quietly waiting. She knew farmers and business men all through the West, she had reported dozens of conventions, served as secretary-treasurer of the Manitoba Dairy Association for five years, circulated market reports, inspected farm machinery, made herself intimately acquainted with dairying, livestock, grain growing. She was ready when J. W. Dafoe, the new editor of the *Winnipeg Free Press*, invited her in 1901 to join the staff. He reminisced in later years: "her field rapidly widened until she became the paper's expert authority on agricultural and marketing questions, and the advisor in these fields in shaping editorial policies. The years of her service cover the whole period of transformation of the West from a primitive economy to a state of high achievement." As for Cora's reaction—she had come home.

One pleasant Sabbath morning at the turn of the century Cora and Aunt Alice made their decorous way to the church of their choice, the Congregational. At the dismissal the Reverend Hugh Pedley, who with his wife was a cheery and frequent visitor to the Hind home, stayed them. He would have them meet a new family, immigrants from England—Mrs. Mantle, her three sons, and Mary. A handshake with the word of greeting, and a life-long friendship had begun which both sides were to cherish among their recollections. Son Frank was installed as Miss Hind's assistant till he left the office to become Deputy Minister of Agriculture of Saskatchewan. "Much I learned from her of fact, of method, of enthusiasm for agriculture," he testified. Killed on the Somme in 1916, his picture hung throughout the unfaded years on her living-room wall. Others were there too, those still living and others now gone: among them beautiful Madge McKinley and the McClungs, Wes and Nellie. There too were Ethel Lindsay (Osborne), her confrère from early newspaper associations, and Miriam Green Ellis, a colleague in the agricultural newspaper field whose successes Cora regarded as practically her own; E. H. Macklin, Harry Sifton, Dr. David Stewart and others, more and more. E. Cora loved Christmas; from many parts of the world came the messages—cards from high places, cards post-marked from some wind-swept prairie hamlet. Socks, yes, she was often knitting socks when the war was on. Socks, parcels, letters must go forward; a pair specially knit for Sammy, "I work on the Free Press, I'm Miss Hind's office boy. She's the smart one": Sammy turned eighteen, Sammy in speckless uniform, Sammy "killed in action."

Dr. Hind perhaps suffered fools with less hilarity than anyone on record, and sometimes her retorts carried a cutting edge even to rudeness. But there was no cutting edge for those who worked in her office, or for those who served in the offices of her friends and at exhibitions and the like, least of all for those who took over the cleaning and polishing chores of her flat. For all these a steady and intelligent interest, for all these a helpful hand when she had the opportunity. "Sometimes in the old days," recounted Ethel Lindsay Osborne, "when the afternoon paper had been put to bed and before the night shift came on we would gather in Cora's office where tea was brewed and the cookie jar stood. There was a woman staff member whom Cora would not have in to these gatherings. True she did often 'put an enemy in her mouth to steal away her brains' but when she fell ill it was Cora quietly put her in the hospital, paid her bill, and started her out again." "Cora's friendship had a fighting quality," observed another friend of long standing, Miss Ethel Johns. "She would defend her friends against all comers. She would also tell you where she thought you were wrong, then it was up to you to put on all your armour." She nursed Aunt Alice with tender patience through the long illness that ended in her death in 1908. Remembering her own typing days, Cora was the first visitor to an anxious young woman who had set up a secretarial bureau. As she observed, "I left as big an order as I could afford. Well I remembered, indeed I was never to forget, the pressing anxiety of being down to five cents."

It was a July morning three years after she had come to the paper, that Miss Hind, eyes snapping, walked from her office to that of Mr. Dafoe and held out a newspaper to that gentleman, who early in his editorship had got over any tendency to be surprised. The sheet announced: "Black rust, wheat ruined, outside estimate 35,000,000 bushels." "It means," elucidated Miss Hind, in answer to his question, "that for speculative purposes Chicago has decided the Canadian crop is ruined."

That night Miss Hind was on the train again, headed west. Her methods of working had been perfected over the years. Now farmers and business men from all parts of the West sent her regular reports on crop conditions in their own areas. She still hired a horse and buggy and drove along prairie roads, climbing a fence now and then to poke the soil to see how moist it was, to rub wheat kernels in her hands, and to look for signs of rust. She talked to everyone she met, asked questions, made notes. She still wore a heavy skirt which in a few years, however, was mercifully exchanged for riding breeches and fine boots laced high over slim ankles and legs. Later she added for high occasions, especially visits to Toronto, a beaded buckskin coat, the gift of the Calgary Stampede board. There was also a gold

mounted cane, a gift of the Winnipeg Stocker and Feeder Show
Board. Toronto perhaps wasn't so much impressed as astounded.

Her crop estimate for 1904 was 55,000,000 bushels. This she stated
when she visited the Duluth Grain Exchange and was introduced
by the president of the Exchange, Julius Barnes. The crowd gave
some polite cheers and some jeers. Fancy, when Chicago had said
2,000,000 bushels less! Finally came word of the official total. It was
54,000,000 bushels. When she called years later on Mr. Barnes in
his office in New York she found he hadn't forgotten the Duluth
occasion. "Miss Hind's file, please," he directed his secretary and
there Cora saw all the crop estimates she had ever made. These
estimates were year by year telegraphed over the world, and her score
was invariably high.

    1905 estimate   85,000,000 bushels, official return   84,506,857
    1907 estimate   71,259,000 bushels, official return   70,922,584
    1909 estimate 118,109,000 bushels, official return 118,119,000

When her 1913 estimate appeared there was an outcry: "It isn't big
enough. Calamity Cora will ruin the country." Miss Hind paid no
attention. Her estimate stood. When the official estimate was tabled
Miss Hind's was found to be correct almost to the last bushel. Some
of the gentlemen who had shouted "Calamity Cora" observed that
they could not bear to have anything said to lower the prestige of
the West. Perhaps they faltered under Miss Hind's cold gaze, that is
if they tried to meet it. "No one loves the West more than I do," she
stated. "It has been my home for thirty years. I have seen it grow
up but very early in my newspaper career I learned that the West
was big enough and strong enough to have the truth told about it on all
occasions."

In 1933 the crop inspections by the *Free Press* were discontinued:
the Canadian Wheat Board had taken over the problems of marketing.
It was announced that of the twenty-nine estimates made, Dr. Hind,
in comparison with government and other official statements, had the
highest number of most closely accurate statements. She treasured
Prime Minister Bennett's speech in the House of Commons in which
he had declared:

For over a quarter of a century the area between the Great Lakes and
the Rocky Mountains in Western Canada was producing millions of

dollars of new wealth year after year in every year in which the effort was made. That has had the most significant influence upon our economic life of any single factor in our development because never have so few people, as far as the ordinary history of the world is concerned, produced so much new wealth in a given time, as has been produced in the last thirty years between the Great Lakes and mountains of this Dominion.

Miss Hind saw more than the blue sky country as she travelled her two hundred miles a day. When she had time she placed her feet in the prints of history already made, and sometimes as she visited a farmstead briefly, she knew history was in the making. But beyond a doubt the big moment was when the estimate was coming out. The Paper waited for it; the Country waited for it; so did the Argentine; so did the United States; so did Europe; so did the Liverpool Corn Trade. Well did the grain trade know that if Cora only would allow one advance peep she could be a wealthy woman. "No one on the Paper from the President down ever asked for it," recounted Dr. Hind. Certainly she wasn't giving it to anyone.

The wheat crop of 1915 had been tremendous—359,187,000 bushels. In 1916 once again the fields of long heads reached far away, even and smooth. Once again the harvest song was swelling to a magnificent orchestration. That July came a steady warm wind from the south, a cursed wind, for, as the evening vapours hovered over the land, the rust spoors dropped. Cora was to see those fields, still bravely standing, but in some way changed from gold to a dirty yellow. Nights, and out from Regina she saw fire creeping along mercifully consigning the stricken fields to oblivion. The rust had struck.

Miss Hind had not been ignorant of this danger during the years of her prairie travelling. She knew the efforts at research in the western universities. She knew of Ottawa's apprehensions. "Let us come out in the open and estimate our danger and take what steps we can to meet it," she pleaded. This was no editorial plural. Cora was enlisted in the fight and so far as her incisive pen could she fought. When Dr. J. H. Grisdale, director of the Dominion Experimental Farms, called a conference of the federal Department of Agriculture and of the universities of Manitoba, Saskatchewan, and Alberta, Dr. Hind was on the invitation list. The University of Manitoba offered green house and laboratory facilities for research and presently Dr.

Hind got to know the scientists there—Dr. D. L. Bailey, Dr. Margaret Newton, Dr. T. Johnson, Dr. C. H. Golden, and Dr. J. B. Harrington of Saskatchewan, and followed as carefully as she could their delicate efforts. She also knew Dr. Reginald Buller and his research with the fungus called "rust." She knew the American confrères who, engaged in the same battle, sometimes came up to see what might be going forward. She kept a careful file. She wrote article after article for her paper so that the public should be intelligently aware of the war. She talked about it in many places but perhaps oftenest when some of her friends were gathered in her pleasant flat, there almost oblivious of the tea as they listened to her recitals. Dr. Hind, no matter how unaware her audience, no matter how far removed from any contact with farming operations, had the gift of making her talks on any agricultural subject alive and breathing. Victory came in 1938 carrying rust resistant wheat in its beneficent arms and much rust resistant wheat was sown. Nineteen thirty-nine and the prairies were freed of the curse.

The depression of the thirties had meanwhile crept along the trails and whirling dismally along them went the dust-laden winds. No rain. No rain. No rain. The fields drifted; the roads drifted; the doors of barns and houses of deserted farms flapped drearily. Miss Hind tried to get out to see it, tried to find some ray of hope. The dust gritted under her feet. It sifted into the trains; it lay heaped in the corners of the grey fields. When she returned to her home from these trips Manitoba's still green leafed trees, still faintly green pastures, met her eyes as though they held a balm for her weary sight. Cora, throughout the years of her journeyings, had always one place in her affections, her home: with its comfortable furniture, its books and china, its carved table laid with fine linen and gleaming silver, its magazines, its cupboard shelves with neat jars of the jellies and pickles she carefully preserved (her aunt's recipes). Perhaps never more than after her survey of the desolation of the drought did this *pied-à-terre* offer its soothing welcome. Remarked Miss Hind, "I never envied any woman her husband, though I have her sons." But not to the exclusion of raising the altar of a home. In 1942, when the rains came, the *Regina Leader Post* wrote of her: "Through the long drought years, she retained her confidence in the productivity of the West. The years when she saw dry lands turn again to green

and gold, her eyes sparkled with pride. This was her West coming
back with the wallop she knew it still possessed."

It was Harold Long, editor of the *Lethbridge Herald,* her companion
on many a crop inspection tour over southern Alberta, who observed,
"She knew wheat but she loved livestock." Every spring found her
on her way to Calgary, to join the ranch folk crowding in from the
plains for the great cattle sale, one of the biggest events of its kind
in the world. "I was connected with the Livestock Association for
forty years and I do not think she ever missed an exhibition or a
spring sale," testified its secretary Ernest Richardson. She went to
Ottawa in 1912 at the invitation of federal government officials to a
meeting of the National Livestock Association, the only woman there
and certainly one of the most attentive in the audience when George
Lane of Calgary mounted the rostrum. She knew Mr. Lane who since
the early ranching days, in winter and summer, by the fires of many
round-ups, had held the range to his heart. He might be a millionaire
now, but his first love stayed with the country where the chinooks
blow. She agreed when he testified that Western Canada was now
importing horses, sheep, and hogs, and not producing nearly the
amount of beef cattle of which it was capable. Into the attentive
silence he threw a challenge: "Our western country is capable of
carrying 300,000 to 500,000 head of beef cattle per year." He had
more to say of ranchers beginning with only their small wages and
climbing on to success "attending to their own business, not loafing
around hotels, bar rooms and billiard halls." He added, and perhaps
Cora's pen moved a trifle faster as she quoted him, "The boys who
come to us from Eastern Canada are the most successful men we
have. The East may well be proud of them."

She was at the first Stampede in 1912. How she enjoyed those
nights at the Palliser when the ranch people, having shed their work
clothes, appeared in black and white and the soft rustle of silk. Cora
had no clothes sense and her hats were often catastrophic, nevertheless
she enjoyed purple and fine linen. That same year she was at the
organization of the Western Canada Livestock Union and became a
member. The annual gatherings rather got into the habit of moving
votes of thanks to Miss Hind, then four years later she held in her
hands an illumined address: "Since the days when as secretary of
the Manitoba Dairy Association you first identified yourself with

western agriculture, your record is one of faithful and invaluable service at all times ungrudgingly given to the interest of the farm and the farmer. Though your work has never shown either fear or favor, every branch of agricultural endeavor having greatly benefited by your able efforts, the livestock men of western Canada feel they have in you an especially loyal and devoted friend." And they handed her a purse of $1,300.

It took Miss Hind a moment to control her trembling hands but she gained composure as she proceeded to salute the men with whom her profession had brought her into contact as the best of comrades: the age of chivalry was not past and she, although a woman and doing work in a field which was regarded as peculiarly that of men, had always been treated with the utmost kindness and courtesy wherever she went. As the years went on Dr. Hind proudly chronicled that Winnipeg stock yards had grown to be the largest in the British Empire. Sometimes nevertheless she remembered that catastrophic year of 1907 in Alberta: the early snow, the sudden cold, the cattle on the ranges; no let-up in the rigid cold, no chinook to clear places where the cattle could forage. Too late the cowboys sought to bring them in and found nothing but dying cattle, nothing but frozen heaps. Fifty per cent of the range cattle perished that year.

It is highly improbable that Miss Hind brought up the subject of sheep when she was at cattle conventions, but she had no such inhibitions at other times. She was at the 1918 conference called by the federal government to consider the position of sheep-breeder and wool-grower associations. Presently she was a shareholder and director of the Canadian Co-operative Wool Growers. This was the company from which she ordered her yarn when "socks for soldiers" occupied her leisure. The Wool Growers of Manitoba at the Brandon Winter Fair once handed over to her title to a pen of twenty-six young ewes.

In 1922 Miss Hind took ship for Great Britain. If she needed anything to keep her mind off the vicissitudes of the "bounding billows" she had the thought of the embargo practised in the United Kingdom against Canadian cattle. But Cora was one of the few who, leaving her shipmates in their bunks below, jauntily dined with the Captain—roast pork on the menu! In her many voyages she "never felt a qualm."

For thirty years Canadian livestock associations had been wasting good paper and stamps writing to the British authorities inquiring about the

Marie Guyart de l'Incarnation

Catharine Parr Traill

Susanna Moodie

Pauline Johnson

Laure Conan

Adelaide Hunter Hoodless

E. Cora Hind

Maude E. Abbott

Emily F. Murphy

Nellie L. McClung

Agnes Macphail

Lucy Maud Montgomery

Emily Carr

Mazo de la Roche

Alice Wilson

Margaret McWilliams

embargo. The cattle trade had started in 1878 and, in spite of the long voyage to the finishing pastures of England and Scotland, had been profitable. The same year came an embargo against cattle from the United States because of the fear of tuberculosis. Canadian cattle were also suspect because of the "three thousand miles of boundary." In 1892 some British veterinarians discovered one of the Canadian immigrant cows was suffering from contagious pleuro-pneumonia. Others of the profession held different opinions but the British Board of Agriculture reached for its pen and placed Canadian cattle also under an embargo. The Canadian Minister of Agriculture had a pen too and soon it was at work. All to no avail. "Once there was a cow," etc. and the fear held that American cattle might be moved across the border and shipped as Canadian.

Enter E. Cora Hind, and the Press. *The Times* sent round a reporter. Cora had her grievances ready. Canada was suffering under the "wholly unjustifiable imputation that her herds were diseased." A second grievance was that a pledge had been given that at the end of the war the embargo would be removed, a pledge apparently repudiated. Thirdly, a royal commission set up at Whitehall had found in favour of the removal of the embargo. Again, Irish Free State cattle were put under no embargo. "It has long been established that Canadian herds are not only healthy, but that they are healthier than the herds of Great Britain—much healthier than the herds of Ireland." Cora had a lot more to say, more interviews to give out to various other publications, more ports and markets to visit, more dealers to interview, more meetings to address. *The Times* came out editorially for the lifting of the embargo, as did several other publications. In the House of Lords, as Cora noted with satisfaction, the Duke of Devonshire rose to defend Canadian cattle. He was well acquainted with them; that was part of his business as Governor-General of Canada. That autumn the embargo was lifted.

Dr. Hind made several trips to Great Britain and the newspapers always gave her a warm welcome. In 1932 it sent out its representatives to meet the incoming *Juventus*, carrying under its Italian flag the first cargo of wheat from Churchill. It also carried its first and only woman passenger, E. Cora Hind, 71 years old. "It does seem the height of effrontery for the East, in view of the terrific expenditures on the part of the Dominion Government to make a port of Montreal, to mention the Churchill and Hudson Bay route in connection with expense. If ever there was a 'daughter of the horse leech' that daughter is Montreal. . . . Churchill will succeed," she wrote. Did she remember her first crop report and the handful of kernels, as the president and members of the Liverpool Corn Exchange, that Mecca of the grain trade, received her and listened eagerly to her talk?

Back in Western Canada her journeyings were followed eagerly by the farmers, by the grain trade, by the great grain organizations, the United Grain Growers, and the Pools (now set up for co-operative handling of wheat). Cora knew all about them. She approved the grain companies but her enthusiasm for the Pools could easily be controlled. "There E. Cora sat," observed a Pool official. "There she sat on that *Juventus* deck, after her remarks that the Pools had taken no interest in the Churchill Port. And every kernel of wheat in the cargo from the pools! There she sat. I wonder at E. Cora. I wonder at her." Cora did not feel any call to repentance. Indeed when on her world trip, 1935–37, she touched down in Australia and was asked "Do you believe in pools?" she shot back her reply, "I do not, either voluntary or compulsory." Individualist through and through, she could not, in her seventies, accept the new demands of the depression and the new concepts of collective merchandising. But, the Canadian wheat pools continued to develop.

On this 1932 trip, scanning the British newspapers, it must have been with a wide smile that she read the *Morning Post* of London:

A woman who can go around and look at wheat fields, and then come home and estimate the Canadian wheat crop, forecasting it so accurately that bankers and grain companies take her estimate as gospel—such a woman is not met with every day. It would be strange enough to us if a man of great experience could soberly and accurately forecast the crop—not just a guess, not just once be lucky but time after time get nearer to the inner future truth than anyone else. But that such a faculty would be centred in a woman—this, for some reason, seems extraordinary even in an era when almost nothing in faculties and doings of women can surprise us.

Dr. Hind had become and was to remain to the press of Great Britain a V.I.P.

Miss Hind did not do all her travelling to the centres of the world. The map in her office with its rows of coloured pins carefully demonstrated the increasing areas of farming as the boundaries of the great

West moved north. Hence followed her trip in 1929 to the banks of the mighty river that gives the Peace district its name. Then came careful descriptions of the region, warning of the difficulties of lack of water; warning about immigration of those who only carried hope in their meagre satchels; warning about difficulties of transportation. There were stories also of good yields and of research being pressed forward by the University of Alberta, and by the federal government department. She found some beginning herds of cattle, with satisfaction she reported creameries here and there—Cora never deserted her first agricultural love—"not many though," she commented, adding "wheat does not have to be milked in the winter."

Dr. Hind frequently gave the lie to the opinion, raised on insufficient evidence, that newspaper folk are a total loss on the public platform. Perhaps, however, there were two outstanding occasions in this capacity for her. The first was on her return from the farmers' marketing trip arranged by the Canadian National Railways to Great Britain when she, with seventy farmers from the West and East but now all Canadians, spent a month in the United Kingdom studying the great market there. The second was on her return from her two-year trip around the world visiting wheat-producing countries, when she addressed a capacity house at the Walker Theatre in Winnipeg.

On the first occasion she stood before the annual meeting of the Saskatchewan Grain Growers Association, in 1905; there were hundreds of its members, men and women ready after a long day session to listen to this woman whom many of them knew personally, whom all of them knew professionally. A small figure she looked among the men arranged about her on the platform, as, clothed in the anonymity of a black velvet dinner dress, she straightened her notes nervously. But not for long. These were her ain folk. She must tell them all she had seen on that month in what was to many of them "back home": seven public receptions, three banquets, nine official luncheons, twenty afternoon teas, one breakfast, five theatre and opera parties, ten educational meetings, visited fifteen outstanding farms, attended one football match and Their Majesties' reception at Buckingham Palace. She told it all, for she had missed none of it, to this audience which listened as though drinking wine. Now and then a face was illumined as some name dear to the listener was mentioned. There was word too of the necessity of studying the market, of keeping up quality and quantity.

The Chairman did his parliamentary procedure best to close the meeting. But the audience had memories with them, questions, hopes that she might have seen this or that. It was long past midnight when the surging crowd consented to release her.

The second occasion was a star-studded fragrant August evening in 1937 in Winnipeg when at the age of seventy-six she came forward on the stage of the Walker Theatre aglow with gladioli and realized that the crowded house before her, which could have been sold out three times over, was welcoming her with salvos of cheers. She was home from a two-year trip around the world visiting wheat-producing countries. All of them had read her articles in the *Free Press*; many were to read her book *Seeing for Myself*, her story of the girl of fifty years ago coming to a pioneer town, unknown, poor and brave, now one of the first citizens of the West.

On she went, the United Kingdom, Russia, Hungary, Austria, Czechoslovakia, Africa, India, Ceylon, Australia, New Zealand, Norway, Germany, Yugoslavia, France, Italy, South Africa, Rhodesia, South America. One hour, two hours, three hours—scarcely a stir in the great audience, only an unwavering attention. Afterwards, some may have marvelled at the rapport which Miss Hind, a stranger, had been able to establish among the many differing peoples with many languages whom she visited. Obviously her interest had reached to them as they presented to her their hopes, their difficulties, their triumphs, and as they showed her their grain fields and flocks and herds. Apparently she had early secured their confidence and they had early realized that here was a visitor who came not to criticize, not to compare unfairly, but to learn what they had to teach. Mingled also in her talk on this night in Winnipeg were some informed encouragement for Canadian agriculture; some critical, pungent incisive words about the less than steady attention to careful marketing in Canada; of the need of immigration agents who knew the language of the country to whose citizens they were selling Canada; of more realization of the need of status for Canada's trade commissioners. The audience had read these observations in her newspaper articles, faithfully sent to her paper; they also read her "findings" in her book. But this was a personal appeal not for herself but for an understanding of Canada, of her position as one of the great trading nations of the world. The small figure behind the reading desk was cheered and cheered again as the audience rose in its hundreds. Dr. Hind received many of her roses when the fragrance was sweet to her, but never more than on that evening in her home city.

On October 6, 1942, Dr. Hind, aged 81, died of a stroke. She lingered only a few days. The story crossed Canada, reached *The Times* in London, was given a column in the *New York Times*. Telegrams, letters, cables poured into the *Free Press* office—plain, crabbed handwriting, letters bearing crests. Over the office the flags hung that day at half mast. She herself had written words that would befit her departure: "Those of us of the old new West who have been privileged to travel the prairie trails in summer heat and winter cold, in the awakening beauty of the spring time, in the promise of summer, and the golden fulfilment of autumn, when we set out alone on the longest trail of all, we shall 'go west' with great content, if the soft southwest wind brings to us the tang of the wild sage and the prairie roses, the beat of a thousand hooves as the herds go down to water, or the sibilant sigh of the wind through miles of ripening wheat."

BIBLIOGRAPHY

Files of newspapers have been especially useful: *Winnipeg Free Press, Regina Leader Post; Lethbridge Herald; Montreal Gazette; Western Producer; The Times* (London); *New York Times; Morning Post* (London). A biography, *Brave Harvest*, by Kennethe Haig (Toronto, 1945) and Cora Hind's *Seeing for Myself* (Toronto, 1937) give fuller accounts. Personal reminiscences have provided background.

8

Maude E. Abbott

1869-1940

JESSIE BOYD SCRIVER

IN 1932 I was travelling in Europe and spending some time in medical centres. Invariably when it was learned that I came from Canada, there came the response, "Ah, then you must know Dr. Maude Ab*bott*" (with the emphasis on the last syllable).

We knew Dr. Abbott*—Maudie to staff and students at McGill—as an institution in herself but had not appreciated the distinction she had achieved and the esteem with which she was regarded abroad at a time when few Canadian medical men and no Canadian medical women had achieved such renown beyond our shores.

Maude Elizabeth Seymour Abbott was born on March 18, 1869, at St. Andrews East, in Quebec, a naturally beautiful village on the

---

*AUTHOR'S NOTE. Graduating in medicine from McGill in 1922, I was a member of the first class to graduate women in that faculty. I have been fortunate in being able to talk about details of Dr. Abbott's early life with Dr. H. E. MacDermot who wrote *Maude Abbott: A Memoir* in 1941, the year after her death. I am indebted to the Macmillan Company for permission to quote from Dr. MacDermot's *Memoir*. I should also like to thank Dr. Sclater Lewis, Dr. Abbott's personal physician, and Dr. Harold Segall, cardiologist who worked with Dr. Abbott, and Dr. Eleanor Percival, a member of that class of 1922, for reviewing with me some of the details of our association with this vital and outstanding Canadian woman.

north shore of the Ottawa River not far from Montreal. We learn from Dr. Abbott's own *Social History of the Congregation of Christ Church, St. Andrews* that this village had been one of the settlements in the Seigneury of Argenteuil, had been a stopping place for the fur-traders as they travelled by canoe from the far north, and later under British régime had "attracted a superior class of settlers from whose efforts a thriving community rapidly developed, which quickly came to contain within itself the best elements of the day." These early settlers "were chiefly U.E. Loyalists who had come to Canada at the time of the American Declaration of Independence, or Americans who had come to Canada for family or business reasons in the succeeding years of unrest, or Scottish emigrants who were brought to develop the land of the Seigneury."

To this settlement there came in 1818, in answer to an appeal for an Anglican clergyman, two brothers, the Rev. Joseph and the Rev. William Abbott. The Rev. Joseph remained in St. Andrews and the Rev. William occupied a charge in what is now known as Abbotsford, P.Q. Later there was controversy as to whether the spelling should be with two T's, honouring the Rev. William and not Sir Walter Scott's residence. However the change was not accomplished. Succeeding his brother Joseph as rector of St. Andrews in 1826, the Rev. William remained there until his death. He was Maude's grandfather. His daughter Elizabeth married the Rev. Jeremiah Babin, but Mrs. Babin died of pulmonary tuberculosis seven months after Maude's birth and later Maude and her sister Alice were legally adopted by their grandmother Mrs. William Abbott and their grandfather's name was bestowed on them by Act of Parliament.

The records describe Mrs. Abbott as a gracious woman of fine character who exerted a profound influence on the lives of the two young girls. Indeed the neighbourhood as a whole strengthened this influence. In Maude's own words, "Probably there are few communities in Canada in which were combined in a more ideal and delightful way, the genial social atmosphere of old world culture and refinement, open-hearted colonial hospitality, sterling qualities of the pioneer life, and the pervading influence of a living religious faith and principle, than in St. Andrews during the last three decades of that eventful half century."

Maude kept a diary and the early entries are those of day-to-day happenings in the household and community. Part of her entry for Christmas 1880 when she was eleven is of interest. ". . . we were not able to get up early to look at our stockings. It was past eight when we did so and I got a gold cross, two yards of wide red ribbon, one of narrow, a black handled penknife, a silver thimble, a black-handled tooth brush, half a dozen handkerchiefs, fifty cents, a pencil case, some frilling, a little box full of candies, a lovely pair of seed bracelets, an orange, some grapes and nuts, raisins and candies, also a coral necklace. After I had emptied my stocking I loitered round until pretty late."

Maude's early education was carried on at home under a governess, with the emphasis on literature and history rather than mathematics and science. Her reading was of a wide range and her intellectual curiosity and good mind gradually developed in her a desire for further learning. Into her diary crept evidence of a restlessness and an ambition to go to a formal school where she might learn more and more. At the same time she chided herself for what must appear as a selfish desire and might be interpreted as dissatisfaction with her present status. This she said would not be true. In the home and in the community Mrs. Abbott, Maude's grandmother, was the very embodiment of unselfishness, and this same unselfishness came to be a dominant trait in Maude's life. In later years her first thought was always for her work or her associates or her friends or her family, not for herself, a fact which was not infrequently to her disadvantage.

In the autumn of 1884, her desire was realized and she was sent to Montreal to the private school of the Misses Symmers and Smith. Here the stimulation of studying with her classmates resulted in further evidence of Maude's ability and excited a desire for even further studies. In December, 1884, she wrote: "We are never satisfied. My next wish is to go to College, and now I am wishing for that almost as ardently as I did last winter for my present good fortune." This dream seemed even more remote of fulfilment than her previous one.

Today, in the latter half of the twentieth century, when university doors for the most part are wide open to women students, it is hard to realize that not so long ago this was not the case. True in Europe and Great Britain and the United States, facilities for higher education for women were available in the first half of the nineteenth century and by mid-century the pioneer Elizabeth Blackwell had received her medical degree from the Geneva Medical College in the State of New York. In Canada the movement was slower in getting started. Trinity College, Toronto, and Queen's University, Kingston, admitted women students earlier than did McGill in the conservative atmosphere of Quebec.

The first consideration of higher education of women at McGill was in 1870. There was some sympathy with the idea among certain members of the staff but the University felt that such a move was impossible. The decision was probably influenced by the prejudice in Quebec against "mixed classes" and by the University's inability to meet the expense of separate classes. Then, too, an attitude prevailed that the increased mental strain of higher studies would be beyond the women's physical endurance! Credit should be given to those faculty members who were willing to lecture to young women and did so under the programme of the Ladies' Educational Association of Montreal. This programme naturally promoted a growing interest in the matter in the community and by 1884 a group of young women made formal application for admission to the Faculty of Arts of McGill. From reports one would gather that the idea of women students attempting higher studies was no longer frowned upon, and Sir William Dawson, the Principal, had looked into the problem abroad. Finances proved the deterrent and Sir William explained to the applicants that McGill was unable to set up separate classes. He was at the same time sympathetic to the idea of increasing the scope of the classes of the Ladies' Educational Association.

One can imagine with what gratification came the announcement in September, 1884, during the meeting in Montreal of the British Association for the Advancement of Science, that Sir Donald A. Smith (later Lord Strathcona) was about to give $50,000 in aid of higher education of women. The financial deterrent removed, plans were made immediately to open classes in October and that autumn saw the first women students admitted to McGill into the Faculty of Arts. Two years later Sir Donald increased his gift to $120,000—a magnificent sum in those days—and the opportunity for higher education was firmly established. The women students were known then and through the years as Donaldas in honour of Sir Donald and if there had been any doubt as to whether they could stand the strain of study, the scholastic records of these young women would have removed it.

Maude entered McGill in the third class to admit women, having been granted a scholarship on the results of the entrance examinations. Feeling that she was needed at home she had been dubious about accepting the scholarship but Miss Symmers was anxious that for the sake of the scholastic reputation of women students she should do so. Accordingly, arrangements were made at home so that she was able to enter classes in the fall of 1886. Her superior ability soon was evident and when she graduated in 1890 she had won the Lord Stanley Gold Medal.

At graduation ceremonies, Maude was Class Valedictorian, a more serious assignment than in later years; the address was given at open Convocation, having been censored first by the Principal. There is not space here to report her speech completely but a few quotations bespeak her mature thinking and earnestness.

Too little has been said to the women students of McGill with regard to their duties and privileges in the University; too little to the citizens of Montreal of this the grand educational opportunities laid open to their daughters. The subject being still in the form of a question, is full of interest, and the eyes of the public are on McGill in her women's classes, noting, criticizing, and approving the princely donation of Sir Donald A. Smith. The 19th century is pre-eminently practical, and it is well that it is so. Work is fundamental to the onward march of science; it is at the bottom of every great and good action that was ever done; it underlies the formation of all true character. And it is the sin of idleness that is to be counted as the deadliest, just because it chokes, with the stifling pressure of stagnation, every noble deed, and eventually every holy aspiration. . . .
Remember that at this early stage of women's education in Canada, you, as members of the advance-guard, are in your own persons to be pointed out as instances of its success or failure. I cannot do better than quote the words of our beloved benefactor, when last autumn he admonished us to strive to be, not only highly educated and learned women, but ladies in the higher sense which used to be designated by the good old English word "Gentlewomen".

Nothing has been said so far about her medical career. Maude says in her autobiography that the idea came in her second year in Arts when a dear friend, Mrs. Eastlake, asked her what she was going to do when she left college. Maude replied that she had not thought about it, to which her friend answered that if she were not an artist she would be a doctor. When Maude went home she asked her grand-mother "May I be a doctor?" Whereupon her grandmother answered "Dear child, you may be anything you like."

The seed was sown and she heard from other university centres where women were studying medicine. Once having made up her mind, she desired to follow her medical studies at her beloved McGill. However when presented with this young woman's application, the medical faculty, whose decisions were independent of the University, firmly refused to consider opening its classes to women, maintaining the same unyielding stand as with previous applications. Undaunted, Maude set out to try to reverse the decision.

It would take too long to recount the story of the efforts of this indomitable young woman, of the interest and financial assistance of influential citizens, the advice of her illustrious cousin Sir John Abbott, the first Canadian-born prime minister of Canada. Actually there were few members of the faculty who really opposed the study of medicine by women, but they did object to teaching "mixed classes." Many letters and opinions were exchanged. In the light of the place of women in the profession today, an excerpt from one of the letters is rather amusing:

In certain subjects certain terms have to be employed which certainly could not be used before women without great embarrassment. Of course if they want to endow a separate college, I have not the smallest objection. They may be useful in some departments in Medicine; but in difficult work, in surgery, for instance, they would not have the nerve. And can you think of a patient in a critical case, waiting for half an hour while the medical lady fixes her bonnet or adjusts her bustle?

The main objection was that co-education in medicine was imprac-ticable and separate classes too expensive. As might be expected, the letter to Miss Abbott from the Registrar finally arrived saying "it could not see its way to undertaking the medical education of women in connection with the Faculty."

Shortly after her graduation in 1890 in Arts, Maude received a message from the medical faculty of the University of Bishop's College that they were prepared to accept women students. The clinical teach-ing of this school was given largely by McGill teaching staff at the Montreal General Hospital; the hospital retained control of permission to enter the wards for teaching, and tickets of admission were issued. This led to a situation which was potentially serious and worth recording. An able student, Miss Grace Ritchie, who had been in the first class in Arts in McGill, and had completed three years at Queen's University in Medicine, transferred to Bishop's for her final year. She obtained her ticket of admission to the ward teaching and was tolerated in the classes. She advised Maude to apply early for her ticket and to pay for it, which she did and obtained her receipt, but the ticket was to follow.

Meantime applications for permission to attend clinics for the summer session at the Montreal General Hospital were received from several women students at Queen's University and the hospital authorities suddenly realized that a firm precedent might be in the offing. To quote Dr. Abbott's own words,

The Committee of Management saw with alarm that they had taken a step that might open the flood gates for an ill-considered innovation and they had accordingly ruled that no more tickets should be issued to women students. So that, in spite of the fact that my $20. had been paid in and acknowledged, the matter was still in abeyance and my ticket withheld.

Help came fortuitously but happily.

It was now July of 1891 and I was beginning to lay my plans to go to Philadelphia, when the newspaper storm broke. It was the time for the payment of annual subscriptions to the Montreal General Hospital, and the situation had somehow got through to the consciousness of the Life Governors. A number of these quite spontaneously and entirely as a matter of fair play, took up the cudgels on my behalf, saying it was unfair to refuse a ticket for hospital attendance to me, an Arts graduate of McGill, when this privilege had just been accorded my fellow graduate Miss Ritchie and in no way abused by her; and they refused to pay in their subscriptions until a ticket had also been issued to me.

The newspapers gave the situation much publicity, a fact which caused Maude unhappiness as she was fundamentally a shy person and also feared what effect it might have on her future training. In the end the publicity had its effect, though only on her personal behalf:

In the middle of it all one day by mail at St. Andrews the ticket reached me. The battle had suddenly been won for me entirely in absentia by men I had never known or seen; but a resolution had been passed by the

Committee of Management that no other tickets for hospital attendance were to be issued to women students.

Thus with the necessary permission she was in full attendance at all the Montreal General Hospital clinics that were open to McGill and Bishop's students. The only woman in the classes (Miss Ritchie had graduated), she said she enjoyed the work greatly and on the whole was very kindly treated. Some of the teachers, appreciating her diligence and dependability, rewarded her work by allotting her extra patients. However in those clinical years she was lonely and although on the whole the attitude of her fellow students was not unchivalrous there was some resentment of her unusual zeal and steadfastness of purpose. Also the camaraderie evident today among men and women medical students was absent in those pioneer days. The reward for four years of hard work came in June 1894 when Maude graduated in Medicine from Bishop's with brilliant honours, winning the senior anatomy prize and the Chancellor's prize for the best examination in the final subjects.

The doors of the Faculty of Medicine at McGill remained closed to women until near the end of World War I when medical personnel was in demand and women's units such as the Scottish Women's Hospital had proven themselves in battle areas such as Salonika. In 1917, four women were admitted as partial students to all the subjects of first-year Medicine—no doubt as a trial run; they were then taken into second year as regular students and were joined by a fifth member who transferred from Toronto. So in the autumn of 1918 women were studying medicine at McGill University without having hammered at its doors or having indulged in any campaign. One should add that all four of that first group were prepared to enter one of the several well-known medical schools in the United States accepting women students.

It is difficult to convey the joy and triumph of Dr. Abbott at that graduation in the spring of 1922 when McGill bestowed for the first time her regular medical degree of M.D., C.M. on five women medical graduates. In 1910 McGill had honoured Dr. Abbott with a McGill M.D., C.M. (*honoris causa*) recognizing her work and reputation and there is no doubt that her reputation had some influence on the final decision to admit women to the study of medicine.

I have described at some length the early training of Maude Abbott because it is well that we should remember the struggle and disappointments which were part of those pioneer days in contrast to the comparatively smooth path of outstanding young women students who choose medicine as a career today.

Immediately after graduation in 1894 Maude planned for postgraduate training. Her grandmother had died in 1890 and consequently Maude and her sister Alice were without family responsibilities. At that time, the Mecca for postgraduate medical training was Vienna where were to be found many of the outstanding teachers of the day and abundant clinical opportunities. With Vienna as her goal, she and her sister Alice sailed for Europe in July, 1894, visiting London first, then spending several months en route to Vienna in various centres to perfect the language—Heidelberg, Berne, Interlaken, Zürich. She bore letters of introduction to important medical teachers in each centre, thus enjoying unusual and stimulating experiences along the way. Alice at the same time was studying music.

Finally in March, 1895, they arrived in Vienna and remained there for the next two years. Maude studied in a number of courses but it was the outstanding grounding she received in internal medicine and in pathology which led to her later work at McGill.

Returning to Montreal in September, 1897, she started practice in the centre of the city. As one reviews the records one appreciates that her goal was not to carry on a large practice but rather that by using her superior training she might be worthy of a place on the teaching staff of her beloved McGill. Chance encounters sometimes shape our ends, and one day when walking through the college grounds, she met Dr. Charles F. Martin who had been on the staff of the Montreal General Hospital when she had been a student there. He was now at the recently opened Royal Victoria Hospital and invited Maude there to do some work. There she met Dr. Adami, the eminent pathologist, and was soon working on a subject which had interested her in Vienna also. Her ability for research in pathology was evident and soon recognized by her superiors. At the same time Dr. Martin had put her to work on a clinical problem, a statistical study of "Functional Heart Murmurs." When this paper was presented at the Medico-Chirurgical Society by Dr. James Stewart, since women were not at that time admitted to membership, it was well received and immediately Dr. Adami nominated her for membership in the Society. Her election to membership meant personal recognition for Dr. Abbott.

A problem in pathological research on pigmentation cirrhosis was ready for publication in December, 1899, and was presented for her by Sir Humphrey Rolleston before the Pathological Society in London in January 1900, the first communication ever made by a woman before that Society.

Having so creditably worked on one problem, she was now assigned to others which demanded her time and unstinted effort but unfortunately were not accompanied by a stipend which would replace income from practice. Her energy knew no bounds but there were times when Maude became very discouraged and viewed her future with misgivings. At the same time she had added family responsibilities as her sister Alice had suffered a nervous breakdown following a serious illness in Europe, and remained a chronic invalid. With deep affection and constant concern for her sister's comfort, Maude bore this demanding responsibility without complaint through the years.

At this time there was a growing realization of the need for organization of the wealth of pathological material which had found its way to the Medical Museum of McGill. These specimens dated back to 1823 and the opening of the Medical School, but unfortunately they had not been described or adequately catalogued. In recognition of her ability and enthusiasm Maude was appointed curator. This was a colossal assignment; there was no established method of classification so that she was faced with an almost pioneer task. Before beginning the work she was sent down to the United States to the large teaching centres to see their museums and also the Army Medical Museum at Washington. It was on this trip that she first met Dr. William Osler, who, through the years until his death in Oxford, was an adviser and inspiration in her work. Her diary and correspondence contain many references to Sir William's influence. In his own inimitable way he was able to call forth extraordinary enthusiasm and effort in any whom he advised.

Maude devoted her energies in her characteristically whole-hearted way to her new Museum task and was rewarded by finding in it much that was of unique and outstanding interest. The abnormal heart specimens became her special pride and formed the basis of the work which later established her world-wide reputation as the authority on congenital cardiac abnormalities.

As she brought order in the Museum, the medical students began to show interest and early morning or evenings would find them conferring with Dr. Abbott and studying from the newly organized material. Of their appreciation we may quote a part of a letter written by the members of the class of 1904.

As the closing hours of our college life grow fewer and fewer . . . we desire as members of the graduating class of '04 to express our gratitude for the kindly interest you have taken in our studies in Pathology, for the unfailing courtesy you have shown us, for the many unselfish hours throughout this whole year that you have spent in our behalf—hours that fell at a very inconvenient time for you, yet you grudged them not. Freely and unstintingly you have given us of your time and of your talents and we have profited, and profited much.

May we ask you to accept as a mere token of our appreciation the enclosed order for books. And we hope that as succeeding classes come and go that it may in some small measure recall to your memory the class of '04 for whom you so zealously laboured.

In 1905 Maude was invited to write the section on congenital cardiac anomalies for Osler's *System of Medicine*. This was a signal honour and as might be expected was done with great thoroughness, with correlation of clinical records and autopsy findings in over 400 cases. When finished her section called forth warm appreciation from Dr. Osler and his letter to Dr. Abbott is worth quoting:

DEAR DR. ABBOTT:

I knew you would write a good article but I did not expect one of such extraordinary merit. It is by far and away the best thing ever written on the subject in English—possibly in any language. I cannot begin to tell you how much I appreciate the care and trouble you have taken, but I know you will find it to have been worth while. For years it will be the standard work on the subject and it is articles of this sort—and there are not many of them—that *make* a system of medicine. Then too, the credit which such a contribution brings to the school is very great. Many, many thanks.

Sincerely yours,
WM. OSLER

This work established her reputation and gradually recognition from faculty members followed. True there were from the beginning several who were helpful and staunch supporters but for the most part those early years were times of little recognition and very inadequate working facilities. However, those who were closely associated with her in her work were ever loyal and devoted, giving long hours to assist in the overwhelming tasks to be done. Under her tireless enthusiasm and boundless energy and hard work the Museum soon assumed an important role in the medical teaching which it had not enjoyed hitherto.

When the Medical Building suffered its disastrous fire in the spring of 1907, the Museum lost many of its specimens but thanks to the intrepid effort of Dr. Abbott, aided by some students and the Museum secretary, many precious specimens were salvaged, as were her catalogues. Immediately she set about re-establishing order and soliciting replacements from other museums in the United States and abroad.

During this same period, when she conferred frequently with curators of other medical museums, it became apparent that an international association could be of great benefit to all concerned. Dr. Abbott pursued the idea and with her relentless personal effort the International Association of Medical Museums was formed and came to play an important role in the reporting and sharing of medical knowledge. She served as the Association's secretary from 1907 to 1938 and also was editor of its *Journal of Technical Methods* and its *Bulletin*. She travelled rather extensively during these years and soon gained an international reputation both for her museum work and for her unique contributions to the knowledge and understanding of congenital cardiac anomalies.

As so often happens, recognition at home followed rather than preceded her recognition abroad, but in 1910 she was honoured by McGill with an M.D., C.M. degree (*honoris causa*). Through the ensuing years she was sought out in consultation as the authority on congenital heart conditions; autopsy specimens were sent to her from all over North America and even from Europe; young cardiologists came from far and near to spend days to weeks studying with her and her associates at McGill were all very happy that Maude was reaping some reward for her hard work, fine mind, and steadfastness of purpose.

Today cardiologists tell me that Dr. Abbott, by the use of her eyes, hands and stethoscope in examining patients and by her meticulous examination of post mortem hearts, laid the foundation for the further scientific investigations carried out by Dr. Helen Taussig, who paid frequent visits to Dr. Abbott. These in turn led on to the brilliant cardiac surgery which now is able to repair many of the congenital abnormalities. The present complicated diagnostic procedures, such as heart catheterization, gas analyses and cine radiography, make accurate diagnosis more available; at the same time they make Dr. Abbott's work even more admirable.

It is with pride too that we record that in the Institute of Cardiology in Mexico City there is a mural painted by the famous Mexican artist Diego di Rivera who was guided by the well-known Spanish medical historian Guerra. Among the noted cardiologists in the painting there is only one Canadian and that one is Dr. Maude Abbott.

She received several invitations to posts at other universities but was loath to leave McGill; in 1923, however, on loan from McGill, she went to the Women's Medical College of Pennsylvania as Professor of Pathology and Bacteriology and Director of Clinical Laboratories where it is reported that she did an excellent job reorganizing the department. On her return to Montreal in 1925 she was appointed Assistant Professor of Medical Research in the McGill University Clinic at the Royal Victoria Hospital under the Director, Jonathan Meakins, who had relinquished his chair of Therapeutics at Edinburgh to head the new department at McGill. It was his desire that Maude should have such facilities as she required to complete or carry on the many projects she had in hand.

The years went on and in 1936 she reached the statutory age for retirement from her academic position at McGill. This was a bitter disappointment for Maude who still had much work planned and still displayed unbounded energy. The disappointment was somewhat relieved by her being granted an honorary LL.D. by McGill, the highest honour her university could give.

Almost immediately thereafter she started on a lecture tour on the Pacific Coast lasting seven weeks, four weeks of which were spent in San Francisco where for part of the time she was the guest of Professor and Mrs. Emil Holman. Dr. Ann Purdy (Mrs. Holman), an eminent cardiologist, has told me what a busy four weeks they were with lectures and clinics every day and dinner parties or social gatherings every evening. Maude loved it all and was truly in her element.

While she was visiting the West Coast she received word that she had been elected an Honorary Member of the New York Academy of Medicine—another honour added to her list.

In the following years she continued to write and one can but be amazed at her accomplishment through the years. Her bibliography lists over 140 titles, bespeaking a tremendous amount of work, and her *Atlas of Congenital Heart Disease*, published in 1936 by the American Heart Association, remains a classic. Not all of her writing, however, was medical. She was keenly interested in history and especially that of early Canada, and with a view to preserving the story of the past of her early home county of Argenteuil, she and several others set about collecting data and records of the early days there. It was a proud day for her when Lord Tweedsmuir, the Governor-General, officially opened the Carillon Museum, where in the Abbott Room were recorded the past and the accomplishments of her illustrious family.

She was a woman of broad sympathies, with a tremendous interest in people, she had an uncanny way of knowing when help or encouragement was needed, and she was always generous in her praise of a piece of work well done. She was very fond of little children who in turn were fond of her and she was always able to produce from her large handbag some picture card or knick-knack for their amusement. When a new baby arrived in the household of any of her co-workers or friends she would turn up very soon, bearing a gift of a sweater or a bonnet or a spoon. When she travelled she remembered her home friends with cards and mementos and on return would regale us with the interesting and amusing details of her trip, such as a ride on a donkey in Greece during her travel there with Dr. and Mrs. Paul White. Warm-hearted and impulsive, generous in her outlook and with a good sense of humour she had many friends and it was said that when she travelled on two continents, doors were open to receive her everywhere she went, and at medical meetings she would be surrounded by former students or friends waiting to have a word with her. Dr. Abbott was herself the soul of hospitality and the return of a former student or the appearance of a friend passing through town was always the occasion of a party. Her parties were great fun, usually not too large dinner parties, with stimulating conversation and reminiscences by the hostess. With her gentle breeding and humility of spirit, in spite of her many honours, she held the affection and respect of her many friends, and although she could be aggressive if need be in connection with her work, any such attitude was never for personal gain.

Maude was fond of good-looking clothes but had little time for their choosing or care and was frequently the despair of her friends trying to help her get ready for an important occasion where she would be the guest of honour. Once about to leave for a party, all coifed and clad in a dark red velvet floor-length gown, she suddenly thought of a specimen which she wished to review. The resulting dribbles of formalin on her dress called for hasty effort to repair the damage. There was never a dull moment if one were associated with Dr. Abbott!

The esteem and respect which was granted her was a cherished experience and was never taken for granted. The late Professor E. G. D. Murray told of an occasion at Cambridge at a meeting of the pathologists of Great Britain in 1929. When Dr. Abbott entered the door at the front of the hall, the presiding officer rose to greet her and the rest of the assembly gave her an ovation, a striking tribute for such a group to pay. As Dr. MacDermot has said "with all the flattering respect she received, however, Maude remained entirely unspoilt. She neither looked for it nor did she disregard it, she would have been more than human not to have been touched by it."

Her energy and power of work were enormous and amid what appeared chaos she was capable of extraordinary concentration working for hours oblivious of her surroundings, and from her desk, which appeared in total disarray, she could at once extract the desired detail. No wonder she exhausted those who tried to keep up with her pace, and acquired the name of "the beneficent tornado" from one of her Pennsylvania friends. In present-day terms Dr. Abbott might be called "accident prone." Aside from minor mishaps she suffered three major accidents, one in 1929 when she was struck by a motor and received a severe concussion. In 1937 she was knocked down by a taxi in New York and suffered broken ribs, and in 1939 she was crushed between two street cars in Montreal. Probably her short-sightedness and her obliviousness to her surroundings while in deep thought were contributing factors. Dr. Sclater Lewis, her personal physician, says that it was a losing battle to try to curtail her activity while she was ill, and in her hospital room she would be surrounded by books and papers and would insist that her secretary keep her supplied with the necessary material.

One of the last honours to be accorded her was the establishment, by an anonymous donor, of a scholarship at McGill "In honour of Dr. Maude Elizabeth Seymour Abbott, in appreciation of her distinguished career, signalized by her work in connection with the history of Canadian Medicine and the Sir William Osler Pathological Collection, and by her outstanding research in congenital cardiac disease, where she is recognized among the pioneers in establishing this subject as a living part of clinical medicine." The terms of the scholarship required that it be given to a worthy student in medicine.

Throughout the years Dr. Abbott maintained a keen interest in medical education for women and was instrumental with Dr. Helen McMurchie in founding the Federation of Medical Women of Canada, which group awards their Maude Abbott Scholarship annually in her memory to a woman medical student.

After her 1939 accident, her health was obviously failing but she insisted on working and refused to be idle. In July 1940 she suffered a cerebral haemorrhage from which she never fully recovered. In her final weeks she was still the same Maude, chafing at idleness, thinking of others and unselfish to the end.

On September 2, 1940, she died, and in the obituary notice in the medical journal *The Lancet* (London) October 15, 1940, are found the following words.

Dr. Abbott came of a family which holds an honoured place in Canadian public life. She was proud of her English stock, and she had many close friends in this country.

Kind-hearted and generous to a fault, she combined a quiet simplicity of mind with great intellectual ability and an energy and enthusiasm which were at once the admiration and despair of her friends. In her long and happy life she had passed through much tribulation—she had had "misfortunes great and sma', but aye a heart abune them a'"—and the memory of her joyous vital enthusiastic personality will ever be treasured by those of us who were privileged to be her friends.

9

Five Persons from Alberta

EMILY MURPHY 1868–1933

NELLIE MCCLUNG 1874–1951

LOUISE MCKINNEY 1868–1933

IRENE PARLBY 1878–1965

HENRIETTA EDWARDS 1849–1933

ELEANOR HARMAN

IN A BOOK of sketches, *Open Trails*, published in 1912, "Janey Canuck" (Emily Murphy) describes a visit to Ottawa and a tour of the Parliament Buildings, in the course of which she arrived at the entrance of the Senate Chamber just as the Opening of Parliament was taking place. She wanted to go in to watch the spectacle, but was wearing none of the furbelows and feathers customary for female guests admitted to the floor and galleries of the Chamber on this gala occasion. However, as happened so often before and afterwards, the determination of the lady from Edmonton overcame all opposition, and she was soon ensconced in an advantageous seat beside an elaborately gowned female, who looked her over with the obvious question in her eye—"How did *you* get in?" As Janey in modest triumph recorded, she had now won "the distinction of being the first woman to hold a seat on the floor of the Senate Chamber in a street suit."

All the other women seated in the Senate that day were there in a purely ornamental rôle, their places of honour reflecting the political achievements of their husbands, fathers, brothers, or sons. Canadian women had no vote in either provincial or federal elections, and the possibility that members of their sex might not only exercise the franchise but also one day be summoned or elected as representatives to either the Upper or Lower Chamber of the House was still only a vision splendid, albeit one that had moved perceptibly nearer than a few decades before.

But the chaos of World War I which followed, the growth of democracy, and the wearing-down of opposition through a further nine years of campaigning brought about the great change at last, and in the Dominion election of 1921, Canadian women participated fully, having been granted both the right to vote and the right to stand for election. One woman, Miss Agnes Macphail, was elected to the Dominion Parliament from Ontario. But even before then, women's organizations vigorously petitioned the Government of the day to appoint women as senators. The nominee often proposed as first Canadian woman to sit in the august Senate Chamber was Emily Murphy—"Janey Canuck."

The choice was a natural one; in 1921, Emily Murphy was one of the most widely known of Canadian women.[1] She was born Emily Ferguson near Cookstown, Ontario, in 1868, and had four Irish grandparents, one of them Ogle Robert Gowan, a member of Parliament for twenty-seven years, and the founder of the Orange Order in Canada. A cousin of Ogle Gowan was Sir James Gowan, a Supreme Court judge who later became Senator. The Ferguson side of the family was also strongly Tory, including Thomas Roberts Ferguson, M.P. for Simcoe and Cardwell, and Mr. Justice Thomas Ferguson of the Ontario Supreme Court. With this background, it was almost inevitable that three of the Ferguson boys should become lawyers, and that their sister Emily should show a decided flair for legal and political matters, together with a high degree of Irish combativeness in all spheres of activity.

The Ferguson family was comfortably well-to-do, and Emily attended Bishop Strachan School in Toronto, while her brothers went

[1]Her life and career have been described in detail in an official biography by Byrne Hope Sanders, *Emily Murphy, Crusader* (Toronto, 1945).

to Upper Canada College. At 19 she married, for love as well as suitably, a young Anglican minister named Arthur Murphy. They spent several years in western Ontario, raising a family of three daughters as they moved from one parish to another. Arthur Murphy for a while seemed headed for a bishopric, and Emily for a serene existence as his consort. Then all changed. Arthur, whose spirit was fundamentally restless, "heeded a call" in 1894 to become a mission preacher. At first the family travelled about Huron Diocese, as Arthur preached salvation for periods of two weeks at a time in one parish after another. His success was such that he was invited to continue his activities in England. Two years were spent in this work in southern England before the family returned to Canada in 1900, settling in Toronto.

All went well after the return, at the outset at least. Arthur continued his missions, travelling about Canada; Emily sometimes accompanied him, and sometimes she remained in Toronto where she had become an active journalist, contributing to a new periodical, the *National Monthly*, and publishing in 1901 a book of her travel sketches, entitled *Janey Canuck Abroad* (she was now regularly using Janey Canuck as a pen-name). Her writing was lively, literate, and perceptive, but sentimental and mannered somewhat in the style of "Elizabeth" (the author of *Elizabeth and Her German Garden*, a favourite book of the turn of the century). The resemblance is accentuated by Emily's weakness for pet names; her clerical husband was always referred to in her volumes as the "Padre." But since she accepted "Dear Old Girl," and "Tubbie"—she was short and plump—honours may be considered even.

Then a series of misfortunes befell the family. Arthur Murphy contracted typhoid, and since he had been weakened by overwork, his illness was serious and his recovery was slow. Simultaneously, the British missionary society that employed him ran out of funds and his income terminated with his appointment. Then Emily herself succumbed to typhoid, and when she was not yet fully herself again, her youngest daughter died of diphtheria. After this blow, the Murphys decided to move west to Manitoba, where Arthur, giving up the ministry for the time being, might improve both his health and his fortunes by developing a timber-limit he had acquired in the Swan River region.

The sudden precipitation of the Murphy family, with its background of education, culture, and moderate luxury into a Manitoba pioneer community in 1903 could not surprise anyone familiar with social patterns in the Canadian West in the first decades of this century. The most unusual personalities were washed up on the shores of remote Western communities—concert pianists, opera singers, portrait painters, authors, very often engaged in fantastically unsuitable occupations. The Murphys, however, reacted vigorously to the stimulus of the new environment. Arthur cruised his timber-limits, Emily and the two daughters explored the community on horseback, and Emily reviewed dozens of books for the *Winnipeg Telegram*.

Although the family had made a successful adjustment to Manitoba, Arthur Murphy was attracted by regions still farther west, and in 1907 the family moved on to Edmonton, leaving behind to memorialize them in Swan River a community skating-rink donated by Arthur and a new hospital which was the fruit of a campaign led by Emily. Edmonton was henceforward home for the Murphys. With enough money (at least in the boom days), an excellent family background, a rising literary reputation, and her own originality and sparkle, Emily opened up like a flower and was soon in the centre of social activity in this lively western city. At the same time, she began to go about the province, sometimes accompanying her husband on business trips (he was engaged in land deals and coal-mining operations), and sometimes by herself looking for material for newspaper or magazine articles. She put together enough material for three more books of sketches, published in 1910, 1912, and 1914. She rapidly became involved in women's activities of all kinds, from church organizations to hospital boards to visiting jails to the women's franchise association; she found a multitude of causes to assist, and friends easily enlisted to help her to support them. Many of these causes had legal or political aspects, and she began to spend a good deal of time looking into statutes, attending the law courts, and listening to sessions in the legislature—all of them occupations congenial and familiar to one with her family background.

Emily's first major "cause" in the field of politics was in behalf of married women's property rights. In the new province of Alberta, so recently carved out of the Northwest Territories, these rights were literally non-existent, because of the custom of early fur-traders and settlers of forming alliances with Indian women, who were hardly in a position to know what their rights should be. Emily's lobbying was so effective that the *Edmonton Journal* prophesied:

Mrs Murphy is so much in earnest over the bill, that its success is as good as accomplished. It may not be this year, nor the next, but this leader of women will keep hammering away until even the most obstinate man will be convinced that it is best to withdraw quietly and without further ado, and let down the bars.[2]

The Alberta legislature passed the Dower Act in 1911.

The appointment that changed Emily Murphy's life came in 1916, and it turned her finally away from journalism and literature to public service. In that year, the same in which women were enfranchised in the province of Alberta, two Edmonton women, despatched by the Law Committee of the Local Council of Women to observe the trial of a group of prostitutes rounded up under circumstances that aroused suspicion, were asked by Crown Counsel to leave the court, on the ground that the evidence in such cases was unsuitable to be heard by a mixed audience. When the ruffled ladies asked Mrs. Murphy's advice, she suggested that they accept their ejection but press for the establishment of a women's court to try cases involving women. She was immediately entrusted by the Council with the job of heading the campaign for it. The result was unexpected. The Attorney-General of Alberta not only acceded to the proposal for a women's court, but asked Emily to become its first magistrate. Mrs. Emily Murphy, sworn in in June of 1916, was the first woman in the British Empire to occupy the post of police magistrate.

While the appointment was applauded enthusiastically by Emily's friends and by feminists everywhere, including some who were still labouring for provincial enfranchisement for themselves, the new magistrate met with rather less than enthusiasm among her colleagues in the courts. During her first day in court, the counsel for one defendant objected to the magistrate's jurisdiction, on the ground that a woman is not a "person" under the British North America Act of 1867. During succeeding months, the point was brought up again from time to time in her court, and argued by counsel, with the judge taking note of their objections, and then proceeding placidly with her judgment. In December of 1916, however, Mrs. Alice Jamieson was appointed magistrate in Calgary, and one of her cases was shortly

2Quoted in B. H. Sanders, *Emily Murphy*, p. 122.

appealed on the grounds of a woman magistrate's qualification. This case was taken to the Supreme Court of Alberta, where Mr. Justice Scott ruled:

... applying the general principle on which the common law rests, namely of reason and good sense, as applied to new conditions, there is at common law no legal disqualification for holding public office in the Government of this country arising from any distinction of sex.[3]

During the years following her appointment as magistrate, Mrs. Murphy managed to find time, in addition to her work in court, to become, among other things, President of the Canadian Women's Press Club, Vice-President of the National Council of Women, and first President of the Federated Women's Institutes of Canada. It was in the latter capacity that she inspired a unanimous resolution from the Institutes in 1919 requesting the Canadian government to appoint a woman to the Senate. The National Council of Women forwarded a similar resolution in that year—which was still two years before women voted generally in a federal election.

The idea of promoting Mrs. Murphy herself as the desired appointee began with a resolution forwarded to the Hon. Arthur Meighen, Prime Minister of Canada, from the Montreal Women's Club in 1921. The president of this organization, Mrs. Isabella Scott, was a dedicated feminist, whose fighting spirit never diminished despite her inability to secure a vote for herself in the province of Quebec. Furthermore, the secretary of the Montreal Club was Mrs. Gertrude Budd, a former Calgarian, who was well aware of the controversy and sniping that preceded Mr. Justice Scott's judgment that in Alberta (at least) women were persons. Mrs. Budd now wrote to Mrs. Murphy the following letter:

We women here want you in the Senate because you are a woman and a worthy representative. In fact, in all of Canada, we feel there is no other to equal Judge Murphy for the appointment. . . . With very best wishes and trust it will not be too long before you are notified that you are going to be "laid on the shelf" with the other Senators, but hoping of course, that you will not be too quiet, I am,

Sincerely and affectionately,
GERTRUDE E. BUDD.[4]

[3]From the Murphy Papers, quoted by Catherine L. Cleverdon in *The Woman Suffrage Movement in Canada* (Toronto, 1950), p. 142.
[4]*Ibid.*, p. 143.

Her biographer records that to this letter in Emily Murphy's papers was pinned a note in Emily's own handwriting saying this was "how it started."

Mr. Meighen's reply to the request of the Montreal Women's Club stated that he had been advised by the Department of Justice that the appointment of a woman was impossible under the British North America Act. However, he was sufficiently impressed by their urging that during the campaign for the general election of 1921 which followed, he promised that he would seek on re-election to have women admitted to the Senate. As he lost the election, he was not called on to redeem this promise.

But the matter was not allowed to drop. During the next five years, the government was frequently petitioned by women's organizations to make the appointment. Hopes rose when Mr. Mackenzie King promised his support in a letter to Mrs. Murphy in 1922, and when Senator A. McCoig gave notice in 1923 of a motion for an amendment to the B.N.A. Act to permit admission of women to the Senate. But Senator McCoig did not proceed with his motion, and Mr. King took no action, although he did assure the Women's Canadian Club in Calgary in 1924 that he would pursue the matter. In 1924, also, the National Council of Women sent a delegation to Ottawa to urge the appointment of a woman senator, a plea that was renewed in 1927 and 1928.

By this time Emily Murphy's fighting blood was up. She was in regular correspondence with her lawyer brothers, one of whom had now become a judge of the Supreme Court of Ontario, regarding the legal aspects of the problem. The B.N.A. Act was ambiguous, indeed inconsistent, in its use of the third person pronoun. Section 21 of the Act, which describes the composition of the Senate, contains nothing to bar females from membership, but Section 23, which describes the qualifications of a Senator, uses only the masculine pronoun. Section 24, the key section, reads:

The Governor-General shall from Time to Time, in the Queen's Name, by Instrument under the Great Seal of Canada, summon qualified Persons to the Senate; and, subject to the Provisions of this Act, every Person so summoned shall become and be a Member of the Senate and a Senator.

The question then was whether women were Persons as conceived under the Act.

Emily's brother William, Mr. Justice Ferguson, suggested that a simple method of resolving the matter would be for the government to go ahead and appoint Emily to the Senate, whereupon the Senate could, if it wished, question her right to sit by reference to the Privileges Committee. However, this ex post facto method of dealing with the issue did not appeal to the government, and the petitioning continued. Then Judge Ferguson drew to Emily's attention Section 60 of the Supreme Court Act, which provides that any five interested persons may petition for an order-in-council directing the Supreme Court of Canada to rule on a constitutional point in the B.N.A. Act. Indeed, if the government considered the matter important enough, the legal costs could be defrayed at public expense. Emily made her application for leave to present such a petition, and was successful.

She had now to find the other four "interested persons," to associate with herself in the case. After careful consideration, she made her choice. All four women selected were residents of Alberta, but were so well known throughout Canada that residence in the province could hardly have been the first criterion. Their presence in Alberta at the same time demonstrates once again the extraordinarily interesting and colourful population of the West at this period. Three of the women lived in rural or semi-rural small communities, and yet held posts in national organizations.

Emily's first choice was a friend and colleague. To Edmonton in December of 1914 had come Nellie Mooney McClung, novelist, suffragette, and temperance worker. She was born in Chatsworth, Ontario, in 1874, of Irish and Scottish parentage, but the family moved to Wawanesa, Manitoba, when Nellie was only six years old. At first there was not even a school in the neighbourhood for her to go to, and she had in all only six years of schooling, including a year at the Normal School in Winnipeg, before she began to teach in Manitou, at the age of 16.[5] When she was 19, Nellie married Robert Wesley McClung, a pharmacist, and the young couple opened a drugstore in Manitou and began to raise a family, eventually of five children. Encouraged by her mother-in-law, Mrs. J. A. McClung, a veteran of the W.C.T.U., Nellie began to write. At first she sold short stories

[5] Her childhood in Manitoba and her experiences as a schoolteacher are delightfully recorded in her autobiography, *Clearing in the West* (Toronto, 1935). She recorded her later life in *The Stream Runs Fast* (Toronto, 1945).

to Methodist Sunday School publications, but in 1908 her first novel, *Sowing Seeds in Danny* (really a series of fictional episodes based on her schoolteaching experiences) was published, and became a best-seller in both Canada and the United States. It ran ultimately into seventeen editions, and is reported to have sold in all more than 100,000 copies, probably making Mrs. McClung Canada's first best-selling author. The book was largely a temperance tract, sentimental and moralistic in the fashion of the time, but it had wit, human understanding, and delightful dialogue. Mrs. J. A. McClung persuaded her daughter-in-law, who had so suddenly blossomed into a noted woman author, to "give readings" from the book in aid of the W.C.T.U. Home for Friendless Girls in Winnipeg, and thus launched her on a public career. For Nellie McClung had found that she could move audiences to laughter and tears, as well as charm them from the printed page. She tells how she made this discovery during an address of welcome to delegates at a W.C.T.U. conference:

For the first time I knew the power of speech. I saw faces brighten, eyes glisten, and felt the atmosphere crackle with a new power. I saw what could be done with words, for I had the vision of a new world as I talked. . . . We believed we could shape the world nearer to our heart's desire if we had a dry Canada and that, we felt would come, if and when women were allowed to vote. We did not believe that women would ever become drinkers. . . .[6]

In 1911, Wesley McClung sold his drugstore in Manitou, which had flourished only too well, so that he was exhausted with long hours and overwork, and entered the insurance business in Winnipeg. Nellie joined the Winnipeg branch of the Canadian Women's Press Club, and plunged into the woman suffrage movement in Manitoba. She was one of the first fifteen members of the Winnipeg Political Equality League, which in the five years of its existence, from 1912 to 1916, provided by far the most spectacular suffragette campaigning ever seen in Canada. Compared with the exploits of the British women who chained themselves to park railings, insulted cabinet ministers, cast themselves under the hooves of police horses, and went on hunger-strikes in prison, Canadian suffragettes were generally none too colourful, with the notable exception of the Winnipeggers.

Since a provincial election was in prospect in Manitoba, the Political

[6]*The Stream Runs Fast*, p. 61.

Equality League solicited the support of the leaders of the political parties. First Nellie herself tackled Sir Rodmond Roblin, the Conservative premier, and offered him the opportunity of inserting into his election platform this popular plank. Roblin looked up at her and said:

"What in the world do women want to vote for? Why do women want to mix in the hurly-burly of politics? My mother was the best woman in the world, and she certainly never wanted to vote! I respect women," he went on, "I honor and reverence women, I lift my hat when I meet a woman.... Now you forget all this nonsense about women voting," he went on in his suavest tones. "You're a fine, smart young woman, I can see that. And take it from me, nice women don't want the vote."[7]

The Political Equality League had enrolled in its ranks practically all the newspaperwomen in Winnipeg, and did not lack therefore for publicity; its major exploits were reported even in the Government newspaper, the *Telegram.* The League printed banners and decorated Winnipeg street-cars with them; it had a booth at the Stampede in August (in those days Winnipeg was thought to be far enough west to be entitled to hold an annual stampede), where it distributed pamphlets, collected signatures to a petition, and made speeches, not all of which were politely received. Speakers were despatched wherever requested from a central bureau set up by Lillian Beynon Thomas, well-known Winnipeg newspaperwoman.

The highlight of the campaign, however, was unquestionably the skit staged in the Walker Theatre on January 28, 1914. The idea of a mock parliament was not a new one, but can seldom have been used more effectively. Plans were carefully laid. On the day before the play, the afternoon of January 27, a delegation from the Political Equality League presented its case for the enfranchisement of women to the Manitoba Legislative Assembly, meeting in Committee of the Whole, with Premier Roblin in the chair. The members of the delegation spoke in turn to the packed House and galleries, stating their case as eloquently as they could, and when they had finished, Sir Rodmond rose to reply. Nellie was in a panic lest a last-minute conversion should take the flavour out of their skit, but the old orator did not fail them. Nellie sat "with every fibre of my brain stretched to absorb his diction and the exact tones of his voice. He was making the speech that I would make in the play in less than thirty-six hours."

[7]*Ibid.*, p. 107.

He told us how he loved his mother, and for her sweet sake, reverenced all women. The present status of women was highly satisfactory. Noble characters had been produced. "Any civilization," he said, "which has produced the noble women I see before me, is good enough for me. . . . Gentle woman, queen of the home . . . set apart, by her great function of motherhood. . . . And you say women are the equal of men." He paused here dramatically, blowing himself up like a balloon and shouted at us: "I tell you you are wrong. You do your sex an injustice which I shall not allow to pass unchallenged. Women are superior to men, now and always!"

He never had a closer listener in his life. . . . I could hardly wait to get home and practice it all before a mirror. . . . I had had two good observers in the audience, Wes and Jack [her son], who was then seventeen, and so I tried my speech on them and received their contributions gladly.[8]

Most of the people who thronged into the Walker Theatre on the evening of January 28 had been present or knew what had taken place in the legislature on the previous afternoon, and hence fully appreciated the irony when Nellie, as the mock premier, welcomed a delegation of men seeking "votes for men" from a parliament composed of women. She praised their manly beauty: "Any system of civilization that can produce such splendid specimens . . . is good enough for me, and if it is good enough for me it is good enough for anybody."[9] "Premier" McClung continued, as reported in the *Winnipeg Free Press*:

Another trouble is that if men start to vote, they will vote too much. Politics unsettles men, and unsettled men mean unsettled bills—broken furniture, broken vows and—divorce. . . . It has been charged that politics is corrupt. I do not know how this report got out but I do most emphatically deny it. I have been in politics for a long time and I never knew of any division of public money among the Members of the House, and you may be sure, if anything of that kind had been going on, I should have been in on it. Ladies and gentlemen, what I mean is that I would have known about it.[10]

The point of the jest was reinforced several months later, when members of Sir Rodmond Roblin's government (but not Sir Rodmond himself, to be fair) were placed on trial for misappropriation of funds in connection with the construction of the Parliament Buildings in Winnipeg. The scandal toppled the Roblin Government.

On January 27, 1916, under the aegis of the new Liberal Govern-

8*Ibid.*, pp. 115–16.   9*Ibid.*, p. 117.
10*Ibid.*, pp. 121–22.

ment headed by T. C. Norris, a bill to grant suffrage to women passed the Manitoba legislature, and the work of the Political Equality League came to a triumphant conclusion. But by that time the McClung family had been living in Edmonton for more than a year, following the appointment of Wesley McClung to head the branch of his insurance agency in that city, and Nellie was already involved in the woman suffrage campaign in Alberta. She joined forces with Mrs. Murphy, Mrs. H. M. Edwards, Mrs. Jamieson, and other workers, and following a call made by the women upon Premier Sifton the Edmonton *Bulletin* reported the Premier's comment: "Mrs. McClung and Mrs. Murphy are very determined women."[11]

In 1921, Mrs. McClung was elected to the Legislative Assembly of Alberta, one of the five Liberals returned from Edmonton, but found herself seated on the Opposition benches, as the province as a whole swung to the new party, the United Farmers of Alberta. In this same election, Mrs. Louise Crummy McKinney, who had been elected from Claresholm in 1917 (the first woman member of any legislative assembly in the British Empire) was defeated, while Mrs. Irene Parlby of Alix was elected on the U.F.A. ticket and entered the Cabinet as Minister without Portfolio.

Mrs. McClung's career as a suffragette has been dealt with here in some detail not only because it is colourful and interesting and deserves to be remembered, but also because it symbolizes vividly the efforts of many women in many parts of Canada for many years. Let us not put these noble heroines on any chilly pedestal. Perhaps it is about time women gave up the effort to admire the pioneers of woman suffrage as heroines at all—never too easy to do because they and their doings are so easily ridiculed—and instead turned just to envying them for the glorious time they had. Here they were, after centuries of contempt, suppression, even slavery, out of the doll's house at last. They honestly believed that when women got the vote, they would create a better, happier world. This was the refrain, "When women have the vote . . ." They did not want the franchise in order to satisfy any personal ambitions or longing for power, but for the sake of the good that might be done. Those of us who are disillusioned about the possibility of reaching some of their objectives, and about the worth of some of the causes they espoused, and who also at times forget how

[11]C. L. Cleverdon, *The Woman Suffrage Movement in Canada*, p. 117.

much of what they fought for is now incorporated in our legislation, can still admire and envy the whole-hearted zeal with which they petitioned, held meetings, passed resolutions, and wrote letters and letters and more letters. To quote again from Nellie McClung (not that she worked harder than many others, but she put it into words):

That summer of 1914 ran like a torrent. Each day was full of excitement— meetings, interviews, statements, contradictions, and through it all the consuming conviction that we were actually making history. I do not think that any of us ever felt either tired or discouraged. Every day felt like the day before Christmas.[12]

Heady stuff!

The second of the four persons selected by Emily Murphy to sign the petition with her was Louise McKinney of Claresholm, ex-M.L.A., who was even more widely known as a temperance campaigner than as a politician. She began her public career as a W.C.T.U. organizer, and was president of the Dominion W.C.T.U. when she died. It is a little hard to present with full sympathy the devotion of women such as Mrs. McKinney to the temperance cause, since it includes a degree of what seems to be fanaticism—such as her efforts to prevent the sending of cigarettes and tobacco to the men in the trenches in World War I. (What a pity it is that so many of those earnest souls who campaigned against the evils of tobacco are not here to read the current medical literature on the subject!) But we have to consider this seeming fanaticism in the context of the times. Most women, no matter how sheltered their lives had been, had seen for themselves the effects of intemperance on the home, and it was not a long step for them to visualize the "liquor traffic" as a kind of super-Mafia. Smoking was another bad habit which they confidently thought could be eliminated by legislation. To take part in the temperance crusade provided a superb training for suffragettes, and since it was well understood that "when women had the vote," Demon Rum would be downed once and for all time, the co-operation and support of the W.C.T.U. in woman suffrage activities was most natural. Nellie McClung was a stout advocate of temperance all her life, although she managed to smile a bit about her own views towards the end. Louise McKinney may, however, have felt that Emily Murphy's Anglican broadmindedness had carried her a bit too far when Emily

12*The Stream Runs Fast,* p. 134.

contributed a statement to a pamphlet issued by the Conservative party in 1926 which included the following paragraph:

Before Government Control became the law of Alberta, I opposed it vigorously, both on the platform and by my pen. It seemed only logical that if the restrictions were removed there would be more drunkenness and crime. No living person could persuade me to the contrary. I had a fine line of arguments on the subject, too . . . I am bound to acknowledge that my fears were largely unfounded.[13]

Louise McKinney's political background was interesting. Although born in Ontario (at Frankville, in 1868), she had taught school in North Dakota, settling in Claresholm, Alberta, following her marriage. She was possibly in touch with political movements in North Dakota, but when the Non-Partisan League, an agrarian movement which advocated public ownership of farmers' utilities such as grain elevators and flour mills, spread into Saskatchewan and Alberta from North Dakota in 1916, Mrs. McKinney became a prominent member. She was elected to the Alberta legislature in 1917 as one of the League's two successful candidates. Subsequently the League was absorbed into the burgeoning United Farmers of Alberta, but Mrs. McKinney, along with one or two other ex-Partisans, did not see eye to eye with the U.F.A. president, Henry Wise Wood, on the rôle which the U.F.A. should play in politics. Wood prevailed, temporarily, and when Mrs. McKinney was defeated in 1921, she did not run again. In joining the progressive movement, Mrs. McKinney was carrying into the political sphere the crusading spirit of her temperance activities, only in this case the traditional political parties became the representatives of the "wealthy interests" that were enriching themselves at the expense of the farmer. Thus in Louise McKinney, Emily Murphy had a co-appellant who represented not only the Dominion-wide temperance movement, but the militant agrarian politics of Alberta.

The fourth of the petitioners, Hon. Irene Parlby, was born Irene Marryat in 1878 (she was a relative of the author Frederick Marryat), and spent her girlhood in India and Ireland. She married Walter Parlby on a visit to Alberta in 1896, and, as she often recalled afterwards,

[13]*Temperance vs. Prohibition, Opinions of Judge Emily F. Murphy and Others* (Toronto, issued by the Liberal Conservative Publicity Bureau, 1925).

began her married life in a sod shack. The Parlbys belonged to that group of British expatriates who engaged in ranching in Alberta in the province's early years, and who, leaving behind the comforts and culture of civilization, enjoyed the beauty and freedom of the new land. As Mrs. Parlby said in a radio broadcast in 1938: "First of all I think came the exhilarating feeling of living where the world was really young, where there were no people crowding in on you with their miserable, silly little conventions and pettinesses and prejudices, and all the other barnacles people grow when they congregate together in a community." Mrs. Parlby entered politics through her efforts to improve the lot of the lonely rural women of Alberta; as secretary of the Alix Countrywoman's Club, she was sent as a delegate to the U.F.A. convention in Calgary in 1916, and suddenly found herself president of the women's branch of that organization.[14] Although she never held a portfolio in the government after her election in 1921, Mrs. Parlby was generally consulted when matters relating to health and welfare were under discussion, and Nellie McClung mentions that during the time they both sat in the legislature, even though they belonged to opposing parties, they were in accord on most matters affecting women. The inclusion of Mrs. Parlby as a co-appellant signified the support of the Government of the Province of Alberta, which was undoubtedly an important factor in securing the co-operation of the Government at Ottawa.

The fifth appellant, Mrs. Henrietta Muir Edwards, was by many years the senior of the five women; she had been born in Montreal in 1849, and moved to Macleod, Alberta, after her marriage. She and her sister organized the Working Girls' Association in Montreal in 1875, a forerunner of the Y.W.C.A., and edited a paper, *The Working Woman of Canada*, which was one of the first of its kind. She was later connected with the Y.W.C.A., but her main career as a feminist was through her work with the National Council of Women, of which she was for thirty-five years convener of the standing committee on laws affecting women and children. As a result she was instrumental in securing much of the legislation which improved social conditions over this period. In the course of her activities, she compiled two standard works on the legal status of women, one for the Province of

14"The Honourable Irene Parlby," unpublished thesis by Clare Mary McKinlay, B.A., University of Alberta, 1953. A microfilm is in the Public Archives, Ottawa.

Alberta and another for the Dominion of Canada. She had been associated with the other appellants in delegations to the Alberta Government during the agitation for woman franchise in that province. Mrs. Edwards brought to the Persons Case the prestige she had established during her long association with the National Council of Women, and, of course, the implicit support of that organization— which had, indeed, already expressed its views directly many times on the question of the admission of women to the Canadian Senate, both by resolution and by personal delegation.

The petition, signed by Mrs. Murphy and her four colleagues, was forwarded to Ottawa at the end of August 1927. In a gesture of self-effacement, Emily Murphy arranged for the signatures of the five persons to be appended in alphabetical order, with the result that Mrs. Edwards' name appeared first, and the case was then and afterwards referred to as *Edwards v. Attorney General of Canada*. From this distance, we can regret it. Emily Murphy's generous impulse led to confusion and embarrassment, despite the ready acknowledgment of the other four women that the chief credit belonged to Mrs. Murphy.

The case reached the Supreme Court in the following March. Hon. Lucien Cannon, K.C., Solicitor-General of Canada, led the counsel supporting the Department of Justice's ruling. The case for the appellants was argued by Hon. Newton Wesley Rowell, who had already demonstrated, as leader of the Liberal Opposition in the Ontario legislature in 1916 and 1917, his advocacy of woman suffrage. The Government of the Province of Quebec indicated its stand on the question by appointing a special counsel to assist the Crown, and the Province of Alberta confirmed its support of the petitioners by asking Mr. Rowell to represent it also.

The most telling points made by Mr. Rowell were based on the Interpretation Act of 1850 and the Dominion Elections Act of 1920. The Interpretation Act, also known as Lord Brougham's Act, was in force at the time of the passage of the B.N.A. Act by the British Parliament, and it provided that in all acts words referring to the masculine gender should also be taken to refer to the feminine gender, unless an exception were expressly stated. Then, too, when the Dominion Elections Act was passed in 1920 by the Parliament of Canada, "persons" in Section 41 of the B.N.A. Act had been interpreted to include females.

The chief argument of the Crown was that the B.N.A. Act must be interpreted precisely as it was intended in the period when the Act was passed, and since women held no public office of any kind in Canada in 1867, the Fathers of Confederation could have had no intention of including women among the "persons" qualified to be summoned to the Senate.

After considering the matter for six weeks, Chief Justice Anglin delivered the judgment of the Court, which substantially took the view of the Crown counsel: under the B.N.A. Act, women were not eligible for appointment to the Senate. The disappointment of the "five persons" may well be imagined. Granted that on the day the decision was read, Hon. Ernest Lapointe, Minister of Justice, stated in the House that the Government would take steps at once to have the B.N.A. Act amended, the difficulties of securing such amendment were considerable. To begin with, there was the well-known objection of the Province of Quebec to any such amendment. Second, there was the possible opposition of the Senate itself, and if it dissented, it might not be possible to secure the joint address of both Houses required for amendment of the constitution. In order not to discourage the Government in any action it might seriously contemplate, Emily Murphy said nothing about her intentions until after Parliament had prorogued, but immediately that had occurred, without any steps being taken to implement Mr. Lapointe's promise, the five persons requested an order-in-council giving them leave to appeal to His Majesty's Privy Council in London. The request was granted, and the Department of Justice co-operated further by consenting to pay the costs of the action. Rowell agreed to take the case again, the Government of Alberta sent along its own Attorney-General to assist him, and even Premier Taschereau of Quebec relented and withdrew his counsel from the case.

The Persons Case was argued for four days in London in July of 1929 before the Judicial Committee of the Privy Council. The Canadian Press carried an account by Lukin Johnston, an eye-witness:

In a quiet room at Number One, Downing Street, five great judges, with the Lord Chancellor of England at their head, and a battery of bewigged lawyers from Canada and from England, are wrestling with a question, propounded on behalf of their sex, by five Alberta women. . . . Deep and intricate questions of constitutional law are debated back and forth. The exact shade of meaning to be placed on certain words is argued to the finest point. . . . And so it goes on, and probably will continue to go on for several days. At the end of all these endless speeches, lessons on Canadian history, and questions by five great judges of England, it will be decided, if one may hazard a guess, that women undoubtedly are Persons. Which one may say, without exaggeration, most of us know already![15]

The judgment of the Privy Council, delivered by Lord Sankey on October 18, 1929, reversed the Canadian Supreme Court decision. The Judicial Committee took the view that the constitution should be interpreted according to the custom of the times, and custom had indeed changed. The law lords considered the wording of the B.N.A. Act with regard to "persons" was ambiguous, and supported Mr. Rowell's contention that the Interpretation Act was applicable. The judgment concluded:

Their lordships have come to the conclusion that the word persons includes members of the male and female sex, and that therefore the question propounded by the Governor-General must be answered in the affirmative; and that women are eligible to be summoned and become members of the Senate of Canada.

The Gilbertian overtones of the case of the "five persons" have not lost their power to raise a smile with the passing of the decades, and the wrangling of the learned counsel about the ambiguity of the pronouns of the B.N.A. Act seems no less amusing to us now than it did to Emily Murphy and her colleagues. But if we put to one side the legal ponderosities and ineffabilities of the judgment, it seems apparent that the Judicial Committee came to the practical conclusion that the admission of women to the Senate was desired by the majority of Canadians.[16] Without belittling in any way the effort made by Emily Murphy herself in the endless correspondence, the poring over statutes, and the conferring with legal counsel on constitutional technicalities, we must recognize that no small part in bringing about final success was the building up of a favourable climate of opinion by women's organizations all across Canada, together with the persistent lobbying that finally convinced the Government of the day that a large body of electors desired the change. The same unwearying enthusiasm and

[15]B. H. Sanders: *Emily Murphy*, pp. 243–44.
[16]The judgment has been severely criticized by some authorities in constitutional law for advancing a new principle of interpretation which views the constitution as "a living tree," in the words of Lord Sankey.

dogged unremitting effort had brought success to the Political Equality League in Winnipeg in 1916–17, and to other organizations in other areas during that crucial decade. The impetus provided by the petition of the five persons was, however, needed to overcome the legal quibble without the prolonged negotiation involved in a constitutional amendment. In evaluating their achievement, it should be noted that women did not secure the right to take their seats (theirs by inheritance) in the House of Lords until twenty-eight years after the decision of the Judicial Committee admitted Canadian women to the Senate.

Was the prize worth the struggle? One might not think so, in view of the continuous downgrading of the Senate by political writers and the press. But the fact remains that the 72 seats in the Canadian Senate are the objects of intense desire by a surprisingly large number of Canadian citizens. The dignity of the title, in a country which has few titles, plus the income for life, makes a summons to the Senate highly prized, and with these perquisites, the appointees seem not to find it too hard to bear the mild persiflage that follows any Senate appointment. But whether many Canadian women really yearn to be summoned to be Senators or not, it was important that the legal disability with regard to their sex should be removed promptly in this as in other areas of politics. It would have remained as a cause of exacerbation until it was ended—a psychological barrier at least to women taking an equal place in the political arena.

Needless to say, Emily Murphy's friends and supporters fully expected that the leader of the five persons would be appointed to the first vacancy in the Senate. This did not occur. Whether the omission reflected resentment of her persistence is impossible to say. Considering the load of tradition encumbering Senate appointments, it may not be too surprising that Emily did not qualify in the eyes of two successive prime ministers of opposing political parties. A prime minister, whose prerogative these appointments are, finds many candidates eager for a few places, and in addition must keep in mind the necessity of providing comfortable stalls for worn-out party hacks, and even, on occasion, for political mavericks who are embarrassing their colleagues. He may also receive such requests as one found by Professor F. A. Kunz in the Meighen Papers:

"My daughters," an ambitious mother wrote to Senator Meighen, "are both married. May I dream of reaching to the Upper House, Ottawa?" To this a remarkably patient Meighen sent the following coolly correct answer: "A Senate seat is a legitimate aspiration of any Canadian."[17]

Mrs. Murphy was a Conservative, and at the time of the Privy Council decision a Liberal government was in power in Ottawa. There have been very few occasions in Canadian history when a member of the opposing political party has been summoned to the Senate. Perhaps this should have been one. Be that as it may, Mackenzie King did appoint a woman Senator in 1931, Mrs. Cairine Wilson, who was not only prominent in women's organizations but a Liberal party-worker. After the defeat of the King Government in 1931, Hon. R. B. Bennett, a Calgary lawyer, became Prime Minister. As Bennett had sponsored Emily's Dower Act in the Alberta House many years before, it might be assumed that he was favourably disposed towards her, and when the Senator for Edmonton died in the January following Mr. Bennett's accession to office, the way seemed cleared for Emily's entrance to the Senate Chamber. However, the appointment had traditionally been made from among Alberta's large Roman Catholic minority, and Mr. Bennett decided not to break with tradition in Emily's favour.

Perhaps the appointment might eventually have come—some aspirants have had to bide for a decade or more—but Emily was not able to wait. She retired from her post as police magistrate in October of 1931, and died suddenly two years later. Both Mrs. McKinney and Mrs. Edwards died in 1931, and thus only Nellie McClung and Hon. Irene Parlby were living when a plaque in honour of the five persons was unveiled in the lobby of the Senate Chamber in Ottawa on June 11, 1938.[18] The campaign waged by the Business and Professional Women's Club in order to achieve this modest memorial would have appealed to Emily Murphy. Thick files in the Public Archives attest to the effort that was required to bring it about, and there are letters in these files, with well-known signatures attached, that would have brought a reminiscent smile to Emily Murphy's face. At one stage the tablet seemed destined to be relegated to the Archives, but the intervention of Senator Dandurand finally resolved the matter; he thus made gallant amends for the opposition of Quebec to the petition of the five persons in the previous decade.

[17]*The Modern Senate of Canada, 1925–1963: A Re-appraisal* (Toronto, 1965).
[18]Mrs. McClung died in Victoria in 1951; Mrs. Parlby lived to the age of 97 and died in Alberta in 1965.

How to give the leader of the five persons just credit in view of the alphabetic order of the names on the original petition was a special difficulty for the committee in charge, but was happily solved in the inscription, which reads:

This Tablet is placed here
by the
Canadian Federation of Business and
Professional Women's Clubs

To Honour

Mrs. Henrietta Muir Edwards,	Macleod
Magistrate Emily F. Murphy,	Edmonton
Mrs. Nellie L. McClung,	Edmonton
Mrs. Louise C. McKinney	Claresholm
Honourable Irene Parlby,	Alix

All of the Province of Alberta

To further the cause of womankind these five
outstanding pioneer women caused steps to be taken
resulting in the recognition by the Privy Council of
women as persons eligible for appointment to the
Senate of Canada

This movement was inaugurated by
Magistrate Emily F. Murphy

10

Agnes Macphail
1890-1954

DORIS FRENCH

In the early spring of 1940, a tall, grim-faced, grey-haired woman, with the long stride of the country-bred, marched up the front steps of the majestic stone building which houses Canada's parliament. She went directly, avoiding the quick smiles of recognition, the attempted greetings of bystanders, to a sixth-floor office which still bore her name on the door panel. A federal election had just been held. The Commons was not yet back in session. Few were about. She proceeded, tight-lipped, to empty her desk and gather her belongings.

Inevitably, a reporter had spotted her coming in, and the phone rang.

"My comments on the election? It wasn't fair. It was called without warning and under the worst possible weather conditions. Try getting out the farm vote through twelve-foot snowdrifts! What I intend to do now is get myself a job! How can I possibly know what I'm going to do? What have I got left to do?"

And she banged the receiver down, as for eighteen years she had wanted to bang receivers, on the insensitive, baiting members of the press.

Agnes Campbell Macphail had passed her fiftieth birthday during that election campaign. As a parliamentarian she was in top form. She was in great vogue throughout Canada and the United States as a public speaker, renowned for her platform wit, her compelling demand for social reform in Canada and peace abroad.

It was the outbreak of war which had defeated her at the polls, though the twelve-foot drifts certainly had cut her support among the farmers of Grey-Bruce constituency in western Ontario. For years Agnes Macphail had, in her usual hell-for-leather style, denounced war and the preparations for war. She had taken particular aim at cadet training in the schools, supported by federal funds, and annually in parliament had moved to do away with this programme, making her speech a tirade against those who had grown faint-hearted in support of the League of Nations.

Now war had come. And with the greatest reluctance, with a sense of soul-shaking depression, Agnes had changed her mind and decided, along with the majority of the C.C.F. party with which she was closely tied, that Hitler must be defeated before Europe was over-run. She had campaigned in a mood of bitter dejection. And the rural voters had turned back to the Liberals, partly because they felt the need of a strong government to conduct the war, and partly to keep out the Conservatives, who just might resort to the measure they feared most—conscription. The C.C.F. founder and leader, J. S. Woodsworth, whom Agnes deeply admired and respected, had broken with his party and held to his pacifist conviction.

The whole world was going up in flames, the long hard struggle for greater human opportunity and welfare seemed swept aside, personal loyalties were broken. And the voters of Grey-Bruce—*her* people—had turned her out of office. For Agnes Macphail, on that March day in 1940, her life and work seemed finished and judged worthless.

She was the first woman elected to Canada's parliament. More than any of the twenty women Members since, she made politics her career, and parliament her home.

Yet it had all come about a step at a time, and as a child, the oldest daughter of a backwoods Ontario farmer, born in a log farmhouse and educated in a little rural school, nothing could have seemed less probable. When she looked back in later life she was inclined to credit her success to her Scottish blood. She visited the small Scottish village of Kilmartin, near the Firth of Lorne, where her great-grand-father had once been head shepherd on a large estate, and she wrote an autobiographical sketch called "My Ain Folk," tracing her own qualities of stubbornness and strong public spirit to the Campbells and Macphails who were her forebears. The sketch itself came from a need to establish the bonds of family, she who had chosen work instead of marriage, politics instead of a husband and children.

She was born on March 24, 1890, in Proton Township in Grey County. Dougal Macphail, her father, had taken up a farm in the Proton district where her grandfather had homesteaded. When Agnes was twelve they moved to a larger farm with a red-brick two-storey house, near Ceylon. There were two younger sisters, Gertha and Lilly. Dougal became an auctioneer, renowned for his quick wit and persuasive tongue. Agnes remembered: "They used to say he could sell haggis to an Englishman on St. George's Day." Her mother, Henrietta Campbell Macphail, was a strict disciplinarian, a woman who stood by what she believed, an industrious housekeeper. Agnes believed she inherited qualities from both: her father's wit, her mother's tenacity. She summed it up: "I owed it to my father that I was elected to Parliament in the first place, but I owed it to my mother that I stuck it out once I got there."

Even a secondary school education was unusual for a country child in those days, and Agnes spent two years arguing with her parents before she was allowed to proceed to high school in Owen Sound. She was sixteen. In two more years, 1908, she had her junior matriculation and was off to Normal School at Stratford. The height of her ambition was to be a schoolteacher. She later taught in several small country schools and enjoyed teaching as well as boarding with farm families.

She had strong views on the importance of education and she never lost interest in this first phase of her career. When she arrived in Ottawa she made a point each year of inviting the young ladies from the local Normal School to have tea with her on Parliament Hill, while she lectured them on the processes of democratic government. She was always a popular speaker at teachers' conventions and luncheons, and she spoke from a sense of warm identity with them.

But though she was happy and proud to be a teacher, she was

ready for the next step when it came. As a teacher she had a certain status not granted to other rural women, and she was drawn into the hotly disputed politics that raged around the 1911 election, fought on the issue of "reciprocity" of trade with the United States. About that time she sent a letter to the *Farmers' Sun*, the organ of the United Farmers of Ontario. She was permitted, again because of her professional status, to become a member of the U.F.O. which, under exceptionally dynamic leadership, was talking of running its own farm candidates in the coming provincial election. Soon she was attending U.F.O. meetings, deeply involved in the lively arguments of the times. At a U.F.O. meeting in 1919, without warning, the chairman recognized Agnes Macphail and asked her to speak. She wanted to refuse. But she had become passionately persuaded that farmers had been silent too long; they must speak and act on their own behalf, if they were to achieve political justice. Obviously she couldn't turn down this challenge. She got to her feet and talked for ten minutes on farm problems. When she finished they cheered her, as much perhaps for her courage as for the words she said.

After that there was no holding back. She spoke at dozens of meetings in support of U.F.O. candidates.

She found herself in December, 1920, appearing before a special commission on tariffs, presided over by the federal Minister of Finance, Sir Henry Drayton. She told him pertly that she had never before stood in the presence of a real knight, she was a plain farmer's daughter. But, she said, she was in a position to know the effect on farmers of the tariff policy, which favoured industry at the expense of agriculture. She knew, for one thing, that it made marrying a farmer a very dubious venture, which she herself refused to embark on. Newsmen covering the drab proceedings of the commission seized on her speech and the story appeared in Toronto papers. Her fame was spreading.

Though the suffragette movement in Canada was now on the point of success, Agnes had never participated in its activities. It was a less flamboyant affair than in England, but a small, dogged Canadian Suffrage Association had presented annual petitions to provincial and federal governments. And World War I had brought the vote to Canadian women as it did to those in Great Britain.

In 1916 the Western provinces granted the female franchise, and in 1917 two women were elected to the Alberta legislature. Ontario passed legislation next. In 1918 the federal government extended the franchise to all women already on provincial voters' lists, and in 1919 followed this up with an act enabling them to seek office as federal candidates.

She had not fought for political rights, but Agnes had no false modesty when some members of the local U.F.O. asked her to run as a federal candidate in Grey-Bruce (then South-East Grey). Her family gave her no encouragement, they felt only doubt and concern. But a strong group of supporters put her name forward at the U.F.O. nominating convention. Several men were also nominated, successive ballotings were held, but her name emerged on top. Even then it was hard for many to accept the result. There were efforts to hold a new convention "in which saner judgment would be possible" as some U.F.O. members said. But Agnes refused to back down. She was by now quite sure she could do as good a job as any of the male candidates. And her determination and obvious appeal to audiences weighed in her favour and brought the united support of the U.F.O. behind her.

Agnes said later that almost any candidate picked by the U.F.O. could have won that election, which was held in December, 1921. The tide of rural revolt was running strong, and the United Farmers of Ontario was joined by the farmers of the West in a national movement they called the Progressive party of Canada. Some sixty Progressives were elected, an unprecedented event in Canadian politics, which had always divided simply into Liberal and Conservative (Grit and Tory) camps. There were many radical opinions among them, but little cohesive direction, and before another election the party had dwindled, with many returning to the Liberal side and others forming a "Ginger Group" which very soon led to the C.C.F.

And so, though it was perhaps true that she owed her first success largely to the wave of strength in the farm movement, this could not be said of the next election test, nor the two after that. Agnes Macphail fought them and won as an Independent, on the force and vigour of her own personality and growing reputation.

When Agnes was elected she recognized the debt she owed the suffragettes, and she took her unique position seriously. She set out to make plain her equality with men in the Commons, never asking for privileges, but insisting on her right to be there: this, she felt, would make things easier for the women Members of the future. She wrote later that the first time she walked the traditional length of corridor to attend the Opening in the Senate Chamber, she was so conscious of leading the way for other women that "I could almost hear them coming."

She was only 31 when she entered the House of Commons. She was a tall, erect young woman, inclined to dress severely, her thick, wavy brown hair shaped close to her head, in the fashion of the twenties. She was sensitive, aware that there were no guide-lines to follow, inclined to be brusque and direct in making up her mind. She was well aware that many considered her a freak, an oddity, and were ready with waspish tongues to criticize whatever she did.

She felt that it was particularly unfair that most women reporters in those first years in Ottawa wrote garbled, careless accounts of her, often spiked with malice. They made her navy serge dress a national joke, finding something hilarious in the fact that she had worn it throughout her campaign and intended to go on wearing it in the House of Commons. As a matter of fact she had chosen it as the most appropriate costume she could think of, in entering what had been a man's world, to take part in what had been man's work. It was carefully made of good wool serge—it was rather a blow to have it ridiculed. And she had decided not to wear a hat; she knew she'd have a headache in no time if she were obliged to sit through a Commons day wearing one. This decision too was treated with great scepticism by the ladies of the press.

In a journal which she kept intermittently in later years she wrote of the ordeal of her early parliamentary life:

The misery of being under observation and being unduly criticized is what I remember most vividly about those first months. Visitors in the Gallery couldn't help seeing one woman among so many men, but they made no effort to disguise the fact that I was a curiosity, and stared whenever I could be seen, in the House, the corridors or the dining room. Eating was the worst; it may be they thought I would eat peas with my knife or cool my tea in my saucer, but for whatever reason I was observed closely. So closely that I lost twelve pounds in the first month I was a Member and after that I ate my food downtown for some months.

Though she was in fact a warm-hearted, friendly person, brought up in a country district that had plenty of social life, she gained a reputation in Ottawa as an austere, sharp-tongued spinster. It was the obvious public reaction to the puritanical, down-to-earth tenor of her first speeches. She insisted, for instance, that people ought to be taxed directly rather than through relatively painless excise and other indirect means. If people knew exactly what they were getting for their money they would accept taxation quite willingly, she declared.

She took the unprecedented step of turning back $1500 of her salary into the public treasury, insisting that $2500 was enough income for anybody. (As a schoolteacher she would have been used to a salary of around $800, and her modest campaign expenses were looked after by the U.F.O.) The Commons had recently raised Members' salaries to $4000, and her first formal motion in the House was to return to the former level. Naturally it was voted down, with a good deal of nasty questioning of motives in the course of the brief debate. Agnes certainly did nothing to endear herself to fellow Members at the beginning of her career.

She was outspoken in her uncompromising view of democracy. Early in the first session she showed her irritation at a discussion of immigration policy when such terms as "common laborers" were tossed about. "We do not sufficiently respect those who toil with their hands!" she said. "I am truly amazed at the sentiments that are expressed by some of our well-groomed, luxuriously-living friends. They evidently have not had their brow wet with sweat for some time!" And she protested a proposal to bring in "servant girls," as though these were a class apart. "If that girl's character and her brains are as good, is she not the equal in every way of the woman of the house who hires a servant simply because her husband is in a financial position to enable her to do so?"

In the beginning she considered herself a champion of the farm people, speaking often of their hard work and great contribution to Canada, the farm women as well as farm men. Soon she was speaking in support of all the welfare measures put forward by the Progressives and presently by the C.C.F.

When Agnes Macphail was elected to Parliament, the phrase "welfare state" was not yet coined. There was no unemployment insurance, no old age or blind person's pension, no family allowance, no government scholarships or support for artists and musicians, no crop failure insurance for farmers, no medical insurance plans. The trade unions were still battling for recognition, with every strike a disastrous encounter with employers who could turn them out at will. As each welfare measure was proposed by the C.C.F. it was denounced as wildly impractical and revolutionary. Dependence on the state is sometimes now deplored, though seldom by the person who faces hard luck and finds a pension there to fill his need. Few, for all their talk, would really choose to go back to the days when an individual was left to cope alone with all the uncertainties of life.

But the coming of the welfare state was not a natural process of evolution. It was fought for tenaciously and in the face of hostile ridicule by a small reform group in the House of Commons. Agnes Macphail stands among them, a strong advocate of co-operative living, of help to those in need, a standard of living sufficient for human dignity and worthy of a young, rich country for which she felt a genuine, unshakable devotion.

Before the end of her first term in parliament she had turned far afield from her prime interest in rural Canada. A strike was on in Glace Bay, Nova Scotia in 1925. It was a particularly bitter strike, a protest against a further wage cut among miners who were already on the bleak edge of poverty. There was much talk of "Red" agitators stirring up trouble. A group of ladies representing a charitable organization visited the place and said the tales of hardship were exaggerated. Sympathy in parliament seemed on the side of the British Empire Steel Corporation which had received the benefits of tariff protection and subsidies.

Agnes Macphail decided to go down to Glace Bay and see for herself. She came back, and made in the course of the budget debate her first major speech in the House of Commons, a compelling, absolutely forthright account of the squalor and injustice she had discovered.

The miners' unions never forgot her intervention on their behalf. She was welcomed in Halifax years later as a friend of the working people. And her name found its way into folk music, a little ballad sung in the late twenties with the opening lines:

> God give us more women like Agnes Macphail;
> When the miners were hungry she never did fail.

She was a strong supporter of the co-operative movement, which in Canada is almost entirely a rural phenomenon. She spent a great deal of time outside the House in helping to organize co-operative stores and marketing agencies in her own riding. During a later period of her life she was a member of the board of directors of the Ontario co-operative union.

Her reputation as a speaker to be reckoned with was well established by the time she moved into her second term in parliament after the elections of 1925 and 1926. By 1927 it was not unusual for a newspaper like the Ottawa *Journal* to publish this editorial tribute: "Miss Macphail's speech had structure and passion, plus a fine and restrained vein of sarcasm, a dancing wit, some passages of pathos, and a deal of good humour. It was far and away the best speech that has been made in the House this year."

She could rip the hide off her opponents when she felt moved to do so. The 1926 election saw the Progressive contingent in the Commons further reduced to 12, Agnes among them. A sizable group of former Progressives now sat on the Liberal benches. Agnes knew very well what blandishments had been used to win them over. She was twice offered a position in Mackenzie King's cabinet if she would switch allegiance.

When the House met after that election she verbally chastised both the renegades and the Liberal politicians who had seduced them. Mitchell Hepburn, later to become Liberal premier of Ontario, was in the Commons at the time and rose after her attack to say that "the forty-minute rule [cutting the length of speeches] was the most humanitarian legislation ever enforced in this House."

For many years she was not accepted by such organizations as the Women's Canadian Club and the I.O.D.E., chiefly because of her outspoken words on militarism and what she called patriotic jingoism. Each year she mounted a bitter protest against cadet training in the schools. It was cruelly dishonest, she said, to glorify the horrible tragedy of war by making it appear so gay and bright and attractive to the young. Instead of cadet training she wanted a peacetime gymnastic programme for boys and girls because, she told the Commons: "Such a system would result in very much improving the health of our school children, and would leave Canada in a perfectly safe position, because if our future citizens have strong, well-developed bodies and unprejudiced and open minds, then Canada need not fear the future." She considered Canada's Royal Military College an outrageous extravagance, dedicated to creating a class of snobs.

She applauded Canada's action in signing the Briand-Kellogg peace pact in 1928, urging the government to go one step further to total disarmament. "I never wanted to be in the Cabinet," she said, "but I would like to be the Minister of Defence for one year, and by that time there would be no need for that department." It was one cabinet post that was never offered her.

From the moment the League of Nations was formed she was an ardent supporter, and a tireless platform speaker for the League of Nations Society. She was the first Canadian woman to go as a delegate to a League of Nations conference, held at Geneva in 1929. She was appointed by Prime Minister Mackenzie King, and was one of a seven-member delegation headed by three cabinet ministers. In Geneva she declined to serve on the Health and Welfare Committee, which to her male colleagues seemed the appropriate place to put a woman. She said she preferred to sit on the committee dealing with disarmament. She had her way, and was the first woman to act as a member of that body.

Also, in Geneva, she put in an embarrassingly low expense account, and other delegates begged her to increase it. She was more frugal with government money than with her own.

A champion of the underprivileged, a spokesman for the farmer, a defender of the industrial worker, an uncompromising advocate of peace—but if Agnes Macphail is remembered for any one contribution to Canada it is her valiant fight for penal reform.

As women M.P.s since her time have discovered, a female parliamentarian is the natural target for everyone in Canada with a hard-luck story. There may be a lingering suspicion that she is an unfeminine creature; nevertheless people in trouble count on her having a soft side more easily touched by tales of misfortune than her male colleagues. Of all the grievances that poured across Agnes's desk, the most shocking were stories of mistreatment in Canada's prisons and unfair discrimination against former convicts who were trying to go straight.

The 1920s pre-dated the welfare state for ordinary citizens. It is even more startling to realize how little had yet been done for the lowest element of society, the convicted criminal. People had scarcely heard about rehabilitation and reform as a practical approach to the treatment of criminals. Prisons were hidden away from the public eye, the domain of petty-minded, all-powerful administrators. A prisoner had no hope of letting the outside world know if he was mishandled by guards or otherwise subjected to inhumane treatment. But some, after their release, and the wives and friends of others, came to Agnes Macphail and poured out their lurid stories—of the strap, an instrument perforated with holes which cut through a prisoner's bare flesh; shackles, which held a prisoner's hands above his head in day-long punishment; uncleanliness, rats and vermin, sadistic guards.

Agnes approached the subject gingerly at first. It was repugnant. She had her hands full keeping the government reminded of the needs of the decent, hard-working members of society.

Her first effort was a resolution which she introduced in 1925, asking for a programme of productive work for prison inmates. She was distressed to think they must wait out their sentences in complete idleness, reduced to a vegetable existence. If they could produce things in prison workshops to sell on the open market, they could be given a small wage which would go to support their families outside, or to build up a credit for them to begin life again when they were released.

Nothing happened to her suggestion the first year. But in March 1926 she brought in the same resolution at a more propitious time. The Mackenzie King Government was a minority, under bitter attack by the Opposition under Arthur Meighen, and prepared to make concessions to Progressive Members for their support. It was in this session of parliament that the House of Commons passed an Old Age Pensions Bill, the result of a straight bargain between J. S. Woodsworth, soon to be leader of the new C.C.F., and Mackenzie King.

Agnes wrung from the Government the passage of her resolution urging a work programme in the federal penitentiaries. It was of course a long way from implementation, but at least it was now on record as a statement of Government policy. Each session after that she found an occasion to refer to the penitentiaries, and the need to begin reforming men instead of merely inflicting punishment. She protested badly trained and poorly paid guards, the fact that such jobs were handed out as political patronage.

A few years later she entered the fight in earnest. In the early 1930s a series of riots broke out in penitentiaries across the country. Fires were started and property damaged. The authorities claimed that Communist prisoners were the cause of the outbreaks. Whippings were administered, sometimes to as many as twenty men at a time, as punishment. Sensational news stories were printed.

Agnes Macphail visited the Kingston penitentiary, insisting on her right as a member of parliament to go inside. No woman had ever before gone through the institution, insisting on seeing the "hole" where prisoners were kept in solitary confinement, the washrooms and eating halls and kitchens. What she saw disgusted her. Bathtubs, she found, were used not only for baths but to wash dishes. There was no segregation for those who were ill. Insane men howled in their cells, ignored by the rest. There were no psychiatrists on staff to treat mentally disturbed prisoners. Heads were shaved. Discipline was so strict that talking at any time among themselves was forbidden, and what appeared to be the most innocent pastimes, such as making little picture frames from cellophane wrappers from cigarette packages, were subject to punishment. For seventeen hours of every day the prisoner was completely alone in his cell, with nothing to occupy his hands or his mind.

In 1934, she moved the appointment of a royal commission, a full-scale inquiry, into Canada's prison system. She clashed head-on with the Minister of Justice in the R. B. Bennett administration, the Honourable Hugh Guthrie. Though she had learned to like and respect many of her honourable opponents in the two major parties, Guthrie was not among her favourites. And he obviously found her questioning an embarrassment, in the midst of the sensational publicity his department was getting. He resorted to an ungentlemanly tactic to silence her.

He found that she had been in touch with an ex-convict, Charles Baynes, and was preparing to use his story to point up the need of reform. Baynes was a tubercular (he claimed that the disease resulted from war service, and drew a pension) and when he was sentenced a second (or third) time to Kingston penitentiary he begged Agnes to intercede with the government and have him moved to a prison farm which he felt would be better for his health. Baynes was the youngest son of a wealthy English family, an intelligent and well-mannered man, and Agnes knew of his efforts to help other veterans receive pensions for war injuries. She was prepared to help him, and to quote his case as an example of brutal neglect of ailing prisoners.

She did not know the details of Baynes's criminal record. She tried to get the information from Guthrie's department, but the Minister saw to it that the information was not supplied. When Agnes was about to present her resolution in the House, word was passed through the Press Gallery that Guthrie planned to give the bothersome lady Member a "merry ride."

In her address, urging the setting up of the Commission, Agnes did refer to Baynes's illness. He happened to be well known to her, she said, and had a "fine social outlook." That was the opening Guthrie had waited for. Armed with the file he had kept from her, he read to the House in full detail the history of Baynes's arrests and convictions from one end of Canada to the other for acts of sexual perversion and "gross indecency."

In 1934, the effect of such a revelation was stunning. Agnes Macphail was publicly humiliated in a most devastating fashion. In private she suffered great anguish over the incident, blaming both Baynes and members of his family for not informing her about the nature of his offence. But she did not give up her battle to bring a breath of clean air into Canada's prisons. In the House of Commons and on public platforms everywhere, she pounded away at the Government's refusal to set up a royal commission.

She learned that further efforts had been made to link her to Charles Baynes as the source of her information on prison conditions— a deliberate attempt to smear and discredit her. She charged that Inspector Dawson from the penitentiaries branch had made a particularly crude remark, in the presence of witnesses. She challenged Guthrie on this, insisting that her honour as an M.P. must be protected against such attack. The Government set up a judicial inquiry, which she felt was far too limited in scope, to investigate Dawson's actions. The inquiry dragged on ineffectually, and the verdict was in favour of the government inspector.

It was an unsatisfactory affair, and the publicity Agnes received was not on the whole very favourable. But in the course of the investigation other statements did come to light, by the prison chaplain among others, about the sorry state of affairs in the Kingston penitentiary. The demand for a full-scale inquiry was mounting in vigour.

In parliament during the remainder of the Bennett Government's term of office Agnes Macphail was in the forefront of the demand for prison reform. She lost no opportunity to hurl statistics—how much it cost to keep a man in jail, instead of rehabilitating him, what percentage of prison inmates were repeaters. She quoted noted penologists like Thomas Nott Osborne who urged an end to the old "eye for an eye" philosophy.

By 1935 she was being supported by other Opposition Members, including Ernest Lapointe of the Liberals, who urged the Government to agree to her demand for a royal commission.

An election was held that year. The Liberals went back into power. Ernest Lapointe became Minister of Justice. The Archambault Commission was established, worked for three years, and in 1938 presented a report which revealed the shocking state of Canada's prisons and became a bible for those who sought reform. Chief Justice Archambault mailed her a personal copy with this inscription: "To Miss Agnes Macphail, M.P., courageous pioneer and untiring worker on behalf of prison reform in Canada."

An even greater tribute was paid to her, when the prisoners in Kingston "Pen" prepared a special issue of their magazine *Telescope*, three years after her death. The editor wrote:

As inmates, most of us are prone to take for granted the privileges we have today, without remembering that it was not always so in this penitentiary. However, those of us who suffered from day to day and lifted our eyes to "Aggie," as she fought for humane treatment of inmates, know that it was not always so and quietly revere and bless her memory, which the passing years have not dimmed.

Aggie is dead but lives on in the hearts of countless prison inmates who knew her and loved her. When the bell tolled for Aggie on February 13, 1954, it tolled for the inmates of every Canadian penitentiary.

The prevalent attitude that politics is dirty and rough keeps most women out of it, preferring to lend their talents to *nicer* occupations, and the safety of their clubs and auxiliaries. But Agnes Macphail entered politics with the highest ideals, believing quite simply in democracy, believing in the fundamental goodness of people and in their right to self-government. Her success as a politician, in winning five successive election victories, was due to the close contact she kept with the people of her riding. She told them she was in Ottawa to serve them. She asked for their opinions. She wrote carefully to the members of her executive when a hard decision had to be made. For example she and the other Progressives had to make up their minds how far they would go in supporting the minority government of Mackenzie King after the 1925 election, and she spelled out the alternatives and asked their advice.

She held meetings throughout the year in every part of her riding, most often in the rural schoolhouse. She wrote a regular weekly column which was printed in each little local paper. It was hard on her secretaries, but the letter went out without fail during all her years in Ottawa. It was mentioned admiringly in the Toronto *Star Weekly* in 1936, with an analysis of the unerring way in which she wrote what the people back home would be most likely to read. King George V had died, and all who came to the House Opening were required to wear mourning: Agnes mentioned that some of her guests had to stay away because they couldn't afford a black dress. She had visited the southern States on a lecture tour so she included a recipe she had enjoyed, suggesting that some readers might like to try it. Said the *Star Weekly*: "Of course they will try it. And at every table where it is served it will be called 'Miss Macphail's recipe' for years to come. How can anyone hope to defeat a woman like that?"

At the end of her first term she had discovered the difference in the cost of city and country living, and the special financial demands on an M.P. She felt she could not continue turning back $1500, as she had for the first four sessions. So she put the facts simply to her 1925 nominating convention, when she offered herself for a second time as a candidate, sure that her people would understand. And they did: no other names were submitted but her own.

Among the political theories she had picked up from the Progressives was "group government," which was an alternative to party organization. The idea was that each major economic group in the country would elect its own members, farmers, industrial workers, the white collar class, and the professionals. Agnes hung on to some of this philosophy throughout her career. She ran under various labels, but chiefly as an Independent. She heaped scorn on the party followers who filled the back benches of the Liberal and Conservative parties.

And many years in Ottawa only confirmed her belief that there must be a better way. She said, "I believe the day will come when the Cabinet will be a body elected by the Members of the House. They will share equally in blame and praise and the situation will not be as it is now, namely, when the Government does something really fine the Opposition is in despair."

How the end of the dual-party system could be prevented from turning into totalitarianism she didn't say, but she did feel a keen dissatisfaction with the political restraints that led so often to compromise or hypocrisy.

Reform groups under many labels were drawn together by the impact of the Great Depression, and at a meeting in Calgary in 1932 the Co-operative Commonwealth Federation (C.C.F.) was formed. The United Farmers of Ontario held their own meetings that fall to decide whether or not to join the C.C.F. Agnes strongly urged them to do so, and they took the step, although they changed their minds a year or so later, and at that point Agnes resumed the "Independent" label, though she continued to sit with the C.C.F. group in parliament and attend their caucus.

Political activity left Agnes with almost no time for other interests or pursuits. She lived alone in Ottawa most of the year, and during the parliamentary recess divided her time between lecture tours, meetings in her home riding, and a few precious weeks of relaxation at her parents' home. When her father retired he bought a substantial red brick house in the village of Ceylon, where her mother devoted herself to raising flowers. Dougal Macphail died in 1930. Agnes became much closer to her mother in later years, and was with her when she died in 1937. She kept in close touch with her two sisters, and was fond of surprising her young nieces with unexpected gifts. And she had a host of friends, attracted by her vivid, outgoing personality and zest for life. Nellie McClung was somewhat older than Agnes but very fond of her. Other friends included Nora Henderson, a controller in the city of Hamilton, and prominent women in New York and the southern States, many of whom she met on her travels as a lecturer. Her two secretaries, Malvina Bolus and later Lilla Bell, were devoted to her.

Throughout her life she had to consider many times over the opposite attractions of marriage or a political career. There seemed to her no practical way of combining them. Politics consumed her time and attention—how could she begin to make room for a home, husband, and children? As a young girl she had felt strongly the right of a woman *to be a person*, to do things in the world at large instead of merely serving as helpmate to a man. A farm woman's life was a round of drudgery. The woman produced children, and if they were boys they were allowed to go off and do big, exciting things, but if they were girls they must be trained to stay at home and repeat the eternal cycle. She rebelled against this future for herself, even in the years when, like any lively young schoolteacher, she was always off to a dance and had followers in quantity.

In Ottawa her name was linked with Preston Elliott and with Robert Gardiner, members of the Progressive group, but though she had proposals of marriage from both she could not take the step into matrimony which she felt would put an end to her independence. In autobiographical notes she wrote:

One of the outstanding features of this age is the number of intelligent women who do not marry. I have talked to hundreds of these fine, alert and very capable women in business, the professions, and the arts, and their reason was the same as mine: *the person* could not be subjected.

In parliament she sometimes spoke acidly on the subject:

When I hear men talk about women being the angel of the home I always, mentally at least, shrug my shoulders in doubt. I do not want to be the angel of any home; I want for myself what I want for other women, absolute equality. After that is secured then men and women can take turns at being angels.

Among her papers stored in the National Archives are a few love letters, kept deliberately because, as she told a close friend, she could not bear the thought of being remembered in history as the frigid spinster much of the contemporary press made her out to be.

Late in 1939 she was prepared to gather up her things and make a permanent home in a bachelor apartment in Ottawa. But permanence in politics is always improbable. In March 1940 she went to the polls and for the first time was defeated. It was a blow to which she never quite became reconciled. Yet much useful work lay ahead of her in the following fourteen years. She survived several anxious years of job-hunting, for her resources were slim, and she had a genuine horror of ending her days in poverty. Presently she was writing a column for the *Globe and Mail* called "Farm Betterment," and she moved to Toronto, renting a large house and taking in roomers to help finance it. But her political differences with George McCullough of the *Globe* led to her leaving his payroll a year later.

At this point, in her fifty-second year, she at last moved completely into the C.C.F. party, with which she had been in close harmony since its inception. She was taken on staff to organize for the party in rural Ontario, and though she had her own highly individual methods of proceeding she kept up this work until the party found itself unable to continue paying her. And in the provincial election of June, 1943, she ran as a candidate for the C.C.F. in East York, and won.

She considered the provincial Assembly something of a come-down, after her years in Ottawa. But she was respected and deferred to, and she put considerable effort into her favourite field of reform institutions, conducting a personal survey of the old Mercer Reformatory for women in Toronto. She played a leading rôle in organizing the Elizabeth Fry Society to aid women prisoners. She spoke strongly on educational and farm needs.

Meanwhile she carried on a personal vendetta with Premier George Drew, whom she heartily disliked. She would set the government benches in an uproar with her blunt attacks on him. When he made what she considered a particularly stuffy pro-British speech she mocked him for "wrapping himself in the Union Jack."

"Don't you like the Union Jack?" needled a Member.

"Yes, but not with the Premier in it."

"You'll never have me, in it or out of it," Mr. Drew retorted.

In 1945 the C.C.F. party fared badly at the polls and Agnes, among others, lost her seat. At the same time she suffered a slight stroke, the beginning of a decline in health which she bitterly resented. After a brief period of rest she continued speaking at C.C.F. meetings, and when another election was called in 1948 she again accepted the East York nomination. Elected once more, she continued to do a useful job as a Member, speaking strongly in support of an increased supplement for old age pensioners, and for the still unproclaimed principle of equal pay for equal work for men and women.

But her health was poor, her temper sometimes short, and there was a sadness in her bearing that distressed those who knew her. She told the legislature one day what a short thing fame is: "I had a letter returned from Ottawa, I think it was yesterday, which said, 'Not known here.'"

In 1951 she again lost out at the polls, in a swing of political fortune which reduced her party's strength in Ontario to two. Shortly afterwards she suffered a second, more severe stroke. She rallied and carried on, though she found her enforced inactivity so irksome that she was often barely civil to those around her. And again she was haunted by the fear of poverty.

A pensions bill for M.P.s with long terms of continuous service was passed at this time in Ottawa, but Agnes just missed qualifying for it. Suggestions were made to the government from many quarters to have her appointed to the Senate. She would have accepted such an offer if it had come, as a last chance to participate once more in the Parliament she loved, even though she had often heaped scorn on the elderly members of the second chamber. Prime Minister St. Laurent gave some verbal assurance that her name would be among those he intended to appoint as Senators in the spring of 1954. But he was a few months too late. In February she had a third and final heart attack, and died in Toronto's Wellesley Hospital.

A bronze bust stands in the North Gallery of the House of Commons, commemorating the first woman Member. Many years later throughout Canada there are hundreds, perhaps more, who can recall her clearly: the deep tones of her voice, the pride of her tall figure and her swinging walk, her straightforward sincerity of purpose. She opened a way into the service of our country which all too few women have followed, and none surely with half the joy and dedication that carried her from a backwoods farm to the halls of Parliament.

BIBLIOGRAPHY

Agnes Macphail Papers. Public Archives, Ottawa.
DR. D. R. FLETCHER, "Agnes Campbell Macphail" (unpublished).
AGNES MACPHAIL, "My Ain Folk" (unpublished).
CATHERINE LYLE CLEVERDON, *The Woman Suffrage Movement in Canada*. Toronto, 1950.
MARGARET STEWART and DORIS FRENCH, *Ask No Quarter*. Toronto, 1959.
Hansard for 1921 to 1940.

Lucy Maud Montgomery

1874-1942

ELIZABETH WATERSTON

She was born on a beautiful island. Her mother died when she was very young. Her father left her with an old lady and an old man, in an apple-orchard, by the sea. When she grew up, she was put under a vow, never to leave the old people. But a young man loved her, and after ten years of waiting he carried her off, away from the island.

This is the language of fairy-tale. It seems to be the first way to tell the story of Lucy Maud Montgomery. Girls following her biography in H. M. Ridley's *Life of L. M. Montgomery* may feel they are reading another romance in the sequence of "Anne" and "Emily" and "Pat" and "Story Girl" books.

Many women *have* lived "fabulous" lives. But in L. M. Montgomery's case the real miracle is that she could exploit her experience in an enduring art-form. She universalized her story; she recreated it against vivid regional settings; she structured it into mythical patterns. She retold the legends she had lived, in haunting and memorable style.

She used her life materials in a way that brought her personal fame, and brought her country's literature a popular international recognition. Literary critics throughout the Western world saw at once the values she had achieved. If subsequent sophisticated criticism agreed to laugh at or to by-pass the creator of "Anne," critics today are less ready to be patronizing.

We find in her life, her letters, her journals, the story of an important craftsman, a professional writer fighting to clarify and improve the conditions of an artist's work. And in her novels we find a subtle and illuminating use of archetypal patterns, particularly of the recurring myths of girlhood.

If we re-examine her life story and look at her books as in part an unconscious supplement to the biography, we come close to watching the miracle of the creative imagination.

Born in 1874, in a North Shore village on Prince Edward Island, Lucy Maud Montgomery was brought as a baby from Clifton to Cavendish, to her mother's family. Her grandmother MacNeill gave her a home when her young mother, Clara Woolner MacNeill Montgomery, died, twenty-one months after Lucy Maud's birth. Her father, Hugh John Montgomery, left the Island to strike out for the West, and settled in Prince Albert.

Lucy Maud Montgomery's memories of childhood were very intense. She could recall "spots of time" from her third year on. She was a bright, quick child: when she started school she moved eagerly through the old P.E.I. "readers," with their characteristic Maritime blend of New England and British writers. Years later she would place on the title-pages of her books verses from that same range of great Romantic and Victorian writers of America and Britain: Whittier, Emerson, Longfellow, Oliver Wendell Holmes; and Tennyson, Byron, Cowper, and Burns.

Life was dominated by the grandparents' notions of how a little girl should dress and behave. She was a solitary child, creating imaginary friends, and living in the book-worlds of Bunyan and Scott and Thackeray. Slowly and sensitively she realized the beauty of her native setting: the apple-orchard slopes of the MacNeill farm; the red-earth, tree-lined road winding past pond and woods to the village of Cavendish; the blueberry barrens; and the circling, sounding sea.

She responded; and she wrote. She phrased her impressions of the world around her in the formal and already old-fashioned diction of

Thomson's *Seasons*. She liked, later, to tell the story of showing her earliest lines to her family—who complained, "It doesn't rhyme!" But one point of the story is that although she defended the "blankness" of her verse, she was willing to re-work it, producing soon reams of rhyme. It was a first, characteristic effort to adjust to critical suggestions. From the beginning it was not just self-expression that she wanted—it was recognition. She wanted to write; but she also wanted to be read. She sent off her first manuscript, hopefully, when she was eleven, to an American magazine, *The Household*. It was returned, but she tried again, this time for a Canadian publication. It would be four years before her first appearance in print, but those years were characterized by an amazing persistence. Composing, copying, mailing, continued in the face of total lack of interest—this would not be in the scope of most twelve-year-old, thirteen-year-old, fourteen-year-old lives.

The first heartening acceptance came for a verse-narrative, reworking a P.E.I. legend, sent to the Charlottetown *Patriot*. This was in the winter of 1889–90, and the manuscript was sent from the far West, for Lucy Maud had now moved out to Prince Albert to join her father. From Prince Albert, while she was in high school, she sent other poems and sketches to Montreal, to Charlottetown, and to New York.

The reunion with her father was brief. He had remarried, and although she enjoyed the company of her step-brother and step-sisters, the adolescent girl did not fit comfortably into the new home. The year, so productive of immediate literary work, never seemed "usable" later: she by-passed it when she was exploiting other events of her girlhood and assigning bits of her own experience to her fictional heroines.

Meanwhile, the young Islander trailed back to Cavendish to finish school and to write entrance examinations for Prince of Wales College. In 1893 she moved to Charlottetown to attend the College (where courses covered the final two years of high school and the first two of university). Her one-year course qualified her for a teacher's licence. In this same year she had her first "pay" for literary work: two subscriptions to the magazine that accepted her poem, "Only a Violet." It was an American magazine.

L. M. Montgomery (as she now signed her manuscripts) continued to write and submit stories and poems to Canadian and American magazines, after she had taken her teacher's licence and begun to work at Bideford School. Most of the manuscripts came back, but enough were accepted (though without any monetary reward) to make the young author decide to get further training in the field of literature. She went to Halifax in 1895, enrolled at Dalhousie College, and took a course in English literature from Archibald MacMechan, himself a poet and short story writer. The alternative for an Islander would be McGill—many of the characters in her stories go to the Montreal university; but L. M. Montgomery's formal education was all in the Maritimes. During her year in Halifax she earned her first money for writings: five dollars from *Golden Days* in Philadelphia; five dollars from the *Halifax Evening Mail*; twelve dollars from the Philadelphia *Youth's Companion*. She was also placing more and more work with the Sunday School papers, enough to encourage her ambition for a career as a writer.

In 1896, back on Prince Edward Island, school-teaching left little time or energy for composition. But for many months she worked at her writing each morning from six to seven, by lamplight, sitting on her feet to keep warm in the old farmhouse where she was boarding.

She resigned her teaching job two years later to return to Cavendish. The death of her grandfather MacNeill in 1898 left her grandmother alone. L. M. Montgomery decided to see if she could make a living by her writing, eked out by the money her grandmother made as local postmistress. Lucy Maud was twenty-two years old; she was selling enough to cover board and clothing; she was improving her work. "I never expect to be famous," she wrote. "I merely want to have a recognized place among good workers in my chosen profession." In the year after her grandfather's death, in double dedication to family and career, she promised her grandmother to stay and work at home.

Briefly, she interrupted her Island life when she accepted a job on the Halifax *Daily Echo* in November, 1901. She moved into a Halifax boarding-house, and for almost a year wrote a weekly gossip column, edited a page of "society letters," proof-read, answered the phone, and did free "write-ups" of the advertisers' goods. She was learning to work under pressure, to produce for a given audience. Meantime she could submit manuscripts to other publications, with a growing percentage of acceptances. She was sending to more sophisticated journals now: *Ainslie's, The Delineator, The Smart Set*, published in the eastern States.

The young author acquired "pen-pals" among other young people aspiring to literary success. She began an interesting correspondence, for instance, with Ephraim Weber, a Kitchener man who had gone homesteading in Alberta, but shared her literary ambitions and frustrations: "We'll be dead long before Canadian literature will be a bread-and-butter affair." By June, 1902, she was writing all her friends to tell them she was going home to the Island, hoping for more free time for writing.

Settled again in Cavendish, she was beginning a long courtship with a young Presbyterian minister, the Reverend Ewan Macdonald, a fine-looking man a few years older than she, and product of the same kind of schooling and family. She worked hard at her sketches and stories, mailing them to a great variety of magazines: *Canadian Magazine, McClure's*, the *Family Herald, Current Literature*, the Boston *National, Sunday School Times*, the Battle Creek *Pilgrim, Modern Women*, New York *Gunton's, Lippincott's*. Her letters are filled with indefatigable zest, and eager interest in the possibilities for publication. She was reading *Trilby, Dr. Jekyll and Mr. Hyde, The Story of an African Farm*, the poetry of Markham, catching up on contemporary best-sellers. She was puzzling over matters of faith, the possibility of psychic experience, the mystery of pain, evolution, the divinity of Christ, eagerly discussing, exploring, opening her mind to any new trend of thought. She was simultaneously re-exploring the Bible, Gibbon's *Decline and Fall of the Roman Empire*, and Emerson. The best way to catch a notion of her work at this time is to read *Further Chronicles of Avonlea*, published much later, but consisting mostly of stories written in her early twenties, "pot-boilers" as she herself scornfully dubbed them, but intriguing in their range of interests.

She could report making $591.85 in 1904. Ideas for stories and poems came fast, caught into notebook jottings, set aside till a mood or a market suggested a way of "working up." She could pass along practical advice: "*To work at once, stick to it*, write something *every day*, even if you burn it up after writing it."

In 1904, she re-read a note-book entry: "Elderly couple apply to orphan asylum for a boy. By a mistake a girl is sent them." Although her first intention was to work this notion into a short story for a Sunday School paper, she found the character "grew on her" so much that the work expanded to book length. She worked on it for eighteen months, keeping other writing on the go at the same time. The manuscript was mailed out hopefully to a publisher, and rejected. Mailed again, three more times, to other possible publishers, including Macmillan. Rejected again—and finally stowed away by the author in discouragement.

Meanwhile she had placed another story, *Kilmeny of the Orchard*, in serial form, with an American magazine, and other stories with the Chicago *Blue Book*, New York *Watson's*, Chicago *Rural Magazine*. She made about $800 in 1906, but by dint of unremitting writing. She rarely left Cavendish; her grandmother was now eighty-two, and the younger woman had almost all the housework to do. She was reading less, and an odd mixture: the Book of Job, Upton Sinclair's "hideous" *The Jungle*, Lewis Carroll's *Alice through the Looking Glass*.

Then spring came, and wonderful news. The manuscript of *Anne of Green Gables*, which she had dug out, re-worked, and sent off to one more publisher, was accepted. "I am blatantly pleased and proud and happy," she said, "and I shan't make any pretence of not being so."

The L. C. Page Company of Boston, "her" publisher, was not a major house, but they did handle Bliss Carman, Charles G. D. Roberts, and other writers well known to Maritime readers. They offered 10 per cent royalties (nine cents on a wholesale price of ninety cents), plus a flat sum for dramatic rights, and bound her to give them first refusal of all her books for the next five years. Pitman's of London would hold the English rights. On the whole, acceptable terms, and certainly a glorious realization of the long, long dream of having a full-length book published.

In June, 1908, the first copy of *Anne of Green Gables* arrived from the publishers, attractively bound, in good clear print on good firm paper—a format that would stand up to the readings and re-readings that awaited it when it reached the hundreds of thousands of its young audience.

The book instantly appealed to an incredibly large market, and one not limited to girls. It brought floods of letters to its author, including a note from Bliss Carman, and one from Mark Twain. The proud author thrilled to Mark Twain's comment: in Anne she had created "the dearest, and most lovable child in fiction since the immortal Alice." *Anne of Green Gables* went into four editions in three months, and rolled on from there into one printing after another.

The terms of the publishers' contract did not include any sliding scale of royalities for this run-away best-seller. If the author wanted to cash in on the "Anne-mania" she must get to work on a sequel. The publishers insisted that she should write "like mad" to meet the demand. She settled into a new routine: two hours of writing, one of transcribing onto the typewriter—thinking out plot and dialogue as she worked around the house. She was less than happy with her new book. It didn't "grow"; she had to "build" it. She blocked it all out in her mind before writing it. "All the incidents have happened . . . and I have only to write about them now."

Meanwhile she house-cleaned, sewed, gardened, played the organ for the church choir. The Reverend Ewan Macdonald was still hovering near, trying to persuade her to marry him. He found adamant refusal for a number of reasons: her grandmother, her writing commitments, her career, her new book—reasonable barriers multiplied. There were still serious puzzles in her religious thinking also: "I call myself a Christian, but oh!"

In November, 1908, she sent off the manuscript of *Anne of Avonlea*. She was feeling tired, head-achey, nervous, worn out by the publicity surrounding "that detestable Anne." "Petty flings of malice and spite" followed local readings of the book. She was brooding over "certain worries and troubles that have seemed ever present in my life for the past six years [i.e., since 1902]. They are caused by people and circumstances over which I have no control, so I am quite helpless in regard to them and when I get rundown I take a too-morbid view of them." A favourite aunt died in 1909. That year she refused an invitation to speak at a World's Congress of Women in Toronto: "couldn't get away."

But in the fall of 1909 she started a new book—beginning by composing the first sentence and the last paragraph. *The Story Girl* she considered "away ahead of *Anne* from a literary point of view." She enjoyed writing this tale of a golden summer, a gathering on the Island of a family group, focused and dramatized by the story-telling skill of the one gifted cousin. Writing this nostalgic book about the "few opulent months" gave the author great pleasure. It occupied her most of 1910. While it was in the making her publishers brought out *Kilmeny of the Orchard* (1910), a re-working of a story previously published serially.

The Story Girl was published in May, 1911. The year had already brought a major change in L. M. Montgomery's life. Her grandmother died, at the age of eighty-seven, thirteen years after the grandfather's death and the restraining promise to stay on. Lucy Maud Montgomery now felt free to marry, in July, 1911, Ewan Macdonald, and to set out on a wedding trip to England and Scotland. Like the teen-age trip to her father in Prince Albert, this long voyage never seemed usable to the author. There are no references in any of her later books to the sights and experiences of this long-dreamt-of tour. She returned to Canada, not to Prince Edward Island, but to Leaskdale, Ontario, where Mr. Macdonald had accepted a call.

When she left the Island, L. M. Montgomery had produced four works of unequal value. *Kilmeny of the Orchard* is fervid in style, melodramatic in plot. It followed a contemporary fad for books about psychosomatic impairment. Kilmeny's dumbness is not unlike the hysterical crippling of the child in *The Secret Garden* (1911), and her pathos is linked with that of "Freckles" in Gene Stratton Porter's novel (1904), her violin-playing with that of *The Girl of the Limberlost* (1912). *Trilby* contributes something to the tone. But L. M. Montgomery set her plot of impediment released by love in an Island setting. Kilmeny in her magic trance is guarded by an old aunt and uncle and a gypsy boy, in the best Gothic tradition, but her Eden is a clearly realized orchard, with "real toads"—and an indoor world of antimacassars.

In *Anne of Green Gables*, the world of dour propriety is assaulted by the daemonic force of a red-headed child brought miraculously from "off the island." This book seems almost untouched by timely fashions in "girls' stories." It opens its casements into timeless myths of youth and growth and the quest for identity. Every incident in it is at the same time vivid and deeply suggestive: Anne comes down a long lane with Matthew, to the old farm where angular Marilla sits between a west window flooded by sunlight and an east window framing a cherry tree in bloom but "greened over by a tangle of vines." Anne dyes her red hair green. She is given first a brown dress by Matthew, then a green one by Marilla. Anne makes her "kindred spirit," Diana, drunk, just before she herself walks a ridge-pole, and breaks an ankle. Midway through the book she breaks a slate over Gilbert's head, then must work out her resentment of him and accept his "friendship" as the book ends. Psychologists today would interpret the story symbolically; they would suggest that reading such a story probably helps young girls accept imaginatively the processes of growing up and edging toward adult physical passion. For the millions of girls who have "identified" with Anne, these deep patterns *may* work in some such subconscious way; but the book satisfies also in its romantic pantheism, its regional humour, and its fresh sense of the excitement of language. L. M. Montgomery knew more than the psychologists about the dreams and the anxieties of adolescent girls: her childhood loneliness, her early power of expression and her suspended maturing had kept open the channel to "lost time."

A glance at *Anne of Avonlea* shows a decrease of power. Anne, "half-past sixteen," putting in a year of teaching, is a "Sleeping Beauty." All action rises from minor characters. They interest, because they represent types that will recur: a cranky old man from New Brunswick; a pair of ill-matched twins; a gifted, poetic "Yankee" boy; a long-waiting spinster. L. M. Montgomery was not yet ready for a real study of late adolescence. Anne's romance builds no suspense. (There are good regional bits still, such as Mrs. Lynde's view of a neighbour: "a slack-twisted creature who washes her dishes sitting down.")

The Story Girl might seem at first reading equally episodic. But the book begins on a May morning on the road to an orchard-farm, and runs rhythmically to November, when "the sharp tops of the spruces" stand "against the silvery sky." It presents three mysteries: that of the old "witch," Peg Bowen; that of the secret chamber of the "Awkward Man"; and that of the family "blue chest," heritage of broken romance. The "Story-Girl," Sara, motherless, gifted, differs from Anne in that her father exists though in the background. (Anne, we remember, dreamt of being called "Cordelia," like Lear's loving daughter.) And Sara's circle can meet with the grown-up world of adults, occasionally, but happily, at twilight, in the orchard. The boy who tells the story knows himself to be only temporarily on "the Island." The identification of island with orchard with spring with youth is tactfully handled and effective. All these things give organic unity to *The Story Girl*. They justify L. M. Montgomery's own fondness for the book.

She had now left Cavendish and the routines of her old home.

The new life would have its new routines: running the manse, helping with parish work, women's groups, choirs, Sunday school. New
duties would be added, a year later, with motherhood. Like most
women-writers of her generation she had always had at least two
lives: that of producing artist and that of conscientious house-keeper.
The "woman's world" was hers by no choice of her own. What woman
in 1912, in a small provincial town, could expect to resign from this
sphere? The artist's world was a different matter. There was nothing
automatic in the intense determination that freed a couple of hours
a day for writing and revising, and kept the imagination active in
undeviating devotion to a régime of steady craftsmanship. L. M. Montgomery had inherited some special talent, and had grown up in a
gossipy community where anecdotes were valued, and a good racon-
teur much admired; she had worked at her craft in hope of money
and a career. But now the real mystery appears: what force, what
drive, what aspirations powered the undeviating drive on through the
long string of successful books, one every other year, from the year
of her marriage till the year before her death? Not only for the royalty
money, welcome as that was in a small-town manse, but for other
rewards, she found time to detach herself from the "real" world of
Leaskdale, to continue the tales of the other "reality," the remembered
island of adolescence.

Chronicles of Avonlea was published in 1912. In this set of Island
stories Anne Shirley appears very briefly, and rarely as a moving force.
These tales of proud poverty, of loneliness, of frustrated courtships
are interesting experiments in point of view. Romance and sensibility
are filtered through the practical viewpoint of matter-of-fact narrators,
the unpoetic neighbours who watch poignant events. "Sentiment and
humour" (as L. M. Montgomery says of one of the *Chronicles*
characters) "wage an equal contest."

The Golden Road (1913) is an elegy on childhood. It completes
the seasonal cycle of *The Story Girl*, running from December through
the riches of summer to "sere" autumn in the orchard setting. Most
mysteries of the earlier book find rather prosaic fulfilment: a bride
for the Awkward Man, a visit to church for the Witch. The "Story-
Girl," Sara, tells a new cycle of tales: Indian and classical legends, and
local folk tales, while her sad alternate, Sara Ray, suffers new repressions. The children's rituals and fears are convincing and funny.

But the family disperses as the book ends, and a sadness tinges the story.

Perhaps the elegiac mood reflected the author's entry into a new phase of life. Her first son, Chester Cameron, was born in 1912. A second infant, Hugh, born in 1914, lived only for a day. In 1915 the birth of Ewan Stuart completed the Macdonalds' family.

By this time, war had broken out, and the manse was touched by the tension in all Canadian life. L. M. Montgomery turned once again to the story of Anne, to satisfy "all the girls all over the world who [had] wanted more." It was a relief to escape to girlhood and romance and the friendships and escapades of student days, "pre-war."

Anne of the Island (1915) takes Anne away to the mainland and to maturity. Anne is at college, involved in the love-stories of her friends, and in a delusive romance with "Royal Gardner." Gilbert lurks near, offering apples. Anne rejects his first offer of love, in a very real moment of tension and fear. The reconciliation at the close is autumnal and subdued. The whole book is perfectly adapted to its audience of adolescent girls, in its timidity, its repressions, and its lyric romanticism and idealism. The book is "real" too in the gentle growth of Anne's friendships with other girls as she comes nearer to a sense of her own identity. The moving climax to this development occurs when a "Mainland" friend takes her to "Bolingbroke," her birthplace, where she feels "not an orphan any longer."

The major weakness in plot is the ending, when Anne's "spell" is broken, and she accepts her love for Gilbert, because of a melo-dramatic sudden illness and miraculous cure. But such a resolution is acceptable in myth; and once again L. M. Montgomery had released mythic energies in the story she had created. She had prepared for such a supervenience of miracle by the recurring use of symbolic settings, suggestive of Eden. The tone of the closing is wistful, per-fect for its insecure audience, and its saddened time.

Emotions stirred by the war had led L. M. Montgomery to a revived activity in poetry. In 1916 she brought out *The Watchman and Other Poems*, dedicated to the Canadian soldiers who had died in the war. The title poem is a meditative monologue on the first Easter, in a manner reminiscent of Browning. The other poems, lyrics of sea, of hills and woods (rather heavily fraught with dryads and dingles and fisher-folk and moonrise) are mostly reprints from a surprisingly long list of magazines, *Youth's Companion*, *Forward*, *Maclean's Magazine*, *East and West*—and fifteen others, all markets for occasional poems. These are Edwardian, water-colour descriptions:

> Elusive shadows linger shyly here
>   And wood-flowers blow, like pale, sweet spirit-bloom,
> And white, slim birches whisper, mirrored clear
>   In the pool's lucent gloom.

This volume marks an important change. It was published by the Canadian firm of McClelland, Goodchild and Stewart in 1916, and by Stokes of New York in 1917. Constable's of London issued an English edition in 1920. The old connection with the Page Company of Boston was broken. The galling sense that she had had less than a fair return for the best-selling *Anne of Green Gables* had irked L. M. Montgomery throughout the five-year period when she was bound to give Page's the first refusal of her new books. Now she moved happily into an arrangement that involved a reputable Canadian publisher along with American and British affiliates. (English rights were later transferred from Constable's to Hodder and Stoughton.)

In the next six years, the new publishers brought out *Anne's House of Dreams* (1917), *Rainbow Valley* (1919), and *Rilla of Ingleside* (1921). All three are shadowed by war. The focus moves from Anne to her family. Even in *Anne's House of Dreams* Anne and Gilbert have become unreal, and their friends seem phoney and sentimental. Owen Ford speaking:

> "The rose is the flower of love—the world has acclaimed it so for centuries. The pink roses are love hopeful and expectant—the white roses are love dead and forsaken—but the red roses—ah, Leslie, what are the red roses?"
> "Love Triumphant," said Leslie in a low voice.

Not low enough, say we—but the author seems unable to suppress this false strain. The real vitality in the book lies in the middle-aged, gossipy ladies, Susan and Miss Cornelia.

The gossip continues in *Rainbow Valley*, easing the shadow of world catastrophe into the small talk of neighbours and pets. Anne's young family are joined by the motherless brood at the nearby manse. Her own children are shadowy, and she herself is reduced to some cliché gestures ("hands clasped before her") and "tag" descriptions

("shining grey eyes"). A newcomer joins the range of types: Mary
Vance, an orphan, but a brassy, skinny, pale-eyed, pugnacious one.
The widowed minister, dreamily abstracted from his children's needs,
is firmly realized also. And how L. M. Montgomery must have enjoyed
"naming" the children of this Presbyterian minister: Jeremy and
Carlyle, turbulent Faith and gentle Una!

The play of names in *Rilla of Ingleside* is thought-provoking too. It
is Walter, named after Anne's father, who is killed—the father dies
again, in a sense. Marilla's namesake adopts a war-baby, Jims, while
Jem, given up as dead, lives again at the end. Nan and Di, the twins,
are "off-stage" most of the time although the notion of twins still seems
to press on L. M. Montgomery's fancy.

The book makes an interesting contrast with *Anne of the Island.*
Anne's daughter waits through a four-year period for her romance, just
as the mother had done, but the inhibition is imposed from without,
by war. In a little experiment with first-person point-of-view, Rilla
recounts her waiting in her journal—a preview of the major method
of the Emily Books which will come soon.

These three "Anne" books were brought out by the new publisher
in a format similar to the earlier volumes. Their sales were excellent.

Trouble flared in 1920 when the former publisher, Page's of Boston,
brought out a collection of early pieces, which had appeared years
before as magazine sketches, under the title *Further Chronicles of
Avonlea.* Their reasoning seems to have been that the author had
owed them "refusal" on these stories. L. M. Montgomery indignantly
protested against "piracy," and decided to sue for invasion of her
rights. The suit dragged on for about nine years, wearying, sometimes
embarrassing and humiliating, always irritating and distracting. This
battle over the publishers' "right" to the book was important for professional writers. It stirred furious discussion in authors' associations,
and spot-lighted the need for business acumen and a readiness to fight
for due rewards. It revived all the old tensions over copyright and
piracy which had so long plagued Canadian writers.

Of the book itself, L. M. Montgomery spoke slightingly. But there
are at least two aspects worth notice. First, a number of ghost stories
in the late Kipling manner reflect the author's interest in psychic
phenomena and her ability to blend new ideas about extra-sensory
perceptions with the old patterns of folk tale. Second, the "Western"

sketch, "Tannis of the Flats," set in Prince Albert, and reminiscent of Bret Harte and Owen Wister, catches attention as a single use of that alien setting experienced briefly when Lucy Maud Montgomery visited her father in the 1880s.

The furore about her lawsuit increased her status among Canadian writers. She was in demand as a speaker at literary societies, and was still bombarded with letters and questions about her methods of working and the "originals" of Anne and of Green Gables.

In 1921 she had the rather unhappy experience of seeing a silent movie based on her book, but distorting many elements in it. Her old contract with the Page Company gave her no royalties for "screen rights," and she had no control over the revision of the story for movie purposes. She particularly objected to the school-room scenes, in which the Stars and Stripes flew bravely over the P.E.I. school-house.

Perhaps the tension over rights to the products of her imagination, combined with this public focus on its processes, led L. M. Montgomery to a new subject. She went back again to the memory of her own girlhood, and began the story of a girl living between the world of fact and the world of words. "Emily" is a character whose joy and release consist of writing—first a letter journal to her dead father, then a set of sketches in her "Jimmy-books" (note-books offered by a sympathetic old cousin) and finally tales and poems, proffered to publishers.

The theme of a writer's ambition had been a sub-current in early "Anne" books. Now it becomes a major strand. In the three "Emily" books (*Emily of New Moon, Emily Climbs*, and *Emily's Quest*), chapters of Emily's journals reflect and intensify the third-person narrative sequence.

Emily of New Moon (1923) is an intriguing book even without this looking-glass effect. In it L. M. Montgomery moves powerfully into a mythical tale of girlhood. Names of people and places half-reveal and half-disguise the undercurrents of meaning and emotion. The little girl named Emily Byrd Starr comes from Maywood to the New Moon farm of her mother's people (the mother was named Juliet). Her false friend is Rhoda (rodent?), her true friend is Ilse (ipse?). Her first teacher is Miss Brownell (who destroys imagination), her second Mr. Carpenter (who, obviously, builds). Midway through the book a priest encourages her to "keep on" writing; but at Wyther

Grange she meets a man *named* Priest—Dean Priest at that—the crippled "Jarback," her own dead father's friend, who brings her to life again, at the cost of possessing her soul. None of this is obtrusive, but it adds a dimension of interest to the surface story. That story is an intriguing though unpretentious version of Wordsworth's *Prelude*, a careful recreation of those "spots of time" in which the creative imagination is nurtured. It clarifies the directions of a growing child's fantasy-life. The story is climaxed by a mysterious vision in which Emily's mind, in delirium, fuses three bits of memory, and prophetically "sees" a hidden truth (the "real" story of Ilse's lost mother). This prophetic second sight restores Ilse to her estranged father, by clearing the dead mother's reputation. It is an effective fable of art. It is also a good solution of the double plot, a fusion of Emily's "real" life among her friends and her life as poetic creator.

Having opened the doors of memory so far, L. M. Montgomery pushed them wider—perilously wider—in her sequel. *Emily Climbs* (1925) recreates the tone of a teen-aged girl's view of life: her sense of being misunderstood and repressed, her obsessive interest in her own identity. Emily had gone to "Shrewsbury" to the town where shrewish Aunt Ruth waits to curb, censor and belittle her. Yet in spite of never being understood Emily manages to enjoy, innocently, most forbidden pleasures. This fantasy of adolescence is a precursor of *Catcher in the Rye, A Separate Peace* and the whole fashionable swarm of such books. It expresses the romance and dreaminess of adolescence, as well as the arrogance, self-pity and inhibitions we have been taught ruefully to recognize. The material is awkwardly handled: the structure and style seem to have some of the clumsiness and unsureness of the adolescent. But the book is a pioneering entry into a difficult and important area.

It is no accident that L. M. Montgomery's first mature attempt at an adult novel came as an interruption of the "Emily" series. *The Blue Castle* (1926) was an effort to "climb" past the stereotypes of girls' books.

In 1925 the permanence of her appeal was marked by the beginning of a re-issue of her work in a "uniform edition" (Harrap, 1925–1935). Her family life had made a welcome shift, from Leaskdale in the rather remote Uxbridge area, to the larger town of Norval, near Toronto, and in the centre of the earlier settled regions of western-central Ontario. Here Mr. Macdonald hoped for an easing of his duties, since his health was not good. The Macdonalds' sons were now boys of thirteen and ten. Perhaps the vigorous reality of their lives suggested a vivid alternative to the retrospective dreams of remembered childhood.

The Blue Castle is energetic and tough. It is an amazingly blunt story of a frustrated woman's attempt to find a real life in defiance of family tabus and conventions. It has a Cinderella plot, but the settings and characters mark a definite break from cliché. The story begins with a pompous family dinner party, which may echo Galsworthy but which certainly precedes *Jalna* (1927). It moves to "the verge of up-back," to the derelict home of a drunken no-good, and from there to a roaring barn-dance brawl at Chidley's Corners. Exactly half-way through, Valancy (what a nice name for an independent Canadian heroine!) accepts joyfully the fact of her love for the mystery man from Muskoka, and moves with him to an enchanted island. In the second half of the book the author piles up improbable plot twists with jaunty unconcern, without losing the sardonic realism of her portraits of the family group left behind in "civilization." Valancy's Dionysian revolt is blurred a little by the third plot thread—her devotion to the romantic nature-writings of "John Foster." But as one young reader says, "You can skip the John Foster stuff," and keep a book with real vitality: a fairy-tale set to a jazz tempo.

The reviewers were not impressed. Professor Desmond Pacey some years later summarized the contemporary reaction: "all the weaknesses of the Anne books and none of their redeeming charm." L. M. Montgomery had an over-developed sensitivity to reviews. She had an old habit of quoting reams of critical comments to her friends, to her correspondents, to lecture audiences. Good or bad, she found reviews very important. In *The Blue Castle*, reviewers had missed the special quality she was aiming for, or had not found it impressive.

In 1927, *Emily's Quest* marked the author's retreat from her experimental venture. This is another "girls' book," in magazine style. The familiar characters are re-assembled, re-aligned, and finally sorted out into romantic pairs. "Jarback Priest," after threatening to become a distinct person, diminishes and fades as conventional poetic romance takes over. The book makes an interesting pair with *The Blue Castle*, so different in tone.

In 1929 another gifted fantasy-child was added to the established pattern, in *Magic for Marigold*.

Then came one more attempt to break the mold. *A Tangled Web* (1931) is an effort at mosaic method in plotting a story for grown-ups. *Aunt Becky Began It* was the English title of this novel—Aunt Becky being the old-witch character who dangles a family treasure before the Dark-Penballow clan, and sets its members to weaving a number of webs in hope of the heirloom. This folk-tale motif of treasure and hag-guardian has recurred in almost every one of L. M. Montgomery's novels. The novel "up-dates" the Island girls, now lipsticked, silk-stockinged, bobbed, and given to small swearings. The author offers a cheap "come-on" in the opening paragraph when she implies that we will learn how Big Sam Dark "learned to appreciate the beauty of the unclothed female form." But in spite of this minor naughtiness the stories are still the conventional tales of "Avonlea," not really lifted into any newly mature vision.

The author had now an impressive list of still-popular books to her credit. A new generation was "growing up on Anne," and the production of new books had settled to a rhythm of one novel every alternate year. A new movie version of *Anne of Green Gables* was in the making (to be released in 1934). A number of tours of Canada, east (every summer) and west, had shown the author how universally popular her books continued to be, and how strong the demand for "more about the Island."

During these years at Norval she added two more to her list of seventeen books: *Pat of Silver Bush* (1933) and *Mistress Pat* (1935). "Pat" is a convincing child, in her deep attachment to her home and her dread of change and chance. "Old Judy Plum," the Irish house-keeper who watches the child's initiation into maturity, becomes weari-some in her stage-Irish mannerisms, but she delighted (and still delights) young readers. Dialect humour holds its appeal for children.

L. M. Montgomery's own "children" were now young men ready for university. Perhaps the give-and-take of their boyhood life together was now far enough distanced in the author's memory to have become accessible for re-creation. Such a theory of the way her imagination worked, at a distance in time from experienced fact, might account for the new strength in the "Pat" books of studies of family life. Brother-and-sister relations, not well handled or handled with false sentimentality in *Rainbow Valley* and *Rilla of Ingleside,* are better managed now, with new variety and a sometimes rueful realism.

Before leaving Norval, L. M. Montgomery found time also to collaborate on a compilation of lives of *Courageous Women* (1934). The list of women includes Pauline Johnson, Marshall Saunders, Madame Albani, and Catharine Parr Traill, along with non-Canadian "heroines" such as Joan of Arc, Florence Nightingale and Helen Keller. The collaborators were Mabel Burns McKinley and Marian Keith (Mrs. Donald MacGregor). Mrs. MacGregor had been a treasured friend since 1911, the year both young women, newly established authors and newly married brides of ministers, had met at a Toronto reception given by the Women's Press Club. It was a friendship that perhaps exerted unfortunate pressures on L. M. Mongomery to conform to the conventions of romantic escapist fiction of the moral uplift sort.

The Macdonald family moved to Toronto in 1935 when Mr. Macdonald retired from the active ministry. Life centred around the activities of the two university students, Chester in law and Stuart in medicine. The Women's Press Club, the Canadian Author's Association, and other groups of professional and amateur artists absorbed time and energy. So did the business of arrangements with publishers, and the still voluminous correspondence with friends, relations and readers. She was herself an omnivorous reader of classics, mystery stories, best sellers, magazines—anything and everything.

In this year of flattering official recognition, 1935, L. M. Montgomery appeared on the King's Silver Jubilee List as an officer in the Order of the British Empire. She was also elected Fellow of the Royal Society of Arts and Letters. The Institut des Lettres et des Arts of France made her a member, and later awarded her a silver medal for literary style.

She set to work again in her new home on Riverside Drive in Toronto, to rebuild the pattern of plotting, writing, and revising, all dove-tailed into the daily chores of housekeeping. Two last "Anne" books were to be written: *Anne of Windy Poplars* (1936) and *Anne of Ingleside* (1939). These stories are concocted to "fill in the gaps" in Anne's story: the years she spent in waiting for Gilbert to finish his medical course (*Windy Poplars*) and the years when her children were small (*Ingleside*). Both books have a warmed-over flavour. The people are "characters" revived from earlier models. Neither book has distinction in structure. The slang is an odd mixture of phrases of the 1930s and the remembered cadences of the 1900–1910 period. Even "Susan" has lost her gossipy vigour. Anne's children are quaint and cute and not very believable.

But there remained one further flame of creativity. One last girl would be added to the roll-call of convincing heroines. *Jane of Lantern Hill* (1937) begins in Toronto. It is a Toronto of dreary grey mansions and more dismal filling-stations, family dinners, and ashy back-yards. But Jane goes every summer from this Toronto to join her father, on Prince Edward Island. Eventually she draws her golden mother with her, back to the Island. This small and poignant version of Orpheus and Eurydice ends in pastoral reunion and fulfilment. It is equally vivid in its Island paradise, where Jane keeps house for her father, and in its Toronto hell, where Jane quakes before Grandmother (who calls her "Victoria"). If, as Professor Northrop Frye says, literature is "two dreams, a wish-fulfilment dream and an anxiety dream, that are focussed together, like a pair of glasses, and become a fully conscious vision," this last book stakes a claim as literature. Not just "children's literature," either, for both Jane's anxiety and her dream are successful metaphors of adult psychic realities. Jane's island paradise is deeply meaningful and satisfying; and not only for children.

L. M. Montgomery was increasingly conscious of her role as myth-maker. She talked mystically about "the Island" as a place of the soul. Asked to contribute an article on P.E.I. to a memorial volume on Canada, designed for presentation by the Canadian Pacific Railway to King George and Queen Elizabeth, L. M. Montgomery side-stepped the expected conventions of travel-book descriptions. She wrote of the Island's beauty, its reality, its peace; the feeling it gave, in "dimming landscape . . . and long, white-sand beach and murmuring ocean . . . homestead lights and the old fields tilled by dead and gone generations who loved them," of being "home."

By 1939, the life of L. M. Montgomery was far from paradisal. Her health was no longer good, and her spirits very depressed. She was deeply distressed by the coming of war. Her husband's ill health was a great worry. She was in correspondence with the Ryerson Press, which planned a Canadian edition of her earlier works. Ryerson had been agents for the old Page Company of Boston; now they were bringing the early books out again in Canada. There would be no change in the royalty arrangements. The whole business revived L. M. Montgomery's resentment over what she considered the exploitation of her efforts by the publishers. Two movie versions of *Anne* had been made, and two three-act plays based on *Anne* appeared in 1937, one by Alice Chadwicke, one by Wilbur Braun. Both, issued by French in New York, brought no returns to L. M. Montgomery, for she had sold all "rights" to dramatic versions for a lump sum back in 1907. She brooded also over the "piracy" suits she had suffered through in the twenties. Illness and depression grew together. She wrote to a correspondent who had paid her a tribute in 1940, "It always gives me pleasure to hear that [my books] have given a little help or enjoyment to my readers. Certainly in the kind of world that this has become we need all the help we can get."

L. M. Montgomery died April 24, 1942. She was buried in Cavendish, in

> the loveliness
> Of cool, far hill, and long remembered shore,
> Finding in it a sweet forgetfulness
> Of all that hurt before.

Her husband died a year later. In Prince Edward Island, a stone monument has been erected at the entrance to Cavendish National Park, and the old "Green Gables" house, near L. M. Montgomery's childhood home, stands as a shrine to her memory and a recognition of the continuing reality of "Anne."

Her death brought a wave of retrospective articles, mostly nostalgic. Her old correspondent, Ephraim Weber, prepared two articles for the *Dalhousie Review*, "L. M. Montgomery as a Letter Writer," October, 1942, and "L. M. Montgomery's 'Anne,' " April, 1944. They remained the major serious contribution to knowledge of the author for many years. Subsequent critics of Canadian literature—such as Arthur Phelps, in *Canadian Writer* (1951), and Desmond Pacey in *Creative Writing* (1952), were patronizing and casual. They spoke of her naïve plotting, her whimsy, her sentiment. Hilda M. Ridley's biography, *The Story of L. M. Montgomery* (1956), blurred some details, and over-emphasized the childhood background of the author.

Wilfrid Eggleston in his graceful edition (1960) of *The Green Gables Letters* (*From L. M. Montgomery to Ephraim Weber, 1905–1909*), has done much to restore our sense of the wisdom and wit of this "lively and attractive personality."

Her established audience—girls between ten and fourteen—continues to read and love the L. M. Montgomery books. But she may also lay increasing claim to our attention as adult critics. The books have an intensity because they *were* written as "children's books." The same kind of sesame that unlocked Lewis Carroll's inhibitions and let him write the classic of fantasy and repression that we now see in *Alice*—that same magic releasing power seems to have operated with the Canadian, late-Victorian, provincial spinster. Writing "for children," she could re-enact the rituals of childhood. Recreating her own remembered yearnings and anxieties, she could create a myth of the hesitant desires and worries of the virginal years.

Modern psychology explains some of the hidden power of L. M. Montgomery's books, especially for adolescent girls. Most teen-aged girls find it hard to get along with their mothers, the psychologists say, yet not daring consciously to dislike the mother, they are torn by mixed emotions of admiration, rivalry, dependence, hostility, all operating at a subconscious level. The heroines of L. M. Montgomery have no mothers. They do have aunts and grandmothers (who can safely be hated). Indeed, they usually have a range of aunts, some restrictive, some permissive. The adolescent reader can discriminate ambivalent feelings by loving one aunt (mother-substitute), while hating another. Also, in adolescence there is a normal intensity of feeling for the father, a feeling that must be outgrown or re-directed, but that is very powerful in the transitional stage between family relations and extra-familial ones, and correlated with the transition from homosexual to heterosexual devotion. In most of L. M. Montgomery's books, the father, safely distanced by death, stirs deep feelings of attachment (usually disapproved of by the aunts or grandmothers).

Other tenets of the psychologists who study adolescence can similarly be illustrated from the Montgomery books. "Girls may feel unconscious jealousy of boys": in the novels girls replace boys, as Anne replaced the asked-for boy orphan, as Valancy replaced her mother's desired son. Many times, also, names are used to suggest a crossing of boundaries: "Peter" in *The Quarantine* is a girl; "Bev," the boy-narrator in the Story Girl series has an ambivalent name, as have "Phil", "Jo", Jamesina, Pat, and a long list of others. The theory would be that reading such tales gives young girls an outlet for their fantasies of changing sex. Another tenet: "The adolescent longs for yet dreads the coming of physical passion." No doubt this accounts for the pleasure girls find in reading the long, long sequence of tales in which consummation of a romance is suspended, usually by some illogical tabu. Item: "The ending of virginity may be symbolically accepted in dreams, as a prelude to reality." Re-reading the L. M. Montgomery books with even a reserved acceptance of Freudian symbolism would surprise most of us! Once again, the theory is that such gentle, sublimated acceptance into the young reader's consciousness can be a healthy form of gradual adjustment. Such a Freudian re-reading, besides increasing our interest in the "Anne" and "Emily" books, may lead to a revaluation of *The Blue Castle*, where many of the suppressed themes are directly stated.

The basic assumption in this revaluation is that L. M. Montgomery was probably not conscious of the forces she was releasing. She was, however, honest enough to use the patterns her memory suggested. Furthermore, she was a good enough craftsman to lift the stories from the level of clinical confession to that of archetypal statement.

We may guess, also, that this author was increasingly conscious of the basic equation she had established, almost by chance, in her first successful novel. "The Island" is adolescence. And adolescence, that time of intense dreaming, of romantic yearning and disturbing hostility, remains as a part of every consciousness. Encircled by the mature sands of logic, pragmatism, utilitarianism and conformity, the island of youth exists for us and in us still. Perhaps art can be the channel by which we rediscover the island. L. M. Montgomery's world of poetry, virginity, and pantheism still opens for the adult reader the way back to his own world of young realization: he "wakes, to dream again."

This brings us to the final claim of L. M. Montgomery on our attention and respect. She is the novelist for the bookish child, the word-conscious child to whom she gives reassurance about a sense of the magic of "naming." She knows that words are her tool, and have been so ever since as a child, by naming, she made her own Island in time.

BIBLIOGRAPHY

WILFRID EGGLESTON (ed.), *The Green Gables Letters*. Toronto, 1960.

NORTHROP FRYE, *The Educated Imagination*. Toronto, C.B.C. Publications, 1963.

S. J. KUNITZ and HOWARD HAYCRAFT, *Twentieth Century Authors*. New York, 1942.

R. E. MUUSS (ed.), *Theories of Adolescence*. New York, 1962.

DESMOND PACEY, *Creative Writing in Canada*, pp. 94, 98. Toronto, 1952.

A. L. PHELPS, *Canadian Writers*, pp. 85–93. Toronto, 1951.

HILDA M. RIDLEY, *The Story of L. M. Montgomery*. Toronto, 1956.

IAN SCLANDERS, "Lucy of Green Gables," *Maclean's Magazine* 64: 12–13, 33–36 (Dec. 15, 1951).

EPHRAIM WEBER, "L. M. Montgomery as a Letter Writer," *Dalhousie Review* 22: 300–310 (Oct., 1942).

——— "L. M. Montgomery's 'Anne'" (Bibliography), *Dalhousie Review* 24: 64–73 (April, 1944).

{ 12 }

Emily Carr

1871-1945

FLORA HAMILTON BURNS

EMILY CARR was born on a night of storm and deep snow—December 13, 1871. In her Journal she wrote, ". . . and the storm has never quite lulled in my life. I've always been tossing and wrestling and buffeting it." The house where she was born was only two blocks from Horseshoe Bay, scene of many of her paintings, where the waves dash high above the cliffs and relentlessly carry away the shoreline.*

*AUTHOR'S NOTE. My grandparents, who came to Victoria in 1851–52, knew the Carr family from the time of their arrival in 1863. Both families were residents of James's Bay and attended the same church. When Emily returned to Victoria to live in 1913 she became an intimate friend of my mother and was deeply grieved by her sudden death in 1924. My close friendship with Emily commenced at that time.

For many years I was the only person who knew that Emily was writing. She asked me to be her critic, and read or sent me her manuscripts for criticism, and in the beginning for typing, before she taught herself to type. This was naturally on a voluntary basis on my part. During her very serious illness in 1940 I typed and edited (as far as anyone could edit Emily Carr—punctuation, paragraphing, sentence structure) the manuscripts of *Klee Wyck* and *The Book of Small* for submission to the publishers. Mr. Ira Dilworth was instrumental in obtaining publication by the Oxford University Press, and thenceforward took over the editing of her manuscripts. My friendship with Emily extended throughout the last twenty years of her life, and I had the happiness of witnessing the late recognition of her as a great artist and writer.

Quotations from *Growing Pains* are made by kind permission of Clarke, Irwin & Company Limited.

Emily was the youngest daughter of Richard Carr, a forceful personality who, after wide travel and many occupations, had made his fortune in the California gold rush and then returned to his native country, England, to be married. He brought his young wife out to California where his two eldest daughters, Edith and Clara, were born. A few years later he retired and decided to settle on Vancouver Island as he wished to bring up his family in a new country but under the British flag. On July 5, 1863, Richard Carr arrived in Victoria with his wife and two little girls. He bought ten acres of choice property opposite Beacon Hill Park, built a graceful and commodious house and laid out a beautiful garden in the English manner. Too vigorous to remain idle, he established a flourishing business as a wholesale importer of wines and provisions.

Three younger daughters, Elizabeth, always called Lizzie, Alice and Emily, and a son Richard, who died in early manhood, were born in Victoria. Edith was almost sixteen when Emily was born, and as Mrs. Carr was delicate and often ill it was Edith who soon assumed many of the duties of looking after the younger children. Mr. Carr had put his free and adventurous youth behind him, but the very forcefulness of his character changed him into a martinet with strong overtones of puritanism so that the children became victims of the patriarchal system. Edith reflected this stern Victorian upbringing, which Lizzie and Alice accepted without question, but from her earliest years Emily showed great independence which often verged on rebellion. She was utterly unlike the rest of the family and so full of spirit, curiosity, and adventure that she was constantly called naughty by her older sisters. Mrs. Carr was a quiet, gentle woman, devoted to her husband and family. Calm and understanding, she held the balance between her husband's rigid ideas of family life and her own sympathetic outlook. Everyone loved Mrs. Carr and the family had many friends.

Emily was intensely affectionate, and although she thought her family disapproved of her she was undoubtedly her parents' favourite child, but their sense of fairness prevented them from showing this. She was passionately fond of animals and spent her happiest hours in the cowyard, singing to the cow and mothering the chickens, ducks, and calves. Her first attempt at art was inspired by watching the family dog for a long time. She ran into the house, spread out a brown paper bag, and with a charred stick from the fireplace drew the dog. When her father saw the drawing he bought her a good paintbox and arranged for lessons. Shortly afterwards she drew a portrait of her father reading. He gave her a $5.00 gold piece, put the picture in a handsome frame, and ordered four copies for her sisters. Emily destroyed almost all of her early work but this picture has survived and foreshadows in a remarkable way the free, confident style of her late and finest work. Her two outstanding characteristics which never changed throughout her life were her overmastering desire to paint and her intense love and sense of kinship with animals.

Emily was fifteen when Mrs. Carr died. She adored her mother who had been a spiritual refuge for the warm-hearted, passionate girl. The bond was so deep that Emily felt totally bereft. Her father, too, was so heart-broken that he shut himself away from his family, leaving them entirely in the hands of Edith who thus, at the age of thirty-two, became the dominant figure in the household. Clara, who was very beautiful, had married during her parents' lifetime.

Mr. Carr died two years after his wife, leaving a substantial estate for his children, but it was all in Edith's name which rendered the younger children dependent upon her. Emily resented this domination, both for herself and for the rest of the family, feeling that they were not allowed to grow up and lead their own lives. Faced with full responsibility for the family, Edith no doubt believed that the only way to control this headstrong, turbulent girl was to impose an unyielding discipline. Being treated as a mere child left such an imprint upon Emily that in her autobiography she frequently refers to herself as years younger than she actually was, and indeed affected her personality to such an extent that in England, in her thirties, she was constantly addressed as "child" by intimate friends.

Emily had attended Girls' Central and Victoria high schools but the usual subjects bored her and she was never a good student. At the age of seventeen she appealed to the gentleman her father had named as her guardian to arrange for her to attend the San Francisco School of Art, now the San Francisco Art Institute, as there was no art school in western Canada. Her guardian consented and in 1889 Emily arrived in San Francisco, complete with straw suitcase and a canary in a battered cage. Filled with the joy of liberation, she remained there for six happy, carefree years. At the end of 1894 the Carr estate suffered financial losses and she was recalled to Victoria. The work she brought back represented the usual art school subjects: portraits, still life, landscapes; she had not yet learned how to express herself in her work.

Emily received a warm welcome home from her sisters and was asked by a friend to start drawing classes for children so she converted the loft above the cow barn into a studio. The children enjoyed their lessons, Emily enjoyed the children, the classes multiplied, and her studio soon became a rendezvous for many friends. Vivacious and full of fun, with softly curling brown hair and strongly marked, winged eyebrows over eloquent grey eyes, Emily was extremely attractive. She had beautiful hands, the fingers long, delicately shaped, but capable of performing the most intricate operations or heavy manual tasks.

Emily was always called Millie by her family and friends. She said that when she signed her pictures Emily Carr no one recognized her so she just stuck in an M, which accounts for her varied signatures, "M. Emily Carr," "M. E. Carr," "E.M.C.," and "M. Carr."

In the summer of 1898 Emily was invited to visit the new Indian mission at Ucluelet on the west coast of Vancouver Island, and she spent several weeks at this tiny, isolated post. Living conditions were stark but she was deeply stirred by the Indians, their way of life and their first unwilling steps to adjust themselves to the white man's ways. The village patriarch accepted her and said she was not "stuck up" and knew how to laugh. Her sense of fun bridged the language gap and they named her "Klee Wyck" (Laughing One), Emily's favourite and truly characteristic nickname. She sketched the people, their boats and houses, but she did not attempt to paint the great, brooding, virgin forest—the wild beauty and grandeur overpowered her. She knew of no artist or art school able to teach her to paint such immensity, and felt she must go to Europe for further study.

This was a climactic year for Emily: she had come to know the Indians in their remote habitations; she had been profoundly moved by the solemn beauty of the vast, untouched forests and rugged shores of Vancouver Island. She wrote in Growing Pains, "Immediately upon my return from the West Coast Mission, I tasted two experiences for the first time—love, and poetry. Poetry was pure joy, love more than half pain. I gave my love where it was not wanted; almost simultaneously an immense love was offered to me which I could neither accept nor return." (Page 108.) Emily had numerous admirers and men friends, but this new friendship was entirely different. She loved deeply, passionately, with all her being, once for all. Until she left for England she believed her love was reciprocated, but no word of their future was ever spoken by the man she loved. This was a profound, traumatic experience which affected her emotional life for years. She told me later, "I don't love many, but when I do I *love hard.*" She was exceedingly proud. Family and friends never knew of her feelings.

By the summer of 1899 Emily had saved enough money to go to England. She was twenty-seven but scarcely more mature than when she had embarked for California ten years before. Totally unsophisticated and unprepared for life in the largest city in the world, Emily found London, its crowds, dust, noise, and miles of dreary streets and houses unbearable. She "ached with homesickness for my West" (page 125). She thought most of the people she met "narrow-minded, snobbish, cold and hard." She had no interest in history or conventional sightseeing, and the art galleries disappointed her.

The Westminster School of Art had been at its peak during the previous ten years when Aubrey Beardsley and other well-known painters had studied there, and among Emily's co-students were Charles Furse and Duncan Grant. In spite of her lack of enthusiasm for English life Emily soon had several devoted friends among the students and others. As usual she received nicknames: in San Francisco they called her "Dummy" because of her lack of sophistication; in London, with cars just coming into use, she was "Carlight" and "Motor," while her closest personal friends called her "Klee Wyck" as soon as they heard the story.

In England, poor health dogged Emily. Shortly after her arrival she had to undergo a serious operation on her foot and was incapacitated for three months. Besides her daily work in the life class she took night courses in design, anatomy, clay modelling. Always tired, she drove herself relentlessly, and when doctor and friends remonstrated she replied that her money was limited and she must utilize every hour of every day. London was inimical to Emily: she was a forest tree transplanted to a city sidewalk—no space to grow, no sun or air to quicken leaves and branches. She wilted physically and spiritually.

To escape London Emily spent a year with the art colony at St. Ives, Cornwall, under Julius Olsson and Algernon Talmage, well-known landscape artists, whom she respected and who recognized her talents, followed by six months at the Herkomer School of Art at Bushey, Hertfordshire. She enjoyed St. Ives and Bushey and her love of life and fun came to the surface. Back in London on her way to St. Ives for a second winter Emily, always in a hurry, always accident-prone, had a serious fall. Her condition was so alarming that her sister Lizzie travelled from Victoria to take her home, but Emily refused to leave. The specialist ordered complete rest in a sanatorium for at least a year since she was suffering from acute anaemia.

Eighteen months of enforced inactivity in alien surroundings combined with unbending regulations reduced Emily to such a state of depression and despair that her condition was regarded as hopeless until a new doctor prescribed fresh treatment. After an intensive course of massage and exercise she was able to return to Canada. On her way home she spent two months with friends in the Cariboo, recuperating in the high, bracing atmosphere. At the end of 1904 she returned to Victoria after an absence of five and a half years. Her youth was over and she felt she had accomplished nothing, but she was back in Canada and her heart sang.

Five and a half years older, Emily felt Victoria had changed, but the change was in herself. Riding astride on Edith's beautiful horse—much to her sisters' consternation—she went into the country, absorbing peace and vitality. In her autobiography she wrote: "The woods standing, standing, holding the cool sap of vegetation were healing, restful after seeing the boil of humanity. . . . After the mellow sweetness of England with its perpetual undertone of humanity it was good to stand in space" (page 273).

Early in 1905 Emily rented a studio in town where shortly afterwards Alfred Watts of the dashing Victoria newspaper, *The Week*, interviewed her. He thought her Cornish paintings charming but considered her Ucluelet sketches of Indian life outstanding. *The Week* engaged her as their current affairs cartoonist, and until she left for Vancouver at the end of the year her witty and original cartoons enlivened its pages.

Victoria was unconscious of art; no one was teaching it, the Arts and Crafts Society was still in the future. Vancouver, however, was rapidly becoming a large and wealthy city and the Ladies' Art Club asked Emily to become their teacher. The engagement proved fleeting: the members were not interested in serious work and criticism and terminated the arrangement. Emily opened classes for children in Vancouver which prospered immediately. She evolved her own system —no copying, everything portrayed direct from live models, still life and painting out of doors in the Park and along the waterfront. Emily found it was vigorous, hard, happy work and she discovered that she had learned more during her frustrated years in England than she had realized.

In 1907 Emily and Alice visited Sitka and the Yukon, seeing many Indian villages with their grand totem poles, painted housefronts and unique grave houses patterned on Russian church architecture. Emily realized that this art was fast disappearing and determined to make as complete a record of it as possible. During the next two summers she went north, going far off the beaten track to reach unspoiled villages and paint the Indian memorials in their own surroundings. With the advice of Dr. C. F. Newcombe, eminent anthropologist, and missionary friends, and through her own indomitable determination she travelled to remote areas by any conveyance available—gasboat, canoe, stage, or wagon.

The sheer power and command of their materials by the Indians, combined with their close relationship to their surroundings and their constant search for "the hidden thing which is felt rather than seen" inspired her and stimulated her creative energy. Yet it imposed on her a need for broader technique and stronger handling, which led to a determination to go forth once more to study.

So in 1910 Emily left for Paris, accompanied by Alice. They took a small flat in the Latin Quarter, Rue Campagne Premier, off Montparnasse Avenue. Emily had a letter of introduction to Harry (William Henry Phelan) Gibb, an English artist who had studied and worked in Paris for years and had been strongly influenced by Cézanne. He was fighting strenuously for the "New Art" and was highly regarded by modern artists and Gertrude Stein. He advised her to study at the Académie Colarossi, successor of the ancient Académie Suisse, the nursery of many of the greatest of the Impressionists—Monet, Pisarro,

Cézanne, Gauguin—and a Mecca for *avant-garde* students. Men and women studied together there and Gibb considered it a great advantage for women painters to see the stronger work of men. With no knowledge of French, Emily found the experience very hard. The rooms were hot, airless and crowded, and in a month or two she was overcome by "that miserable, chalky lifelessness" which had seized her in London. Gibb recommended her to the large studio of John Duncan Fergusson, who had also worked in Paris for many years as a follower of Manet, the Fauves and the Rhythm Group. Fergusson employed the finest critics in Paris but within a few weeks Emily was in hospital—measles, with complications—and was seriously ill for three months. Her French doctor, like the London physicians, said that she must keep out of large cities or die (page 291). He recommended that she take the hot salt baths in Sweden.

"Why did cities hate, thwart, damage me so?" brooded Emily. The sensitivity of the true artist is far greater than that of the average person. Gauguin never felt well in Paris which drained him of all energy and strength: he disliked the crowds, the rush, the tension and competition; Paris depressed Cézanne and forced him to escape to the country; Van Gogh could not bear Paris, and fled.

The salt baths benefited Emily, and she and Alice enjoyed Sweden which reminded them of their own West Coast. In the spring of 1911 Alice went back to Canada and Emily returned to France. She joined a landscape class which Harry Gibb had formed at Cressy-en-Brie and in Brittany. Tramping the countryside, sketch sack on shoulder, Emily was well and happy. She loved the picturesque villages and the unspoiled, laughing people. Harry Gibb was impressed by her painting, and when she asked to see some of his sketches he refused, saying, "Your work must not be influenced by mine. You will be one of the painters,—woman painters—of your day." "You work too hard! Always at it. Easy! Easy!" (pages 294-5). At Concarneau, beloved of artists, she painted a succession of sharply realized, brilliant marine sketches, unmistakably individual in style.

Culminating her eighteen months of study, two of her paintings were accepted and well hung at the famous Salon d'Automne, among such well-known contemporaries as Bonnard, Vlaminck, Rouault, Segonzac, Marquet.

Paris in 1911 was exciting for modern artists. Over sixteen of the greatest Impressionist painters, including Monet, Renoir and Degas, were working in Paris at that time. The galleries and dealers' showrooms were filled with their pictures but the Louvre had refused to recognize or accept any of their work. Count de Camondo, who died early in 1911, bequeathed his unrivalled art collection, including fifty-six Impressionist paintings, to the Louvre on condition that all be accepted and exhibited. On May 8, 1911, the Louvre accepted this munificent gift. At last, after forty years of struggle and denial, the Impressionists were admitted to the Louvre. France gave Emily a new vision of the painters' world—a revelation of light, colour, and simplification of form. She was so in tune with the work then being done in France that its benefits were greater than those she had derived from her sojourn in England, but she was still baffled as to how to paint the immensity of the West.

At the end of the year Emily returned to Vancouver where she held an exhibition of her work. It was probably the first time modern paintings had been seen in British Columbia and neither critics nor public liked them. The press notices were humiliating and schools where she had taught refused to employ her again. In spite of this Emily did not regret "the new way of seeing." During the summer of 1912 she took tremendous journeys to the almost inaccessible, storm-shrouded Queen Charlotte Islands and to the most distant Indian villages at the headquarters of the Skeena and the Naas. She slept in mission houses, schoolhouses, lighthouses, Indian houses or a tent, carrying her own food and bedding and always accompanied by her large Old English sheep dog "Billie." Many of her finest historical canvases are dated 1912.

Part of the Carr property was to be sold in 1913 and Emily returned to Victoria where she built an apartment house and studio on an unsold lot, expecting that with an income from the apartments she could devote herself to painting. She opened the "House of All Sorts" with an "At Home" and an exhibition of her latest work. In its column "Late Society News," *The Week* carried a long list of her guests but no mention of her pictures. This epitomized the reaction of Victoria at that time. The great totem poles with their bold, grotesque contours and strong colours shocked and mystified Victorians, and the freshness, brilliance and charm of her French pictures went unnoticed. Those who did not loudly condemn felt that the less said the better, but Dr.

Newcombe, an acknowledged authority on Indian art, bought eight or
nine of her paintings and Mrs. Dennis Harris, a talented amateur artist
and daughter of Sir James Douglas, together with my mother,
approached the provincial government to buy one or more of Emily's
important canvases. There was no response. The British Columbia
government never bought a painting by Emily until after her death
when public opinion demanded it. She exhibited fifteen pictures at
the fourth Exhibition of the Arts and Crafts Club at Victoria in 1913
but the Club did not show any of her pictures again until 1924,
when four of her paintings were exhibited. Her sisters begged her to
abandon the "new way of seeing" but Emily said she would rather
starve. She had steeled herself to the disapproval of the family but
the total rejection of her art was a bitter blow. She told me,

I feel about my paintings exactly as if they were my children. They are
my children, of my body, my mind, my innermost being. When people
call them horrible and hideous I resent it deeply—I can't help it. I know
people don't have to like my pictures but when they condemn them I
feel like a mother protecting her young. I don't wish to speak about them
to those who are unsympathetic towards them.

There followed fourteen years of frustration and relentless struggle
to make a living. With the outbreak of war in 1914 property and rents
sank and income from the apartments was insufficient to cover upkeep
and living expenses. Emily converted all her own quarters, including
the studio, into apartments or rooms for boarders, and took refuge in
a tiny attic where, on the under side of the shingled roof, she painted
two enormous eagles, wings outspread. She could not afford help but
became an excellent cook and turned her constructive talents into
mastering all minor repairs.

Emily was temperamentally unsuited to the position of landlady,
and hated it. She was too impatient, too imperious, too intolerant of
others' ways, and too quick-tempered to handle tenants with ease and
tact. In the early days, owing to her inexperience, unscrupulous persons tried to take advantage of her and at times there were unseemly
disputes, including an occasion when, exasperated beyond words by
a tenant, she turned the hose upon him. To those whom she liked
and respected she was warm hearted and generous and some of her
tenants remained for years. During the depression of the 1930s she

told one of them that even if he were unable to pay his rent, he would always have a home there.

In addition to children's classes and political cartoons for Western Women's Weekly (Vancouver), Emily bred Old English bobtailed sheep dogs for sale, and when their maintenance became too expensive she filled her kennels with the new, small breed of Belgian griffons. Her kennels were always a source of great pleasure and pride to her. To increase her income she also took up pottery making, gathering and preparing the special clay herself. She moulded each piece by hand, without a wheel, using Indian designs as decoration, unglazed, and built her own kiln. With none of the usual mechanical devices she fired 500 pieces at a time—a nightmare ordeal lasting three days and nights. She enjoyed the modelling and designing but the entire process was gruelling, exhausting work. In spite of all these activities Emily could not pay off the mortgage, with its threat of foreclosure. These were searing years; she had no time or inclination to paint, and in 1923 she underwent a serious operation which was not completely successful. In the mid-twenties part of the Carr property formerly in Edith's name was sold, and Lizzie and Alice helped Emily to pay off the mortgage on her house.

During those years Emily became deeply attached to one of her young pupils, Carol Williams, who adored her and loved animals almost as much as Emily did, and who wanted to be an artist. The freshness and ardour of her mind and her affectionate nature endeared her strongly to Emily who had always longed for a daughter, and she wished to adopt her. Naturally Carol's parents would not entertain such an idea, but Carol spent part of every year with Emily until, very young, she married and went to Ontario. The unique bond between Emily and Carol (Mrs. Pearson) continued throughout Emily's life.

My family had known the Carrs intimately ever since the latter settled in Victoria but my close personal friendship with Emily began in 1925. In spite of her arduous life she was a most exhilarating companion, acutely observant, and with a great wit—at times almost too biting. Her sense of comedy was spontaneous and refreshing, and she had had so many amazing and unusual adventures that there was never a dull moment in her company. Although she was fifty-four at that time one could never think of age in connection with Emily. Indeed she seemed younger than many people half her age. She never spoke of her painting and detested any kind of "art jargon" or hypocritical pretence in connection with it. Impulsive and generous, Emily was inclined to hide this side of herself under the guise of impatience of sentimentality, yet in certain respects she was curiously sentimental. She loved children and delighted in inventing games and toys to amuse them. Her menagerie of pets was famous, of which the griffon dogs—Koko, Ginger Pop, and Tantrum—Susie the white rat, and Woo, her little Javanese monkey, were her favourites. When Lizzie first saw Woo she was almost speechless. "Millie! I never, never, *never*, thought a relation of mine would sink to a-a-a *baboon!*" (*Heart of a Peacock*, p. 169.)

Edith had died in 1919. Lizzie, a highly trained physiotherapist, was living in the big house and Alice carried on her popular kindergarten in the house she had built on the Carr property. Each sister led her own life; they did not think alike, or see things from the same point of view, but in spite of a good deal of bluntness on all sides there was a great depth of affection between the trio, "Bigger, Middle and Small," as Emily called them in *The Book of Small*. They visited back and forth almost daily, Sunday dinner was always at Lizzie's house, supper at Emily's, while Alice baked delicious bread for the three of them.

In 1926 Marius Barbeau, ethnologist at the National Museum, Ottawa, paid his third visit to Emily Carr. He had first heard of her paintings at Fort Simpson in 1916 from his Indian interpreter, Lazarus Moody, who had been Emily's guide on her journey up the Skeena in 1912. M. Barbeau immediately sought her out but at that time she refused to show him her pictures, believing that he asked out of idle curiosity. He had visited her again in 1920 when he saw some of her canvases, and on this third visit he came to select sixty of her pictures for the exhibition of Canadian West Coast art to be held at the National Gallery of Canada in 1927. Emily was sceptical about sending her pictures east and said she knew nothing about the National Gallery. Finally Eric Brown, Director of the Gallery, came to Victoria himself to persuade Emily to allow the Gallery to exhibit her pictures, pottery and beautiful hooked rugs, and invited her to attend the exhibition in person. M. Barbeau arranged with the Canadian National Railways for a complimentary ticket for the journey and invited Emily to be his guest in Ottawa. Alice and Lizzie were thrilled by this amazing invitation and insisted, "You must go. We will look after the house."

Until this exhibition art circles in eastern Canada or anywhere else knew nothing of Emily Carr or her painting. Her work was a revelation to the Group of Seven and they welcomed her with open arms. But if Emily Carr was a revelation to the Group of Seven, the work of the Group was a revelation to Emily Carr. Here were the artists she had dreamed of, painting the lands of Canada as she felt they needed to be painted, with the majesty, strength, and austere beauty which their vastness demanded. She felt the task was too great for her, but her fellow artists assured her that she alone could meet the inexorable challenge flung at her by the land of her birth. The climax of her trip was her visit to the studio of Lawren Harris. In her autobiography she wrote:

The day I . . . was met by Mr. Harris and led into his tranquil studio,— that day my idea of Art wholly changed. I was done with the boil and ferment of restless, resentful artists, cudgelling their brains as to how to make Art pay, how to "please the public". Mr. Harris did not paint to please the public, he did not have to, but he would not have done so anyway. (Page 340)

The Group was enthusiastic about her work but she begged Mr. Harris to criticize her paintings "hard." He replied:

"Your work is impressive . . . I really have, nor can have, nothing to say by way of criticism. . . . The pictures are works of art in their own right . . . have creative life in them . . . they breathe." (Page 319–20)

A new era thus opened in the life of Emily Carr. Uplifted and reinvigorated, she returned to Victoria and resumed her painting. When she bemoaned her isolation from the centres of art she was stimulated and consoled by the letters of Lawren Harris, Eric Brown and Frederick Housser, author of *A Canadian Art Movement*. Lawren Harris reiterated what her teachers in England and France told her, that her isolation was an essential factor in the development of her art.

Emily was 57 when she entered upon the most prolific, potent, and dynamic years of her life. In 1928 she went north for the last time, encountering greater physical hardships than any she had endured in the past. She spent incredible days and nights on Indian and Japanese fishboats in a wild Pacific storm; in torrential rains, sheltering, wet to the skin, in ruined grave houses; tormented almost beyond endurance by mosquitoes, she reached the most remote outposts of Indian life and penetrated even to the hostile, forbidden village of Kitwancool. In planning these journeys she had the invaluable help of Mr. "Willie" Newcombe, an authority on Indian life and traditions, who became one of her most devoted friends and her practical helper during the rest of her life. Historical paintings of great power resulted from these journeys but the Indians had abandoned their ancient beliefs and art, and Emily felt she, too, had outgrown these subjects. She turned wholly to the creative task of interpreting the majestic landscapes of British Columbia, and her art underwent a dynamic change. Light, space and pulsating atmosphere dominated her paintings.

Events moved swiftly. During the next ten years her pictures were shown at sixteen exhibitions of international standing, including the American Federation of Arts, Washington; the Stedelijk Museum, Amsterdam; the Paris International Exposition; the Tate Gallery, London; and the Group of Seven, Toronto. Her first one-man show in Victoria was sponsored by the Women's Canadian Club in 1930. She was made an honorary member of the Group of Seven and took two more trips to the east, including New York and Chicago, and the National Gallery of Canada bought six of her paintings. In 1928–9 the American artist, Mark Tobey, twice visited Victoria where he was Emily's guest, and she derived great enjoyment and stimulation from their studio work together in the study of basic form, but she was deaf to his suggestions that she adopt abstract art. As her paintings became known in Canada and abroad she made many new friends and her studio became a gathering place for visiting artists, writers and musicians, among whom were the American writer, Mrs. Kathrene Pinkerton, living in Victoria in 1930; Mrs. Nan Lawson Cheney, the artist; and Dr. Duncan Campbell Scott. Emily also had an intimate circle of young art students then in Victoria, which included Edith Hembroff (Mrs. E. Brand Schleicher), Jack Shadbolt, Max Maynard, and others, whom she was always anxious to help in any way she could.

Emily wished to write and in 1926 persuaded me to enrol with her in a short story course with the Palmer Institute of Authorship, Los Angeles. She was away to a flying start with her first assignment, a later version of which was published as "In the Shadow of the Eagle," and other stories which have since appeared in *The Heart of a Peacock*. Every week or two she would read me her latest story, ask for my criticism and compare it with that of the Palmer Institute. With her spontaneous gifts of vivid writing and story telling she soon outstripped anything the Palmer Institute could teach her. She attended night school classes conducted by Mrs. N. de B. Shaw, and her story "The Hully-up Letter" in *The Heart of a Peacock* won the prize. For years we went over together stories which have since been published in *Klee Wyck* and *The Book of Small*. Emily's handwriting was a stumbling block and as her manuscripts multiplied she bought an ancient typewriter and taught herself to type.

In 1933 Emily bought an old trailer-caravan and had it towed to whatever site she chose. There, surrounded by her "creatures," she camped and painted for a few weeks each summer. She said the animals were a bridge between her and the world of nature and helped her to paint. Her greatest source of joy and inspiration was the woods and seashore where she could sit in silence and absorb the all-pervading vibrations of earth, sea and sky, light and shadow, soaring trees and dancing saplings, and then paint with great rapidity, powerfully aware that she and all things were parts of an Infinite Whole—the Living Universe. She was a mystic, deeply religious, but not in any conventional sectarian manner. Some of her artist friends were influenced by theosophy and felt that its teachings would be helpful to her art. She was interested, but after several years' study of its principles she told her friends that she did not feel that theosophy was for her; she was content with simple Christianity. With her twofold nature—the egoist and the idealist—she was constantly aware of her need of a Redeemer. She was closely atune to the poems and ideas of Walt Whitman and always kept his *Leaves of Grass* by her side.

In spite of Emily's reputation in the art world picture sales were few. Lizzie died in 1936, Alice was almost blind, and Emily experienced the first indications of heart trouble. The House of All Sorts consumed time, money, and strength but she could not find a purchaser, so in 1936 she exchanged it for a bungalow with some rental value while she herself moved to a small, old-fashioned cottage a few blocks from Alice where, freed from the burdens of a landlady, she could concentrate on her painting and writing.

Life never ran smoothly for Emily. Suddenly, in 1937, while preparing for the Coronation Exhibition at the National Gallery, she was stricken with an extremely severe heart attack. Her condition was critical and a long period of hospital care and rest was essential, with no physical activity, including painting, permitted. Emily was in despair; acute financial worry, added to the terrible prospect of not being able to resume an active life, jeopardized her recovery. Through my sister and friends in the East representations were made to Eric Brown of the National Gallery, asking what could be done to ease Emily's immediate financial situation. He replied by telegraphing Mr. Eric Newton, noted English art critic who was then visiting western Canada, to go to Victoria and select fifteen of Emily's pictures to be sent east and placed before prospective purchasers. When Newton saw Emily in hospital he told her, "As I drove over the Island Highway I saw *Emily Carr pictures* no matter in what direction I looked. You have caught the Western spirit. . . . Get better; these hands are too clever to lie idle." (Page 357.) Later he was to say, "Emily Carr is not merely a good woman painter, she is the greatest woman painter who has yet lived." His visit was the turning point in Emily's recovery. Her convalescence was slow and her subsequent health precarious, but she was allowed to paint as long as no other physical exertion was involved.

There were no more solitary camping trips but whenever her health permitted during the next few years she took a country cottage for a few weeks and painted with such freedom, power and sense of spiritual exaltation that she reached the highest pinnacle of her art. Her output was incredible, and it seemed that with the lessening of physical activity she received an outpouring of spiritual power.

With her activities curtailed Emily turned seriously to writing and Eric Brown urged that she write her autobiography. Miss Ruth Humphrey, Professor of English at Victoria College, whose advice and criticism Emily sought, brought her manuscripts to the attention of Dr. G. G. Sedgewick, head of the English Department of the University of British Columbia. He was enchanted by them; he read several of her stories over the C.B.C. network and introduced them to

Ira Dilworth, regional director of the Canadian Broadcasting Corporation. Dilworth was so impressed that he came to Victoria to see Emily and arrange for further broadcasts, and to assist her in finding a publisher as previous attempts had failed.

Early in 1940 Emily decided to move to Alice's house; the war was in progress, it was almost impossible to obtain household help, and Alice was now blind. Emily did not consult Alice but announced that she would move in and build on a bedroom, bathroom, and kitchen for herself, use the big schoolroom for her studio and Alice's spare room for her maid. Alice was speechless but her own plans for a companion were submerged by the speed and dominance of Emily's arrangements, which were quickly carried out.

At the end of May I was shocked to hear that Emily was again in hospital—a stroke; she was so ill that she could barely speak, but insisted she must see me immediately. In a darkened room, her voice only a whisper, she told me Ira Dilworth was leaving for the East in a day or two and wanted to take *all* her stories to a publisher. She asked me to bring her the great box of manuscripts from which she indicated the versions for publication.

Some in pencil, some crudely typed, all had to be edited for spelling, paragraphing, punctuation, and correctly typed. Would Emily object if I transposed words to improve sentence structure? Would she survive? Amid a sea of manuscripts I ploughed on, the deadline was met and Ira took them to Toronto. In spite of wartime difficulties the Oxford University Press accepted the stories for publication.

Impatient to resume her writing, Emily left hospital before she could walk unaided. She improvised a "scoot box" to enable her to move about her room, but the next few months were a nightmare for her and blind Alice. She was obliged to spend a great deal of time in bed, and during the rest of her life an easel with one of her latest paintings stood at the foot of it. She seldom retouched her pictures, but from time to time she would rise and add a few brush strokes until she was completely satisfied. Occasionally friends drove her into the country for a few hours' painting which always refreshed her.

During 1941 Emily was buoyed up by preparations for the publication of her books. Ira Dilworth came to Victoria frequently to discuss details with her and the Oxford University Press spared neither time, money, nor effort to make her first publication, *Klee Wyck*, "a show piece of Canadian bookmaking." The book was ready for the Christmas trade and Emily was acclaimed across Canada as a great Canadian writer. *Klee Wyck* was awarded the Governor-General's Gold Medal for general literature. Emily was embarrassed by the press notices and told me, "I am so dumb when suddenly confronted with appreciation. It always astonishes me and makes me feel very humble and unworthy."

The University Women's Club of Victoria made Emily an honorary member and on December 12, 1941, the President, Mrs. Henry Esson Young, gave a large reception at her home to celebrate Emily's seventieth birthday and the publication of *Klee Wyck*. It was a gala affair, attended by representatives of the Lieutenant-Governor and Premier of British Columbia, the Mayor and Reeve of Victoria and Oak Bay, the Chief of the Cowichan Indians, members of every important organization in Victoria as well as Emily's closest friends. After the speeches, presentations, telegrams, and toasts Ira Dilworth read extracts from *Klee Wyck*. Emily was deeply moved but to her surprise her voice "rang out like a bull" when she said:

"Thank you, everybody, for giving me such a splendid, happy birthday and being so kind to Klee Wyck. I would rather have the good will and kind wishes of my home town, the people I have lived among all my life, than the praise of the whole world. . . . I relived the villages of Klee Wyck. . . . After fifty years they were as fresh in my mind as they were then because while I painted I had lived them deep." (Page 372)

The following year Emily founded the Emily Carr Trust Collection by which she willed 170 of her best work in oils, watercolour, and black and white to the Province of British Columbia on condition that they be permanently housed and exhibited at the Vancouver Art Gallery as there was then no gallery in Victoria. In addition she left 500 other works to be sold for the benefit of the Emily Carr Scholarship Fund to assist young, talented British Columbia artists. Of the 170 works the greater portion represent an historical pageant of the myths and cultures of the British Columbia Indians. By these two unique and magnificent gifts Emily Carr enriched the artistic and historical heritage of the people of British Columbia.

In 1942 the woods called urgently to Emily; she felt they had something more to say to her and "the longing was too terrific to subdue" (page 379). She went to a cottage on the verge of Mount Douglas Park where a farmer's wife looked after her. Eight days later she was brought into hospital on a stretcher. In a tremendous outburst of creative ardor and energy she had painted fifteen large oil sketches but this prodigious achievement precipitated an almost fatal heart attack. In hospital she told me, "This 'trombone stuff' is a slow business. Guess I was 'most a goner, but I'm catfish in my many lives. Anyhow I enjoyed Mount Douglas and was careful. I'm being very 'pie' because I want to finish my work."

The Book of Small appeared at the end of 1942 amid an avalanche of enthusiastic press notices, followed by the *House of All Sorts* in 1944. She had completed her autobiography, *Growing Pains*, but stipulated that it should not be published during her lifetime (it was published in 1946). She was working on *Pause*, her experiences in the sanitorium. Most of the stories in *The Heart of a Peacock* had been written many years previously, but it and *Pause* were published posthumously in 1953. *Klee Wyck* and *The Book of Small* are masterpieces of Canadian literature, but in *Pause* and the last chapters of *Growing Pains* the effects of her serious illnesses, which precluded the exacting revision bestowed on her earlier books, can be detected.

The last three years of Emily's life were a ceaseless struggle between the dynamic urgency of her creative genius and her failing physical strength, and she was constantly in and out of hospital and nursing homes. Throughout, gentle, selfless Alice was her mainstay and unassuming support but this added to Emily's frustration as she had always thought that she would take care of Alice. There were, however, shining aspects in the recurring pattern of light and darkness in Emily's life. Sales of her books and pictures relieved her of financial worry. During these years her paintings were being shown all over the continent at important exhibitions, for which she always submitted new work as she felt that pictures more than two years old did not represent her feelings. She was right. Her last paintings are her greatest, with a sense of freedom and joy in living which lifts them onto the plane of spiritual revelation.

In 1944 Max Stern, the renowned Montreal art dealer, exhibited sixty of her paintings at the Dominion Gallery, Montreal. He considered Emily Carr Canada's only authentic genius, and sold fifty-six of her pictures within two weeks. That year Emily suffered another stroke which impaired the use of her left arm, but from her bed she continued to write and work on her many paintings.

In the early months of 1945 Emily was constantly at work preparing for an exhibition at the Vancouver Art Gallery in April. By the end of February she had completed and mounted on plywood thirty-five large oil-on-paper sketches and felt extremely tired. Taking her type-writer with her, she went for a rest to St. Mary's Priory, a few yards across the road from her childhood home. After a day or two she seemed rested and better, and talked of doing some writing which always calmed her. A day later, on March 2, 1945, peacefully and without warning, Emily Carr passed beyond this world.

Through her paintings and her books Emily Carr has written her own biography and they speak for themselves. Her books give us many of the events of her life but her paintings show us the unfolding of her soul. The eye of the artist revealed the appearance of things, but the soul of the mystic sought behind the appearance for the underlying meaning, the ultimate reality.

As a figure of world stature Emily Carr was too big to fit into the Victoria frame in the early twentieth century. She has been called a genius and like all geniuses, she overflowed and outran her time.

BIBLIOGRAPHY

This bibliography refers only to works which are sources of biographical information. For critical material the *Canadian Periodical Index* should be consulted.

BOOKS

EMILY CARR, *Book of Small.* Toronto, Oxford, 1942.

—— *Growing Pains: The Autobiography of Emily Carr.* Toronto, Oxford, 1946.

—— *Heart of a Peacock.* Toronto, Oxford, 1953.

—— *House of All Sorts.* Toronto, Oxford, 1944.

—— *Klee Wyck.* Toronto, Oxford, 1941.

—— *Pause: A Sketch Book.* Toronto, Clarke, Irwin, 1954.

—— *Hundreds and Thousands: Journal of Emily Carr.* Toronto, Clarke, Irwin, 1966.

IRA DILWORTH and LAWREN HARRIS, *Emily Carr: Her Paintings and Sketches.* Toronto, Oxford, 1945.

CAROL PEARSON, *Emily Carr as I Knew Her.* Toronto, Clarke, Irwin, 1954.

BYRNE HOPE SANDERS, "Emily Carr" in *Famous Women,* pp. 3–43. Canadian Portrait Series. Toronto, Clarke, Irwin, 1958.

MAGAZINES

RUTH HUMPHREY, "Emily Carr—An Appreciation," *Queen's Quarterly,* 65 (Summer 1958).

FLORA HAMILTON BURNS, "Emily Carr and the Newcombe Collection," *The Beaver* #293 (Summer 1962). Reproduced for Catalogue of Hudson's Bay Company's Exhibition *The World of Emily Carr,* Victoria and Vancouver, July–August, 1962.

J. K. NESBITT, "The Genius We Laughed At," *Maclean's Magazine,* 64 (Jan. 1, 1951).

SPECIAL REFERENCES

F. MAUD BROWN, *Breaking Barriers: Eric Brown and the National Gallery,* pp. 102–6. Ottawa, Society for Art Publications, 1964.

DOROTHY EBER, "Head of the House that Art Built" (Max Stern) *Maclean's Magazine,* vol. 79 (Feb. 5, 1966).

{13}

Mazo de la Roche

1879-1961

DOROTHY LIVESAY

I. Impressions

When I was entering adolescence I had one clearly defined ambition: to be a novelist: It was with keenest interest, therefore, that I learned from my father, J. F. B. Livesay, that our new neighbour at "Woodlot" in Clarkson, Ontario, was a woman writer, Mazo de la Roche. Her short stories, it seemed, had been published in the *Atlantic Monthly*, winning her the interest and friendship of the American novelist, Christopher Morley. Later, when published as a book, *Explorers of the Dawn* (1922), they met with some critical success. But Mazo's first novel, *Possession*, published in 1923, was what truly interested me. Here, for the first time, was a Canadian writer who dealt with real life. Here was a story Hardyesque in its vivid perception of character, its psychological intricacy of relationship. The theme was a New World one with a setting and locale somewhere along the shore of Lake Ontario near where we lived; and in the heart of the fruit country, which stretched in those days from Toronto to Hamilton.

The book *Possession* does not suffer in any respect from a beginning writer's lapses and hesitations. The style is crisp and clear, to the point. It is not overloaded with adjectives or with pompous vocabulary.

Thumbnail sketches of characters are set down sharply, as in this passage about a country auction sale:

The morning broke cloudy and cold. Jagged lines of foam curled across a steel grey lake. Farmers driving by had their collars turned up to their ears. Jock, the collie, raced up and down the road barking ceaselessly. Derek decided to take Windmill with him for company. He would have liked to give the four men half a holiday that they might all go, but he was afraid of Mrs. Machin. There was no doubt about it, he was afraid of her.

There she stood on the flagstones outside the kitchen door, the wind blowing her apron in snowy folds about her stiff person, her lips twisted in a smile of contempt for the hurrying passerby.

'Fools', she said. 'Tumblin' over themselves to pay fancy prices fur cows that's no better than any other cows only they're fed rice till their bags is fit to burst. You stop crammin' the high-priced feed down 'em and they soon stop their fancy milkin'. Them Jerrolds make me sick. I can tell you, your uncle had no use for them.'   (*Possession*, pages 37, 38)

In many a passage such as this Mazo de la Roche's first novel shows that she was already a practised hand at conveying atmosphere, setting, and character in an economical, vivid style. True, the method is traditional, reminding one of Hardy or Galsworthy. There is no stream of consciousness, no flashback technique. But the story moves forward, as realistic narrative should, under the impetus of dialogue. Indeed, when I first came upon this writing, I believed that Mazo de la Roche's flair for dialogue was unequalled in Canadian prose.

Not only could she deal with various British accents which were so marked in Ontario at the turn of the century—the Scottish, the Irish, the Somerset, the Cockney—but she caught the local farmers' turn of speech. The only unreal element in her recording of her characters' speech occurs in the level of language used by Derek, her Haligonian hero. He speaks as if he had just left English public school, a jargon that intrudes with a jarring note on the realistic speech of the minor characters.

How was it possible that a woman apparently so young and inexperienced could write with such masculine vigour and competence? The mystery deepened when I got to know Mazo, second-handedly as it were, through my parents' eyes and from the respectful distance of my own fifteen years. At that time we were living right next door to Mazo and her cousin Caroline Clement. We shared woodland lots, parcels of land from a large estate called "Benares," settled on by Arthur Harris and his wife Mary, and made into a suburban development by Anne Harris Sayers. Miss de la Roche's purpose in coming to Clarkson was to find a retreat where she could write undisturbed, where there would be no telephone and no interruptions while she worked. Her cousin or "adopted sister" commuted to her office job in Toronto, walking through our woodland trail early in the morning on the way to the train. Mazo, left free to write, worked with a burning intensity at Trail Cottage, only sauntering out, mid-morning, to give her blind Scottie dog, Bunty, a run on the way to the farm for milk. Thus I first saw her, tall, gaunt, with short ruddy-brown hair glinting in the sun. Sometimes she would stop to talk to my mother in the rose garden, sometimes she would exchange lively banter with my father bent over his seedlings. When she spoke the nervousness of her appearance, her shakiness, would disappear into a full deep laugh, loud enough to ring clear through the woods. She seemed, indeed, a part of those woods with her long narrow face, her tawny brown eyes which even behind spectacles gave one a sense of animal life. Behind her trembling, frail, somewhat neuter frame, one sensed a passionate intensity.

All through these Clarkson years Mazo remained for me a fascinating mystery. Where had she been reared? Somewhere in Ontario, or Toronto itself? Was her ancestry really French? At what age had she begun to write? Not until 1957 did her own autobiography appear, *Ringing the Changes*. I went to it with gusto, hoping at last to find the answer to many questions about this inscrutable novelist. Again I was disappointed. Although the book does throw psychological insight upon her early years, a quarter of it is devoted to forebears who are described in a haphazard, unchronological way. To create a family tree from the quick sketches given would be no small task! To make matters worse, the photographs of the ancestors are published without their names being attached. Why, one asks, all this obfuscation? The next interesting part of the story concerns the internal life of Mazo as the beginning writer, but this takes up less than half the book. The latter half of the autobiography is the least entertaining; a series of random jottings about travel or places visited, English houses lived in, servants hired and fired, dogs bought and reared, two children adopted. So much attention is given to small insignificant details and so little attention to time and places that the effect sometimes is that of listening to a soap opera. As for comments on literature, reactions to books read, response to social and political conditions, there are almost none. Domestic trivia seem to have absorbed the whole person, once she emerged from working at a novel. Although Mazo met many interesting people, such as the St. John Irvines and George Bernard Shaw, there are few enlivening anecdotes or thumbnail sketches such as have made Edith Sitwell's autobiography so wickedly delightful. She seemed deliberately to avoid meeting strangers and many reporters have commented on her fear of publicity (in a personal sense) and her desire to be a recluse.

Mystery, then, there was. Recent research has elucidated some of the difficulties, and problems of time and place will doubtless be cleared up when the full-length biography by Ronald Hambleton is published.[1] In the meantime I shall set down as clearly as possible the known facts of Mazo de la Roche's life experience. Throughout I must bear in mind Mazo's own warning about biographers: "Even two biographers can make a mystery of a man—no matter how open his life." She disliked the thought of writing in the first person singular, "always repellent to me," and she was not given to introspection or self-brooding. "Those who work in the field of the imagination have no need to explain either their actions or their failures—except to themselves."

II. Influences

The bare facts of Mazo de la Roche's life have been hard to come by. In her own autobiography, *Ringing the Changes*, she is curiously reticent as to time and place. Such an attitude might be condoned during her lifetime, but it would now seem to be in the interests of accurate literary history in Canada to have the facts set down plainly.

The first point to be established is the date and place of birth. Most of the literary encyclopedias, including the biographical dictionary *Canadian Writers* (Ryerson, 1964) give the author's birthdate as 1885 and the birthplace as Toronto, Ontario. In *Ringing the Changes* the author describes her birth in this way:

[1] I am indebted to Mr. Hambleton for giving me access to information contained in the manuscript of his biography, *Mazo de la Roche of Jalna* (Toronto: General Publishing Company, 1966).

I was not born where I should have been, in my father's house, but in my grandfather's. My mother was visiting there and made a call at the Rectory where a member of the family was down with scarlet fever. She contracted the disease. She was terribly ill and so not able to go home to have her child. (Page 29)

Well, the doctor came to the house where my mother was lying ill. The disease had not yet been diagnosed. He took off his sealskin cap, raised his head and sniffed the air. 'I smell scarlet fever', he said. . . . A few hours later I was born, while outside a blizzard raged and the temperature fell to twenty below zero. When my father saw me he said to my mother, 'let me name this one and you may name all the others.' And so he named me and there never were any others. Mazo had been the name of a girl to whom he had once been attached. (Page 31)

The facts omitted in this passage would have intrigued Charles Dickens (Mazo's favourite novelist). The only "place" clearly designated is her maternal grandmother's house (but no town, no street). The only "time" mentioned is winter. Since the baby weighed only three and a half pounds when born—"a fledgling"—it might be presumed that she was premature. Furthermore, the doctor in attendance was a member of the family: Dr. Bradford Patterson "whose third wife was my Great-Aunt Fanny." Other than these there are no "facts" given and now both the birthdate and the place have been proven wrong. The truth as recorded by Ontario Government vital statistics is that Mazo de la Roche was born January 15, 1879, in Newmarket, Ontario. Her parents were registered as William Richmond de la Roche and Alberta Lundy. It has been verified by Ronald Hambleton that this couple had been married in Newmarket on October 17, 1877; so Newmarket appears to have been the family home for some years and the place where Mazo de la Roche began to grow up. But there was more than one Lundy family scattered through that part of Ontario, so she probably had visited other country places in the neighbourhood, and seen something of farm life such as is described in her novel, *Growth of a Man*. Mazo's pioneer grandfather was Daniel Ambrose Lundy, who married Louise Willson. The father of Louise was Hiram Willson, half-brother to that David Willson who founded the religious community, "Children of Peace," at Sharon, Ontario. (This founding-place is twice described by Mazo: first, in the midway novel *Growth of a Man* and second in *Ringing the Changes*.) The community may well have had great significance for Mazo, for Louise Willson Lundy had among her descendants Mazo de la Roche, H. R. Macmillan, and Caroline Clement, the cousin who was to become Mazo's lifelong companion.

The Lundy family itself—grandparents, aunts, and uncles—seems to have been a source of fascination for the writer. These strong-willed, Protestant characters had come from the United States as United Empire Loyalists, to settle first in Nova Scotia. They were strongly motivated by non-conformist religious beliefs and although they never did anything remarkable they were unusual people, self-educated in the best sense, conscious of their good breeding. They might bear comparison with British colonists anywhere in the world: Australia, Africa, India. Their ties with the old country, though tenuous in a material sense, were never emotionally cut. Presumably their pattern of life is recorded in the picture of the Whiteoaks family in *Jalna*.

Another genealogical matter that requires clarification is the origin of Mazo's father's family. In *Ringing the Changes* she gives no hint other than that her grandfather de la Roche had connections in Ireland, but was of French origin. A Roman Catholic, this dashing paternal grandfather was named John François and his middle son, William Richmond, retained the prefix 'de la' when it gave him status in a social context. Caroline Clement remarks that "sometimes he had to drop it for business reasons—travelling salesman as he was, in Orange protestant Ontario." However, according to Beer's genealogical table, the story varies: it is recorded that Alberta Lundy married "William Roach." Mr. Hambleton's research offers the likelihood that the Roaches came from County Limerick, Ireland. The fact that their descendant, Mazo, chose to use the prefix indicates how strongly she was drawn, in imagination, to an established aristocratic way of life. Her own childhood was anything but settled, anything but rooted.

Mazo's parents appear to have left Newmarket and the maternal family when she was still a small child, and by 1911 her mother had lived in "seventeen houses." One of the towns where Mazo records that the family spent three years was Galt, Ontario—the home of her mother's relatives, the Warnocks. Although no dates are mentioned in *Ringing the Changes* external evidence points to the fact that the stay in Galt took place during the years 1889 to 1892. Mazo's playmate of those years was Mina Sylvester, a little girl whose birth and death are recorded on the cemetery headstone as "Born 1881; died July 31, 1891."

Of these years of late childhood and early adolescence the time spent in Galt seems to have been the most formative for Mazo. It must have been a rather curious life for a child, living in the old Queen's Hotel with its three long tiers of balcony, left very much alone with her mother, a longtime invalid. Her illness was apparently never diagnosed, but it may have been an arrested case of tuberculosis. Mazo's anxiety over this is apparent in *Ringing the Changes*. But she did get out to attend classes at a Dame school, Miss Bains'; and she read voraciously. As a family group the two adults and the half-grown child tackled such writers as Dickens, Stevenson, and Shakespeare. Thus began a lifelong interest in reading aloud about which Mazo remarked, in an interview many years later, "I am an inveterate reader-alouder. It is a great test of a book."

In Galt there developed, as she describes it, that strong psychological and emotional link with her father. He was the second of three sons of that "gentleman adventurer," John de la Roche, who ran off to the United States, leaving his wife, the Irish Sarah Danford, to cope with the rearing of his children. The boy, William Richmond, grew up without any definite direction in his schooling. Later he appears to have been a devoted husband and father, yet he inherited some of the extravagances of his runaway parent. He too liked fine clothes and fine living; he too had little idea of how to cope with the world of commerce and competition. It is interesting that in choosing an occupation he lit upon that of selling French wines—a somewhat exotic trade surely, for that day and age. Mr. de la Roche seems to have been away from home a great deal, travelling to Montreal and other parts of the country. The child Mazo lived for the moment when he would come home. Of this period she writes:

Often my father and I read the same book at the same time, his six foot three extended in an easy chair, my growing length draped against his chest. . . . So I remember reading *The White Company, Harry Lorrequer, Allan Quatermain* by Rider Haggard. . . . I think it was in those days, when we first began to read together that the bond between my father and me strengthened into a deep understanding and we became the most loved of friends. As he waited for my slower grasp of the page to catch up to his, as his large shapely hand was raised to turn a page, a palpable emotion stirred within us. My love for my mother was instinctive. I took her devo-

tion for granted. But he was my hero, my protector, my gay companion.
. . . As I grew older and young men appeared on the scene I invariably
compared them with him, to their disadvantage—till the day when one
arrived who could better compare with him. (*Ringing the Changes*, page
53)

It is clear from the foregoing and other like passages in *Ringing
the Changes* that although there was strong emotional security for
Mazo in her parents' affection for each other and for her, there was
in the background of their life a hovering insecurity. The family
moved about many times, always gravitating to the house of the
maternal grandmother in the Toronto area. The child must have had
a feeling, sometimes, of being on unsafe ground; she would have had
to make constant adaptations to new surroundings, new schools. So
perhaps it was as an escape from these uncertainties that, like the
Bronte sisters, she sought refuge in an imagined world. How fortunate
she was to find another child, lonely as herself, who could share that
world! This was her slightly younger cousin, Caroline Clement, a
girl who had been left in the care of relatives when her own elderly
parents had died. She first met Mazo in the home of the Lundy
grandparents and she responded immediately, instinctively, to the
leadership of the commanding "sister"—the older, more vigorous Mazo.

The curious thing about Mazo's account of this lifelong attachment
is that although she dedicates *Ringing the Changes*: "For Caroline,
from first to last," there is little development of Caroline's point of
view in the book. But of their devotion there is no question. In their
childhood years, whenever they were alone, they plunged themselves
into their imagined world, "The Play," acting out and rehearsing the
lives of invented characters whom Mazo had been the first to set on
the dream stage. And Mazo relates, of the days in their teens when
Caroline returned to live permanently with Mazo's grandparents in
Parkdale, Toronto:

It was marvellous to see how she improved in health and looks. Even I,
as a child, was conscious of it. From being a sallow little girl, with high
cheek-bones, she became round-cheeked, red-lipped, full of a gentle vitality.
Soon she had reached her full height of five feet but I kept on growing
and growing. My face became more pointed, my eyes more eagerly enquir-
ing, my hair longer and thicker, my body longer and thinner. Caroline
was serious. I was always ready to smile. She was shy. I was forward.

Both were what today would be called ridiculously sensitive. A rebuke from a grown-up would dissolve us in tears. But there were few rebukes. We lived sheltered in the family, our pleasures were simple. (*Ringing the Changes,* page 68)

The girls' most dominant interest was in the theatre and in play-making. Mazo liked to create and play the parts of the "dashing cavalier. . . . Almost always Caroline was the heroine. . . . Always the costumes were picturesque. The most successful was one in which I was a gypsy fortune-teller. The scene was in Spain during the Napoleonic wars." (*Ibid.,* pages 74, 75.)

As well as making structured plays the adolescent girls lived in a private world of the imagination, even as they had done as children. After Caroline had had her first disappointment in love, Mazo set out to make her smile again.

How well I succeeded! New characters were introduced. All the characters, of both sexes and divers stations and ages, were equally divided between us and remained so always.

They took on a new significance. Their relations with each other became more intense. The passing of time too became controlled. No longer would we hasten through a year in a few days or anchor a loved character to a desired age. . . . One thing I could not yet control was my desire to invent new characters. At every slightest flagging of interest a new character would be brought in to swell the cumbersome cast. Yet never did we forget any of them or leave them to languish in the wings. . . .

Now we learned something new. That was to feel affection for our characters. Certain ones we grew to love, as beings quite separate from ourselves, yet irrevocably bound to us, since no other actor would ever play that part. . . . During our Play one of these characters met a violent end. We had not been prepared for the devastating effect this would have on us. All the night through we mourned and cried our eyes out. It was only at dawn that we fell into an uneasy sleep.

The next morning my mother remarked on my pallor. 'And you have such blue rings about your eyes,' she said. 'Are you sure you are well?'

'I'm perfectly well,' I answered, feeling strangely guilty.

Never again did we risk such a bereavement in our Play . . . there was quite enough suffering in our own lives. (*Ringing the Changes,* pages 85, 86)

It is abundantly clear from this and similar descriptions that the experience of play-acting with Caroline created Mazo de la Roche the novelist. Without Caroline there would have been no *Jalna.*

Such then were the influences on the growing girl that were to create a writer. Mazo de la Roche was educated and found her wellspring through family life. Some formal education she obtained. After leaving Galt, as a young girl in her teens she spent a year with the grandparents in Orillia, and attended Orillia Collegiate.[2] When the grandparents settled in Parkdale, Toronto, Mazo completed her high school education (presumably at Parkdale Collegiate); and would have gone on to university but for the family doctor, who ruled that she was too "delicate." Since she had always loved drawing and painting she decided to attend the Ontario College of Art, where G. A. Reid was her teacher. The over-all impression one gets, in reading *Ringing the Changes*, is that Mazo was not so much interested in intellectual or academic pursuits as in reading, and in observing people. She was not a withdrawn person as a child, not an "isolate." The outdoor life, long walks with her parents, simple excursions, devotion to dogs and horses—these were the strong attractions, all to be stored away in diaries, in vividly remembered conversations. They were to provide the material for the boldly painted descriptions of landscapes and animals that enliven the pages of all her books.

III. Achievements

There is abundant evidence that Mazo de la Roche was a creative child. The account of her first story, written at the age of nine and sent to a children's competition, sets the pattern. Always she was either writing or drawing. The only struggle she seems to have met with in the field of the arts was with her music. The stress and distress she experienced when face to face with her music master at Galt indicates a degree of psychological tension that required attention. But her mother seems only to have chided the music master gently for his severity, and to have failed to see the signs of strain and nervousness in her daughter. Instead she held before Mazo the demand for excellence, for perfection. One can see a certain parallel here with the early years of another creative woman, Edith Sitwell, who was forced by her parents to take up the playing of instruments and to

[2]Information given the writer by Mrs. Helen Macpherson, now of Vancouver. Mrs. Macpherson grew up in Orillia, attended the Collegiate and remembers being for one year in the same classroom with "Maizie Roach." She herself was born in 1878 and was probably not more than a year older than the school friend who became Mazo de la Roche.

participate in robust games. Her salvation also lay in a retreat to an imaginary world.

During that winter I had been subject to hours of strange melancholy. The sense of my own smallness and helplessness in the world oppressed me. The constant coming and going in the hotel made me aware of my aloneness. I watched myself as an actor alone on a great stage. The spectacular and elemental Greek gods, on whom I brooded, were more congenial to me than my schoolfellows. I would stand long on the bridge watching the dark flow of the river below. There was no such flood as there had been last spring[3] but one day I witnessed a happening on the bridge which left an indelible impression of calamity on my mind.

Some farm hands were driving a small herd of cattle across the bridge to be slaughtered. One of them, an immense white beast, refused to cross. The others had been driven over but no matter how he was beaten and prodded, he refused. Again and again they had him on the bridge, but each time he eluded them and plunged back, wild and exhausted, to the safety of the road. There was nobility in him. He would accept his doom but he would not cross the bridge. I watched horrified and at last saw him sink to his knees, a great white bulk, about to die.

When I returned later he was gone, but there was a pool of blood at the edge of the bridge where he had been slaughtered. (*Ringing the Changes*, page 64)

Curiously enough that experience, which marked the end of the stay in Galt and the end of her childhood, was recreated again by Mazo de la Roche in a story called *The Sacred Bullock*. True, the setting has been changed—it is set in a lyrical poetic landscape in Wales, with a boy and girl lover both entranced by a great white bull. In the end, the bull gores the boy who cared for him. That story was published in a collection, in 1939. It would be interesting to know when it was written. The style and the mythical emphasis would suggest the hand of quite a young writer.

There seems no doubt that in late adolescence, from 18 years old on, Mazo's imagination was on fire. The story of her first success is told simply and happily in *Ringing the Changes*. She was not really a secret author (an Emily Brontë or an Emily Dickinson) but from the first showed a strong ambition, a wish to reach the public. We are told that while she was continually sketching and attending art

[3]The Grand River in Galt, Ontario, where eventually the Conestoga Dam was built to stem the floods.

classes "something new was stirring in me. I discovered that I wanted to write a story." No sooner said than done. She chose a French-Canadian setting (familiar perhaps because of her father's frequent business visits to Quebec), wrote the story in secret and mailed it in secret to *Munsey's Magazine*. Like magic, it would seem, the editor wrote back an acceptance, and a fifty-dollar cheque. In her autobiography Mazo implies that she was about 18 when this event occurred and her cousin confirms this impression. Ronald Hambleton, however, has seen the story, published under the name of Mazo de la Roche, in *Munsey's Magazine* for October, 1902. In that year she would have been 23.

The young writer seemed to be well launched: confident of success, and with a motivation for writing. "What a writer of fiction needs," she wrote in her old age, "—first, last and all the time—is a public. Its interest is the steady wind that fans the fire of his creative ability. All his 'agonizing' will not create a public for him." But her youth was far from being free from this "agonizing." She describes how she had to work herself up into a state of excitement before she could write what was in her mind. "I would lie on the sofa in the dim room, my body rigid, my mind hallucinated by the pictures which passed before it. Then I would rise, take up my paper and pencil and write. Again I would stretch myself on the sofa. Again I would write."

Since so much nervous strain was put into this activity it was no small wonder that something would break. The shock came when for the first time Mazo sent out a story for which she received no acknowledgment. In desperation she came to the conclusion that it had been sent off unstamped:

My manuscript was lost. I had no postage on it. . . . Strange how the pavement appeared to slant—as though falling away from me. I had a feeling of strange excitement, yet I felt weary as never before. When I returned home I found that the floor sloped away from me to the pavement had done, as though into an abyss. (*Ringing the Changes*, page 102)

Thus began an illness which Mazo refers to as a "nervous breakdown," although there seems to have been no medical diagnosis. It has been established (by Ronald Hambleton) that between the time of her first published story, in 1902, and 1911, when the family moved to the farm at Bronte, Mazo lived in and around the Toronto area. She describes her convalescence as being aided by the timely offer of a studio belonging to her art teacher and by summer visits to a cottage at Lake Simcoe. These were painful years, when the ability to set pen to paper was fraught with difficulty; when financial insecurity, dependence on maternal relatives, family illnesses all made their demands on the only child—now a young woman in her late twenties. But all members of the family seem to have taken on a new lease of life when Mr. de la Roche gave up his commercial career and invested in a fruit farm near Bronte, overlooking Lake Ontario. It was here that Mazo, accompanied by the devoted Caroline Clement, began to enjoy some peace of mind. It was there that her romantic association with the man she names "Pierre" began—and ended. It was there that she had many of her experiences with domestic and farm animals, of which she was to write so often, and so absorbingly. And it was there she came to know the community of Indian berry pickers whose lives appear vividly in *Possession, Delight*, and in the Jalna series. The theme of the "outsider," of different background or race, brought by circumstances or passion into the quieter lives of pioneer folk, is a recurrent one in several of the important novels. It is often the catalytic element used to evoke a sense of mystery, of fate.

Another element equally strong in the early novels is the realism of description. Accurate, closely observed details of life in rural market towns are fused with sharply etched descriptions of nature and the countryside. Lake Ontario, vast as an inland sea, with its alternating storms and silences, stirred the young writer deeply. The following passage, for instance, published later as a personal recollection, appeared first in *Possession* as the keynote theme.

I shall never forget the storm of that night. The lake gathered itself together and hurled its strength against the shore. But its thunder could not drown the shrieking of the wind. At times it seemed that a great army was marching down the road. There was the tramp of soldiers' boots on frozen ground—the heavy beat of drums—the playing of bugles—the scream of bagpipes. The crackling air vibrated to the blare of wild martial music . . . the music would cease and in its place the thunder of battle shook the shore. Then came the shrieks of the wounded, and, as they died, the keening of mourners. Over and over throughout the night the turmoil of this tragic drama was enacted. . . .

But, in the morning, a brilliant calm brought icy stillness to our shore. A few particles of snow floated in the air. Ice hummocks and caverns had been fashioned by the storm and beyond them the waves tumbled in wintry abandon. The bridge across the creek had become massive in ice. Telegraph wires sagged under the weight of a thousand icicles. It was bitterly cold. The soles of shoes which had been damp when I set them on the floor of the coat cupboard were frozen fast there.

It was a scene that would have stirred Charlotte Brontë, who would have handled it in the same way: first as a diary and secondly as the dramatic "key" scene in a novel. The approach is one where realism dominates, yet the tone is romantic. Such a passage illustrates how the writer found the transition from regional realism to the romantic idyll an easy leap.

Yet, in addition to these temperamental inclinations towards romanticism, there may well have been external reasons which led Mazo into an imagined world of escape. On the Bronte farm after the outbreak of World War I it was difficult to get help; the farm was failing financially. Then Mazo suffered a great physical and emotional loss in the death of her father in 1915. Mazo, her mother, and Caroline had to make their way back to Toronto where they lived in some penury until Caroline obtained an office job. When Mazo's stories began to be accepted by magazines like the *Atlantic*, the taste of success must have been sweet—and the payment welcome.

At the same time it must not be forgotten that there was a real "pull" towards realism amongst writers in Canada in the twenties. Thus, Mazo's first two novels were in the realistic genre being created by other prose writers like F. P. Grove, Martha Ostenso, and Raymond Knister. All their works, though centred on the *land*, were concerned with real people in a real situation. This feeling was in the air, so it is justifiable to ask what made Mazo de la Roche turn from that direction? I believe myself it had a good deal to do with reader-response. The Canadian public was not ready, if indeed it ever will be, to face itself in the mirror. People were resentful and suspicious of writers who tried to do this. So Martha Ostenso went to the United States, F. P. Grove struggled with poverty and school teaching for decades until he gained a grudging recognition. Raymond Knister died at 32, after a terrible struggle with poverty whilst he was attempting to write serious stories centred in Ontario farm life.

And Mazo? I believe when she and Caroline first came to live in Trail Cottage at Clarkson (following the death of her mother), from about 1925 onwards, she had at first no conscious aim vis-à-vis her public. As has been recorded, her life with her imagined characters was complete and absorbing. But perhaps, remembering her own family past, she began to think in more historical terms. This may have lifted her out of immediate realism—the post-war world, the depression—into a vision of the past as she had heard it talked about around the Lundy family table. Moreover she found that the same social pattern which her own people had experienced north of Toronto had prevailed also in the old days in Mississauga County. Near us on the old Harris estate at Clarkson was a house that may well have been the prototype for Jalna. It was called "Benares," after a post in India where the pioneer family had originally been stationed. Benares meant, for me, a gracious, square brick house with a wide front porch and a long scullery at the back built of yellow sandstone (part of the original house that had burned down)—a house that had fascinated me as a prairie child when my father first took me there to visit relatives. The driveway through pine and oak forest, laden in spring with periwinkle and lily-of-the-valley; the old coachhouse, reached by a short drive which then curved around to the front of the house with its wide view of pasture and apple orchard; and indoors, to the right, "the library," where the grandmother always sat, rocking by the fire; and to the left the drawing-room with its gilt mirrors, family portraits, delicate Victorian chairs and oriental rugs; then, in the hall itself, the beautifully carved walnut staircase below which were the servants' quarters and huge kitchen—these are details that remain vividly in my memory. And how close, in description and atmosphere, is Mazo de la Roche's creation of Jalna:

It was a square house of dark red brick, with a wide stone porch, a deep basement where the kitchens and servants' quarters were situated, an immense drawing-room, a library (called so, but more properly a sitting-room, since few books lived there), a dining-room, and a bedroom on the ground floor; and six large bedrooms on the floor above, topped by a long, low attic divided into two bedrooms. The wainscotting and doors were of walnut. From five fireplaces the smoke ascended through picturesque chimneys that rose among the treetops.

In a burst of romantic feeling, Philip and Adeline named the place Jalna, after the military station where they first met. . . . Under their clustering chimneys, in the midst of their unpretentious park with its short, curving drive, with all their thousand acres spread like a green mantle around them, the Whiteoaks were as happy as the sons of man can be.

Whether or no the imaginary Jalna drew its setting from Benares is perhaps only of local interest. What is exciting, however, is the speed with which the book was written and the fame it achieved. It was my mother, a constant reader of literary magazines, who first saw the advertisement of the $10,000 novel prize offered by the *Atlantic Monthly*. As soon as she told Mazo about it the novelist was in a quandary. She would so like to send her newly finished novel, "Jalna," to the contest! But she had already committed it to Macmillan's in Toronto and Hugh Eayrs had agreed to publish it. After discussions with Mr. Eayrs, and probably as a result of his sympathetic consideration for Miss de la Roche's financial need, she was persuaded to submit the novel to the *Atlantic*. I have described that waiting period as follows:

Suddenly one day Mazo told my mother of the possibility: she had received a telephone call from Boston informing her that she was one of the runners-up for the prize. Her excitement, her nervous trembling, knew no bounds. She and Caroline went to Toronto to await further news; and she was really nervously ill by the time the message finally came through from editor Edward Weeks: the judges had decided in favour of *Jalna*.

We all wept for joy. It was not merely that a Canadian writer had been recognized in the United States, it was not merely that we felt that Mazo de la Roche's work deserved recognition, but it was also the fact that she who had been really poor would be able to write without the gnawing fear of poverty. From that time on, she never turned back.

Now, seeing it all in retrospect, I feel sure that it was the unprecedented success of *Jalna* on three fronts—literary, popular, and financial —that led Mazo de la Roche to abandon her interest in regional realism. Almost without realizing the change in herself she ploughed ahead, mapping out with ever greater proliferations the story of those interacting characters who form the long history of the Whiteoaks family. In the end she forced the critics to look at her achievement, not as the author of two or three delightful and amusing romantic idylls, but as the creator of a saga, in seventeen volumes. Recently a French-Canadian critic, André le Grand, called the work a "roman-fleuve." The image of this novel as a river does indeed illuminate the significance of *Jalna* as "a point of departure but also a cornerstone."

This critic observes, most appropriately, that the Whiteoak family lived through a century "on the margins of Canadian life, whether that life were political, social or cultural. In the landscape of *Jalna* as in that of *Maria Chapdelaine*, nothing must change." In short, as the English-Canadian critic Desmond Pacey noted some years ago, "*Jalna* is a landscape of the imagination which has its own reality and is far more vivid than most photographs of actual places."

Small wonder then that as the author found her audience moving deeper and deeper into involvement with the world of *Jalna* she responded to that interest and poured herself into the task. Had she not said all along, "What a writer needs is a public"? She ended up with seventeen Jalna novels, books which during her lifetime were translated into fourteen languages; books which I found, on visiting West Germany after the war, had represented the culture of England, of the English-speaking world, to German teachers who had had to live within Nazi walls. On this very topic Caroline Clement writes me, from Mazo's study in the last house which they shared in Forest Hill Village:

Just recently two of her European publishers have begun bringing out new editions of the entire series in cloth bindings—very attractively done. I should like this to be known in Canada where her books have always had a very poor sale. Indeed I think it is not a book-loving or book-buying country.

It is interesting to note that although Caroline Clement is most loyal to her sister-cousin as author of the Whiteoaks series, she herself considers *Growth of a Man* as Mazo's best novel. And this is a return to the realistic novel, published in 1938! It is the psychological story of a young, sensitive farm boy who after many struggles with poverty and ill-health, "makes good." It purports to be the life story of Mazo's cousin, H. R. Macmillan, the lumber magnate, who grew up near Newmarket, in that same part of Ontario that Mazo knew so well. In so far as the novel deals with Ontario farm people and rural life at the turn of the century it is extremely interesting and well written. The latter half of the novel, however, dealing with a man's world, is less convincing. When a final critical analysis is made of her work that novel will have to be seriously considered, as of special interest to Canadians.

Mazo de la Roche was confined to a wheel-chair for two years before her death in Toronto on July 12, 1961, aged 82. Besides the *Jalna* series she had written several plays, had had *Whiteoaks* successfully played on stage in London and New York, had published a dozen other full-length books, mainly about children and animals, and had written her autobiography. In view of these achievements it is surely time now, in 1966, that her life and work be reappraised by the Canadian public and that she gain her rightful place as our most productive, most imaginative novelist. And as a person, what an amazing human being she was! With what an unusual beginning, middle, and end! In the long run one epithet comes to mind, one abstract noun: courage. Courage to rise above circumstances; to defy convention; to tear from the people around her their hearts' secrets. To this was added the sure ear, the showman's ability to give the audience what they wanted. They loved it—and so did she. It was a contribution to Canadian letters that cannot be forgotten.

ACKNOWLEDGMENTS

My thanks are due to Miss Caroline Clement for her own reminiscences of Mazo de la Roche; and to Mr. Ronald Hambleton for verification of certain data noted in the text; also to the Macmillan Company of Canada and Miss Clement for permission to reprint sections from *Possession*, *Jalna*, and *Ringing the Changes*. I gratefully acknowledge help in ascertaining the facts given by Mrs. Helen Teskey Macpherson, Vancouver (formerly of Orillia, Ont.); Mrs. Katherine Hebblethwaite, Galt, Ont.; Mr. Tim Classey, Toronto; Mrs. Anne Sayers, Clarkson, Ont.

{14}

Alice Wilson

1881-1964

ANNE MONTAGNES

"THE EARTH TOUCHES every life," wrote Alice Wilson, Canada's first woman geologist. "Everyone should receive some understanding of it." This simple conviction highlights much that is puzzling about the woman: why a large-eyed girl from a scholarly Victorian home should want to don trousers and scrabble over fences and up cliffs in search of facts about the earth; what sustained her when men in her profession restricted her to routine and refused her the time and the money for her own research; and why, although many geologists remember and respect her scientific descriptions of the Ordovician strata of the Ottawa–St. Lawrence Lowland, thousands of students, children, and taxpayers also remember the warm patient "rock doctor" who brought to life the shell fish which inhabited long vanished seas around Ottawa four hundred million years ago.

Alice Wilson was tall and painfully thin. She moved with dignity, observing the world gravely. Different photographers saw different Alices. An unknown photographer of her girlhood at the turn of the century posed her and a group of friends conventionally, thoughtful young ladies in ruffled blouses innocently challenging the future. Karsh, in 1939, saw the white-haired pioneer, her mouth resolute but sad; her gold-rimmed *pince-nez* firm, but quite unable to mask the wary contemplative staring from her enormous dark eyes. In 1963, when she was 82, the National Film Board saw her in the field, wrinkled, battered, ancient, wearing her beret (she'd worn it for thirty years)—a legend in her own time quickened by the radiant smile she beamed on the young students around her.

Geology was her career and her hobby. "If I ever stopped working," she remarked in later years, "I'd drop." But she had too much sense of fun ever to be stuffy about it. Her mischievous smile would brighten her dark eyes, and she would write: "As I get older I wonder more and more about our classifications. I look at a woman who gets into my bus. She needs two seats; and then look at me. Certainly if our bones were on the outside we would be put into two species, not to say two genera."

Behind the grave eyes, the reserve, the dignity, the humour there was a will of iron. Without it she could never have triumphed as she did or even survived. A friend explains: "Once she told me she would live to be seventy-five. I asked her why she was so sure—she looked like death at the time—and she said, 'Oh I have a project in hand and it will take me till then to finish it.'" When she did die, at 83, another friend could only remark, "Whatever happened to her will-power?"

When Alice Evelyn Wilson was born in 1881, Cobourg, Ontario, her birthplace, was a college town. Victoria University had been there, serving Upper Canada for forty-five years, and for a good part of that time two of her relatives had been connected with it. Her great-uncle was John Wilson, a somewhat free-spoken Professor of Classics, and her maternal grandfather was William Kingston, Professor of Mathematics.

Even before she began school Alice learned Greek and Latin declensions, and she and her mother, Adelia, grew into a way of expressing their thoughts to one another through biblical quotations; but the classical inheritance lost out to the scientific in the Wilson family. Adelia, a witty talented woman, had as a girl shown a mathematical aptitude, and William Kingston, her father, a bearded Methodist scholar, had fed it in a way. "Her mathematical education went much beyond that of a girl of her generation," we read, "and was stopped only because her father thought she had proceeded further than any girl should go." Not for Adelia the responsibility of knocking on the doors of male halls of learning; that was for the next generation.

But this excessive nurturing of her aptitude bore fruit; Adelia's second son, Norman, was a mathematical genius. He galloped through Cobourg Collegiate in three years, found at fourteen that he was too young for university and finally, trailing scholarships, entered the University of Toronto at sixteen. He went on to distinguish himself, writing papers noted for their strong individual character and close reasoning. He became head of the Department of Mathematics at the University of Manitoba; but he never became the earth-shaking scholar his youthful genius promised: an opponent in a basketball game accidentally stuck his fingers in Norman's eyes and the life-long effects of the injury kept him from the hours over books and papers thorough research needs.

The Wilsons were a very close family. Strangers often thought them dour. But they reserved their fun and talk for one another. Together they would tackle anything for the mind, range round it and probe it with no barriers. For several impressionable years Alice had two older brothers, one astonishing his teachers at Cobourg Collegiate, the other performing brilliantly at Victoria, arriving home daily bursting with news of what they had learned. Virtue, demonstrably, lay in scholarship. Alfred, Alice's older brother, was also sixteen when he entered university in 1889, four years before Victoria left Cobourg for Toronto. He won a gold medal in natural sciences when he graduated from Victoria, took his doctorate at Harvard and went on to become chief consultant of the Mines Branch for the Government of Canada.

Obviously the place to try one's paces if one were a Wilson was the field of scientific scholarship. Alice Wilson deeply respected and sought after formal education, but in a biographical sketch she was once required to write—she called it "my obituary"—she said: "An informal education of equal and lasting value was the free out-of-door life of childhood with her brothers, in canoes and boats on Lake Ontario and nearby Rice Lake, tramping all the country between, and camping in the north country long before it became a tourist's mecca." It was her father, Richard Wilson, a druggist, who led his children outdoors, awakening them to the world around them, teaching them how to raise a tent and make a fire, even helping them build a canoe.

Richard Wilson was Mayor of Cobourg for a short time when Alice Wilson was a girl, and from his sense of civic responsibility, typical of the Wilsons, and from his respect for natural beauties, there grew a family legend, disproved by dates, that it was he who forced the railway to go to the north of Cobourg leaving the lakeshore open for parkland. As a girl Alice Wilson used to roam along this lakeshore, looking at the fossils in the limestone formations, wondering why more organisms collected in one spot than another, coming, perhaps, to conclusions about controlling mechanisms: that in a shallow sandy cove, where only gentle ripples penetrated and sunlight filtered warmly through the water, brachiopods—ancient bivalved organisms—would find more food than in the open sea.

Alice Wilson, then, differed from girls of her generation by the standards of academic achievement and the awareness of the outdoors her family valued. But like any small-town Ontario youngster before 1900 she loved on winter Sundays to jingle home from church in the family's horse-drawn sleigh, snuggled down with her brothers in warm fur blankets; she found the woodshed, with its discarded chairs and old baskets and a three-legged, grey green, copper kettle, a good hidey place; and she played tennis on the Wilsons' mud court, well, being so tall, but had to spend almost as much time weeding it as playing on it.

Like her brothers she went to Cobourg Collegiate, but she did not do brilliantly there. Although she would never admit it, fought always to disguise it, she suffered throughout her life from pernicious anaemia. The humorous disgust with which she regarded this bodily frailty shows in the way she spoke of cod liver oil: "Have you that 'tired feeling,'" she wrote, "or are you too thin? Then along comes someone, friend or foe, and suggests or insists that you take cod-liver oil. They may dress it up as an emulsion, or make it into a pill, but it is cod-liver oil, and not very nice or it would not have to be disguised." Cod liver oil, iron tonics, liver, blood transfusions, treatments at salt spring sanatoriums—at one time or another she tried them all. "They all help," she conceded, "if not to make people well, at least to make them better." For her part, however, she would rather exert will-power, and often will-power triumphed.

She was twenty when she entered Victoria University, expecting to follow the only profession readily open to women in 1901, teaching. "I belonged to a generation where educated people were supposed to have the classics," she recognized, and so she enrolled in Modern Languages and History. She didn't like it much. Languages didn't stick with her. Once, later, when she was on a geological trip in Quebec, she encountered a large animal in a pasture and anxiously asked the French farmer whether she were likely to be attacked by "Monsieur le vache"; and at forty, when her perch at the Geological Survey was trembling insecurely, the idea that having the use of a foreign language might make her more useful for Eastern Ontario field trips, prompted her to go to a French mademoiselle for coaching. She dropped out of Victoria before she took her degree. But she didn't waste the years in language study. Perhaps she would be compelled to teach French; meanwhile there she was at the University, the University gave lectures in science and, woman or no, she would steal into them, take her share of what her brothers had received so freely. "I got no credits," she said; but did credits matter? "I picked up a great many things."

The year 1904 was a turning point. Her father died and she suffered one of the lengthy attacks of illness which conquered her tremendous will to achieve two or three times in her life. She did not return to the University for her final year, and while she was ill the question why she should ever return became more and more insistent. Her brother Alfred was lecturing in Mining Engineering at McGill University. Her brother Norman had just been promoted to the professorship of Mathematics at Wesley College in Winnipeg. Why should she, just because she was a woman, be relegated to the classics when she knew that her bent was to science? Her rebellion was not in the least violent. She was always a lady, gentle, dignified, but Wilsons faced difficulties squarely and took constructive action. When she was well she went to work in the Mineralogy division of the University of Toronto Museum as a clerk, rearranging specimens, becoming familiar with the complete series. Not very inspiring work and considered rather odd for a girl, but at least she was in science. She was there two years.

In 1909 it became obvious that the forty-four dollars a month she earned at Toronto just would not do. Her brother Alfred had recently been appointed to the Department of Mines in Ottawa. Through him she heard of an opening at eight hundred dollars a year at the Geological Survey of Canada. She applied for the position and was accepted.

"Soon after I arrived in Ottawa," she recalled later, "I looked at the Precambrian ramparts of the Canadian Shield across the Ottawa River, and wondered about the earth we live on." She spent the rest of her life satisfying this curiosity at the Geological Survey.

The Geological Survey is a government department which explores Canada gathering information about its geological structure. It prepares geological and topographical maps, searches out and examines underground natural resources and publishes papers, bulletins, and maps based on its findings. Today the Survey occupies part of a handsome new building in Ottawa on Booth Street; on its palaeontological staff alone there are twenty people. When Alice Wilson joined the Survey in 1909 it was housed in the old Clarendon Hotel and the palaeontological staff was four: a vertebrate palaeontologist, an invertebrate palaeontologist, an artist, and clerk Wilson.

A palaeontologist is a scientist who studies the life of past ages through fossils. In geology he works with sedimentary rocks, those laid down by the seas, rather than with igneous rocks which originate in the cooling and solidification of molten matter from inside the earth. Suspended and dissolved in water are bits of igneous rock. These, and the bodies of organisms living in the water, consolidate in layers on the seas' floor, making sedimentary rocks. The palaeontologist's service to the geologist is to tell him the ages of rock strata by identifying and dating the fossils.

Alice Wilson was hired to help the Invertebrate Palaeontologist, Percy Raymond—labelling fossils, recording specimens in a great ledger, dusting the collection. But the origins of these ancient clams, snails, starfish, sea-lilies, trilobites—like ones she and her brothers had picked up on hikes—intrigued her, and she began to take notice of the names she was copying and to ask questions. Raymond was an inspiring man to work under. He saw no reason why any intelligent inquiring mind should not be educated. He encouraged her to read on her own, told her that without a degree she'd always be a clerk, and got her official leave to go back to Victoria. Armed with her B.A. in Modern Languages and History, aged thirty, she returned to the Survey in 1911. The Survey bowed, and she became Museum Assistant, the first woman ever to have a professional position there.

There was now the brand new Victoria Memorial Museum building on Metcalfe Street. During the move there Alice Wilson had been so useful in crating, uncrating, and redisplaying the collections that, when the Survey began a series of bulletins to mark its new dignity, she was included in the general invitation to contribute. She wrote a short but thorough description of a new brachiopod.

Armchair palaeontology—examining, identifying, and writing about fossils—is nice clean work and ought, the Survey considered in 1913, to be the absolute peak of a woman's aspirations. It befitted her nature to stay at home, minding the house, while the men, the geologists, climbed mountains, wielded hammers, camped rudely, and sent their trophies home to be dated; so that they could take up brushes and mark the appropriate colour on their maps. But armchair palaeontology is boring and frustrating. Rarely the occasion arises when one may append one's name to even a short but thorough report, among others, in a bulletin; more often, after six or eight months' painstaking research, one's findings end up as a footnote in someone else's report.

Moreover, Alice Wilson set her sights scandalously high. It wasn't just that she refused to remain a Museum Assistant; not even the rank of Palaeontologist was appropriate to what she thought she could do. She wanted to be a Geologist, to go out and map with the men; and she would prove that she deserved to be one. It was, of course, unthinkable in 1913 that she should board ship for the Arctic in the company of pipe-smoking scientists who might forget to shave for months on end. To men alone lay the honour of dying for science on the ice of the Chuckchee Sea. But it didn't matter; for right outside Ottawa's back door lay a classical region for geology, the Ottawa–St. Lawrence Lowland.

This Lowland, about ten thousand square miles, is the area drained by the Ottawa and St. Lawrence rivers. On the north and west it is framed by the Canadian Shield, and on the south by the Adirondack Mountains. The crest of a fold in the earth's crust, at Beauharnois, marks the eastern boundary. From Brockville to Montreal, from Hull to the Adirondacks—this is the Lowland.

During risings and fallings of the earth's surface more than four hundred million years ago, seas flowed over the Lowland seven times, covering the Precambrian base with layers of sedimentary rock imbedded with fossils—the Ordovician period. After it, the Lowland again rose and for three hundred million years no sediments were deposited, or if there were they have been eroded away; but during this period the rising of the Appalachian Mountains strained the crust of the earth in the Lowland. Cracks, and then great faults occurred in the horizontal strata of sedimentary rock so that today the layers of limestone, sandstone, and shale are tilted, squeezed, and shattered. The youngest strata, some red shales, may be faulted down two thousand feet in relation to the strata on the other side of the fault. The rocks covering these Ordovician strata are only about a million years old: glacial deposits, and then the unconsolidated sea shells, sands, and clays of a later invasion by the sea.

Geologically this Lowland is important because it is one place in Canada where there is a relatively complete record of the Ordovician period. All over the area, where river or wind have worn away newer deposits, edges of the strata appear in outcroppings; wells, borings, quarries for building stone or sculptor's marble expose the thickness of strata. Alice Wilson determined to make this area her own geological province and in 1913, under the sympathetic guidance of Percy Raymond, she began to go out and measure outcroppings and collect fossils, the first woman ever to be sent on field work by the Survey.

Mapping the various sedimentary formations of the Ottawa–St. Lawrence Lowland, determining their chronological sequence, and describing their fossils was to be Alice Wilson's greatest contribution to geological science, and it looked, at the beginning of the First World War, as if she were smoothly launched on this work. Percy Raymond got summer study-leave for her in 1915. She spent six weeks at the Marine Biological Laboratory in Cold Spring Harbor, Long Island, dredging for organisms for comparative study in her laboratory work. In 1915, the *Ottawa Naturalist* published her description of a new Ordovician pelecypod from the Ottawa district; she also contributed to the Museum's second bulletin, and she and a colleague wrote a synopsis of the fossils found around Kingston for the Ontario government. The calm seas at the Survey cast sunny reflections into the Wilson living-room on long Sunday afternoons when, after church and lunch, she and her mother would linger over a huge pot of coffee, discussing everything under the sun, illustrating their ethical deductions with biblical quotation. Adelia Wilson never set spurs into her daughter to make her gallop headlong and carelessly into this men's world, but she supported her in her work always with wit and breadth and the Kingston constructive view of things.

Shoals and storms lay ahead. The war, draining men from non-essential jobs, brought a slowdown to the work of the Survey. And on February 3, 1916, the Centre Block of the Parliament Buildings in Ottawa burned down. The government immediately requisitioned the Victoria Memorial Museum to meet in. Overnight the flats and cases of thousands of valuable geological specimens had to be boxed, labelled, and stored. Alice Wilson, as Museum Assistant, supervising a crew of public works men, got this enormous fiddly job done for the division of Palaeontology with so little confusion that only a few boxes of specimens were lost.

Alice Wilson hated violence. Naturally, at the Survey, where intelligent men were crowded together, each struggling, as she described it, "to piece together the broken and isolated facts of the mosaic of the story of the earth," ink would sometimes spill, a specimen disappear and then the pressure would erupt in lost tempers and harsh words. For all anyone knew Alice Wilson might have been deaf for she never noticed, never raised her eyes from her book, never spoke a harsh word herself. She hated war too, but it could not be ignored and she converted her hatred into an ardent patriotism. In 1916 she volunteered for service in the Canadian equivalent of the Women's Land Army, and when the war was over she watched with the moved and silent crowd as the Princess Pats marched home, the only sound the nails in their worn boots sparking against the streetcar tracks.

War or no, she kept on working. The Survey saw that it didn't cost much to send her, during summers, on short field trips around Ottawa, and that she could stay respectably in little hotels and boarding houses, and they let her go. She worked and observed intensely, bringing her knowledge and intuition together to make sense out of each new discovery. During general reclassification at the Museum in 1919 she became Assistant Palaeontologist, and in 1921 her field work in the Lowland saw light in the Survey's Bulletin 33: *The Range of Certain Lower Ordovician Faunas of the Ottawa Valley with Descriptions of Some New Species.* G. Winston Sinclair, who took over much of Alice Wilson's work at the Survey when she retired, calls this bulletin, written by a forty-year-old Modern Language and History graduate with little more than on-the-job training in geology and only the rank of Assistant Palaeontologist, "a very fine contribution to geological science."

But the Ordovician seas left fossils in other parts of the world, in Wales, in New York State, in the Rockies, along the west shore of Lake Winnipeg; and these far fields, where she might enlarge her knowledge of her period, lured her. With the help of her brother Alfred, she and Madeleine Fritz, one of the first young women to pursue a conventional study of geology, organised a six weeks' field trip to Lake Winnipeg in the summer of 1921. It was a risky adventure. Lake Winnipeg is shallow, never more than seventy feet deep, and therefore extremely stormy and dangerous. They had only a twenty-foot cedar skiff and in one storm they almost drowned. Alice Wilson was so exhausted when they reached shore that she fell asleep, her arm mooring the boat. Indians, mosquitoes, and snakes, which Alice Wilson heartily disliked, troubled them somewhat.

Mostly they camped alone, fishing the abundant waters with a net, sleeping on the beach in silk sleeping-bags. But to get from one site to another they hitched lifts from fishermen. Once when they were crossing a rough stretch of water aboard a lift, a storm trapped them and they lurched sickeningly all night in the high waves, dizzied by thunder and lightning. In the morning they found the skiff had broken tow with all their notes, specimens, and camping equipment. Miraculously it had been driven to shore and they retrieved it and all its precious cargo.

The Lake Winnipeg shore had been worked before and it was from earlier surveys that they knew which were the fertile sites. Nonetheless the trip proved that women geologists could rough it; and they gathered experience from tapping fossils out of the sedimentary rocks with hammers, writing and tying labels on the fossils, putting them in sacks and then in boxes for the men at the Geological Survey.

Back at the Survey the wind had changed and Alice Wilson's position began to founder. "My first director at the Survey was a broadminded man," she said once, "but subsequent directors didn't always take kindly to a woman on their staff." Percy Raymond, who had encouraged her to get ahead, had left the Survey, and there was no one now who would fight for her. Then she must fight for herself. In the field, people remember, she was always first: the first to spot a wild flower, a high flying bird, the gathering storm, always the first over the farmer's fence. Of course she was first; she had to be. She must show them that being a woman made no difference to being a good geologist, even if, when she got home, she couldn't eat for exhaustion.

There were various ways the Survey could keep her in her place: not allowing her time to work on her own; not promoting her; not publishing her work; not giving her a car for field work when they were being issued to all the men. They gave her a bicycle. Women shouldn't drive cars, they said. Without complaining, without a word to anyone but her mother, Alice Wilson went out and bought a Model T Ford, fastened her bicycle to the side and drove off down the Ottawa Valley. How on earth, they wondered at the Survey, did the woman cover so much ground?

For she kept up her study of the Ottawa–St. Lawrence Lowland. Dressed for hiking in a Cossack suit designed for her by a little Russian tailor and in knee-length boots that had to be specially made to fit her long narrow feet, she walked hundreds of miles. Once she fell upon an illicit still but the moonshiners decided that this tall, gaunt, oddly dressed woman with the large eyes was harmless; they let her pass. Not so the dog who bit her as she crossed a farm yard one day. "If you were a gentleman," said Alice Wilson softly to the farmer, "you would have restrained your dog." "If you were a lady," retorted the farmer, "you wouldn't be wearing them pants."

She was a lady and a Wilson, and her honour decreed that she stick to her job. And so although it seemed at times that the only things in this world of men and science that spoke a language she could understand were the rocks, the wild flowers, the geese flying overhead, she hung on.

Without formal training and a degree in geology she knew she'd never be more than Assistant Palaeontologist. Since 1916 she'd been asking, without success, for educational leave. At last, after ten years, the Survey granted her permission to compete for a thousand-dollar fellowship offered annually by the Canadian Federation of University Women. She won, and the Federation announced the award at a tea for Sir Charles G. D. Roberts in Toronto in March, 1926.

With quiet triumph she explained to a reporter that she would work on material revealed during "a preliminary survey made by the Canadian and United States governments for a St. Lawrence deep water way and electric power project." The occasion was too formal to let out that she'd been lowered in a basket down one of the probing shafts to look at strata before it was filled in; or that she'd had to forego Harvard, where Alfred had taken his Ph.D. and where Percy Raymond was now, because Raymond had been unable to get the regulations adapted to admit a woman. She intended to go to the University of Chicago.

Now the Survey woke up to what was happening. She had been ill for two years early in the twenties; so, said the Survey, there was no sense her getting more education, for she wouldn't live long enough to make use of it. She procured a doctor's certificate proving the contrary. Moreover, the Survey now found, her services were too necessary; it was impossible to give her time off. She found a friend, another woman geologist from the States, who would substitute for her while she went without pay. But no, said the Survey; "extended leave of any kind for this purpose cannot be recommended in the interests of the department." The fact was, Alice Wilson wrote to the C.F.U.W., that her degree "would make a woman eligible for the highest positions in the Survey"; and that could not be borne.

Well, if this was the sort of strength the male world could exert, she would show them that women in concert could be equally strong. She appealed to the C.F.U.W. and the women began to lobby for her. Telegrams were sent to men of influence; letters were written to ministers of the Crown; a plan was arranged, if necessary, to tackle Prime Minister William Lyon Mackenzie King. The hand above moved and the Survey backed down. "We felt we were rushing in where angels might fear to tread," confided the C.F.U.W., "but we felt very strongly about the aspect of the matter as it affected the economic position of Canadian women scholars. We will seldom have so splendid a case to push for further scope for women."

Having put on record that it was impossible to do without her services, the Survey could not now turn around and find that it was possible. Therefore, to make up her year's residence at Chicago, she might have leave, without pay, for two periods of six months, provided that in the intervening six months she completed all the work she would normally get through in a year. At this time men seeking educational leave were readily granted a year or more and full pay. In later years Alice Wilson used to say injustices like this were "only a matter of evolution." Possibly: but not even the evolving trilobite enjoys battling for its place in the cove. Later, perhaps, when the new race is established, the evolutionary pattern comes clear; but at the time, in 1926, Alice Wilson was very bitter. What she and Adelia Wilson said to each other is not on record; Isaiah 59:4 may have come into it: "None calleth for justice, nor any pleadeth for truth: they trust in vanity, and speak lies; they conceive mischief, and bring forth iniquity."

Alice Wilson was forty-five when she went to Chicago, with seventeen years' research at the Geological Survey behind her. Stuart Weller, an outstanding palaeontologist and head of that division at Chicago, wrote that there would be "practically no question in regard to your receiving University credit for the work you have been doing with the Survey." She began her work under Weller but he died at the university field station in 1927. A young assistant professor, Carey Croneis, took over supervision of her work. "The situation was a mite ludicrous," he writes. "She was considerably older than I, and probably a more experienced geologist.

"I greatly respected her ability and judgment and to a degree at least, Miss Wilson reciprocated, for she confided in me a seemingly trivial personal matter—her great fondness for tea."

She asked if she could establish an afternoon tea break in our laboratories at the University's Walker Museum, and I readily agreed. Gradually, other students, in addition to geologists, began to drop in. The tea breaks turned into semi-social, semi-professional gatherings at which a good deal of scientific work was reported and criticized. Eventually they became so popular that graduate students from half a dozen other departments petitioned to attend. We had to take up small collections for the tea and crumpets. Finally, when close to a hundred people had appeared one afternoon, we were forced to set up rules regulating the attendance of outsiders; so much had Miss Wilson's tea become the thing.

Her dissertation described the geology of the district around Cornwall, the early St. Lawrence seaway work she had done for the Survey, and on December 17, 1929, Alice Wilson became Doctor of Philosophy. Adelia Wilson, the one person who would have wholeheartedly shared this hard-earned achievement, had died in March. As far as promotion or increase of pay went, the Survey took no notice of her degree for seven years. Economies, they said, prevented publishing even a report of her dissertation. In 1932 the Royal Society of Canada filled this gap.

Hard, unhappy years. The Survey had been receiving collections of fossils from newly explored Ordovician regions—Baffinland and the Canadian Rockies. They came to her to be identified and, although her dating of them has been superseded by later knowledge, her descriptions of them laid a foundation on which younger workers have built. Five days a week for other people's fossils; but on Saturdays and Sundays and summer holidays, off she would dash in her Cossack suit and knee-length boots and her Model T to collect fossils, to measure outcroppings, to sketch field maps. Over the years she worked most of the line fences and all the roads in the Lowland.

It is said that because of Alice Wilson the shapes of Canada and the United States have changed; she discovered that a fault dividing the countries at Long Sault followed a course different from the one the charts showed, and the authorities had to agree to change the boundary. There is even a legend, somewhat questionable, that she was the first woman to make a trip down the Mackenzie River, up to the Porcupine and down the Yukon—alone. For she was becoming a legendary figure, the sort of person to whom things happened and who got things done: first woman with the Geological Survey; first woman sent into the field; zealous and popular guide for the region around Ottawa; defier of authority's decision not to allow a woman in the Civil Service to improve her qualifications with a higher degree.

And so when the Bennett government was looking for a woman in the Civil Service to honour in 1935 they chose Alice Wilson; she became a Member of the Order of the British Empire. In 1936 a major shake-up at the Survey tumbled down two trophies: for the first time in ten years the Survey published a piece of her work, some results of her studies of the Ordovician in Ontario, Quebec, and New York State; and, by-passing minor palaeontological ranks, they made her Assistant Geologist. In 1936 she joined her brother Alfred in the Geological Society of America as the first Canadian woman Fellow. And in 1938 she joined her brother Norman in the Royal Society of Canada as the first woman Fellow. Finally she became an honorary member of the Geological Association of Canada. Honours, professional recognition, and fame: how proud Adelia Wilson would have been, "my cup runneth . . ."; but that was a private world. To a reporter, curious about her reaction to these events, she replied, laughing gently, "Scientists aren't supposed to have any feelings."

She began to travel, seeing with an eye brightened by her

knowledge of the earth. She went to Utah and drove over the salt shore of Great Salt Lake. She discovered a peat bog still in use in a lonely countryside. But most ambitiously she and a companion set off one winter to hitch rides from coastal freighters across the Caribbean, through the Panama Canal, and down the west coast of South America. When she came back to Ottawa the Wilson sense of civic responsibility encouraged her to share her experiences with the Ottawa Field Naturalists, the University Women's Club, and Saturday morning children's groups at the Museum. She told them how dark greasy oil spilled on deck during loading at sea off Trinidad made her think of the organisms of hundreds of millions of years ago whose bodies had made the oil. Tree ferns on Martinique recalled to her the Carboniferous age. In the Pacific off Talara in Peru she had seen oil derricks marching down the cliff right into the sea to tap under-water oil-bearing rocks. She had flown over the Andes, thrilled to see for the first time in three dimensions the geological structures she knew about only from the printed page; and she had seen, a few miles from the Pacific coast, the headwaters of the Amazon River.

One of her duties at the Survey was to receive taxpayers who came in with fossils to be identified, a duty that became, for both her and the taxpayer, a real pleasure. She loved teaching, had a great gift for evoking what it felt like to be a shell fish in the warm shallow Ordovician seas of four hundred million years ago. One visitor recalls her reception by Alice Wilson:

My family, like many in Ottawa, had picked up some fossil trilobites on afternoon jaunts and I had been told that these incomplete fragments were the remains of butterflies. I didn't quite believe this, and so—age about six—I took the largest and set off one summer day to the Museum. The guard must have been surprised, but he took me up to the working part of the Museum to Dr. Wilson.

Many busy people would have turned me away with little attention, but that was not her way. Gravely she showed me the many trays of trilobites, explaining what they were, and what their life in the shallow seas was like. She explained how they came to be embedded forever in the shale, and how important it was to seek and find fossils for study. In the end she accepted my trilobite, the largest ever collected in the district and not complete, taking down what particulars I could muster, and in return she gave me a smaller duplicate from the collection.

Alice Wilson used to say, "You have to teach people to dislike things," and she found children particularly responsive to the sense of wonder with which she regarded the earth and its phenomena. About this time she discarded the rather formidable Cossack suit and knee boots for slacks and brogues. "Even the school children were running away from me," she said, "and that I couldn't stand; I love children." She loved taking them hiking, finding a bird's egg and leading the talk around to what went on inside it; explaining why igneous rocks, though prettily coloured, don't skip across water as well as grey sedimentary rocks which split into flat layers. This interest in children began to form into a new project, a book for them about the earth, its shape, its habits, and its resources. It wouldn't be a textbook. She would write it just as she talked to children, telling them about the old, grey green, copper kettle in the woodshed; about cod liver oil, the oil spilled on the ship's deck, and the derricks at Talara; about swimming in salt water off Long Island, drinking the waters of salt springs, and driving along the salt shore in Utah; about the giant ferns and the adventures of a drop of water—everything that would help children understand the origins of minerals in the earth.

She approached Macmillan of Canada in 1940 and they encouraged her to go on with the book. And in 1940 the Survey made her Associate Geologist. But there was war again. The book was shelved and she devoted herself to the Survey. She reported on possible new sources in Ontario of the oil and gas so essential to the war effort; but with men gone most of her work was caretaking. At the end of the war she was rewarded by being made full Geologist, and in 1946 she retired compulsorily at the age of sixty-five. They say at the Survey that they had to hire five men to take her place.

Had Alice Wilson's career ended then it would have been a public triumph for she had forever smoothed the way for women in the field of geology, but it would have been a private tragedy. So much time had been spent in routine work and in struggling for recognition that the things that excited her, young people and travel, had entered her life only peripherally. And most of the research on her own geological province, the Ottawa–St. Lawrence Lowland, still lay about in collections, notes, and sketch maps. For the next seventeen years she threw herself into the business of living, piling up honours and achievements like layers of consolidated rock. These were happy years. Their record sets no heart skipping as it witnesses battles only just won; their beauty lies in seeing the earth inherited by one who deserves it.

As a retired geologist she kept her office at the Survey. Every working day, until she was 82, in heat wave or blizzard, she went to work. In 1946, the year she retired, the Survey published Memoir 241, her comprehensive description of the geology of the Ottawa–St. Lawrence Lowland. Her eyes were never good enough to do microscope work and the description of the microscopic organisms of the area was done by Madeleine Fritz now at the University of Toronto. Then she began a series of bulletins systematically describing the various groups of Lowland fossil organisms she had collected. The last of these ten bulletins, some of which were published in the *Transactions* of the Royal Society of Canada, appeared in 1961. In 1956 she gathered all this material together in a monograph for the *Canadian Field Naturalist* which had published many of her articles and whose club members she had often taken on tours around Ottawa. This sprightly guide to the Ottawa district captures her vigorous colloquial approach to naturalists and amateur geologists.

In 1947 *The Earth beneath Our Feet,* her book for young people, was published and in 1948 she joined the staff of Carleton College as a sessional lecturer in palaeontology and some branches of soft rock geology. "There's no question in my mind that I remember her more than any other professor," one enthusiastic student says.

She was just a fantastic person, a bug for technical detail in the drawings she made us do. She was so involved in geology that her thought sped her tongue along much faster than our pens could follow, but she was terribly patient with us too, dropping everything for one student who was having religious doubts. She agreed that it was hard for scientists to accept much religious dogma, but she said that no scientist could deny some all-wise overall power. She said that she was always comforted by certain passages in the Psalms.

We never understood how she could do all she did in a day, first to the Survey, then a two hour lecture with us, then back to the Survey, and then a field trip in the afternoon. She always let us browse a little first on a field trip to wear off our outdoors high spirits, but then she would start in describing fossils, making the ancient creatures seem to smile they became so real. On the drive there and back she would lay out for us the whole history of the area.

Between 1949 and 1952 she was one of the most successful editors of the Canadian Federation of University Women's *Chronicle*; with typical thoroughness she got ready for this job by enrolling in a creative writing course. In 1954 a scholarship which the University Women's Club of Ottawa had established in 1952 was named in her honour. The scholarship, worth a hundred dollars, goes annually to a student attending Carleton.

At 78 she was still hankering after far distant places. "When I'm old and decrepit," she told one of the many reporters who came regularly now to interview this white-haired Canadian celebrity, "I can go to Europe in a wheelchair." Over the past fifteen years she had flown over the Rockies; searched out Ordovician fossils in Wales at an International Geological Congress; cruised two thousand miles up the Amazon; gone to Edmonton for a C.F.U.W. conference by way of a bus trip through the Yukon; and, to the astonishment of her colleagues in Mexico, had adjusted her long legs to the short stirrups of a burro to climb through the black dust of Paracutin, the volcano that grew from a cornfield. This trip to another International Geological Congress when she was 75 was the last big one she made, but whenever the occasion arose she was off into the Ontario country-side, taking twice as long as most people to get where she was going because she stopped for every wild flower and every rock outcropping, tossing specimens into the back of her car for the men at the Survey, never wearying of the earth around her.

In November, 1959, she completed her fiftieth year with the Survey. She had been most indignant to find, when the Survey left the Victoria Memorial Museum for Booth Street, that the skirtings in the new building were made from imported black marble. Why import it when her own Ottawa Valley had a perfectly good quarry? she grumbled. Indeed, said a colleague. Would Miss Wilson show her this quarry? Miss Wilson did; and at her fiftieth anniversary celebration at the Logan Club she was astonished and happy to receive, instead of the usual plaque of appreciation, bookends and a paperweight bearing a bronze crest of the Geological Survey of Canada made of this native black marble. The menu at this celebration was itemized in Latin fauna, sly reference to the classical education which had enabled her to correct the endings of the proper names of fossils in her colleagues' papers.

The colleague of the black marble trick was a woman; for Alice Wilson had lived long enough to see other women trooping along the trail she had blazed. At first there were only one or two and over them she had spread a somewhat motherly wing, but by the end of her life they came in such bands to the universities, to the Survey, to the oil companies, that the distinction between men and women became ridiculous. "We were all just young geologists to her," a Carleton graduate explains.

Carleton University conferred upon her the last of her many firsts. On May 20, 1960, she became the first woman to receive its honorary degree of Doctor of Laws. "Explorer of the secrets beneath us," proclaims her citation. "Animator of the young." In 1963 she gave up her office at the Geological Survey, and in April, 1964, she died.

The new home of the Geological Survey sits high on an outcropping of grey Ordovician limestone that falls in steps down to Booth Street. Soon after it was finished workmen arrived with earth and sod, and set about landscaping the rocky slope. When Alice Wilson caught them at it her indignation knew no bounds. Cover up the bedrock of the Ottawa Valley! she cried. Gloss over the fundaments of civic pride! Is this the meaning of geology? Work ceased, and the slope rested in an ambiguous state for some time. Eventually a compromise was reached. Most of the slope was sodded over, but next to the sidewalk a strip of Alice Wilson's "Ottawa limestone" was left bare, and a notice identifying it was mounted for all the children and students and taxpayers passing by to see. Friends, admirers, and her colleagues the geologists agree, from their various points of view, that this slope symbolizes Alice Wilson's contribution to the science of geology to which she gave her life.

BIBLIOGRAPHY

ANON. "In Memoriam: Alice Evelyn Wilson," Canadian Federation of University Women Chronicle, 1964, p. 29.

L. S. RUSSELL, "Alice Evelyn Wilson," Canadian Field Naturalist, 79: 159–61 (1965).

G. W. SINCLAIR, "Memorial to Alice Evelyn Wilson," Proceedings of the Geological Association of Canada, 16: 127–28 (June 1965).

ALICE E. WILSON, Geology of Ottawa–St. Lawrence Lowland, Ontario and Quebec. Geological Survey of Canada, Mem. 241, 1946. 65 pp., maps.

—— The Earth beneath Our Feet. Toronto, 1947. 294 pp., ill.

—— A Guide to the Geology of the Ottawa District. Monograph issue of The Canadian Field-Naturalist (1956). 68 pp., 12 fig.

Private correspondence and personal interviews.

{ 15 }

Margaret McWilliams

1875-1952

BETTY JANE WYLIE

MARGARET MCWILLIAMS' history as well as her career seems virtually to have begun when she arrived in Winnipeg in 1910 at the age of thirty-five. The information about her life before that time serves merely as a clue to her future brilliant career of public service to her community and country.

Maggie May Stovel was born in Toronto on January 27, 1875. She disliked the name she was christened and had it legally changed to Margaret when she was older. Only a few Stovel cousins in Winnipeg persisted in calling her Maggie. She was the eldest child and only daughter of Samuel Stovel and Thomasina Etterick Callaway. Her father was a tailor, the most fashionable tailor in Toronto at that time, and the family enjoyed comfortable circumstances. He died when Maggie was five but left a fair estate for his young family of three. Maggie never remembered her mother smiling after her father's death but the fact that the family had become ardent Plymouth Brethren may have had something to do with Tassy Stovel's rather joyless outlook on life. She died before Margaret was ten and the three orphaned children lived briefly with an uncle and then were separated and farmed out to other relatives in different cities. Maggie May lived with her Uncle Bill and Aunt Emma Callaway in Toronto until they moved to Minneapolis during her college days.

She was a frail and sickly child and did not attend public school regularly until she was fifteen. She learned to read and write before that, and her Aunt Emma taught her to cook and to sew. Her talent as a needlewoman came not only from her father but also from her grandmother, her mother's mother, a clever forceful woman whom Margaret resembled in looks and ability. Margaret often used to say in later years that her grandmother "rode on her shoulders and made her do everything." Margaret also always attributed her later considerable skill as a cook to these early stay-at-home years in her aunt's kitchen. Certainly her love for music and books, especially poetry, developed in those quiet lonely years. Nothing was lacking in the way of material comfort. The only thing missing was the give-and-take and casual happiness of normal family life. In later life she seldom referred to her childhood; she seemed to have wiped it out of her mind as she was inclined to do with anything or anyone she found unpleasant. Kathleen Strange, writing about Margaret McWilliams in *Chatelaine* magazine in 1950, suggests that the denial of Margaret's childhood may have impelled her to seek the limelight and to crave the approbation of the public and the affection of others. But this is too simple. Everyone desires recognition but not many people choose such selfless ways of getting it as did Margaret McWilliams.

When Margaret did finally start public school she went through very quickly and headed her class all the way. She attended Harbord Collegiate Institute where she was strongly influenced by the great educationist Gertrude Lawler. And now the frailty disappears and she begins to demonstrate some of the boundless energy which characterized her for the rest of her life. She was on the executive of the Literary Society and contributed lively articles to the literary magazine.

She was a tall girl, about five foot six, and quite sturdy but never inclined to fat. Fashion did not demand the emaciated slenderness then that it does now. Her hair was brown and she wore it simply most of her life, parted in the middle and pulled back in a bun or a French roll. It was not until she became chatelaine of Government House in Winnipeg that she started experimenting with glamour and softened and varied her hair styles, and by then her hair was beautifully white. She had blue eyes, lively and twinkling when she was dancing or responding to other people's wit, but frequently icy when something or someone threatened her relentless purpose. She loved to dance. A letter from her husband in later years to Prime Minister Mackenzie King reminds Mr. King of Margaret "for they particularly enjoyed dancing together at university."

From high school Margaret Stovel went on to the University of Toronto, graduating with honours in 1898 in Political Science, the first woman to take that course. She stood third in her class. Her aunt and uncle left Toronto as she was finishing her second year and she moved into a boarding house where she was joined by her brother Hodder, five years her junior, who was attending high school. These were lean years; a bank failure had depleted their inheritance and they had to live off the interest of their dwindled estate after paying their tuition. The experience taught Margaret a valuable lesson in money management which was to serve her well in years to come.

The 1898 *Torontonensis* was the first yearbook published by the University of Toronto and Margaret Stovel was a member of the editorial board. Her yearbook biography says, in part: "Her energy, amiability, zeal and executive and literary ability soon brought her into prominence and during her brilliant course she has held many important offices with great credit to herself." She was curator of the Ladies' Glee Club, then vice-president, and president (unanimously elected) in her senior year. She was corresponding secretary of the Women's Literary Society in her second year, and on the editorial board of the *Varsity* in third year, a staff contributor in her senior year and, as already mentioned, one of the editors of the yearbook. Further, "she this year leads the amazons of the Ladies' Lit of University College in their annual debate against the Victoria Ladies' Lit." There it is, an adumbration of her future: the abundant energy which enabled her throughout her life, no matter how tired, to lie down for ten minutes, make her mind a blank, and rise completely refreshed and ready for anything; the ingratiating amiability which made her not only passionately devoted life-long friends in her adopted home town, Winnipeg, but which elicited confidences from fellow passengers on a train in Russia and from hotel porters in Japan and wiped out age barriers in her dealings with young people throughout her life. Her zeal allowed nothing to stand in the way of her cause, and she was to have many causes. She brought the same endless capacity for enthusiasm to anything she tackled, whether it was a new recipe for jam, a new policy of municipal administration, the injustice of a parking ticket or a war for men's souls, and she must have literally overwhelmed any opposition she encountered. Opposition, of course, was a word she did not recognize, and therein lay the secret of her executive ability: people found themselves working for her causes, borne along by her lucid arguments and forthright insistence.

One shy young man, indeed, may have had the whole course of his life altered by her "executive ability." It was when Margaret McWilliams was chairman of the first committee in Canada to investigate the Blue Cross Hospital Plan. A young neighbour of hers on Stradbrook Avenue in Winnipeg was going to university, taking the Agriculture diploma course. She called him in and told him he was just the person to take the plan and sell it to the public. "Forget your agriculture course. You're not really interested in that. This is what you should be doing, meeting people and talking to them." The young man found himself agreeing to Mrs. McWilliams' demands, although later, when he was ready to tackle his first presentation, he had to walk around the block for half an hour while he built up the courage. He never went back to his Agriculture course. The young man was Duff Roblin. He is now the Premier of the province of Manitoba.

Margaret's literary ability too, so early displayed, was later to bear fruit in many ways, and led her to her first job, in a newspaper office. She went first to the *Minneapolis Journal* where she was *pro tem.* women's editor for a year while the editor was in Europe. She lived again for the year in her uncle's home and it was from this home that she was married four years later. But in the interval she spent three and a half years in Detroit working as the music critic for the now defunct *Detroit Journal*. Her early quiet years with music and books and her four years with the Ladies' Glee Club must have stood her in good stead for nothing in her elected courses prepared her for this job.

Margaret Stovel accomplished two things at the *Detroit Journal* which were characteristic of her. She noticed that when the newspaper went to bed for the day, the men would retire to a nearby bar for drinks. She disapproved. She was and continued to be for her whole life a staunch advocate of temperance. She went out and searched the second-hand stores of Detroit and found a samovar and some china cups and saucers and began serving Russian tea, with lemon and cloves and the whole ritual, at press time. Somehow the idea caught on—it may well have been the forerunner of the ubiquitous coffee break observed in offices everywhere in North America. Why the men would eschew their drinks in the bar in favour of a tea hour with the few ladies in the office is not such a mystery when one considers the personality of Margaret Stovel. All her life men enjoyed talking to her. She had an extremely lucid mind, a grasp of what was going on in the world around her equal to any man's, and a direct forthright way of expressing herself. The editorial offices of the *Detroit Journal* must have taken on some of the aspects of a salon during the three and a half years Margaret Stovel worked there, where good conversation and a free flow of ideas proved as stimulating as a few drinks with the boys.

Margaret's next contribution to the people at the *Journal* followed logically from this close personal contact. She was always quick to spot a problem, equally quick to compassion, with action as a logical corollary. "Words by themselves are no good," she was to say years later, and she lived by that precept. She always put her action where her faith was. So, when she saw the real hardships encountered by her fellow-workers during sickness, she acted. She organized and persuaded them to participate in a kind of health-insurance plan on a contributory basis, a forerunner of the Blue Cross Hospital Plan which she was to organize and help launch in Canada almost forty years later.

Margaret had met Roland McWilliams at university and they corresponded while she went off to work and he took his law degree and then established himself in practice in his home town of Peterborough. They were married in 1903 and Margaret set up housekeeping in Peterborough. The women of Peterborough are said to have distrusted her at first, thinking she was an American and an extreme feminist, having worked in a newspaper office for the last four years. However, she won them over by her obvious enthusiasm for and skill at her homemaking duties. She was a good cook but more than that, she had style. She took her samovar with her and continued to use it. It is now in the Margaret McWilliams Room at the University Women's Club in Winnipeg and one can look at it and imagine the tea parties its warm little heart must have presided over. She enjoyed sewing and gardening too, and used her skill at these pursuits as an ornament to her home. Later, when she was an alderman of the city of Winnipeg, a reporter was to comment that many of the prettiest dresses worn by Alderman McWilliams were those she had made herself. It is a fact that, with all the outside activites she was to undertake, Margaret McWilliams never neglected her home.

In 1907 R. F. McWilliams was elected Mayor of Peterborough and Margaret had her first taste of public life. The first taste was not pleasant. Mr. McWilliams had the dubious distinction of being the only man in the first sixty-four years of Peterborough's municipal history who did not serve two years as mayor after being elected. Mayor McWilliams was criticized for talking too much and not presiding enough in the mayor's chair, and he was unfortunately unaware of a "sewer muddle" which occurred during his term of office when a pipe that had been laid in quicksand separated at almost all its joints and cost the city money, the city engineering department its reputation, and the mayor considerable damage to his record by the city assessors. Assessment increased on "everything but dogs" during Mayor McWilliams' first term. When the time came for the customary election by acclamation for his second term, a petition by six hundred ratepayers to another man to accept the nomination embarrassed Mayor McWilliams. The other man won the election by a majority in every poll and completed the public humiliation of a young man who was to become in later life one of the best lieutenant-governors Manitoba ever had.

This was the major reason why Margaret and Roland McWilliams left Peterborough. This, and the boom that the west had been enjoying for the previous ten years. A lawyer friend in Winnipeg had written Roland McWilliams, urging him to come West and telling him of the great prospects in Winnipeg. The young Peterborough lawyer apparently needed no second telling. He came, found a good position in a law firm, and when he was settled sent for Margaret. In 1910 Margaret McWilliams' career really began.

She knew by this time that she would never have children and she plunged herself into community activities. It is touching that the first major project with which she allied herself was that of a babies' milk depot which she helped to organize and then served as a board member for several years. She was also vice-president on the board of a free kindergarten. She joined the University Women's Club of Winnipeg, which had only been in existence since 1909; and the Women's Canadian Club, of which she was secretary for two years from 1912 to 1914; and the Local Council of Women, in which she served as secretary and then as president from 1916 to 1920. She was elected president of the University Women's Club in 1913 and served for two years. She promptly instituted a social service committee in the club to study conditions affecting working women in Winnipeg and founded, outside the club, a Social Science Club, an association of some thirty women who met to study economic problems. Later, in 1919, she formed an International Relations group at the U.W.C. which remains (but there are two of them now) one of the outstanding features of the Winnipeg club today.

The infant club had eighty-four members in 1913 and no clubhouse but it had national longings and a breadth of outlook emanating in no small way from its enthusiastic president. Margaret was a prime mover in the most vigorous programme the club had undertaken as yet, sponsoring visiting lectures by the famous Professor Moulton of Chicago and by Helen Keller and her teacher Mrs. Macy. A series of organ recitals was arranged in various parts of the city. Margaret also led the club in its war effort during the first year of the war and her second year as president, substituting sewing meetings for the regular sessions when the members worked on dressing gowns for hospitalized soldiers.

There were relatively few women university graduates then and they were anxious to maintain and extend their hard-won, new-found vision of the world around them. The feminist movement in England and the United States had spread its influence to Canada and Canadian clubwomen felt rightly that they were on the brink of an exciting emancipation. The First World War brought the whole movement of women's rights to a head. Few men could deny the competent effective work done by women during the war and more women had a taste of being effective individuals in their own right. By January,

1916, the women of Manitoba were granted the franchise and the right to hold public office, the first in Canada to be so recognized. Margaret McWilliams always believed that women must take advantage of this right, "to undergo the ordeal of election." To her, the key to such action was education, so she took it upon herself to educate as many people around her as she could, to render them capable of informed action.

Her World Events classes, which were to become a highlight of Winnipeg's winter season, began in a small way in her own church during the early months of the war. Using a blackboard and chalk, a map and a pointer, Margaret tried to clarify some of the events and geography of the war for her fellow church workers. The classes did not stop for thirty-two years. At one time the membership reached eight hundred and was, in fact, split. Margaret taught a morning class in her own home and a much larger group as an evening class in a public lecture hall.

By 1919 Margaret had joined the university clubwomen in other Canadian cities who were synthesizing the national and international stirrings of the university club movement into the formation of the Canadian Federation of University Women, of which she was the first president. The C.F.U.W. has as its objectives the opening to university women of an opportunity for concerted action on matters affecting their interests, the encouragement of research by women, social intercourse and co-operation between women from different universities, and stimulation of the interest of university women in public life. The number of affiliated local clubs has climbed to over one hundred and the C.F.U.W. gives each year valuable fellowships to women in both the humanities and science.

The scope of co-operation between university women was soon extended by the organization of the International Federation of University Women of which Margaret McWilliams was vice-president. And now her field was international, as befitted a woman with her breadth of vision. Her qualities as a public speaker, demonstrated in the early days of the debating society at university, were to win her international recognition. She never wrote out a speech, preferring to speak from notes. "When you make a talk," she said once, "you take so much time away from people. I believe that it is a spiritual sin not to leave at least one good idea with your audience." She was to have many opportunities to leave at least one good idea with audiences all over the world, and her first such opportunities came to her through her university federation work. She represented the C.F.U.W. at the I.F.U.W. conference in Paris in 1922; and her own province at the I.F.U.W. conference in Oslo two years later.

But she never forgot her own little club where it all began. In 1920 she became House Chairman of the houseless club, appointed to investigate the possibilities of finding a permanent home. She never lost sight of this dream and when, eighteen years later, the opportunity finally presented itself, she wielded her influence. She acted as a kind of liaison between the city of Winnipeg, which had come into possession of the Ralph Connor house, and the University Women's Club, and nothing prevented Alderman McWilliams from speaking and voting for the city's lease of the house to the club.

In 1923 Margaret became president of the Women's Canadian Club and, with the help of the club secretary, conducted a series of personal interviews with some of the pioneers still living about the early days of Manitoba. W. J. Healy, former provincial librarian, prepared the material for publication in the book titled *Women of Red River*.

In the meantime, she had been sitting on the council of the University of Manitoba since 1917, an appointment which one suspects was originally made out of courtesy in the light of the increasing effectiveness of the women's rights movement and of the fact that Margaret's husband had acted as legal advisor in regard to the Act of 1917 which created the Board of Governors and the Council which took over the government of the university. In any case, the appointment was renewed at three-year intervals until October, 1933, when Margaret resigned in protest against the "ignoring of appointments of women to the new Board of Governors." She never went back.

Margaret first met her lifelong teacher friend, Avis Clark, at the home of one of her Stovel cousins shortly after she came to Winnipeg. Avis was younger than she but both women had graduated from Harbord Collegiate, were members of the University Women's Club, and lived in the same apartment block, Devon Court in downtown Winnipeg. Once Margaret learned from a common friend that Avis

was ill and popped in with some food to see her—this practice of
private charities and daily thoughtfulness of others continued throughout Margaret's busy life. There followed invitations to dinner because
an extra potato had been put in the pot or because there was too
much for Roly and Margaret. When the block discontinued its public
dining-room where Avis usually took her meals, Margaret suggested
that Avis go "halvers" with the McWilliams on the upkeep of a house
and it was all settled. Avis Clark lived with the McWilliams from
1923 on. The two women became like sisters and were often mistaken
for each other. Roland complained that they never finished sentences
to each other because each knew what the other wished to say. But
the three of them were fast friends and Roland married Avis after
Margaret's death.

In 1926 Roland McWilliams was a delegate to a world meeting of
the Y.M.C.A. in Amsterdam and Margaret accompanied him. Following the conference, the pair made a trip into Russia, so recently
emerged from the Revolution and just launching into the communist
experiment. They wrote a book about it, *Russia in 1926*. Roland wrote
the introduction and the general conclusions they drew about their
journey; Margaret wrote a sort of daily journal, giving her personal
impressions and the information they gleaned as they went along.
It is still a very readable book and one can learn a great deal about
Margaret McWilliams from it. At their first stop, Leningrad, Margaret
noticed on her first walk around the streets how shabbily dressed the
women were and how few of them wore—possessed—gloves. She put
hers away and did not wear them any more. This is the kind of
sensitive reaction she had to people's feelings all her life, a kind of
instinct for putting others at their ease with her. And where instinct
failed her, her second thoughts invariably corrected her human short-
comings. When, on the last train ride which was to take them out
of Russia, Margaret and Roland found they had to accept the equivalent of a third-class carriage, she confessed a snobbish dismay as to
what kind of people they would have to sit with. But then on second
thought, she was ashamed of her reluctance and was in fact the first
to make overtures to her fellow passengers, expressing her lively
interest in them in spite of what might have seemed to any other
woman insurmountable language barriers. One of the women on the
train turned out to have a son in Canada from whom she had had

no word for some time. On her return, Margaret searched for and found the man's whereabouts and persuaded him to write his mother. Her sincerity was always more than lip service.

But all her books give us more than a self-portrait of a lady. She had a fine intelligence, well trained, an acute sense of history and an ability to see directly to the heart of an issue. Thus in *Russia in 1926* she was profoundly moved by the challenge Communism presented to Christianity. Five years later, as a delegate for Canada to a Pacific conference in Shanghai, Margaret McWilliams foresaw China's future communism. She concluded a series of articles reporting on the conference with this: "With all Asia's millions turned to Communism what would be the fate of western civilization? It may look like a small war waged in a local area [Manchuria]. Wise men in the Orient say it holds a threat for the entire western world." She never stopped emphasizing all her life that the war between Communism and liberal democracy would be a "war for men's souls."

Perhaps stimulated by the success of *Russia in 1926* and eager to try her hand at history, Margaret wrote and published *Manitoba Milestones* in 1928. She intended it to be a living history of Manitoba for the man-on-the-street, and she succeeded in her intention. She displays a sense of vivid detail, a feeling for suspense, and a remarkably human touch. She had said when she became president of the University Women's Club that she did not feel she yet deserved to be called a Westerner. With *Manitoba Milestones* she claimed the West as her own. A little booklet published in 1930 called *All Along the River* also illustrates her intense pride in her adopted community.

In 1930 Margaret was sent to Geneva as an adviser to the federal government's delegation to the International Labour Office Conference and in 1931 she attended the conference already mentioned, held by the Institute of Pacific Relations in Shanghai, paying one-third of her travelling expenses out of her own pocket. In that same year, when the depression had settled in grimly, a book called *If I Were King of Canada* was published, written by one Oliver Stowell. "Oliver Stowell" was a pseudonym which Margaret and Roland McWilliams used for their collaborative effort in a fantasy-based book of practical economics and politics, their solutions for the economic crisis Canada found herself in at that time.

The book could have been written yesterday for the grasp it has of the problems of our society today. The McWilliams forecast much of the social legislation which has been enacted in the last twenty-five years. They recommended credit control, and an economic advisory staff similar to the General Staff in time of war, to be called the Economic General Staff. They proposed a banking system directly responsible to the federal government rather than to private share-holders, which would control money and credit for the benefit of the country as a whole. (Parliament authorized the creation of the Bank of Canada in 1934.) They saw the growing tendency towards socialism in the twentieth century and acknowledged the necessity for public ownership of public services, state-organized medical services, and a wide extension of hospital insurance and pension plans on a contributory basis, as well as a national housing scheme with capital available to home-owners at low interest rates.

The McWilliams valued education above everything else as the key to Canada's future and warned against turning the institutions of higher education into mills intent on manufacturing quantity instead of quality. They foresaw the increasing problem of the right use of leisure as a "matter of the gravest consequence to the individual and to the state," and they recommended continuing education for adults using the valuable "plants [for the young] which stand idle so many hours of the year." They evaluated Canadian culture and, acknowledging the fact that "art cannot be manufactured," they recommended private and public subsidy to encourage artistic develop-ment in Canada, free from American influence. They were fully aware of the "almost unparalleled difficulties" in achieving national unity but were optimistic about the results, commenting on "that most difficult of international problems in the world of our time—that of racial minorities."

"We cannot continue, at a time when the difficulties in our country are so great, with a system which, all across Canada, produces city councils so generally futile and incompetent," wrote Oliver Stowell in *If I Were King of Canada*. It is any wonder, then, that Margaret McWilliams ran for City Council in Winnipeg's Ward One in 1933? She was elected, the second woman to be elected an alderman in Winnipeg and, during her incumbency, the only woman on City Council. Alderman McWilliams continued to serve and be elected until 1940 when her husband was appointed Lieutenant-Governor of Manitoba and she resigned.

Her record of achievements in this field is staggering. She was chairman of a Special Committee on Centralized Purchasing, a committee which was set up on her motion and which saved the city money in every department. She was vice-chairman of the Library Committee, which was set up through her efforts and which in its first year saw the first large increase of books in the city libraries in several years. As a matter of fact, Margaret made a direct appeal to the citizens of Winnipeg which alone resulted in an acquisition of 7,000 books. She was a member for three years of the Special Committee on Housing, and worked incessantly for a demonstration in Winnipeg of low-cost housing. She tried to get a slum clearance project started in Winnipeg and organized a survey report which for years stood as the authoritative document on slum conditions in the city. In 1937 she attended an international convention on housing in Paris as the delegate of the city of Winnipeg. She was chairman of the Medical Sub-Committee of the city's Unemployment Relief Commission, and as vice-chairman of Unemployment Relief recommended and helped establish a social service department to help families on relief. She also thought of and helped to organize a training school for household workers which enabled untrained women to become self-supporting.

She always believed that one should help others to help themselves and to this end she supported the government plan whereby men receiving unemployment relief earned their money by working on city projects. "Idleness is no bonanza," she used to say at council meetings. She was resented and criticized for this for years afterwards. Even after she was chatelaine of Government House she used to get anonymous telephone calls telling her how hard and unfeeling she was. But she was not. One of the first things she did when she went on the U.R. committee was to take the food allowance and test it for herself. For a week she and her husband and Avis Clark lived on the stringent economy and monotony which a tight relief budget imposed. She always believed that in action lies hope, and this personal test of hers confirmed her in her opinion that any welfare system must offer a human being self-respect as well as subsistence and a release

from the dull hopelessness of inactivity if he was to remain a decent
responsible citizen.

In addition to these major activities, Alderman McWilliams was a
member of the Standing Committee on Legislation and Reception,
the Social Welfare Commission, the Parks Board, the General Hospital
Board, the Special Committee on Unemployment Relief Works, and
she worked enthusiastically on smaller pet projects: cleaner streets,
noise control, co-ordination of the city's business, improved traffic
control. Once, when she had received a parking ticket, she blasted
the traffic police for concentrating on over-parked cars instead of
attending to serious traffic violations, and carried this enthusiasm into
an advisory traffic commission meeting where, when she attempted
to make a motion, found out to her blushing embarrassment that she
was at the wrong meeting, not a member, and not entitled to make
a motion. It was the only time she was ever caught out. It must be
admitted that there were some sighs of relief in some quarters at
City Hall when the energetic Alderman McWilliams finally left the
scene.

Evangeline Booth came to Winnipeg in October, 1937. The papers
simply reported that at a giant rally Alderman McWilliams thanked
the Salvation Army General and called on the audience to show their
appreciation. Margaret herself recalled the event years later in an
interview saying that it marked a significant turning point in her own
religious life. She and Roland had been Presbyterians but with
Church Union in 1925 became members of the United Church of
Canada. She had always been deeply religious but had kept her
religion to herself. She realized, however, that in thanking Evangeline
Booth, she must make her own commitment public. After the rally, a
woman spoke to her. "Mrs. McWilliams!" she said, "I didn't know
you were like that!" and Margaret felt as if she had been struck
between the eyes. From then on, in all her public speaking she made
very clear her alignment on the side of the angels. During the war
years and after, she was constantly to remind her audiences of Jesus'
injunction to feed the hungry, clothe the naked and heal the sick. Her
whole life could be said to have centred on these three aims, and one
other: bring light to the mind.

"Take for your master excellence," she would urge people, acknowledging the influence of Sir Richard Livingstone whose lectures she

heard at the University of Toronto in 1943. "Never be satisfied with anything less than first-rate. The first-rate," she said, "means in actual day-by-day living never doing less than we can; never doing anything less well than we can."

In 1940, with the appointment of her husband as Lieutenant-Governor of the province of Manitoba, Margaret McWilliams moved on to a wider social sphere. She resigned from office as an alderman of the city of Winnipeg and became chatelaine of a house at least five times bigger than any house she had ever run before, and this at an age when most woman might be justified in slowing down. Her homemaking which, while efficient and gracious, had always been subordinated to her public service, now came to the fore. The maid of all work who had been with the McWilliams for some years in their private life and whom Margaret had taught to cook, moved with them to become the housekeeper-cook at Government House. They added a cook's helper, a housemaid, an upstairs maid, a gardener and a chauffeur, all necessary to the new life the McWilliams were to lead.

In 1941, the first complete year of their charge, the McWilliams held 17 formal dinner parties, the largest of which, for 29 people, was in honour of Princess Alice. There were 23 luncheons; 14 receptions, ranging in size from 19 guests to 890 members and wives of the Canadian Medical Association; 8 small teas, averaging 40 or 50 guests; 8 small box parties (before the theatre) and two functions: the annual New Year's Day levée, at which Margaret began the custom, since discontinued, of having the brides of the year serve at the civilian reception; and a never-to-be-repeated at-home by Mrs. McWilliams. There were also four supper parties and five celebrity concert parties for five or six guests. One category was missing from this first year: during the McWilliams' term there were seven annual meetings held at Government House, four of them for the Girl Guides, whose provincial honorary president Margaret was.

This, then, was entertaining on a grand scale, though it must be noted that the frequency of any kind of event never was as great as it was during the first year. There is little doubt that the reason for a slightly more moderate scale of entertaining was purely economic. When the McWilliams took office, the Lieutenant-Governor of Manitoba still received the salary settled upon at Manitoba's entrance to Confederation in 1870. There was a modest allowance to cover the salaries of the housekeeper-cook and the chauffeur and the house was rent-free with heat and light included. But there was no entertainment allowance whatsoever, nor any car allowance. Mr. McWilliams bought and maintained his own automobile as well as all the expenses of the extra travelling he had to do in it. The McWilliams never refused an invitation to speak, to open a church or a country fair or a tea or address a graduating class, and they paid their own way in silver collections and bazaar table and home cooking sales. They were not wealthy people; their private resources were extremely limited. Even Margaret's books did not start making royalty payments until a year after her death. Yet they managed—more than managed. A lieutenant-governor in another province is said to have asked, on taking office, how he should go about his duties which seemed to him rather nebulous. "Just follow the example of the McWilliams of Manitoba," he was told, "and you won't go far wrong." His Honour Mr. McWilliams and his wife were acknowledged by the people of Manitoba to be truly the first Lieutenant-Governor and chatelaine of the whole province and not merely of Winnipeg.

How did she manage? Margaret McWilliams planned the menus and did her own shopping, watching for bargains at the grocery store as carefully as any housewife. She made a budget and struggled to keep within it and it must have been a struggle, especially since it was wartime, there was rationing and prices were high. Her early training in college days of living within the limited means of her inheritance stood her in good stead now. And yet she managed to carry out, in addition to the entertaining, a four-year plan of refurbishing the beautiful sixty-year-old house she was living in.

It is quite likely that the McWilliams' practice of temperance at Government House was bolstered by straight economic necessity but it was entirely consistent with their behaviour all their lives. They had always been temperance advocates. Liquor had never been served in their private homes and they simply continued their policy at Government House. Indeed, they became famous for their hot buttered tomato juice and their fruit punch. Margaret used a special kind of berry she had brought in from the north for her fruit punch and she was deeply hurt and offended when a Toronto newspaper waggishly referred to the "swamp-berry juice" served at Manitoba's Government House. Whatever the McWilliams' guests received, they were charmed by their hosts; one highly honoured visitor delighted Margaret when he thanked her for the "dignified informality" he had enjoyed.

When the then Princess Elizabeth and the Duke of Edinburgh came to Winnipeg in October of 1951 the McWilliams held the largest dinner party they ever had at Government House. There were sixty-nine guests. Mr. McWilliams asked the Princess if she would like wine with her dinner, since she was accustomed to it. The Princess asked what their custom was, and Mr. McWilliams admitted that they did not serve it. "Don't do it for us," said the Princess, and the McWilliams did not. This dinner was notable for another reason. It finally made the government aware that the lieutenant-governor of Manitoba had to be a man of some private wealth if he was not to suffer unduly the expenses of his office, and that some allowance should be made for entertaining. The entertainment allowance finally came through, a year after Margaret McWilliams' death.

The World Events classes continued, one morning a week at Government House, until January, 1948, when the last class was finally dismissed. The demands on Margaret as a public speaker increased rather than diminished. She was made a member of the Speakers' Bureau of the Wartime Information Board in Washington and continued to speak locally as well as out of town. For example, she went to Chicago in May of 1945 to speak four times at four meetings held under the auspices of the Build for Peace Organization. She had gone to Ottawa in January of 1943 to attend a meeting of the Committee on Reconstruction appointed by the federal government and subsequently took the chairmanship of the special sub-committee on post-war problems of women. In 1944 she was Canada's only woman delegate to the United Nations Relief and Rehabilitation Administration Conference at Montreal, where she was a member of the Misplaced Persons Committee and an alternate on the Welfare Committee. In an interview on her return she was asked, "How do you keep up with world affairs, in addition to your other duties?" "I just do it," she said simply.

The Historical and Scientific Society of Manitoba which had for years been a rather dormant organization suddenly shook itself and came to life again in 1944 with the aid of Professor W. L. Morton and Margaret McWilliams. Margaret served as president from 1944 to 1947 and instigated a project very dear to her heart. This was a fellowship award for ethnic studies on the Mennonite, Ukrainian, Icelandic, Polish, and French settlers in Manitoba. Today the Society remembers her work with the Margaret McWilliams Medal Competition, an annual award made in eight categories for writing about some aspect of Manitoba history. The award was made possible by a fund established in trust with the Society by Roland McWilliams in 1955.

But Margaret was honoured in her lifetime as well. In 1946 she received an honorary Doctor of Laws degree from the University of Manitoba. She was delighted with the title and used it. In June of that same year the University Women's Club of Winnipeg conferred its first life membership on Dr. Margaret McWilliams "for her contribution to the Winnipeg club and for her continuous efforts towards international understanding." Then in 1948 her alma mater, the University of Toronto, gave her the honorary degree of Doctor of Literature. There is no doubt that she could have earned either of her honorary degrees academically if she had chosen to do so. It was only fitting that they should have been conferred on her in recognition of her outstanding qualities and years of public service.

And still she found time to write. *This New Canada* was published in 1948. Intended as a text-book for Canadian high school students, the revised edition is still on the British Columbia school curriculum, the only one of Margaret McWilliams' books which is still drawing (increasing) royalty payments. But the book found an audience among adult readers both in and out of Canada. It is a lucid readable informative book and it is amazing to realize that the author was 73 years old when she wrote it.

The librarian at the Provincial Library in Manitoba recalls that Mrs. McWilliams always did her own research. In her position she could have requested that it be done for her but that was not her way. She typed her own work, too, with her own hunt-and-peck method rather than having recourse to dictation. Once, when she had asked the library to have some material ready for her, she did not come over to pick it up as arranged. The next day she phoned to apologize. "I made jam instead," she explained.

Early in the morning, spring and summer, she could be seen on her knees working outside in the Government House gardens, and the conservatory was a constant source of joy to her. She filled the rooms with bouquets of flowers and there was always a posy on her desk. Even on the afternoon of her death, the day before Easter Sunday, she wanted to see to the Easter flowers she was sending her friends, and was only persuaded to lie down again when Avis Clark promised that she and James the chauffeur would attend to them.

Her will, in the end, was stronger than her body. It is thought that she must have suffered some advance warning of her fatal coronary occlusion but she gave no indication of it to anyone, least of all her husband or her doctor. The last week of her life in April, 1952, was, in a way, typical of her whole life. On the Monday night she went to the final concert for the Musical Festival winners with her husband and two of the adjudicators and was heard during the intermission describing the famous Red River cart, giving a small lesson in Canadian history to the English adjudicators. Tuesday night she was guest speaker at the annual meeting of the Junior League of Winnipeg, which she had helped start twenty-six years before as the Girls' Service League with her encouragement and advice on organization and parliamentary procedure. During the week she had completed her revision of *This New Canada* and prepared for a holiday trip to the coast with her husband. They were planning to leave on Easter Monday.

On Thursday night she had an executive meeting of the Manitoba Historical Society, of which she was then second vice-president, and saw the final arrangements made for the ethnic histories she had worked so hard to achieve. The meeting was over at one A.M. and she told Avis and her husband: "I've finished everything. Everything's done. My responsibilities are all taken care of and I can go away as light as air."

She died on Saturday, April 12.

A quotation was found in one of her little notebooks, copied out in her small neat script, and this was inscribed on her tombstone:

> God give me work
> Till my life shall end
> And life
> Till my work is done.

BIBLIOGRAPHY

MAUDE COSKEY, Record of Alderman Margaret McWilliams, Jan. 1938, *Free Press* Library.

G. WILSON CRAW, "Mayor's Talents Recognized Everywhere—Except in Peterborough," *Peterborough Examiner*, April 4, 1964.

Government House, Winnipeg: "Distinguished People Entertained at Government House by His Honour Lieutenant-Governor and Mrs. R. F. McWilliams." (This document is in the R. F. McWilliams estate.)

MARGARET McWILLIAMS, *Russia in Nineteen Twenty-Six* (with R. F. McWilliams). London and Toronto, 1927.

—— *Manitoba Milestones*. Toronto and London, 1928.

—— *All Along the River*. Winnipeg, 1930.

—— *This New Canada*, Toronto and Vancouver, 1948.

—— "Institute of Pacific Relations Conference" (nine articles), *Winnipeg Free Press*, Nov.–Dec., 1931.

—— "A Constructive Philosophy for Our Time—What Must I Do?" *Saturday Night*, June 28, 1947.

—— "Hail Manitoba", CBC school broadcast recording, 1951 (R. F. McWilliams estate).

—— Speech notes and notebooks, unpublished (R. F. McWilliams estate).

CONSTANCE KERR SISSONS, "Gifted—and All Canadian," *Western Home Monthly*, Aug., 1931.

KATHLEEN STRANGE, "Margaret McWilliams of Manitoba," *Chatelaine*, 1950.

J. HODDER STOVEL, Memoirs (unpublished; J. Hodder Stovel estate).

OLIVER STOWELL, *If I Were King of Canada*, Toronto and Vancouver, 1931.

Torontonensis, yearbook of the University of Toronto for 1898.

UNIVERSITY WOMEN'S CLUB OF WINNIPEG, Fiftieth Anniversary Pamphlet.

Winnipeg Free Press, City Council Scrapbooks, file on Margaret McWilliams.

BOOKS ABOUT OTHER CANADIAN WOMEN

This list can only suggest the number and variety of such books. It is arranged by date of publication.

WITHROW, W. H., *Barbara Heck*, Toronto Methodist Book Rooms, 1895.

Women of Canada: Their Life and Work, compiled by the National Council of Women, 1900.

STEWART, FRANCES, *Our Forest Home*, Montreal, 1902.

HERRINGTON, W. S., *Heroines of Canadian History*, William Briggs, Toronto, 1909.

SYKES, ELLA C., *A Home-Help in Canada*, London, 1912.

MORGAN, H. J., *Canadian Men and Women of the Time*, Toronto, 1912.

CURRIE, EMMA A., *The Story of Laura Secord*, St. Catharines, 1913.

DOUGHTY, A. G., *A Daughter of New France* [Madeleine de Verchères] Ottawa, 1916.

HEALY, W. J., *Women of Red River*, Winnipeg, 1923.

SMITH, W. L., *Pioneers of Old Ontario*, Toronto, 1923.

GARVIN, A. B. (Katherine Hale), *Isabella Valancy Crawford*, Toronto, 1923.

SKELTON, ISOBEL, *The Backwoodswoman*, Toronto, 1924.

LOGAN, J. D. and FRENCH, DONALD G., *Highways of Canadian Literature*, Toronto, 1924.

DAVELUY, MARIE-CLAIRE, *Dix fondatrices canadiennes-françaises: Profils mystiques*, Montréal, Ed. Le Devoir, 1925.

PIERCE, LORNE, *Marjorie Pickthall*, Toronto, 1925.

HETT, F. P., *Memoirs of Susan Sibbald*, London, 1926.

STEVENSON, O. J., *A People's Best*, Toronto, 1927.

FORAN, J. K., *Jeanne Mance*, Montreal, 1931.

WALLACE, W. S., *The Story of Laura Secord*, Toronto, 1932.

JACKSON, MARY PERCY, *On the Last Frontier*, Toronto, 1933.

KELLS, EDNA, *Mrs. George McDougall*, United Church Publishing House, Toronto, 1933.

BENOIT, P., *La Vie inspirée de Jeanne Mance*, Montréal, 1934.

La Femme canadienne-française, Montréal, Albert Lévesque, 1936 (numéro spécial de l'*Almanach de la langue française*, 1936).

SMALLWOOD, JOSEPH, *The Book of Newfoundland*, 2 vols., St. John's, 1937.

HUGUENIN, MADELEINE-GLEASON, *Portraits de femmes*, Montréal, Ed. La Patrie, 1938.

BLACK, MARTHA L., *My Seventy Years*, London, 1938.

SALVERSON, LAURA G., *Confessions of an Immigrant's Daughter*, Toronto, 1939.

BROWN, A. A., *Log of a Lame Duck*, Macmillan, 1939.

SISTER ST. IGNATIUS DOYLE, *Marguerite Bourgeoys and her Congregation*, Garden City Press, Gardenvale, Quebec, 1940.

JAMESON, ANNA, *Winter Studies and Summer Rambles in Canada*. The latest Canadian edition (selections) is in the New Canadian Library series of McClelland and Stewart, Toronto, 1965.

STRANGE, KATHLEEN, *With the West in her Eyes*, Toronto, 1945.

THOMAS, CLARA, *Canadian Novelists, 1920–1945*, Toronto, 1946.

Loyalist Narratives from Upper Canada, ed. J. J. TALMAN, Champlain Society Publications, Toronto, 1946.

TESSIER, MGR ALBERT, *Canadiennes*, Montréal, Ed. Fides, 1946.

The Letters of Letitia Hargrave, 1813–1854, Champlain Society Publications, Toronto, 1947.

EATON, EVELYN, *Every Month was May*, New York, 1947.

PERCIVAL, W., *Leading Canadian Poets*, Toronto, 1948.

LANGTON, ANNE, *A Gentlewoman in Upper Canada*, ed. H. H. LANGTON, Toronto, 1950.

CLEVERDON, CATHERINE LYLE, *The Woman Suffrage Movement in Canada*, University of Toronto Press, 1950.

BANFILL, B. J., *Labrador Nurse*, Toronto, 1952.

AITKEN, MARGARET and BYRNE HOPE SANDERS, *Hey Ma! I Did It*, Toronto, 1953.

MACBETH, MADGE, *Over My Shoulder*, Toronto, 1953.

NEEDLER, G. H., *Otonabee Pioneers*, Toronto, 1953.

MAGRATH, THOMAS, *Authentic Letters from Upper Canada*, Toronto, 1953.

BUEHRLE, M. C., *Kateri of the Mohawks*, Milwaukee, 1954.

MacGILL, ELSIE, *My Mother the Judge*, Toronto, 1955.

HIEMSTRA, MARY, *Gully Farm*, Toronto, 1955.

SHIPLEY, NAN, *Anna and the Indians*, Toronto, 1955.

EATON, FLORA McCREA, *Memory's Wall*, Toronto, 1956.

AITKEN, KATE, *Never a Day so Bright*, Toronto, 1956.

SHIPLEY, NAN, *Frances and the Crees*, Toronto, 1957.

SANDERS, BYRNE HOPE, *Famous Women* in "Canadian Portraits," Toronto, 1958.

CORMACK, BARBARA V., *The Red Cross Lady*, 1960.

CADELL, G. LINCOLN, *Barbara Heck, Pioneer Methodist*, Cleveland, Tenn., 1961.

BERTON, LAURA B., *I Married the Klondike*, Toronto, 1961.

ANDERSON, W. A., *Angel of Hudson Bay*, Toronto, 1961.

Les Ecrits de Mère Bourgeoys: autobiographie et testament spirituel, Montréal, Congrégation de Notre Dame, 1964.

SYLVESTRE, GUY, *Ecrivains canadiens*, Montreal, H. M. H., 1964.

COPELAND, DONALDA and EUGENIE LOUISE MYLES, *Nurse among the Eskimos*, 1964.

ALLAIRE, EMILIA BOIVIN, *Têtes de femmes: essais biographiques*, Québec, Editions de l'Equinoxe, 1964.

ROBINSON, MARION O., *Give my Heart: The Dr. Marion Hilliard Story*, New York, 1964.

Literary History of Canada, general ed. C. F. KLINCK, University of Toronto Press, 1965.

Mrs. Simcoe's Diary, ed. MARY QUAYLE INNIS, Toronto, 1965.

Dictionary of Canadian Biography, vol. I, University of Toronto Press, 1966.

CANADIAN FEDERATION OF UNIVERSITY WOMEN
ASSOCIATION DES FEMMES DIPLÔMÉES DES UNIVERSITÉS

This book was made possible through generous donations from many University Women's Clubs and Alumnae Associations and a few individual members. Other Clubs and Associations participated wholeheartedly in local Centenary projects in a number of imaginative ways. Some did both.

The Directory of University Women's Clubs and Alumnae Associations of the Canadian Federation of University Women/Association des Femmes diplômées des universités for the year 1966–67 is as follows:

ALBERTA

Calgary, Edmonton, Lethbridge, Medicine Hat, Red Deer

BRITISH COLUMBIA

Chilliwack, Kamloops, Kelowna, Maple Ridge, Mission City, Ladner, Nanaimo, New Westminster, Prince George, Trail, Vancouver, Vernon, Victoria, West Vancouver, White Rock, Williams Lake

YUKON, N.W.T.

Whitehorse

MANITOBA

Brandon, Portage la Prairie, Winnipeg

NEW BRUNSWICK

Fredericton, Moncton, Sackville, Saint John

NEWFOUNDLAND

Corner Brook, Grand Falls, St. John's

NOVA SCOTIA

Dartmouth, Halifax, Truro, Wolfville

ONTARIO

Arnprior, Barrie, Belleville & District, Brampton & District, Brantford, Burlington, Chatham-Kent, Cornwall, Elliot Lake, Etobicoke, Galt, Guelph, Hamilton, Kapuskasing, Kingston, Kirkland Lake, Kitchener-Waterloo, Leaside–East York, London, Milton, Mount Forest, Niagara Falls, Norfolk County, North Bay, North York, Oakville, Orillia, Oshawa, Ottawa (2), Parry Sound, Pembroke & District, Peterborough, Picton & District, Port Credit, Renfrew, St. Catharines, St. Thomas, Sarnia, Sault Ste. Marie, Scarborough, Smiths Falls, South Temiskaming, Stratford, Sudbury, Thunder Bay, Toronto, Welland, Weston, Windsor, Woodstock, York County

PRINCE EDWARD ISLAND

Charlottetown

QUEBEC

Arvida, Hull, Montreal, Quebec, Montreal Inc., Montreal-Lakeshore, Quebec, Richelieu Valley–Belœil, Rosemere, Ste. Anne de Bellevue, Shawinigan, South Shore (Montreal)

SASKATCHEWAN

The Battlefords, Moose Jaw, Prince Albert, Regina, Saskatoon, Swift Current, Weyburn, Yorkton

ALUMNAE ASSOCIATIONS

Marianopolis College, McGill Alumnae, Queen's University Alumnae Association, St. Hilda's College Alumnae Association, University College Alumnae Association (Toronto), University of New Brunswick Associated Alumnae, Victoria College Alumnae Association (Toronto), Marguerite Bourgeoys Alumnae Association